LANGUAGE, GRAMMAR, AND COMMUNICATION

A Course for Teachers of English

LANGUAGE, GRAMMAR, AND COMMUNICATION

A Course for Teachers of English

Gerald P. Delahunty
Colorado State University

James J. Garvey
Colorado State University

McGRAW-HILL, INC.
New York   St. Louis   San Francisco   Auckland   Bogotá
Caracas   Lisbon   London   Madrid   Mexico City   Milan   Montreal
New Delhi   San Juan   Singapore   Sydney   Tokyo   Toronto

This book was developed by STEVEN PENSINGER, Inc.

LANGUAGE, GRAMMAR, AND COMMUNICATION
A Course for Teachers of English

This book is printed on acid-free paper.

1 2 3 4 5 6 7 8 9 0   DOC   DOC   9 0 9 8 7 6 5 4

ISBN 0-07-022911-2

This book was set in Berkeley Oldstyle Book by ComCom, Inc.
The editors were Steve Pensinger and James R. Belser;
the designer was Leon Bolognese;
the production supervisor was Kathryn Porzio.
R. R. Donnelley & Sons Company was printer and binder.

Library of Congress Cataloging-in-Publication Data

Delahunty, Gerald Patrick.
    Language, grammar, and communication: a course for teachers of
  English / Gerald P. Delahunty, James J. Garvey.
       p.   cm.
    ISBN 0-07-022911-2
    1. Linguistics.   2. Language and languages.   3. English language.
  I. Garvey, James J.   II. Title.
  P121.D38   1994
  410—dc20   93-39640

ABOUT THE AUTHORS

GERALD P. DELAHUNTY has taught at the University of California, Irvine, San Diego State University, and Colorado State University, where he is Associate Professor of English and Linguistics. He received his B.A. (1968) and M.A. (1970) from University College, Dublin, and his Ph.D. from the University of California, Irvine (1981). He has published on syntactic theory, English syntax, the textual functions of syntactic structures, sociolinguistics, and Irish archaeology. His current projects are aimed at developing connections and dialogue among linguistics, English studies, and English education.

JAMES J. GARVEY received his B.A. from Loyola University, Chicago, in 1966. He pursued graduate studies at the University of Michigan (M.A. 1967, Ph.D. 1971). He has taught for over 20 years at Colorado State University, where he is an Associate Professor of English. In addition to syntax and semantics, his interests lie in the connections among linguistics and education, composition, and literature as well as in the humanities, including the visual arts, music, mythology, and biblical studies. His publications include work on characterization in narrative and on the computer analysis of writing.

TO MARNA AND CIAN

TO ANN AND JOSEPH

CONTENTS

PREFACE

Teachers of English require knowledge and skills in many areas, including literature, writing, and language. In this book, we approach the last of these areas not simply as a means for teaching the first two, but rather, as a topic worthy of serious study in itself. We have attempted to provide future teachers with the fundamentals that they will need to explore, along with their students, the nature of language and the nature of the English language, particularly its grammar and its meaning systems. Any further extension of language study to literature or composition, we believe, will be successful only insofar as it rests upon a deep understanding of language in its many forms.

The title of this book indicates its major points of focus. By "language" we mean primarily the system of rules that exist in the minds of speakers as a result of acquiring English in the first 6 to 10 years of their lives and largely independently of their schooling. Chapter 1 examines this notion of **linguistic competence,** the central concept which the rest of the book develops. Secondarily, the term "language" applies to those domains of knowledge that are learned in the classroom. Chapters 12 to 14 in Part Three address such issues under the headings of the relations between speech and writing, regional and social variation, and usage.

The grammar component of this book is presented in Part Two. Although some texts simply catalog facts about language and thus are useful for reference purposes, they require a great deal of memorization. *Language, Grammar and Communication,* in contrast, presents the study of language in terms of an ongoing critical process of analysis and discovery. While facts may be important, they take a secondary place to the **principles** that guide students' and teachers' encounters with novel and often open-ended problems. In the process of applying these principles, students will encounter both broad patterns and details and will internalize them without conscious memorization. In many cases, students will discover independently exactly what many textbooks present as facts or as appropriate analyses. This situation is not only inevitable, it's desirable. One who reinvents the wheel is as much a genius as the original inventor.

Our approach to grammar, moreover, is synthetic. That is, it blends the three views of grammar that a teacher should be prepared to encounter in the classroom. **Traditional grammar,** with its roots in Greek and Roman culture, provides an extensive vocabulary for talking about grammar. **American structural grammar** refines traditional practices by basing them on exacting and clearly articulated analytic procedures rather than on the haphazard intuitions that traditional approaches depend on. **Transformational-Generative grammar,** the dominant paradigm in linguistics in the latter half of the twentieth century, establishes language study as a quest for an understanding of the human mind. While losing none of the rigor of structuralism, it raises issues that would concern Plato and Aristotle were they reincarnated as contemporary philosophers.

Finally, our treatment of "communication"—i.e., the communication of meaning—is focused in Chapter 2, but in fact, circulates throughout the book. Grammar isn't appropriately limited to a self-contained mechanical system. Rather, it's the vehicle for the expression of meanings of various sorts. Under the headings of **semantics and pragmatics,** we refine the crude notions of denotation and connotation, examine the mechanisms that define meanings, and provide the reader with a vocabulary for talking about meanings.

TO THE STUDENT

Many students find the study of language challenging. To help you deal with the abundance of new terminology, we have indicated key terms in bold type, often in the context that contains their definitions. Also, a glossary of terms appears at the end of each chapter. Read these definitions carefully and try to resist the temptation to translate them into casual language, which may distort their precision. You don't have to memorize them, for as you work with the concepts, they should become ingrained in your consciousness.

More importantly, language study may challenge your personal values. Some students of literature believe that literary language is "pure," "sublime," and "meaningful," while the discourse of the ordinary person is "corrupt," "mundane," or "meaningless." Such a view isn't simply elitist, it's factually false. This book will show again and again that even the most "ordinary" sentence realizes a marvelously—even miraculously—complex system that defines in large part what it means to be human. Literature, in this perspective, is a miracle of miracles, not just something that is merely better than the ordinary.

To succeed with this book—and ultimately to succeed as a teacher—you will need to approach it in several ways. First, *be patient.* The knowledge and skills presented here will not emerge on a casual first reading. Regular and persistent review and exercises are necessary to help you to internalize knowledge and to develop analytical skills to the level of automatic responses. Second, you will need to *reexamine your writing practices.* Writing about language, like writing about literature, is a distinct form of technical writing. The precise use of technical notions is important, and the process of analysis must often be made quite explicit. Third, *ask questions.* Like your future students, you may be puzzled by some of the material that you find here. But you can safely assume that any gaps in your understanding will be shared by many others in the class. Finally, you should *open your mind* to the study of language in its myriad forms as an infinite resource for meeting human needs both common and rare, general and specialized, serious and humorous, informative and coercive—in short, as one of the most valuable resources that we have as humans.

TO THE INSTRUCTOR

We have written this book with a variety of needs in mind. At Colorado State University, we teach the book in a two-semester course specifically for English teaching certificate majors, supplementing it with readings on language acquisition and the history of English, as required by the Colorado Board of Education. A single-semester course might focus on Chapter 1, Chapters 5 through 10, and Chapter 13.

Chapter 1 describes the systematicity of human language and introduces the important distinctions between competence and performance and between descriptive and prescriptive approaches to language. Chapters 5 to 10 describe the words, phrases, clause, and sentence types of English. Chapter 13 discusses the inevitability of linguistic variation and the values and attitudes associated with social, ethnic, and gender varieties. It also discusses the difficulties of language assessment, especially of students who don't belong to the most favored groups in a society.

The chapters on phonology (3) and morphology (4), may be excerpted to provide brief exposure to these topics. We have found that some students may benefit more from Chapter 2 after they have had some exposure to grammar, so it may be read later in the term. Since students rarely have any vocabulary for describing meaning, we strongly urge that this chapter be included.

We have incorporated exercises throughout chapters rather than sequestering them at the end. Often these exercises provide comprehension checks and practice on previous material. They also help to develop the cognitive strategies required for analytic and critical thinking. Some are open-ended and ask students to consider difficulties with analysis. We recommend that students do them before proceeding to the next section.

We would like to thank Elizabeth-Anne F. Duke, Virginia Commonwealth University; Nancy P. McKee, Washington State University; and Ronald Shook, Utah State University, for their very helpful critiques of the manuscript. We also gratefully acknowledge our teachers and mentors Richard Bailey, Peter Culicover, James Downer, Conn O'Cléirigh, and Jay Roluison.

Gerald P. Delahunty
James J. Garvey

Introduction to the Study of Language

KEY CONCEPTS

Language
Language in education
The organization of this book
Hints for success

English teachers typically view their role as twofold: (1) to promote in their students both an appreciation and an understanding of literature and (2) to develop their students' writing abilities. Recently, a third role has appeared, that of teaching **critical thinking.** This skill has many facets, ranging from syllogistic reasoning to detecting covert claims in arguments to deciphering instructions for the assembly of barbecue grills. Critical thinking also forms a major component of the teaching of literature and of writing. For instance, students must be able to understand literary language whose difficulty may be compounded by archaisms, rhetorical figures, complex grammar, and willful grammatical and semantic violations (Dillon, 1978). In writing, students think critically when they analyze their personal preconceptions and biases, when they assess the relevance and effectiveness of their ideas, and when they deliberate on the exact formulation of those ideas in words.

Fulfilling the goals of English instruction becomes particularly important in a world growing in technological complexity and social diversity. Teachers can no longer expect more than a minute fraction of their students to share their passions for literature or for the well-turned phrase. On the contrary, teachers can reasonably assume that the vast majority of junior and senior high school students have interests, sometimes quite powerful, in the physical and social sciences, in business, or in other areas of intellectual pursuit. Unfortunately, many students see the study of English as the province of sissies and secretaries.

The reasons for this situation lie beyond the numbing effect of the popular media on young people's minds and beyond the narrow desire for a secure job. They rest on some unexamined assumptions about education. One such assumption is that English and "real-world" studies such as the sciences are irreconcilably opposed. The sciences, it is alleged, deal with hard facts. Literature, in contrast, provides an avenue into universal values, apart from any ideological, historical, sociological, psychological, and aesthetic considerations.

Recent developments in literary theory and in the philosophy of science have challenged these assumptions. Approaches to literature from feminist, historicist, sociological, and psychological perspectives have alerted us to the ideological (i.e., hypothetical and theoretical) underpinnings of our reading of literature. On the other hand, the philosophy of science has explored the hypothetical and theoretical foundations of what was once taken for granted as "objectivity." The result is a convergence in our awareness of the similarity in the reasoning processes common to disciplines once thought to be opposed. Both the sciences and the humanities proceed from theoretical assumptions (stated or unstated) about the objects and the process of understanding.

This bridge of a long-standing schism between the "two cultures" of science and the humanities has numerous practical consequences. Composition courses have begun to deal with "English across the curriculum" and to examine with respect the styles of the sciences and other disciplines. Research in composition now employs empirical methodologies that use experimental designs and statistics. And, of course, there is the computer, which has already given us spell-checkers and style analyzers and which promises such brave new worlds as *King Lear* on CD-ROM.

The brave new world that you will enter as English teachers comes complete with a complex set of responsibilities. Parents, boards of education, and legislators look increasingly to the school system to prepare students for the demands of the future. Worries that Americans have started to lag behind the other developed countries translate directly into concerns with public funding (i.e., taxes) and accountability in education. Signs of pressure appear in the form of increasingly shrill demands for success on standardized tests, proposals for increased private education and for longer school years, and the prospect of ongoing competency testing for teachers.

Your major responsibility, however, is to your future students. Educational philosophy has come to recognize the importance of meeting the needs of the learner rather than of simply presenting material on a take-it-or-leave-it basis. As a result, the **learnability** of classroom material becomes a more important concept than its **teachability**.

Moreover, in the coming generation, the classroom will change dramatically in the diversity of its students. U.S. Census Bureau figures estimate population increases from 1985 to 2000 at 23 percent for Blacks, 46 percent for Hispanics, 6.5 percent for white non-Hispanics, and 48 percent for other groups (Chinese, Japanese, Philippino, Arab, etc.).

For teachers, the forces we have noted have serious consequences. Those presently in the system must work to keep up with internal changes and to deal with external pressures. Students preparing for the profession at least have the chance to prepare themselves with the intellectual and psychological equipment that they will need in their careers. But doing so may require some serious attitude adjustment. While literature and composition will no doubt continue as focal topics, they quite likely will be taught in ways different from those that you experienced in your precollege years. Moreover, critical thinking will take on an increased role in the curriculum. Finally, integration of the humanities with the sciences will become inevitable.

LANGUAGE

While the educational situation portrayed above may look like the worst of times, in fact you may be entering the best. For the first time in generations, the means—as well as the need—for healing the rift of the two cultures of the sciences and the humanities is available. We believe that one means of reconciliation is *not* the computer, which is simply a tool, but rather, the recognition of the importance of language in every area of education. Language provides a fundamental unifying ground for the sciences and the humanities.

Within English studies, indications of the centrality of language appear in several ways. Nearly every current approach to literature—feminist, Marxist, psychoanalytic, reader response, etc.—stresses the power of language, sometimes referred to as **discourse,** to define the nature of reality. Composition research, particularly the process model, examines how inarticulate thought comes to take linguistic form and how writers and readers interact by way of the written word. Philosophers of the twentieth century (particularly the schools of **logical positivism** and **ordinary language philosophy**) have paid particular attention to language and its role in the construction of arguments.

Language also represents one of the key elements of your future students' social, cultural, and personal identities. As an English teacher, you have a potentially powerful effect on their lives. Literature expresses values to your students that may be unavailable to them elsewhere in the culture. In their writing, they express to you their personal and social values.

Your response to their language will shape their attitudes as adults. Children have a fascination with language and almost no inhibitions about it. Adults, in contrast, typically display considerable anxiety about their language, an anxiety known as **linguistic insecurity.** This insecurity doesn't develop naturally; it's the consequence of repeated—and mostly negative—interactions with teachers wielding red pens, subtly disparaging the native speech of their pupils.

EXERCISES   1. How do you feel about your ability as a singer? Would you be willing to sing "Home on the Range" in front of your English class? What experiences with singing have formed your attitude? What attitudes about singing do children have? What light does this shed on linguistic insecurity?

2. How many words do you have in your vocabulary? Consider first your **active** vocabulary—those words that you use in (a) speaking and (b) writing. Then estimate your **passive** vocabulary. Estimates based on objective study appear at the end of this introduction.

LANGUAGE IN EDUCATION

Language is central to education for several reasons. It's the means of education; it's an object of study; it's an object of beliefs that are important in education; it poses potential problems in education largely because of the beliefs we have about it; and it's a valuable resource for those who know how to make use of it.

Language is a *means of education* in that it's the medium that students and teachers use to communicate and the medium of communication between textbooks and students.

Language is an *object of education* because it's the fabric out of which pieces of literature are woven and because language itself is the object of study in grammar and composition courses. We focus on language as we learn to edit our essays and speeches. We learn to control the genres required for adult life and the specific characteristics expected in those genres. Language is also an object of study insofar as we develop our skills in using it to communicate, to acquire knowledge from lectures and books, to integrate new information with old, to replace false beliefs with new true ones, and to increase or decrease our estimates of the likelihood that some belief we hold is true.

Language is also an *object of our beliefs.* Many people believe that some forms of English are good and others bad; that people who speak nonstandard varieties are uneducated, perhaps stupid, and unworthy of certain types of jobs.

Language is a *potential problem,* to the extent that it—or the beliefs we hold about it—impedes students' acquisition of knowledge and skills. If we believe that students who speak English with a Hispanic accent, or who speak Black English will be unable to keep up in our classes, then very likely they will not, for teachers' expectations are very powerful determinants of students' success in school.

Language is a *potential resource for teaching critical thinking.* We can evaluate our attitudes about other languages and other dialects and their speakers; we can collect linguistic data, observe its patterns, articulate those patterns as hypotheses which we can then test; and we can evaluate the ways we talk about language for their precision and come to appreciate the value of precision in language use generally.

In this book, we offer you one of several different approaches to language—that of modern linguistics. Of the various conceptions of language available, linguistics offers the one most closely tied to critical thinking and composition studies; it also provides a link with literature that reaches back to the nineteenth century and is flourishing today (Traugott and Pratt, 1980). Linguistics also provides a conception of language that is tied to philosophy and to contemporary sciences, both social and physical.

The majority of this book deals with English grammar. Aside from the fact that the general public expects English teachers to have a mastery of grammar, you will probably be expected to teach the subject in one form or another. We don't suggest that you teach your students by using this book as a syllabus. There is far too much material here and it's not geared to a junior or senior high school audience. We do hope that you will find the analytic and critical methods of exploring language exemplified in the book to be more productive and interesting than the more conventional handbook-exposition-cum-drill-and-practice approach.

More importantly, we hope that you will present to your students the broader conceptions about language that underlie this book and that are exemplified by the study of grammar. These conceptions are presented initially in Chapter 1 but are developed in various ways in the other chapters.

In the rest of this introduction, we will explain the organization of this book and provide some hints for working successfully with it.

EXERCISE   In your college library, consult the journal *Linguistics and Education*. Report back
to the class on (1) the types of topics covered in the journal and (2) one article that
interested you.

THE ORGANIZATION OF THIS BOOK

Part One contains two chapters. The first provides a definition of a language,
along with the key notions associated with that definition. Don't worry if the various terms are somewhat abstract. We will refer regularly to material in this chapter as we go along, and soon the general concepts will become fixed in your
mind. The second chapter explores the various types of linguistic meaning,
grouped under **semantics** and **pragmatics.** Since meaning is central to language
and communication, you will emerge from the chapter with concepts and terminology that will allow you to talk more precisely about meaning. Semantic and
pragmatic notions will also appear in the remainder of the book. Indeed, one of
our goals is to show how closely grammar is linked to meaning. In addition, the
material in this chapter has been very influential in current work on literature
and composition.

Part Two gives you the "nuts and bolts" not only of English grammar (including a brief introduction to its sound system) but also of critical thinking
within linguistics. You should pay particular attention to the way in which grammar is presented. We regularly use an analytic method where we formulate a general hypothesis about a word or construction, then test our hypothesis against
data and then reformulate it. Frequently, we ask you to do similar activities in
the exercises, sometimes by gathering data, sometimes by analyzing material that
lies just a step beyond what is covered in the text.

Part Three deals with three selected topics of particular importance to English teachers: (1) spoken and written language, (2) variation in language, and
(3) usage. Our presentation brings together some current studies in each of these
areas and prepares you to read applied studies that you will encounter in your career. The chapters in this part can be read independently of Part Two, although
on occasion you will find some cross-references to earlier chapters, along with
some phonetic notation that will send you back to Chapter 3.

These final three chapters are far from covering the wealth of information
on topics that you might be interested in as an English teacher. Other pertinent
issues are first language acquisition, second language acquisition (bilingualism
and English as a second language), literary language, composition, reading, spelling, the history of English and of language study, language disorders, classroom

activities for teaching language, language testing, translation, and many more. Just to survey all of these would require at least another book. We encourage you to consult your instructor for further references and bibliographical resources.

HINTS FOR SUCCESS

The study of the English language is difficult. First, you will find yourself confronting challenges to linguistic assumptions (and even prejudices) that have become ingrained in you through your culture. Second, you will find yourself in a mode of analysis somewhat different from that of your literary studies. Third, you will confront a large number of new terms.

Like your future students, you have different learning styles. Some (a minority) will pick up the material in this book almost intuitively. Most others will need to work slowly through the chapters. *Don't expect to master this material in a single reading.* The best strategy for most people is to do a preliminary reading, attend class where the selection is discussed, do assigned exercises, and then return to the reading. If you run into problems, don't despair. The key strategy is to identify the source of the difficulty. Often, verbalizing your thought process aloud will help. Don't be afraid to ask questions of your instructor; if you're having problems, the chances are strong that many of your classmates are too.

Exercises are provided in many instances, and your instructor may give you more. Most people cannot learn linguistics or grammar without doing a good deal of hands-on work. If you have problems, try to identify them as specifically as possible. If you get an incorrect answer, make sure also to get an explanation of the correct one. Try to retrace the thinking that led you to miss the question. Often, you can learn more from mistakes than from perfection. One of our goals is to develop your skills in independent language analysis. As teachers, you will regularly be called upon to answer questions that you cannot find information about in your textbooks. Exercises provide an essential means to independence.

Terminology is plentiful in linguistics. Remember that technical terms have a degree of precision that will not allow you to simplify them in ordinary words. We have provided a glossary at the end of each chapter to help you identify definitions; you should consult it often. Be particularly careful with terms (e.g., **competence**) that have a familiar meaning in ordinary language; frequently, the ordinary meaning will differ significantly from that used in linguistics. *Definitions* should be supplemented with *explanations,* fuller elaborations of the minimal statements in the glossary. Explanations may be taken from the text or from your class notes. Finally, try to have a concrete *example* of each term. Select an example that is clear to you and also is uncontroversial.

Memorization has a bad press, but it's necessary more often than we think (e.g., for exams). We don't encourage memorization for its own sake, but rather, to make your passive knowledge more active. The best time to memorize is after you have become familiar with a concept through much exposure. For long lists (e.g., the prepositions of English) never try to remember every item; select one or a few items, and then only to illustrate a key term. As you gain experience, try to add gradually to that short list. Memorization of terminology should be limited to those key items singled out by your instructor. Remember, though, to use precise language in defining terms. Linguists like to think of themselves as scientists and so value precision and accuracy greatly.

At the head of each chapter, we have listed the key concepts developed therein. We imagine these topics as serving as the focus for essays that might form a part of your examinations. The internal parts of the chapters are clearly indicated by numbers; these subdivisions will provide handy outlines for essays.

REFERENCES AND RESOURCES

Aitchison, Jean. 1987. *Words in the Mind: An Introduction to the Mental Lexicon.* Oxford: Basil Blackwell.

Dillon, George. 1978. *Language Processing and the Reading of Literature.* Bloomington: Indiana University Press.

Traugott, Elizabeth, and Mary Louise Pratt. 1980. *Linguistics for Students of Literature.* New York: Harcourt Brace Jovanovich, Inc.

How many words are in your vocabulary? According to Aitchison (1987), "the number of words known by an educated adult . . . is unlikely to be less than 50,000 and may be as high as 250,000." We may have active control over as much as 90 percent of these words.

GLOSSARY

Active vocabulary: those words that we have ready access to for speaking and writing.

Critical thinking: intellectual skills ranging from syllogistic reasoning to detecting covert claims in arguments to deciphering instructions and technical information.

Discourse: language, ranging in length from a single word to a novel, that occurs in a particular situational context and that forms a coherent whole.

Learnability: the ease with which material can be learned by students.

Linguistic insecurity: the widespread feeling or belief that one's language is in some way deficient, for example, that one's accent is not as good as other accents.

Logical positivism: early twentieth-century philosophy which held that scientific investigation should focus only on concrete, observable phenomena, thus excluding from linguistics any concern for meaning.

Ordinary language philosophy: mid-twentieth-century philosophy concerned with the meanings and uses of language.

Passive vocabulary: those words whose meanings we recognize when we hear them spoken or see them written but cannot easily bring to mind in speaking or writing.

Pragmatics: see Chapter Two.

Teachability: the ease with which material can be organized for presentation in classrooms.

Semantics: see Chapter Two.

1 CONCEPTS OF LANGUAGE

KEY CONCEPTS

A language as a system of rules

Defining a language

Approaches to language study: prescriptive, descriptive, theoretical, analytic, and applied

Competence and performance

1.0 A LANGUAGE AS A SYSTEM OF RULES

The study of language and of the texts and discourses created with it occupies a significant part of primary and secondary school curricula, as it has for many centuries. Because of this, it's very important that teachers have an understanding of language and of the presuppositions underlying the various approaches to language that they encounter. Grammars are analyses of language, but every grammar is a representative, stated or otherwise, of a particular point of view, of particular assumptions about the nature of language, and of the human beings that learn and use it. It's important therefore to understand just what, often unstated, assumptions come with the grammar or handbook of style chosen by a school or school district.

Grammarians have been writing grammars for thousands of years. Many early attempts were second language teaching textbooks, mainly for Greek and Latin. But from the earliest times, grammarians attempted to use their analysis of language to understand the nature of the human mind. For example, Aristotelian philosophers thought that classifying objects was a basic mental activity and that, if they could understand language, then they could intimately understand the mind. Still later, grammarians in Alexandria, Egypt, had become librarians and much concerned about the authenticity of ancient, classical Greek texts. The grammars they wrote reflected their concern with language purity and accuracy. Many came to believe that the language of the ancient texts was a purer, uncorrupted language, of which the language of the day was merely a distant and degenerate relation. It's not unusual, even today, for grammarians to be primarily interested in the purity of language and in correcting grammatical errors. This view of grammarians is held by many people who are neither grammarians nor linguists.

The primary object of language study until the late eighteenth century was written language, particularly the language of literature. At the end of the eighteenth and throughout the nineteenth centuries, grammarians, like many other scholars, became caught up in the Romantic movement and, reacting to the classicism of the eighteenth century, developed interests in the history and folkways of Europe (and other areas). Thus began an interest in the spoken varieties of languages and the development of theories of the histories of the languages of Europe and of their relationships to each other. This interest in spoken and nonstandard language expanded the concept of what could be regarded as a language. Consequently, a major debate began regarding the roles that dictionaries should play. This debate continues. To many people, now as then, dictionaries define a language. If a word is not in the dictionary, it's not a real word. If a spelling is not in the dictionary, it's not a legitimate spelling. If a meaning for a word is not in the dictionary, then the word cannot have that meaning.

Early dictionary editors and compilers often saw themselves as authorities for their readers, providing them with the correct spelling, pronunciation, and interpretations of words. In the middle of the nineteenth century, the *Oxford English Dictionary* (OED) project got underway and developed a dictionary which attempted to change that emphasis, away from prescribing what is correct and toward describing the words that people actually use and the ways in which they use them. Many people saw this as a gross dereliction of dictionary duty, and even today, as new volumes are published, OED editors receive lots of mail from angry readers complaining that various words have been included which they believe shouldn't have been.

We recognize that teachers are caught between apparently irreconcilable forces. They must ensure that their students master the forms of English that are regarded as **acceptable,** correct, educated, i.e., as **standard.** However, educational linguistic research demonstrates that unless teachers respect students' native ethnic, regional, and social varieties, students who natively speak nonstandard varieties will not learn the conventions of standard English. Similarly, studies in bilingualism show that young children whose native language is not respected in the community or in the school are at great risk of failing in the school system. Because language is such an important component, not only of education, but of individuals' personal, ethnic, and social identities, teachers must tread a fine line between teaching the standard variety required for social mobility in our society and respecting and accepting students' native varieties as reflections of their identities. Just as every child has a right to expect teachers to respect his or her sex, ethnicity, social class, color, and creed, so every child has the right to expect teachers to respect his or her language. It's a lot easier to accept linguistic variation if we understand both it and our own attitudes toward it. We deal with this issue in more depth in Chapters 13 and 14.

In the rest of this chapter, we will consider some basic premises about language that permeate this book.

1.1   DEFINING A LANGUAGE

As teachers of language, you need to have a concrete notion of what it is that you teach. Surprisingly, few people have even the most rudimentary conception of a language, even though they use it in nearly every waking moment of their lives—as well as in their dreams. Ordinary people may lead perfectly adequate lives without clear conceptions. For instance, they don't need a precise understanding of physical notions such as *force, work,* or *energy* to build houses or to hit home runs. But education aims to lead people out of unarticulated lives into realms of understanding that explain the mundane behavior that we take for granted. Language is no exception. In fact, it's the premier case of the marvelous complexity that underlies human communication—ranging from the most ordinary to the most profound.

It's important to ask the right question. We don't ask, "What is language?" because this formulation leads to premature abstraction. The key question is, What is *a* language? By "a language," we mean a real-life system for human communication. This formulation of the question isn't uncontroversial. What about animal communication? Why do we view language as systematic rather than chaotic? The answers to these questions will become clearer as we explore in this section the fundamental notions of modern linguistics.

1.1.1 A language communicates meaning

Most people conceive of meaning in terms of *information*—ideas about the external world or about our internal thoughts and beliefs. Such **referential meaning** no doubt accounts for a large portion of communication, but it's not the whole story. **Expressive meaning** reflects the emotional state of a speaker. *Ouch!* has no referential status but expresses pain. **Conative meaning** refers to the intended impact of an utterance on its hearer. *Can you pass the salt?* is only incidentally a question about your physical ability; rather, it attempts to get you to perform the action indicated. **Phatic meaning,** as in expressions such as *Hi!* and *How are you?*, establishes and maintains social contact between communicators. **Metalinguistic meaning** addresses matters concerning the language itself. Definitions or word puzzles are metalinguistic. (For example, what English word has three double letters in a row? See the end of this chapter for the answer.) Finally, **poetic** or **stylistic meaning** reflects nuances of interpretation brought about by the manner in which information is expressed. For instance, Dickens might have opened *A Tale of Two Cities* with [1a] rather than with [1b]:

[1a] In some ways, the times were good and in some ways, the times were bad.
 [b] It was the best of times, it was the worst of times, . . .

The addition of what literature teachers call paradox, the sense of apparent contradiction with an underlying resolution, is part of the poetic meaning of [1b] that is absent from [1a].

Many types of communication are composites of these six types of meaning. Consider the bumper sticker *If guns are outlawed, only outlaws will have guns.* Referentially, it has two propositions (*guns are outlawed* and *outlaws have guns*) joined by an *if-then* connective. Its conative meaning is that guns should not be outlawed. Its poetic meaning rests in the order of the key elements—*guns/outlawed: :outlaws/guns*—a mirror image device called *chiasmus* (Jakobson, 1960).

Meaning can be divided into two categories, *what is expressed* and *what is meant.* What is expressed is a broad category that includes the total meaning that can be gained from a situation. If you meet a person with a gravy stain on his tie, you might infer that that person is sloppy. If you meet someone with a black eye, you might conjecture that she has been in a fight or has had an accident with a door. In both cases, you have received (referential) information, but in neither case has the information been meant. The information has arisen through natural causes rather than through the intentions of the communicators. In contrast, if you had arranged with the first person that he would wear a gravy-stained tie rather than a clean one to convey some message, then the tie would represent intended information. The key notion is that of *intention*. **Linguistic meaning** arises because human beings intend others to derive information by recognizing their intention to convey that information. All of the types of meaning in the previous paragraphs are intended meanings.

Meaning can be expressed either directly (*literally*) or indirectly (*nonliterally*). For example, the sentence *The window is open*, literally describes the current state of a particular window. In certain contexts, however, it could mean—nonliterally—something like "Please close the window." We will explore this distinction further in Chapter 2, under the headings of semantics and pragmatics.

EXERCISE   Give an example of a type of communication that illustrates each of the following sorts of meaning:
- a. conative meaning
- b. referential and conative meaning
- c. intended phatic meaning
- d. unintended phatic meaning
- e. unintended poetic meaning
- f. literal expressive meaning
- g. nonliteral expressive meaning

1.1.2   A language uses sound as its primary means of expression

Meanings aren't magically created; they're based on physical expression, primarily through the medium of speech. While meanings can be conveyed in writing, most of our communication doesn't take this form. Sign languages of the deaf, of course, use manual expression of meaning, but they're not the most common form of language. Speech is primary for several reasons besides the frequency of its use. Children learn to talk before they learn to write. Also, languages exist that have no writing systems. Moreover, writing is a comparatively recent historical development, being only a few thousand years old. Spoken language is at least 30,000 years old.

We can, somewhat simplistically, look at a language as a means to relate sounds to meanings. In this view, one distinctive characteristic of a language is its **arbitrariness.** That is, there is no necessary connection between any meaning and any single sound or group of sounds. Thus the sound of the word *I* has no particular connection to the speaker; we could equally designate ourselves by the sounds *je* (French), *yo* (Spanish), *ich* (German), *wǒ* (Chinese), or thousands of other expressions that exist in other languages. Indeed, most sounds in English are meaningless by themselves—p, f, n, h, e—except as names for letters. Likewise, the sounds of a word are arbitrarily related to its meaning. An English *apple* is a French *pomme,* and a Spanish *manzana*. The word *explosion* can be said either loudly or softly, as can *whisper. Giant* and *dwarf* have the same number of sounds, despite the different sizes of the things they refer to. *Lilliputian* is a big word meaning "small"; *big* and *huge* are small words for the opposite meaning.

There are a few aspects of language that appear to be **motivated**—i.e., nonarbitrary. One common example is the **onomatopoeic** words for animal noises, e.g., *moo, bow wow,* and *quack-quack*. Note that the last two of these suggest that dogs and ducks normally make noises in pairs and that speakers can distinguish a dog's *bow* from its *wow*. However, an Irish dog goes *amh-amh* and a Serbo-Croatian dog goes *av-av*. Another type of apparent motivation is **sound symbolism,** the association of certain sounds with certain meanings, as the two vowel sounds of *teeny,* represented by the phonetic symbol [i]. One can find evidence of this use of [i] in other languages. For example, Spanish uses the suffix *-ito* to designate small things and children. However, it can hardly be said that [i] carries diminutive meaning independently of the meaning of the word in which it occurs. Thus no hint of smallness appears in words like *beefy, treaty, keep,* or *heal*. And similarities with other languages may be purely accidental. The diminutive suffix of German, a language much more closely related to English than is Spanish, is *-chen*.

EXERCISE   What apparent sound symbolism occurs in the following English words? What words can you think of that don't fit the stereotypes?
a. snob, slop, snip, slut, slime, slovenly
b. moose, huge, humongous
c. gonzo, macho, mucho

1.1.3 A language is distinctively human

The word *language* is often used loosely to indicate any means of conveying meaning—e.g., the language of dance, the language of flowers, animal language. This usage is misleading, although it has some truth to it. The discipline of **semiotics** has developed in recent years to study the languagelike characteristics of various forms of communication. The range of semiotic (meaningful) systems is great, encompassing language, gestures, spatial relations, animal communication, film, advertising logos, traffic signals, clothing, and a myriad of other forms and subtypes of communication. Much semiotic research draws on either general or specific linguistic notions.

Semiotic studies have demonstrated the richness of human communication but have never uncovered any means of communication superior to language in its range of meanings. This is hardly surprising. One could hardly imagine translating the Constitution of the United States into body language or into the communication of the most sophisticated chimpanzee. While semiotics has dramatically enlarged our awareness of the scope of communication, it has produced no challengers to language on either quantitative or qualitative grounds. Likewise, research into animal communication has vastly improved our appreciation of the natural communication of primates, dolphins, birds, and fish; but it has presented no rivals to human communication, again on either qualitative or quantitative grounds. A few primates have learned, usually with intensive training, to communicate in English-like ways through sign language, plastic symbols, and computers. Their success tells us a good deal about their intelligence, but their communicative system can hardly be claimed to be that of English or of any other human language (Hockett, 1960; Sebeok, 1981; Sebeok and Rosenthal, 1981; Terrace, 1981).

Another perspective on this issue is the relationship between intelligence and language. Assuming (controversially) that IQ provides a reliable index of intelligence, language abilities are not significantly absent even at dramatically low levels:

> Language begins in the same manner in retardates as in the normal population. We found that it is impossible to train a child with, say, mongolism to parrot a sentence if he has not learned the underlying principles of *syntax*. However, the general principle underlying *naming* is grasped at once and immediately generalized. Naming behavior may be observed even in low-grade idiots; only individuals so retarded as to be deficient in stance, gait, and bowel control fail to attain this lowest stage of language acquisition. Incidentally, it is interesting to note that generalization of naming is beyond the capacity of gorilla or chimpanzee. Children whose I.Q. is 50 at age 12 and about 30 at age 20 are completely in possession of language though their articulation may be poor and an occasional grammatical mistake may occur. (Lenneberg, 1964: pp. 41–42)

1.1.4   Knowledge of language is unconsciously present in the mind

Consider the following questions:

[2a]   Do you like duckling?
 [b]   Do you like snorkeling?
 [c]   Do you like Kipling?

Without the slightest bit of thought, you know that only one of these sentences can be answered "Yes, I like to . . . ." You know this without any knowledge of grammatical terminology such as the fact that *snorkel* is a verb. And although you probably don't know terms such as **morpheme** and **diminutive** (*-ling* in [2a]), you do know that *duckling* has two meaningful parts but that *Kipling* has only one. You also know the grammatical form and function of the *snorkeling* in [2b], although you might not be able to state that it's a **gerund** functioning as a direct object (see Chapter 10). Knowing a language, then, isn't the same as knowing terminology; it isn't the same as being able to articulate grammatical descriptions. Your knowledge of language is unconscious knowledge. No amount of introspection, meditation, psychotherapy, or brain surgery will allow you to view it directly.

One's unconscious knowledge of language is called **linguistic competence.** The clearest sign of unconscious knowledge is the presence of **linguistic intuitions**—gut feelings about language that could not be accounted for in any other way besides the existence of unconscious knowledge. These intuitions, by the way, are *not* the product of education; a totally illiterate person has them. They derive from genetic capacities that are specific to humans and from the process of acquiring language. We will consider these issues further when we discuss linguistic competence below.

1.1.5   A language consists of rules

The word *rule* conjures up exactly the wrong image of language knowledge, suggesting the prescriptions of right and wrong that one finds in style manuals. Linguistic usage employs the word to mean something much different. A **rule** is a part of one's unconscious knowledge of language (one's competence). It's a generalization about a limited part of the language, e.g., pronunciation or sentence structure. For example, English speakers know that the language has a basic subject-verb-object word order and that questions are formed when a part of the verbal element (e.g., *have, be, do*) appears before the subject. Of course, these rules are internalized without specific labels such as *subject* and *verb*. By attempting to formulate rules in words, we are building a **model** of the rule. Our model isn't the rule itself, which remains forever invisible.

When we study language from a linguistic perspective, then, we actually explore our unconscious mind. The motivation for stating rules and devising terminology isn't to improve our writing or to allow us to pass a test. It leads us to the innermost core of our mind, that part of us that makes us distinctively human. Fortunately, information about language is abundant, visible, and inexpensive. If they know the proper approach, teachers and even their youngest students can create complex and fascinating models of their competence. At more advanced levels, the precise articulation of models and refinements of analysis lead students to higher levels of critical thinking.

EXERCISE   What sort of rule can you formulate that might underlie the following sentences? (The symbol * means **ungrammatical,** i.e., not in conformity with the rules of competence.)

a.   Harry sent a present to Mary.
b.   Harry sent Mary a present.
c.   Harry sent a package to Boston.
d.   *Harry sent Boston a package.

1.1.6   A language is a system

Rules aren't distributed randomly in the mind like potatoes in a sack. Rather, they're intricately related to one another in what linguists call a system. It's easiest to envision this conception on the analogy with a stereophonic system. The music system has a set of **components** (receiver, amplifier, tape deck, CD player, etc.) whose overall function is to convert electronic signals of various sorts into sound. Components can interact with each other; for instance, you can play a CD, using the amplifier, while at the same time recording the music on the tape deck. The components also contain smaller parts, all of which interact in precise, though limited, ways with each other and with parts of other components.

Language systems likewise have components. The most commonly cited ones are **phonology, morphology, syntax, semantics,** and **pragmatics. Phonology** concerns the sounds of language, **morphology** the structure of words, **syntax** the principles of sentence structure, **semantics** the literal meanings of words and sentences, and **pragmatics** the meanings that arise when sentences are used in contexts. As we proceed further in this book, you will learn in much more detail the intricate ways in which the system operates. Doing so is one of the joys of language study.

For the moment, let's look at one concrete example of how the system creates interdependencies among its rules and components. The syntactic rule for yes-no questions is connected to the rules of pronunciation, specifically to intonation, the musical pattern of speech. Thus a question has a different pattern of pitches from its statement counterpart:

[3a]   They're leaving at 6:00.
 [b]   Are they leaving at 6:00?

The syntactic rule for statements relates also to semantic and pragmatic rules for the issuing of indirect requests for action. Thus [4] can be interpreted as a request for someone to close the window:

[4]   The window is open.

Pragmatic rules specify that a statement can be a request for action if it designates a state contrary to the one ultimately intended, i.e., the window's being closed. Such rules also specify how an utterance fits into its context:

[5a]   It's cold in here.
 [b]   The canary is gone.

Following [5a], [4] is a request for action. Following [5b], [4] is a suggestion about the canary's escape route. There are many more interdependencies among phonology, syntax, and pragmatics. A syntactic statement can be changed into an exclamatory question by raising the voice pitch at the end of the sentence; this can be roughly indicated through punctuation:

[6]   The window is *open*!!??

By quickly raising and lowering the pitch on *open,* we can create a nonliteral (i.e., pragmatic) implication of contrastive denial:

[7]   The window is *open.* [not closed]

1.1.7   Summary

We can assemble the various elements of our definition of a language in the following definition:

A language is a system of rules, unconsciously present in the mind, that enables humans to relate sounds and meanings.

1.2 APPROACHES TO LANGUAGE STUDY: PRESCRIPTIVE, DESCRIPTIVE, THEORETICAL, ANALYTIC, AND APPLIED

Prescriptive grammarians are mainly concerned with the conventions that govern formal, written communication. Their goal is to maintain a standardized variety of a language so that it can function as the variety of the major domains of a state, such as education, government, commerce, and law, as well as among people separated by great distances, by great cultural differences, and by considerable spans of time. This requires a set of widely accepted conventions that are codified in grammars and dictionaries and style manuals. Such conventions ensure that people using the standard variety will use the same forms in the same ways and with the same meanings, thus presumably facilitating clear and unambiguous communication. Chapter 14 of this book addresses prescriptive grammar in more detail.

Descriptive grammarians are interested primarily in people's linguistic knowledge and behavior, in what they say and how they say it. They don't judge it as correct or incorrect. Generally, they believe that if a community of native speakers of a language consistently speaks in such and such a way, then so be it. That, for the descriptive grammarian, is correct, regardless of how prescriptive grammarians view the behavior. Descriptive grammarians attempt to put aside their own linguistic prejudices (yes, we all have them) and accept and describe what they observe.

EXERCISE   Find three expressions (e.g., *ain't*) that English speakers regularly use but which prescriptive grammarians claim that they shouldn't use. (You may have to look in a prescriptive grammar or handbook of style for this.)

To make the differences between these two approaches more concrete, let's consider an example. We will look at the phenomenon of **preposition stranding**—removing the noun phrase that a preposition governs, as in:

[8]   Bill is impossible to live with.

The preposition *with* typically occurs before a noun phrase, e.g., *with Bill.* In [8], *Bill,* the object of *with,* has been "moved" to the beginning of the sentence (actually into the subject position of the main clause). Prescriptive grammarians have objected to stranded prepositions, especially at the ends of sentences, for two centuries. Their reasons have been many and varied. For instance, the very influential eighteenth-century grammarian, Lindley Murray, regarded them as "inelegant." Currently, editors of various kinds of documents try to eliminate prepositions that end sentences, often for vague reasons or, indeed, for no reasons at all.

1. Find a prescriptive grammar which objects to preposition stranding and report on the reasons it gives for its objection.
2. Besides preposition stranding, what other phenomena do editors, etc. advise us to avoid? Why?

Descriptive linguists respond that speakers of English strand prepositions frequently, both within and at the ends of sentences. We do it naturally. We don't correct each other for it. In fact, we don't even notice stranded prepositions unless our attention is drawn to them. In this regard, we behave differently from how we react to other kinds of errors. For example, we may correct each other's pronunciation (sometimes subtly, sometimes not). We have all felt the strangeness of pronouncing a word seen in print but never heard. We may remark on variant pronunciations of words like *tomato,* joking with people from Britain or Ireland about their pronunciation of the middle vowel. We never do this with stranded prepositions. Stranding prepositions is therefore not a mistake. It's not odd or objectionable. It's not a matter of regional, national, social, or ethnic variation. It does have some stylistic implications. Preposition stranding occurs in all but the most formal types of English.

The descriptive approach to language encompasses a much wider range of inquiry than just grammar. In the following section, we sketch the spectrum of interests that descriptive linguists have pursued. In so doing, we hope to stimulate your curiosity about topics that will one day inform your own teaching. During your career as a teacher, research on many of these topics will yield insights into classroom practice.

The three dimensions of descriptive language study are: (1) theoretical, (2) analytic, and (3) applied. We will examine these areas in the next three sections.

1.2.1   Theoretical linguistics

It's important that we declare the basic assumptions that we make about language. To do anything less is intellectually and ethically unjustifiable, as well as practically imprudent. Theoretical linguists try to articulate exactly what assumptions about language one can reasonably make. For example, they argue that language: (1) is systematic; (2) is rule-governed; (3) is based on unconscious knowledge; and (4) has components such as phonology, syntax, and semantics. Any of these assumptions can be tested, confirmed, or disproved. They are interpretations of facts. They are not themselves facts.

Theoretical linguists take a descriptive attitude, but they want to go beyond merely analyzing language. Their goals are to understand what they observe and to explain why human languages are as they are. To do this, they construct **models of language.** Models are graphic portrayals of the design of languages. For instance, a model might sketch out a syntactic component with different types of rules, as we will see in Chapter 11. In so doing, theoretical linguists try to formulate general statements about what is and what isn't possible in human languages. For example, a theoretical linguist might try to determine the reasons why no human language asks questions by simply reversing the word order of a statement.

Theoretical linguists thus can identify some very general principles that govern language. In science, as in many other fields, if a statement follows logically from general principles, then it's regarded as *explained*. In linguistics, if the rules proposed by linguists for a language follow logically from general assumptions about the nature of human language, then they're regarded as explanations and the general hypotheses are supported. For example, suppose a linguist proposed the following rule for a language called Jibbrish:

[9]   To ask a question in Jibbrish, interchange the first and second words of a statement.

A theoretical linguist would immediately recognize this rule as impossible for a human language—although it might be possible for an extraterrestrial being. The reason is that the rule in [9] violates the general principle of **structural dependency.** This principle states that no human language makes use of numbered positions in its rules but, rather, creates rules on the basis of grammatical categories such as subjects, objects, nouns, and verbs.

Theoretical linguists also define the principles of subdisciplines within the field and devise analytic techniques that can be used in the study of language. These subdisciplines include, among others, phonetics, phonology, morphology, syntax, semantics, pragmatics, and discourse analysis. Theoreticians are interested in how these fields and their basic concepts are internally organized and how they're interrelated.

To consider a concrete example of theoretical linguistics, let's return to preposition stranding. Theoreticians would want to know where the object of a preposition can and cannot be moved to in English. They would want to know what other characteristics of language preposition stranding is related to. They wonder why, and attempt to explain why, English speakers may strand prepositions, but French speakers may not:

[10]   *Bill est impossible vivre/habiter avec.

They wonder what preposition stranding can tell them about the nature of language and about the differences between languages that allow it and those that don't. They attempt to develop theories in which these facts follow naturally from very general, and often from very abstract, assumptions about language. For both descriptive and theoretical linguists, sentences like [10] are **ungrammatical** in French but quite **grammatical** in English, although they may be **unacceptable** to some English speakers in very formal contexts.

EXERCISE   Why do you think that English allows preposition stranding but French doesn't? Speculate a bit on how you might explain this difference.

Theoretical linguists tend to think of themselves as scientists and of their activities as following the methodology of science. They observe phenomena, make general statements to describe their observations, hypothesize what else should be true if their generalizations are true, and test whether they were correct. If they're correct, theoretical linguists create more hypotheses and test again. If they're incorrect, they revise their generalizations and hypotheses and test again. In a sense, they want to be wrong. When they find where they're wrong, they can improve their original formulation and account for a wider range of data than before. Linguistic study, from this point of view, is a dynamic, ongoing, creative task, subject to constant criticism and revision. It's important to understand this because not to do so leads to several misconceptions.

EXERCISE   How would you test your explanation of the difference between English and French regarding preposition stranding?

Language rules from this perspective are not a body of immutable laws discovered or imposed by scholars. They are, rather, reflections of our current understanding of the phenomena of natural language. It follows that what from one linguist's vantage point are exceptional aspects of a language, are from another's perfectly regular features. What I believe today to be regular features may, upon tomorrow's reevaluation, turn out to be exceptional. Exceptions from this general point of view are facts that don't fit within a proposed general rule or statement. Once the statement has been changed, the set of exceptions may change.

It's also important not to see this as either an academic shell-game or an endorsement of the view that anything goes in English these days. In the last century and a half, linguists have discovered an enormous amount about many individual languages and much about natural language in general. Consequently, particularly in the last generation, new understandings about the nature of human beings and the human mind have emerged. These have provided far richer models of how human beings learn, remember, and solve problems than were available before. Furthermore, we have discovered a great deal about the relationships among language, culture, and society. It turns out that we are far more complex than we had given ourselves credit for.

EXERCISE   In what ways do you think the scientific study of language might have affected psychology, computer science, education, and law?

As we noted, we don't believe that "anything goes" in English or in any other language. Languages and language varieties are rule-governed. Some forms are meaningful, grammatical, or acceptable; others are meaningless, ungrammatical, or unacceptable. The status of an expression is judged against the rules that constitute the grammar of the language or variety and the rules of appropriateness of utterances to specific situations. If the grammar cannot assign a meaning to the utterance, then it will be either completely or partially **meaningless.** If the utterance isn't in accord with the structural rules of the language, then it's **ungrammatical.** If the utterance is inappropriate in a given situation, then it's **unacceptable.**

EXERCISE   Construct three meaningless sentences, three ungrammatical sentences, and three sentences that are inappropriate in some context. Don't forget to specify the context.

1.2.2   Analytic linguistics

Language theorists don't work in a vacuum. Rather, they base their hypotheses on the careful examination of language done by either themselves or other linguists. Linguistic analysis draws upon the theories and the analytic tools noted above to provide a description of the facts and rules of entire languages or of portions of a language. For example, Franz Boas and Ella Deloria's *Dakota Grammar* (1939) uses the American structuralist model of language to describe the phonetics, morphology, and syntax of this plains Indian language. In linguistic description, the term **grammar** can refer either narrowly to the rules of sentence formation (syntax) or more broadly to the overall analysis of a language.

Linguistic analysis extends into many fields. The study of regional variation (**dialectology**) and of social variation (**sociolinguistics**) has contributed much to our awareness of the diversity of English (see Chapter 13). Research has broadened our understanding of first and second language acquisition, of the role of language in psychology, computer science, and law. In education, analytic linguistics has contributed to areas such as syntax, lexicography, usage, reading, writing, and literature. These accomplishments concern mostly the present state of the language, a perspective called **synchronic linguistics.** Analysis also extends to the historical study of languages, a perspective called **diachronic** (or **historical**) **linguistics.**

1.2.3   Applied linguistics

Applied linguists draw upon theoretical models and analytic work for practical purposes. Computer parsers, artificial intelligence (e.g., speech recognition and synthesis), and machine translation form the computational side of the applied linguistic family. Linguists have been hired as consultants to help in the simplification of legal documents and in documenting the identities of tape-recorded human voices in trials. They have helped the governments of emerging nations devise alphabets and establish public policies on language. In education, they have provided methods of language teaching (e.g., foreign languages, including English as a foreign or second language, and bilingual education). And there are linguistic underpinnings to innovative designs for English curricula, such as the Whole Language approach.

In spite of many contributions, linguistics hasn't made its full impact on education. Perhaps teachers fear the technicalities of a discipline that claims English study to be a science. Some may see linguistics as a threat to traditional values in teaching. But the future of English education, we are convinced, lies with the broadening of the artificial borders in which the discipline has confined itself since the nineteenth century.

Teachers are the key figures in healing the rift between the sciences and the humanities. One of the aims of this book is to initiate you into the linguistic point of view and to provide you with the linguistic literacy that you will need to enter the next century. As we have tried to show in this section, applied work grows out of theoretical and analytical frameworks. Without those contexts, application is nothing more than sterile gadgetry doomed to failure for lack of intellectual roots. Moreover, theoretical and analytic notions can provide you and your students with intellectually stimulating and rewarding classroom activities. Many of the exercises in this book exemplify such activities.

EXERCISE   Go to your college library and visit the language section. Identify three areas that interest you (e.g., child language acquisition, regional dialects) and report on the books available on the subject. Try to find journals on the topic too and note the types of articles that appear in them. If you have time, consult the ERIC system; you may do so either with hard copy or on a computer if one is available. See the ERIC thesaurus of descriptors, under the heading of "language." (*Note:* This exercise is a good way to get started on a course project or paper.)

1.3   COMPETENCE AND PERFORMANCE

Current theoretical linguists distinguish between the knowledge that speakers of a language must have in order to be able to function in that language and the use speakers make of that knowledge to speak, understand, read, or write. They call our knowledge of the rules that constitute the language **competence,** and they call our linguistic activities **performance.** These activities demonstrate that we possess linguistic competence. From this point of view, the primary task of a theoretical linguist is to discover and create a hypothetical model of the rules that constitute a speaker's competence. Linguists often use the term **grammar** or **internalized grammar** to designate competence; this usage should be carefully distinguished from the two earlier uses of the term.

Performance provides ample evidence of competence. For instance, we can use our ability to specify just what is and what isn't **grammatical** (in accord with unconscious rules) in our language. Consider the following:

[11]   *The blocking the entrance protester was arrested.

Although we can certainly make sense of the sentence, we know that it isn't natural. (It *would* be if translated into German with this word order.) Of course, we may not know exactly what makes the sentence unnatural; nor is it likely that we have been taught anything explicitly about this structure. Likewise, you can determine hidden grammatical relations:

[12a]   Joan is eager to please.
  [b]   Joan is easy to please.

In [12a], Joan will do the pleasing; in [12b] someone else will please Joan. Such "understood" relations are quite common in language. You can also perceive **ambiguity** (two or more distinct interpretations):

[13]   Molly told Angela about herself.

Here Molly is talking about *either* Molly *or* Angela.

The notion of competence depends on certain necessary fictions. Many linguists, though by no means all, assume that all speakers of a language have the same set of rules in their competence. This is a conscious simplification, made with full awareness of the variety inherent in natural language. It's done to allow linguists to develop models of competence without being distracted by phenomena that don't appear to necessitate altering the models' basic principles and architecture. This assumption is not uncontroversial. It has occasionally been viewed as an attempt to ignore the social, discourse, and textual functions of language, which some linguists believe to be crucial in understanding language structure. It has also been viewed, because the majority of linguists are white, male, and middle class, as a thinly disguised attempt to define their variety of English as the grammatical model for all language and all varieties, much as Latin grammar was until recently (and in many situations still is) the model for the grammars of other European languages.

While neither criticism is justified in its extreme version, both point up limitations of the language-as-competence approach. They also point up the need to understand language as a social artifact used by social beings in social contexts for social purposes.

Because many modern theoretical linguists begin from the assumption that what they're modeling is knowledge, it follows that their theories have implications for psychologists and ultimately for biologists. Many believe that language is a very specialized, perhaps unique, kind of knowledge. They believe that it isn't acquired in the ways that other kinds of knowledge are acquired, such as writing or arithmetic. They point out, in support of this belief, that children can learn the language (or languages) of their environments without any instruction from parents or peers. Moreover, children learn a vastly complex system in a very short time, and all children acquire very similar grammars of a given language regardless of the differences in what they hear about them, and (up to a point) regardless of their differences in intelligence. On the basis of these observations, and the (abstract) similarities among languages, these linguists argue that humanity is specifically endowed by nature and genetics with a capacity to acquire natural languages with particular kinds of rule systems. They argue that linguistic knowledge is different in kind from other knowledge because it's based on specialized mental structures, which in turn appear to be based on specialized brain structures.

In support of this neurobiological claim, linguists point out that damage to certain parts of the brain, mainly in the left hemisphere, affects people's linguistic abilities, whereas damage to corresponding areas in the right hemisphere doesn't. Thus the language capacity appears to be (at least partially) localized in the brain. If this point of view is correct, it explains why, even with intense and specific training, no nonhumans, even the most intelligent ones, have ever learned a human language.

EXERCISES

1. What kinds of errors have you observed people to make in learning a second language?
2. Find a description of one of the many attempts to teach an ape a human language. Describe the teaching methods and the results. How do they compare to the ways in which children acquire languages? How do these animals' linguistic skills compare with the linguistic skills of ordinary people?

This point of view regarding language and grammar makes some very important claims about the nature of knowledge, at least linguistic knowledge. It used to be thought that all knowledge, whether acquired by humans or birds, was essentially a matter of habit. One learned to respond in various ways to particular things that occurred in the environment, and the strength of the habit was a function of the number of times a particular stimulus and response were associated by the learner. From this point of view, understanding a sentence would be a matter of associating a particular response with it. And learning a language is a matter of learning just which responses go with which sentences. The process was viewed by behaviorist psychologists as in principle identical to the process by which a laboratory pigeon learns to peck at different colors or shapes.

In 1957, Noam Chomsky published a remarkable little book, *Syntactic Structures,* in which he pointed out that the behaviorist approach to language cannot in principle account for language, its acquisition, and its use. Language is vast. In fact, the number of sentences that any language contains is **infinite.** You can demonstrate this for yourself in a number of ways.

Select what you believe to be the longest sentence of the language. Once you have your candidate, put the words *I believe that* before it. Now you have created a sentence even longer than the first. This must now be the longest sentence of the language. But even to this we can add *Fred thinks that* to create an even longer sentence. To make an (infinitely) long story short, there is no longest sentence in English or any other natural language. Language allows us, in principle, if not in actuality, to create infinitely long sentences, and consequently, to create an infinite number of sentences. We do this by inserting one sentence within another, within another, within another . . . . *ad infinitum.* This property of inserting a sentence within a sentence is called **recursion.** It's because natural languages are recursive that they allow for the creation of an infinite number of sentences. All natural human languages have this property. So do all varieties of human languages. It follows that all languages and varieties are equal from this point of view.

Now, while our languages may be infinite, our memories aren't. Consequently, our knowledge of our language, our competence, cannot be just a set of sentences. It must be a set of devices that allow us to create sentences as we need them. Thus we can produce and understand an indefinite number of sentences that we have never heard or uttered before. We do this, partially, by matching what we hear with the rules of language that we keep in our heads.

EXERCISES   1. Create another demonstration of the infinity of natural language.
2. Reread this chapter until you find ten sentences that you had never read or heard before. Try to find one sentence in this chapter that you *have* read or heard before.

REFERENCES AND RESOURCES

Boas, Franz, and Ella Deloria. 1939. *Dakota Grammar*. Washington, DC: U.S. Government Printing Office, vol. 23, 2, Memoirs of the National Academy of Sciences.

Chomsky, Noam. 1957. *Syntactic Structures*. The Hague: Mouton.

Hockett, Charles. 1960, 1981. "The Origin of Speech." *Scientific American,* 203 (3):88–95. Also in

William S-Y. Yang, ed., *Human Communication: Language and Its Psychobiological Bases.* San Francisco: W. H. Freeman and Co., 4–12.

Jakobson, Roman. 1960. "Closing Statement: Linguistics and Poetics." In Thomas A. Sebeok, ed., *Style in Language.* Cambridge, MA: MIT Press, 350–377.

Lenneberg, Eric. 1964. "A Biological Perspective of Language." In R. C. Oldfield and J. C. Marshall, eds., *Language.* Harmondsworth, England: Penguin Books, 32–47.

Terrace, Herbert. 1981. "A Report to the Academy." In Sebeok and Rosenthal, eds., *The Clever Hans Phenomenon: Communication with Horses, Whales, Apes, and People.* Annals of the New York Academy of Sciences 364. New York: The New York Academy of Sciences, 94–114.

Sebeok, Thomas A. 1981. "The Ultimate Enigma of 'Clever Hans': The Union of Nature and Culture." In Sebeok and Rosenthal, eds., *The Clever Hans Phenomenon: Communication with Horses, Whales, Apes, and People.* Annals of the New York Academy of Sciences 364. New York: The New York Academy of Sciences, 199–205.

———, and Robert Rosenthal, eds., 1981. *The Clever Hans Phenomenon: Communication with Horses, Whales, Apes, and People.* Annals of the New York Academy of Sciences 364. New York: The New York Academy of Sciences.

The word *bookkeeper* has three double letters in a row.

GLOSSARY

Acceptable: in accord with *both* descriptive and prescriptive rules. See **grammatical, unacceptable.**

Ambiguous: having two or more clearly distinct interpretations.

Analytic (also called **"descriptive"**) **linguistics:** the branch of language study that attempts to analyze whole languages or parts of languages, proposing descriptive rules.

Applied linguistics: the branch of language study that (ideally) employs theory and description for practical purposes—e.g., first language teaching, especially composition; second language teaching; translation; language policy; etc.

Arbitrariness: the lack of natural connection between a sign (e.g., the sounds of a language) and its meanings.

Competence (also called **"internalized grammar"**): native speakers' unconscious knowledge of the rules of their language.

Components of language: the interrelated subparts of a model of language, specifically phonology, morphology, syntax, semantics, and pragmatics. Each component is made up of rules.

Conative meaning: the intended communicative effect of an utterance on its hearer.

Diachronic linguistics: the study of historical change in languages. See **synchronic linguistics.**

Dialectology: the study of regional variation in a language.

Diminutive: a part of a word indicating smallness or youth; e.g., Bill**y.**

Expressive meaning: a meaning that indicates the emotional state of a speaker.

Grammar (descriptive): (1) an overall systematic description of a language, written by a linguist or some other person; (2) the syntactic part (component) of the overall description, describing the systematic rules of sentence structure; (3) linguistic competence, i.e., the unconscious but systematic knowledge of the rules of one's native language (also called "**internalized grammar**"); (4) the systematic rules in one's linguistic competence that apply to sentence structure.

Grammar (prescriptive): an unsystematic list of language variations with the claim that one of the variants is right/correct/proper and the others aren't.

Grammatical (descriptive): (1) in accord with rules of competence; (2) pertaining to sentence structure.

Grammatical (prescriptive): in accord with rules of correctness. See **grammar (prescriptive).**

Infinity of language: the capacity of language to express an indefinite number of sentences, as well as an endlessly long sentence.

Internalized grammar: see **competence.**

Language: a system of rules, unconsciously present in the mind, that enables humans to relate sounds (also gestures or graphic symbols) and meanings.

Language acquisition: a process by which children develop the rules of competence in their native language; based on genetic predisposition and exposure to language rather than on formal teaching.

Linguistic competence: see **competence.**

Linguistic intuition: the natural sense of grammaticality, ambiguity, and structure in one's native language.

Linguistic meaning: a meaning that arises from semantic and pragmatic factors of an utterance, as a result of a hearer's perceiving a speaker's intention.

Meaningless (descriptive): making no sense whatever.

Meaningless (prescriptive): not adhering to logic or to rules of correctness.

Metalinguistic meaning: a meaning focusing on items of the language system.

Model of language: a linguist's schematic representation of a rule, a component of language, or of an entire language.

Morphology: linguistic component dealing with the units (**morphemes**) that can be combined to make up words.

Motivated: having nonarbitrary connections between a sign (e.g., a sequence of sounds) and its meaning.

Onomatopoeia: a word or phrase whose sound appears to imitate the object it refers to.

Performance: the use of language in specific situations (speaking, writing, listening, reading); subject to interferences such as slips of the tongue, etc.

Phatic meaning: a meaning that maintains social contact between communicators.

Phonology: the linguistic component dealing with the system of pronunciation.

Poetic meaning (also called "**stylistic meaning**"): meanings conveyed through the manner in which a piece of information is expressed.

Pragmatics: the linguistic component dealing with the system of nonliteral word and sentence meanings in a language. See **semantics.**

Preposition stranding: ending a sentence with a preposition.

Recursion: a property of competence and of rules by which they repeat themselves, resulting in an infinity of structures.

Referential meaning: a meaning concerned with information about the external world or about internal thoughts or beliefs.

Rule of language (descriptive): (1) the mental representation in competence of some specific regularity in the language and (2) a statement that attempts to describe that regularity—i.e., a partial model of competence.

Rule of language (prescriptive): a statement that specifies a correct or an incorrect use of language.

Semantics: the linguistic component dealing with the system of literal meanings of words and sentences. See **pragmatics.**

Semiotics: the study of communicative (sign) systems, including language but also such systems as gestures, spatial relations, animal communication, film, advertising logos, traffic signals, clothing, etc.

Sociolinguistics: the study of language variation according to social class, ethnicity, gender, and formality.

Sound symbolism: aspects of the pronunciation of words that suggest their meanings; e.g., the vowel sound of *teeny* as suggestive of smallness.

Standard: see Chapter 13.

Structural dependency: the principle that all human languages create rules on the basis of grammatical categories such as subjects, objects, nouns, and verbs.

Stylistic meaning: see **poetic meaning.**

Synchronic linguistics: the study of a language at a particular time: i.e., as abstracted from historical change.

Syntax: the linguistic component dealing with the system of sentence structure.

Theoretical linguistics: the branch of language study that attempts to specify (1) the nature of language, its acquisition, and its use; (2) appropriate models and other technical devices used to describe language.

Unacceptable: evoking a negative response for *any reason* whatever; the broadest category of disapproval of language.

Ungrammatical (descriptive): not in accord with linguistic competence; i.e., not natural, normal, in agreement with the intuitions of the ordinary native speaker.

Ungrammatical (prescriptive): not in accord with rules of correctness.

2 MEANING AND COMMUNICATION

KEY CONCEPTS

Popular views of meaning
A linguistic view of meaning
Semantics
Word meanings and lexical relations
Sentence meanings
Pragmatics
Reference and deixis
Presupposition
Speech acts
Speakers' intended meanings
Discourse and text analysis

2.0 POPULAR VIEWS OF MEANING

Probably no aspect of language is more important than meaning. However, because meaning is so many-faceted, we still don't understand it fully. To get a hint of the complexity of the topic, consider just the range of interpretations of the forms of the word *mean* that occur in the following sentences:

[1] I didn't mean to offend you.
[2] Those clouds mean rain.
[3] Gautama finally discovered what life means.
[4] The word *cactus* means *a plant with spines*.
[5] The word *cactus* means *a plant with areoles*.
[6] When I say *Close the window*. I mean *Close the window*.
[7] When Elmer said *no*, he really meant *maybe*.

In its various forms, the word *mean* can designate notions such as *intention* [1], [6], and [7]; *causal relation* [2]; *overall intelligibility* [3]; and *simple definition* [4] and [5].

One currently popular view of meaning is that it's essentially subjective. Suppose that you're arguing to no conclusion with someone on the issue of when human life begins. You or your opponent might remark *What do you mean by "life"? It's all a matter of semantics.* Such an example suggests that individuals are free to assign any meaning that they want to words. (Such a position, of course, runs contrary to what we have said about language—namely, that it's a shared system of rules.)

Another, and closely related, popular view of meaning suggests that much communication is actually *mis*communication. The assumption is that speakers and hearers start off with quite divergent ideas about whatever they're discussing, and only after subsequent negotiation come to an approximate consensus on the notions associated with their words. The emphasis on miscommunication is closely allied with the idea that meaning is a mental image. This assumes that the meaning of a word is the image it prompts in the minds of its users. We will return to this idea shortly.

A third popular view about meaning is that it's a single phenomenon. Examples [1] to [7] should be sufficient to convince you that the word *meaning* includes a variety of different types of communication. This variety follows from several observations: First, not only words, but sentences, have meaning; second, meaning can be expressed directly (i.e., literally) and indirectly (i.e., nonliterally). To illustrate these two points, consider:

[8] The window is open.

We might define the words *window* and *open* by using a dictionary (*the* and *is* are more problematic). We could describe the literal meaning of [8] as a relationship between a state of affairs—openness—and an object—a window, specifically that the object is in the state of openness. This simple, literal gloss expands if we consider the **context** in which [8] is uttered. Let's construct that context as [9]:

[9] *Don:* I'm cold.
   Dawn: The window is open.

In this situation, the expression *The window is open* takes on further meaning beyond the literal. It expresses not just a statement about a situation but also a *suggestion* as to what Don should do to remedy the situation, or perhaps an *explanation* of why he's cold. Any attempt to understand the nature of meaning must be prepared to deal with the literal, decontextualized interpretations of words and sentences and their interpretations in context.

2.1   A LINGUISTIC VIEW OF MEANING

Our discussion suggests a diagram such as Table 2.1, which lays out the various aspects of meaning and the disciplines that study them. **Semantics** deals with the literal meaning of words and sentences. **Pragmatics** deals with nonliteral meanings that arise in context. We can expand the definition of pragmatics further by contrasting two senses of the word **context**—(1) **linguistic context,** the actual words and sentences that precede and follow an utterance, and (2) **situational context** (AKA **extralinguistic context**), the situation

TABLE 2.1   Types of Meanings and Contexts

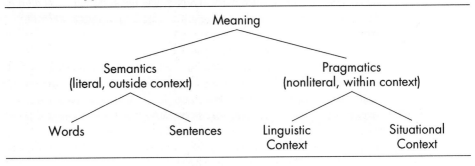

that accompanies the utterance. Extralinguistic context is quite variable and includes: (1) objects in the immediate environment, (2) knowledge shared by the speaker and the hearer, and (3) level of formality, among others.

EXERCISES
1. Identify one clear-cut instance of miscommunication, i.e., faulty conveyance or understanding of meaning. In your example, where does the fault lie, with the speaker/writer or with the hearer/reader? What linguistic resources contribute to the miscommunication? What is the difference between NONcommunication and MIScommunication?

2. Consider the theory that the meanings of words consist of the images they bring to mind. Which of the words below allow you to form clear images? Be sure to identify the images clearly and to relate them to the specific words.
   a. automobile
   b. triangle
   c. fortitude
   d. arrive
   e. ordinary
   f. frequently
   g. and
   h. of

What image do you form as the supposed meaning of the following:
   i. The cat sat on the mat.
   j. The Middle Ages gave way to the Renaissance.
   k. No man is an island.

To what extent do your images do justice to the meanings of examples a to k? On this basis, what do you see as weaknesses of the image theory? Refer to word versus sentence meaning and to literal versus nonliteral meaning.

As the exercises above suggest, the image theory of meaning leads to significant difficulties because of words such as *and, of, ordinary, belong,* and *fortitude.* The image theory emphasizes the relation between words and the external, visible world, as well as the human ability to visualize. However, language, especially in the form of sentences, is used for many more tasks than indicating visible states. And while we are certainly capable of visualizing very creatively about words and sentences, there is little reason to think that we do so in actual communication. This isn't to downplay the connection between words and the world. Linguists and philosophers use the term **reference** to designate this connection. **Referring expressions** include the following:

[10] The rose in the vase
[11] Students with 4.0 GPAs

These expressions designate real-world entities, although you will notice that they consist of more than one word. In fact, it's difficult to make a single word such as *rose* refer in communication, unless one is speaking Tarzanese and pointing to a specific flower. Example [11] indicates a further problem; you might visualize one or a dozen students with 4.0 GPAs, but the potential reference is infinite. And you might ask how many such students you would have to visualize before you knew the meaning of [11].

The simple point is that, however important it is in communication, and whatever complications it involves, *reference is not meaning*. For this reason also, the image theory isn't a valid account of meaning.

The rest of this chapter will examine meaning from the perspectives of semantics and pragmatics. We will refer to popular beliefs about meaning only occasionally. In general, linguists invoke the following working assumptions about meaning:

[12a] Meaning involves a system shared by speakers of the language.
 [b] For the most part, communication of meaning is successful.
 [c] Meaning can best be understood by studying how it occurs successfully.
 [d] Meaning has many different forms.
 [e] Meaning can be studied through two broad categories, semantics and pragmatics.
 [f] Semantics includes the literal meanings of words and sentences.
 [g] Pragmatics includes many other types of meaning.
 [h] Other types of meaning indicators (e.g., tone of voice, body language, volume, tempo, etc.) can be understood within the framework of pragmatics.

The remainder of this chapter will follow the distinction between semantics and pragmatics—i.e., between literal meaning and meaning-in-context. We turn now to semantics.

EXERCISE How does our distinction between semantics and pragmatics relate to and differ from your previous thinking about meaning? (*Hint:* You might want to explore such matters as the distinction between "What one says." and "What one means."; between language as communication and language as manipulation.)

2.2 SEMANTICS

As we have indicated, semantics involves (1) the literal meaning of words and (2) the literal meanings of sentences considered outside their contexts. To this we add one further point:

The literal meaning includes unstated meanings that are very closely tied to stated meanings. For instance, sentence [13] is closely linked to sentence [14]:

[13] I gave Mary a rose.
[14] I gave Mary a flower.

The reason for the close connection between [13] and [14] lies in the relation between the words *rose* and *flower*. In particular, the notion of being a flower is included in the definition of *rose*. We will return to this issue below. For the present, we will simply note that sentence [13] **entails** sentence [14]—but not vice versa. The terms *entail* and *entailment* are terms denoting specific semantic relations between sentences. We will deal with them in more detail below.

2.2.1 Word meaning

In Chapter 1, we observed that your linguistic competence allows you to do many things—e.g., to distinguish between well- and ill-formed strings of words, to detect grammatical structure, and to detect ambiguity. In the domain of semantics, we can also identify abilities that indicate the presence of competence. (Recall that competence is unconscious knowledge; examples such as the ones below tell us only that such knowledge must exist, not what it actually is.) Consider examples [15] to [17]:

[15] Colorless green ideas sleep furiously.
[16a] violin-fiddle
  [b] elbow-arm
  [c] big-small; above-below; open-closed
[17] I'll meet you at the bank.

Sentence [15] is a *grammatically* well-formed sentence; compare it with *Old green jalopies deteriorate rapidly*. However, the meanings of the words don't literally "fit together," thus rendering the sentence semantically ill-formed. The pairs in [16] show **semantic relationships** between words, such as **synonymy** (i.e., sameness of meaning) [16a], **meronymy** (part-whole) [16b], and **antonymy** (oppositeness of meaning) [16c]. Finally, sentence [17] shows that a grammatical structure may be ambiguous because a word may have more than one meaning (*bank* = "repository for money" or "side of a river"). In such a case, then, we have purely semantic ambiguity.

Examples such as the above could easily be multiplied, but these few should make clear a simple idea: *Linguistic competence includes an unconscious knowledge of the literal meanings of words*. While this conclusion might seem trivial, it conceals several less than obvious points. First, it suggests that speakers carry around in their minds something like a dictionary of their language. However, there is no good evidence that speakers' dictionaries resemble the published dictionaries of a language. For instance, no ordinary dictionary will tell you that the words *idea* and *sleep* cannot literally be combined as subject and predicate. (Linguists often use the terms *lexicon* or *mental lexicon* to refer to this aspect of our linguistic competence and to emphasize its difference from standard dictionaries.) In fact, the nature of the mental lexicon is still unclear; we will explore below two attempts to represent its contents.

Second, you shouldn't confuse knowing the meaning of a word with being able to give a satisfactory definition of that word. Definition-stating is a learned ability and is only marginally necessary in most communication; it's also far beyond the normal capacities of people. The eminent lexicographer Sidney Landau expresses the point simply (by "general definer," he means one versed in common, rather than technical, vocabulary):

> It is difficult to find highly skilled general definers. Such people are about as rare as good poets . . . there are probably fewer than a hundred experienced general definers in the whole of the United States. (Landau, 1984: p. 235)

Third, whatever the nature of the mental lexicon, it clearly must show that *words are related to one another*. To put it negatively, words aren't just *listed* in our competence, in alphabetical or any other simple order. Rather, they are interconnected in complex ways. Interconnections determine which words can and cannot occur together in grammatical constructions—e.g., as in [15]. Interconnections concern families (or **semantic fields**) of words related by concepts such as synonymy, meronymy, and antonymy—as in [16].

Interconnections obtain even within a single word, as in the case where a single word such as *mouth* has several *related* meanings, including a part of an animate being, of a river, or of a bottle. The technical name for this type of interrelatedness is **polysemy** (literally, "many meanings" of a single word).

EXERCISE   Without consulting a dictionary, state the meaning(s) of the words below:
a. situation
b. Pong (as in "Ping Pong ball")
c. if
d. of
e. vacillate

What problems did you run into? How did you solve them?

2.2.2 Explaining word meaning

Since published dictionaries don't offer a very useful model of our **lexical competence,** linguists have struggled to present more plausible ones. Besides having to account for the observations noted above, they must also explain the fact that, while the human brain is finite, an individual's vocabulary may be very large. Estimates for an educated person's vocabulary run anywhere from 50,000 to 250,000 words. The largest unabridged dictionary of English, Merriam-Webster's *Third New International Dictionary* (Merriam-Webster, 1961, with supplements in 1983 and in 1986) contains well over half a million definitions. Clearly, no two individuals have exactly the same vocabulary. If this is so, how can we hope to describe the vastness and variability of lexical competence? A general solution is to describe not the vocabulary of a single individual or the entire word-hoard of English, but instead, to envisage the *general properties* according to which the vocabulary of any individual—or of any language—can be constructed. There are two such viable models of lexical structure, the componential model and the network model.

2.2.2.1   The componential model

The **componential model (C-model)** is based on the premise that words are collections of many smaller units of meaning. These units are usually called **components,** although sometimes you will hear them referred to as **features.** Components are often regarded as *pure concepts,* not to be equated with the words of any language. A word is essentially a shorthand way of grouping a set of concepts under a single label. Some of the concepts that have been proposed by various linguists as components are listed in Table 2.2.

TABLE 2.2   Some Proposed Semantic Components

ANIMATE (ALIVE)	NOT	PLACE
HUMAN	CAUSE	SIZE
MALE	BECOME	HORIZONTAL
FEMALE	KNOW	VERTICAL
YOUNG	INGEST	FLAT
OLD	INTENTION	CURVED
MARRIED		

Table 2.2 includes only a fraction of the possible semantic components in language. But they're adequate to illustrate the thrust of the C-model. For instance, the word *die* is a shorthand for the components BECOME, NOT, ALIVE. The word *kill* adds to these three the component of CAUSE. The word *suicide,* includes, among others, these four plus the notion of SELF. (You should note that the components are independent of the part of speech to which they apply.) The word *cannibal* contains at least the components of INGEST and HUMAN. This example shows that certain features are irrelevant to certain words. A cannibal simply ingests humans, whether or not they're young, old, male, female, or married.

Now you might object that such definitions are grossly oversimplified. That objection is valid only in part. First, it does show the need to distinguish between universal and language-specific components. The features mentioned in Table 2.2 are quite likely to be universal, but many others may not be. In a language spoken by cannibals, the word *cannibal* may have many other literal components limited to that language—if, indeed, the language has a word for *cannibal* at all. On the other hand, if you object that *cannibal* suggests primitiveness, warfare, initiation, or absorption of the characteristics of the person devoured, your objection would not be well founded. This is because these aren't *essential* components of the meaning of *cannibal;* a cannibal is still a cannibal even if he's a highly educated rugby player. So such suggestions, however valid in one sense, don't concern the *literal* meaning of the word. And the literal meaning is all that semantics is concerned with.

EXERCISES　　1. Examine the words below. Which of the components from Table 2.2 might the words contain? For each word, identify one component that isn't in Table 2.2.
　　a. bachelor　　　d. skyscraper
　　b. spinster　　　e. table
　　c. teach　　　　f. thicken

2. Indicate words that contain the following combinations of components. If no such word exists in English, indicate that fact. If you know a language besides English, try to find a word that corresponds to the set of components.
　　a. YOUNG+HUMAN+FEMALE
　　b. YOUNG+HUMAN+MALE
　　c. YOUNG+NOT+HUMAN
　　d. YOUNG+NOT+HUMAN+EQUINE
　　e. YOUNG+NOT+HUMAN+FELINE
　　f. NOT+HUMAN+MALE+EQUINE
　　g. NOT+HUMAN+FEMALE+EQUINE
　　h. CAUSE+NOT+INGEST

3. Examine your analyses in Exercises (1) and (2). What technical problems arose in applying the C-model? For example, consider the use of NOT.

4. Examine your analyses in Exercises (1) and (2). Do you see any cultural bias in your analysis or in the C-model in general? If so, what is that bias? How would you go about correcting it within the framework of the C-model?

How effectively does the C-model account for lexical competence? Actually, quite well. First, it can deal with semantic anomaly by suggesting that words that occur together—e.g., as subject and predicate—must have compatible components. Thus in [15] the subject *ideas* has the components NOT+ANIMATE; in contrast, the predicate *sleep* requires that its subject have the component ANIMATE. Actually, the components must be seen as specifications of how words can combine with each other as well as definitions of individual words. Such specifications are called **selectional restrictions**; they identify the semantic (literal) limitations on the components of words put together in close grammatical relationships such as subject and predicate, verb and object, etc. Semantic anomaly, in short, will result when selectional restrictions are violated.

Second, semantic relations can be indicated in terms of components. Synonyms share all components. (Remember we are thinking semantically, i.e., literally!) Antonyms share all components except a very few; e.g., *alive* and *dead* share the component ANIMATE, although the latter has the component NOT.

Finally, lexical ambiguity is represented in the C-model by assigning to the same word two different sets of components. **Polysemy** is explained as having at least one common component, with at least one different component. So the various senses of *mouth* will share the component of OPENING and will be distinguished by such components as ANIMATE, SIZE, FLAT, and CURVED.

EXERCISES

1. Explain the following semantic oddities by noting the selectional restrictions that the sentence violates. Try to identify the meaning that you get from the sentence. How does that meaning arise? (Don't hesitate to use components beyond those mentioned in Table 2.2.)
   a. ?Monica elapsed.
   b. ?John accidentally resembled his sister.
   c. ?I lost my dog a grief ago.
2. For each pair of words, indicate which components they share and which components distinguish them. (Again, use components beyond those noted in Table 2.2.)
   a. car—automobile   c. huge—humongous
   b. chase—follow   d. building—skyscraper
3. Write down as many meanings as you can think of for each of the following words. (Don't use a dictionary.) Which of the meanings are related and which aren't? How can you show this difference using semantic components?
   a. ring   c. order (verb)
   b. order (noun)   d. of

2.2.2.2 The network model

While the C-model holds that **primitive concepts** lie at the root of meaning, the **network model (N-model)** posits that such concepts don't exist. Semantic competence, in contrast, is to be explained on the assumption that words—conceived of as whole entities and not broken down into components—have certain **primitive relations** with each other. In other words, our semantic competence doesn't consist of knowing definitions at all, but rather, of knowing how words relate to each other.

The primitive relations most commonly explored in the N-model are indicated in Table 2.3.

Let's examine the notions more closely. **Synonyms** aren't characterized in the familiar way as words that have the same meaning. It's quite likely that no two words have exactly the same meaning. In her lively and lucid study *Words in the Mind,* Jean Aitchison (1987) observes that we tend to *pursue* something desirable (e.g., knowledge, a career) but *chase*

TABLE 2.3 Lexical Relations in the Network Model

	Characteristics	Examples
Synonymy	Extensive overlap in meaning	large-big chase-pursue
Antonymy	Opposite of meaning along related dimensions	large-small strong-weak
Hyponymy	Inclusion of meaning	rose-flower
Meronymy	Part-whole relationship	elbow-arm

things such as runaway horses (p. 82). For some speakers, chasing evokes the notion of speed, while pursuing doesn't necessarily do so. Synonyms thus have to be thought of as two "circles of meaning" which overlap to a greater or lesser extent. In other words, synonymy allows variation in the degree of similarity between words.

Antonymy retains its traditional characteristic of oppositeness, but with the recognition of a close relationship between antonyms. *Large* and *small* share the criterial notion of size. However, *apple* and *eraser* aren't antonyms because they share little, if any, meaning aside from being physical objects. **Antonyms** like *strong/weak* are called **scalar** (or **gradable**) because they indicate dimensions on a scale, in this case of strength. **Absolute (nongradable) antonyms** such as *alive* and *dead* indicate sharp boundaries in the semantic spectrum of animacy; if one is alive, one isn't dead and vice versa. Other types of antonyms are **reversives** such as *open* and *close* and **converses** such as *above* and *below* (if x is above y, then conversely, y is below x) (Cruse, 1986).

Hyponymy, a term not familiar in traditional lexical study, highlights the common situation in language where word meanings are organized in a hierarchical taxonomy. The meaning of the word *rose* includes the meaning of the word *flower*. Consequently, if something is a rose, it's also a flower. Moreover, the set of things that we call *roses* is included in the set of things that we call *flowers*. The word referring to the subset (e.g., *rose*) in hyponomy is called a **hyponym;** the broader term (e.g., *flower*) is called the **superordinate** or **hypernym.**

Meronymy, another unfamiliar term, designates the situation where one word represents something that is a part of some whole represented by another word, e.g., *head/body*. Partitive relationships needn't apply only to physical objects but may extend to temporal relationships (e.g., *day/week*), to events (*inning/baseball game*), and even to quite abstract entities (e.g., *self-control/maturity*).

Although there are many other lexical relations, these are the most frequently mentioned in the network literature. For further elaboration, see Cruse (1986).

The network model becomes more complex because it describes the relationships not between single words but between what are called the **senses** of individual words. For instance, if you look up the noun *order* in a dictionary, you will find its meanings broken down by numerals and letters to include such different notions as: (1) "a condition of arrangement," (2) "a customary procedure," (3) "something requested for purchase," (4) "a monastic group," etc. Each one of these senses would be subject to different network relations to the senses of other words. For instance, sense 1 of *order* would be an antonym of one sense of *disorder;* sense 3 might refer to a whole of which the word *dinner* (in a restaurant) is a part.

One network relationship that deserves attention is **metaphoricity.** It appears occasionally as a connection between two different words but quite frequently between two different senses of the same word. For instance, the word *mouth* has one central sense and one metaphorical sense applying to a part of a river and another applying to the mouth of a bottle. Metaphorical senses arise historically later than their central, more literal sense. Some extensions may be haphazard; e.g., we don't think of the nose of a river or bottle. But there may be some general principles in language for metaphorical growth. For instance, English seems to have a principle by which color words may be extended to psychological states: e.g., *blue* (sad), *red* (with anger), *green* (with envy), *yellow* (cowardly), *black* (mood).

EXERCISES   1. Using the N-model, indicate how each of the following words are related. Write down any difficulties you have in coming to a decision.
a. forward—backward
b. casual—formal
c. car—wheels
d. car—passenger
e. journey (verb)—travel (verb)
f. week—semester
g. freshman—sophomore
h. turkey (fowl)—turkey (undesirable person)
i. brain (body part)—brain (very intelligent person)
2. Using the N-model, indicate the semantic relations among the words in each of the groups below. To simplify your work, write the group of words in a circle and draw lines between related words; label each line with one of the network relations. Later, redraw your diagram to show relations clearly.
a. car, truck, locomotive, wheels, trunk, hood, horn, vehicle
b. delay, linger, loiter, procrastinate, hasten, hurry, stampede (all as intransitive verbs)
c. selfish, egocentric, altruistic, giving

2.2.2.3   Relationships between the C-model and the N-model

Which of the two approaches to word meaning is valid? On the one hand, you might favor the N-model on the grounds that, when asked the meaning of a word, people tend to provide synonyms rather than fully specified definitions. The ability to state adequate definitions is beyond the capabilities of most speakers; recall Landau's remark above. Psycholinguistic experiments likewise favor the N-model as the more natural. (See Chapter 7 of Aitchison, 1987.)

On the other hand, there is some overlap between the two approaches. Synonymy and antonymy, at least, seem to be cover terms suggesting that two (or more) words share a certain number of components. One might argue that just as speakers are unable to articulate the rules of their grammatical competence, so they're incapable of identifying components or of stating definitions.

Notice that both approaches fall short of fully describing the meanings of words, e.g., the familiar lack of "complete synonymy" between words such as *stampede* and *scatter,* where the former typically is applied to cattle and the latter to a much wider range of entities (e.g., humans, animals, marbles). This objection can be overcome by relegating such matters to pragmatics. So on this score, the two approaches both come out as adequate in what they propose to accomplish as *semantic* theories.

It may be possible to combine the two approaches, in the form of a "componentially augmented network," which would combine the strengths of both approaches.

Semantic networks may well serve as devices to abbreviate redundant or repetitive semantic details. For instance, the fact that anything with the component HUMAN is also

ANIMATE is a major redundancy that might be represented in people's minds through a taxonomy of animate beings as hyponyms of the superordinate category of animacy. Put simply:

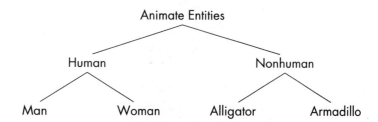

So a lower category inherits or includes the characteristics of all the categories above it on the tree. For example, women are human and animate.

The vast number of lexical items in any language makes it unlikely that a small set of lexical relationships will suffice to differentiate all words. For example, we know that *height* and *depth* have a great deal of meaning in common—e.g., measurement, vertical—but they are distinguished, as is shown by the anomalies in [18] and [19]:

[18]   The river is 50 feet deep/*high.
[19]   The mountain is 14,000 feet *deep/high.

Height and *depth* and their derivatives are thus not synonyms; the first indicates "measurement to the top"; the second denotes "measurement to the bottom" (Room, 1981: p. 62). However unable speakers might be to articulate this difference, the consistency of their semantic judgments in cases such as [18] and [19] indicates that they do know the meaning of these items. It's hard to see how a network model alone might account for such cases. Future work in semantics will no doubt shed light on the interrelationships of the two models.

EXERCISES
1. Room's *Dictionary of Distinguishables* (1981) identifies groups of words that are closely related semantically but differ in meaning. Below are some words from Room. For each group, indicate the semantic distinctions between the words. (*Hint:* For semantic distinguishables, you should be able to create sentences such as [18] and [19].)
   a. astronomy—astrology
   b. crime—offense
   c. regret—remorse
2. Standard dictionaries often attempt to distinguish the following pairs. What are the semantic differences between the members of each pair. To what extent are these differences matters of competence?
   d. infer—imply
   e. include—comprise

2.2.3   The semantics of sentences

One common belief about language is that words are the sole, or at least the primary, bearers of meaning. This notion surfaces, for instance, in the almost religious reverence paid to dictionaries. A moment's reflection should easily dispel this belief.

One would hardly be able to learn a foreign language simply by memorizing its individual words. We might be more likely to begin by either memorizing expressions from a phrase book or studying some of its basic grammar. In the phrase-book approach, we would recognize that combinations of words such as *bon jour, auf Wiedersehen,* or *hasta mañana* carry the meaning. Even single words actually serve as shorthand for longer expressions; words for "yes," such as *oui, ja,* and *si* have no meaning outside larger contexts. Clearly, the same holds true of your native language.

Adopting a grammar-centered approach to a foreign language suggests that syntactic constructions add meaning. Consider an example from English:

[20]   The aardvark chased the armadillo.
[21]   The armadillo chased the aardvark.

These sentences have exactly the same words, but convey different meanings, in this case a difference between the chaser and the chasee. Obviously, word order influences the way in which sentences—their subjects and objects—are interpreted. In this way, grammatical meaning is interwoven with word meaning.

Linguists have explored several aspects of the meaning of structures larger than words. For the moment, we will examine those that concern the literal meaning of sentences.

2.2.3.1   Propositional analysis

One approach to the study of the literal meaning of sentences is **propositional analysis**. In this type of analysis, we identify the **proposition** or propositions expressed by a sentence and represent them in a special notation. A proposition is a claim which is specific enough to be evaluated as true or false. A sentence may express one or more propositions, or indeed, may not express a complete proposition at all. Ambiguous sentences, by definition, must be represented by two or more propositions. In this section, we introduce the rudiments of the way in which propositions are represented by logicians and linguists.

The notation we introduce here depends on identifying the main communicative elements of sentences—most importantly, the main verb along with phrases that depend on it, typically its subject and objects. The result is a representation of the sentence which expresses its basic sense. In this section, we present an informal, brief, and simplified illustration of this type of analysis. For example, sentences [22] to [25] can be represented as [26] to [29]:

[22]   Oscar is laughing.
[23]   Ranger Rick is feeding Smokey.
[24]   Waldo is giving Esmeralda Fido.
[25]   Angus is superstitious.

[26] laughing(Oscar)
[27] feeding(Ranger Rick, Smokey)
[28] giving(Waldo, Esmeralda, Fido)
[29] superstitious(Angus)

Example [26] indicates an action (laughing) by Oscar; [27] represents a relationship (feeding) between Ranger Rick and Smokey; [28] represents a relationship (giving) among Waldo, Esmeralda, and Fido; and [29] denotes that Angus is in a state (superstitious).

Notice that each expression in [26] to [29] consists of an expression to the left of the parentheses, which we will call the **predicate**, and one or more expressions within parentheses, which we will refer to as the **arguments** of the predicate. Schematically, our propositions are represented in the form: Predicate (arguments). Arguments are implied or required by predicates, which may have one, two, or three of them. Thus *laughing* requires a laugher; *feeding* requires a feeder and a thing fed; *giving* requires a giver, a thing given, and a recipient. If any of these arguments are omitted, the expression is incomplete and we wouldn't be able to determine whether the proposition it's intended to express is true or false. If you already are familiar with the distinction among intransitive, transitive, and linking verbs, this analysis should pose no problems for you. If you are familiar with calculators, you may recognize operators (predicates) such as +, −, and ×, and numbers (arguments) in our notation.

In our simplified propositional analysis, we will ignore the contributions of words such as the verb *be* and of such grammatical items as tense. Of course, such details need to be accounted for. However, they don't form a part of this simple propositional analysis because they indicate only the relative time at which an event occurred or at which a state applied, not the major semantic dependencies in which we're currently interested.

No doubt you noticed that our propositions don't observe English word order. The reason for this is that word order is a matter of the grammar of specific languages rather than of semantics, and we would like our system to treat all languages equally. The choice of representation is largely a matter of convention and convenience; for example, we could have placed the predicates after the arguments (as in "reverse Polish notation" on some calculators):

[30] (Ranger Rick, Smokey)feeding

Generally, the predicate of a proposition represents the main verb of a sentence, as in [26] to [28]—*laugh, feed, give*. However, in [29], we have treated *superstitious* as a predicate. This is because *superstitious* is like a verb in that it implies someone who is superstitious, just as *laugh* implies someone who laughs.

While a simple proposition contains only one predicate, it may have up to three arguments. The order in which we list arguments is significant. Most simply, the first argument represents the subject of the sentence, and others represent various objects.

EXERCISE Identify the propositional structure of the following sentences. Ignore the tense of the verbs. Write the propositions using [26] to [29] as a model.

a. Lassie is howling.
b. Smokey bit Ranger Rick.
c. Oscar sends Smokey caviar.
d. Angus became suspicious.
e. Smokey seems confused.

Keep a record of any difficulties that you run into.

The principles of propositional analysis are very simple, but with minor modification, they will allow you to study some fairly complicated semantic structures. Let's briefly examine some of these complexities.

You may have assumed that any sentence with one grammatical clause expresses one proposition. On the contrary, a single clause may express two—or more!—propositions. In fact, there is no limit to the number of propositions that a single sentence can express. For example, consider sentence [31]:

[31]   Hungry wolves howl.

Various grammatical structures (e.g., adjectives that premodify nouns) can conceal entire propositions. So [31] could be appropriately represented as [32] or [33]:

[32]   howl(hungry(wolves))
[33]

```
                          Proposition
                         /          \
                Predicate            Argument
                   |                 /        \
                  howl          Predicate      Argument
                                   |              |
                                 hungry         wolves
```

In [32], the argument of *howl* is itself a proposition (examine the parentheses), composed of the predicate *hungry* and the argument *wolves*. These relationships are clearly labeled in the diagram in [33].

Ambiguous sentences may represent two or more distinct and unrelated propositions. For example, [34a] expresses the two propositions [34b] and [34c]:

[34a]   John saw her duck.
  [b]   saw(John, her duck); i.e., John saw Mary's waterfowl.
  [c]   saw(John, (duck(she))); i.e., John saw Mary lower her head.

Some pairs of sentences represent the same proposition, i.e., they're synonymous. For example, the following three (and many other related sentences) all express the proposition [27]:

[35a] Ranger Rick is feeding Smokey.
  [b] Smokey is being fed by Ranger Rick.
  [c] It's Smokey that Ranger Rick is feeding.

Many sentences overtly contain two clauses. In such cases, the analysis will show at least two propositions and will indicate how they're connected:

[36] Smokey growls and Ranger Rick leaves.
[37] Either Smokey growls or Ranger Rick leaves.
[38] If Smokey growls, then Ranger Rick leaves.

Sentences [36] to [38] each contain two propositions and demonstrate that we need to represent not only isolated propositions but also their connections. Propositional analysis provides a very limited set of connectors, far fewer than those available in human language. The idea is that the basic semantic meanings of the natural language connectors can be analyzed as these logical connectors. The standard logical connectors are *and* (&), *or* (V), and *if-then* ($\rightarrow$). We can represent sentences [36] to [38] by identifying individual propositions and then connecting them by the appropriate symbol:

[39] [= 36] (growl(Smokey)) & (leave (Ranger Rick))
[40] [= 37] (growl(Smokey)) V (leave(Ranger Rick))
[41] [= 38] (growl(Smokey)) $\rightarrow$ (leave(Ranger Rick))

Note that we have added extra parentheses around each proposition; this is to keep propositions clearly distinguished.

Another important logical symbol is that of negation, represented by a tilde (~) placed before the proposition. So sentence [42a] would be represented as [42b]:

[42a] Ranger Rick didn't/did not leave.
  [b] ~(leave (Ranger Rick))

We must be careful to indicate which proposition the negative applies to. Examples [43a] to [43c] have different interpretations:

[43a] ~(growl(Smokey)) & (leave(Ranger Rick))
  [b] (growl(Smokey)) & ~(leave (Ranger Rick))
  [c] ~(growl(Smokey)) & ~(leave(Ranger Rick))

Take a moment to examine these three formulas, noting the location of the negative sign and the parentheses. (The apparent complexity presents more of a visual than logical difficulty.) Now try to state different sentences for each formula.

The results that you arrive at should be close in meaning to [43d] to [43f] (as usual ignoring tense):

[43d] Smokey didn't growl and Ranger Rick left.
  [e] Smokey growled and Ranger Rick didn't leave.
  [f] Smokey didn't growl and Ranger Rick didn't leave.

Note that some of these paraphrases are somewhat artificial. In [43d], for instance, we would normally use the word *but* rather than *and*. Sentence [43e] might be more naturally expressed as [44]:

[44] Even though Smokey growled, Ranger Rick didn't leave.

Sentence [43f] sounds better if *so* replaces *and*. Propositional analysis currently provides no means of representing the individual meanings of expressions such as *but, even though,* and *so*; instead, it lumps them together under the cover-symbol & because, as we mentioned earlier, the meaning represented by & is the basic semantic meaning of these expressions.

EXERCISES
  1. Convert the following sentences with connectives to propositions.
      a. Fall comes and apples ripen.
      b. Either Oscar fainted or Lady Marshmallow is mistaken.
      c. If the Earth stops, Oscar will get off.
      d. They don't work, so they don't eat.
  2. Convert the following propositions into sentences (pay close attention to the parentheses):
      a. (eat(George, mushrooms)) & ~(become(sick(George)))
      b. (come(Fall)) → (ripen(apples))
      c. ~(come(Fall)) → ~(ripen(apples))

The final elements of propositional analysis that we deal with here are called **quantifiers**. These symbols represent two notions: The first is the notion of *all*, indicated by the **universal quantifier (∀)**. The second represents the notion of *existence*, indicated by the **existential quantifier (∃)**. Both quantifiers typically apply to arguments of propositions. They're written in a special way and are prefixed to the proposition. Let's consider some examples:

[45a] All cats like mice.
  [b] Every cat likes mice.
  [c] For every cat, it likes mice.
  [d] If something is a cat, it likes mice.

Different as they seem, the sentences in [45] have exactly the same semantic meaning; they all express the same proposition. That is, all of them are true under exactly the same conditions. Logicians argue that [45d] is closest to the propositional representation for all of these sentences. This may surprise you since [45d] actually has two propositions.

But as we have just seen, a single grammatical clause may express more than one proposition. Sentence [45d] also contains one of the connectives—the *if-then* conditional. The English word *something* corresponds to what logicians call a **variable,** a linguistic wild-card. Variables are represented by the last letters of the alphabet: x, y, z.

The propositional structure common to the sentences in [45] is:

[46] $\forall x((cat\ (x)) \rightarrow (like\ (x,\ mice)))$

Reading this formula in its most long-winded version, you get something like: *For all things, if a thing is a cat, then that thing likes mice.* While this version will not win a Pulitzer prize for style, it does have the virtue of being quite exact about the meaning of the sentences in [45].

The existential quantifier works in a similar way. The sentences in [47] all have the same literal meaning; they express the same proposition:

[47a] A Smurf exists.
  [b] There exists a Smurf.
  [c] There is (at least one) Smurf.
  [d] There exists (at least one) Smurf.

As you might suspect, the longest-winded variant is the closest to the propositional form, which is stated below:

[48] $\exists x(Smurf(x))$

Reading even more painstakingly, we can render this formula as: *There exists at least one entity that is a Smurf.* Notice that, in this analysis, the grammatical noun *Smurf* is interpreted as a predicate. Propositional analysis once again departs from the grammar of English. Its characteristics were developed to allow logicians to express in a single consistent form the propositional meaning which might be expressed by various natural language sentences and to distinguish the several propositions that are expressed by a single ambiguous natural language sentence.

Existential quantifiers may be concealed in sentences, as in [49], which has the propositional form [50]:

[49] Some exams are easy.
[50] $\exists x((exam(x))\ \&\ (easy\ (x)))$

In other words, there exists at least one thing that is an exam and is easy.

Negation, universal quantifiers, and existential quantifiers may also be combined:

[51a] No exam is easy.
  [b] $\sim\exists x((exam\ (x))\ \&\ (easy\ (x)))$
[52a] Nobody likes Victor.
  [b] $\forall x \sim(like\ (x,\ Victor))$

[53a] Not everybody likes Victor.
  [b] ~Vx(like (x, Victor))

EXERCISE   Give English sentences that *exactly* paraphrase the formulas in [51b], [52b], and [53b].

2.2.3.2 Entailment

Entailment is a very important semantic relationship between propositions (although we will treat it here as a relation between sentences). For example, [54a] entails [54b] to [54d]:

[54a] Trigger is a stallion.
  [b] Trigger is a horse.
  [c] Trigger is an animal.
  [d] Something is a horse.

If [54a] is true, then [54b], [54c], and [54d] must also be true. In general, one sentence **entails** another if (and only if) when one is true, the other must also be true. Notice that if [54b], [54c], or [54d] were false, then [54a] could not be true; more generally, if the entailed sentence is false, the entailing sentence cannot be true.

It's important to remember that entailments are relations between sentences and not between words. We dealt earlier with the lexical relation of hyponymy that exists among *animal, horse,* and *stallion.* Thus *stallion* doesn't entail *horse* or *animal;* they're its superordinate terms. However, the sentence [54a] entails the sentences [54b] to [54d].

We can also view entailments as the conditions that must be met for a sentence to be true, i.e., as its **truth conditions.** Some linguists hold that the entailments or truth conditions of a sentence define its literal meaning. They hold that to understand a sentence is to know what conditions must be met for the sentence to be true. It follows from this point of view that if two sentences have the same entailments, they have the same meaning; or vice versa, for two sentences to have the same meaning they must have the same truth conditions. Logically oriented linguists aim (1) to represent the meaning of sentences in a notation that allows its entailments or truth conditions to be derived, (2) to provide one such representation for every meaning of an ambigous sentence, and (3) to provide equivalent representations for synonymous sentences, as we outlined in the previous section.

2.3   PRAGMATICS

The word *pragmatics* is related to the words *practice* and *practical.* It refers to the study of language use, as opposed to the study of language structure. Perhaps the most straightforward way to think about pragmatics is as the study of the meanings of utterances in context. This contrasts with the study of the literal or decontextualized meanings of sentences, which is the domain of semantics.

To get a sense of the differences between literal and contextualized meanings, consider the following sentence:

[55]   He intends to question him about the murder.

Literally, this means that some male intends to question some other male about some murder. Without context, however, we have no way of knowing just who *he* and *him* refer to, nor of knowing which murder is involved. If it occurred in one of Agatha Christie's Poirot stories, *he* might refer to Poirot and *him* to his suspect. If it occurred in a Columbo movie, then *he* might refer to Columbo, and *him* to a different suspect. If it occurred immediately after:

[56]   Chief Inspector Langrishe has arrested Father Dowling.

then we would quite naturally interpret *he* as referring to Langrishe and *him* to Dowling.

Of course, the pronouns in a sentence such as [55] could refer to individuals in the physical, nonlinguistic context. We will discuss such uses later, when we deal with deixis.

2.3.1   Reference

One of the most important jobs that expressions do in context is refer. That is, linguistic expressions pick out things (people, places, objects, activities, qualities, relations, etc., etc.) in the real world or in a fictional one. Such expressions are called **referring expressions.**

Some referring expressions pick out their referents quite straightforwardly. The name *Oscar Wilde* probably picks out only the individual who lived at the end of the last century, and who wrote *The Importance of Being Earnest, The Ballad of Reading Gaol,* and *The Picture of Dorian Grey.* Generally, **proper names** are assumed to pick out unique referents. There is, as far as we know, no Oscar Wilde other than the one we just described. Nor, again as far as we know, is there a New York City other than the one on the Hudson River. So *Oscar Wilde* and *New York City* can be used safely without confusion regarding their referents.

Other referring expressions aren't so fortunate. We (the authors), for example, have two colleagues named *David.* To avoid confusion, we sometimes must add these people's last names. There are, nonetheless, only two Davids in our department, so we can avoid confusion easily. However, the expression *The President of the United States* could refer to any of thirty or so individuals. *The Pope* can refer to a great many more. And *he* or *she* refers to an indefinite number. Clearly, when we speak or write we try to make sure that our hearers and readers know which David, president, or pope we have in mind by ensuring that the context limits the possible referents of these expressions to just one.

2.3.2   Deixis and deictics

Deictic expressions are an important class of referring expression whose referents may "shift" from one use to another. The term itself derives from the Greek word *deiktein* meaning "to point." The class includes the personal pronouns, adverbs such as *today, yesterday, now,* *then, here, there,* and verb tenses. In [57], *yesterday* refers to March 1, 1992 when uttered on March 2, 1992, but refers to March 1, 1993 when uttered on March 2, 1993:

[57]   We finished that chapter yesterday.

For a hearer or reader to know what day *yesterday* refers to, she must know when the expression was uttered. If we found [57] on a piece of paper without a date, we wouldn't know what day or date *yesterday* referred to.

Because the referent of a deictic expression may change from one use of the expression to another, deictics have also been called "shifters." Their shiftiness is assumed to distinguish them from proper names, whose referents are assumed to remain constant from one occurrence to another. From the point of view of a theory that identifies the meaning of a sentence with the truth or falsity of the proposition it represents, deictics (and the relative indeterminacy of reference generally) are a considerable problem. To determine the truth or falsity of a proposition, we must know the persons or things referred to by its referring expressions. These identities depend on the context in which the sentence is uttered.

Analysts distinguish the **deictic center** and three types of deixis: **personal, spatial, and temporal.** The **deictic center** is the point of reference from which the entities, places, and times denoted in an utterance can be identified. The three types of deixis constitute aspects of this point of reference. The speaker (*I*) is the personal deictic center in an utterance; the place where the utterance is made (*here*) is its spatial deictic center; and the time at which it is made (*now*) is its temporal deictic center (Levinson, 1983).

Consider, for example, the following expression uttered in the context in which there are two people and two pieces of furniture:

[58]   *John:* I asked you to move this over here.
         Jan: Oh, I thought you wanted me to put *this here*.

Here we have two *I*'s, each referring to a different individual, in each case to the speaker of the expression in which it occurs. We also have three past tense verbs (*asked, thought, wanted*) indicating that the events they refer to took place before the time at which the utterances occurred. And we have a demonstrative expression, *this,* which occurs twice, referring to a different entity in each case. The first refers to some entity close to John; the second to an entity close to Jan. Finally, there are the two occurrences of the spatial expression *here. Here* indicates a location close to the speaker. On its first occurrence, it refers to a location close to John; on its second, to one close to Jan.

In contrast, *you* represents the addressee, *there* represents a place that doesn't include *here,* and *then* represents a time that doesn't include *now.* So deictic expressions connect language with the context in which they're used, and they're interpreted by reference to aspects of the deictic center in a speech event, i.e., its speaker, time, and place of the utterance.

Verbs too may have a deictic component in their meanings, particularly verbs such as *come* and *go* or *bring* and *take.* Thus we say *Come on over here to me,* but not *??Go on over here to me,* or *Bring that over here to me,* but not *??Take that over here to me.* The second member of each pair is odd because the deictic center is where the speaker is, but *go* and *take* denote motion away from the deictic center, and so the sentences are contradictory. *Come* and *bring* denote motion toward the deictic center.

However, we can say *I'll come over there to you* without contradiction. This is because we have some limited options that allow us to shift the deictic center away from the speaker, in this case to the addressee.

2.3.3 Presupposition

Another important pragmatic category is that of **presupposition**. Consider, for example, the difference between [59a] and [59b]:

[59a] Oscar enjoyed his trip west.
  [b] It was his trip west that Oscar enjoyed.

While [59a] could be appropriately uttered in a broad range of contexts, [59b] (called a **cleft sentence**) is appropriate only in contexts in which the speaker (and perhaps also the hearer) assumes (presupposes) that Oscar enjoyed something. The negative cleft sentence, [59c], also presupposes that Oscar enjoyed something:

[59c] It wasn't his trip west that Oscar enjoyed.

Sentence [59b] asserts that his trip west was what Oscar enjoyed; [59c] asserts that whatever Oscar enjoyed, it wasn't his trip west. But both [59b] and [59c] assume that Oscar enjoyed something. In general, a sentence (e.g., *Oscar enjoyed something*) is **presupposed** if it follows from both the positive and the negative versions of another sentence (e.g., [59b] and [59c]).

Sentence [60], called a **pseudocleft sentence**, has the same presupposition as [59b] and [59c]:

[60] What Oscar enjoyed was (not) his trip west.

The notion of presupposition is also used to distinguish among cases such as:

[61a] Bill believes that the circus has left.
  [b] Bill regrets that the circus has left.
  [c] Bill doesn't regret that the circus has left.

Sentence [61a] may be true whether or not the circus has left; sentences [61b] and [61c] can be true only if the circus has left. Predicates (including both verbs and adjectives) such as *regret,* whose complements are presupposed, are called **factive predicates.** Other factive predicates are: *remember, realize, be amazed.*

Sentence subjects tend to be presupposed. If the subject is a noun phrase, then the existence of its referent tends to be presupposed, [62a] and [62b]; if it is a clause, then the clause is generally assumed to be true, [63a] and [63b]. (Note the hedges *tend* and *generally* here.) Consider the following:

[62a] Pflegosaurs were (not) carnivorous.
  [b] Pflegosaurs existed.
[63a] That the Earth is round is (not) very surprising.
  [b] The Earth is round.

Sentence [62a] presupposes that [62b] is true, and [63a] presupposes that the Earth is round; i.e., that [63b] is true. The claim that subject noun phrases tend to be referential and that subject clauses are generally presupposed to be true is compatible with the traditional notion that a sentence consists of a subject which refers to something and a predicate which says something about the subject's referent.

2.3.4   Speech acts

Consider the utterance *Out* in the following scenarios:

[64a] A poker game and the dealer asks *Are you in or out?* You answer, *Out*.
  [b] You are playing softball against a pitcher who is having a super day. He pitches another three strikes and once again the umpire yells, *Out*.
  [c] You tried for 15 minutes to ignore your cat but finally he's got you so steamed that you get up, walk swiftly to the door, open it, and pointing toward the snow, say sternly, *Out*.

The point here is obviously the fact that the same utterance, *Out,* is used to communicate three different meanings. In the first, the expression communicates the assertion, *I am out.* In the second, it's the ump's declaration that *You are hereby declared out.* And in the third, it expresses the order, *I hereby order you to get out.* Clearly, when we speak we not only refer to entities and predicate something of them, we make assertions, declare decisions, give orders, ask questions, give advice, make promises, or make requests, to name but a few. These acts are called **speech acts** and have been extensively studied by linguists and philosophers.

Speech acts can be either explicit or implicit. An explicit promise is one in which the speaker actually says *I promise . . . ,* e.g., *I promise that I will return the money tomorrow.* That is, the utterance contains an expression, usually a verb, which makes the intended act explicit by naming it.

But we don't have to say *I promise . . .* in order to make a genuine promise. We can merely say *I will return the money tomorrow.* When the speech act isn't named by a specific verb in the sentence, we are performing the speech act implicitly.

What matters in performing a speech act isn't whether it's explicitly named but whether the act meets certain contextual or background conditions, called **felicity** or **appropriateness conditions.** For example, imagine a situation in which you promise your instructor to finish an assignment by the beginning of the next class period. For this to count as a genuine promise, you must say something to the effect that you will finish the assignment by the next class period; the instructor must want you to complete the assignment by that time; you must be able to carry out this task; you must sincerely intend to finish the assignment by that time; and you must intend your instructor to interpret your remarks as your commitment to finish the assignment by the next class time.

No doubt these conditions all seem perfectly ordinary. However, articulating them makes explicit what we usually take for granted and which we pay attention to only when things go wrong. They're also very useful in helping us to characterize the differences between speech acts. Promises are distinct from threats, for example, in that a promised act is one desired by the addressee, whereas a threatened act is one which the addressee would prefer not to happen. That is, they fulfill distinct felicity conditions.

Analysts typically distinguish among four types of felicity conditions:

1. The **propositional content condition** expresses the content of the act. Thus *I will return the book tomorrow* denotes the promised act, i.e., returning the book tomorrow. Sometimes conventions require that a precisely specified expression be used. For example, in some marriage ceremonies, the bride and groom must respond *I will* to the question *Will you Joan take John to be your lawfully wedded husband?* No other form, even if it means *I will*, is acceptable.
2. The **preparatory condition(s)** express the contextual background required for a particular act. For example, *I will* constitutes a marriage vow only in the context of a real wedding; a promise requires that the promiser be able to perform what s/he promises; a speaker making an assertion must have evidence to support the assertion.
3. The **sincerity condition** requires that the speaker be sincere. For example, a promiser must willingly intend to keep the promise; a speaker who makes an assertion must believe what s/he asserts.
4. The **essential condition** is that the speaker intends the utterance to have a certain force. For example, someone uttering *I promise to return tomorrow* must intend this utterance to be a commitment to return tomorrow; an assertor must intend the utterance to represent a true representation of a state of affairs. (Searle, 1970)

In sum, for an utterance such as [65]:

[65]   (I promise that) I will return the book tomorrow.

to be a "felicitous" promise, (1) it must denote the promised act, (2) the addressee must want the book to be returned tomorrow, (3) the speaker must intend to return the book tomorrow, and (4) the speaker must intend the addressee to take the utterance to be a promise to return the book tomorrow.

Various classifications of speech acts have been proposed, but the one most widely used classifies speech acts as:

1. **Representatives,** which denote states of affairs, or at least speakers' purported beliefs about states of affairs, including assertions, descriptions, reports, statements;

2. **Directives,** which attempt to get the addressee to do something, including questions, requests, orders;
3. **Commissives,** which commit a speaker to a course of action, including promises, threats, vows;
4. **Declarations,** which bring about states of affairs, including namings, firings, hirings, pardons, resignations;
5. **Expressives,** which denote a speaker's psychological state or attitude, including apologies, compliments, greetings, thankings; and
6. **Verdictives,** which denote an assessment or judgment, including assessments, appraisals, judgments, verdicts.

Speech act analysts distinguish between the **locution** (or **locutionary act** or **force**), i.e., the form of the utterance, and the **illocution** (or **illocutionary act** or **force**), i.e., the communicative goal that the speaker intends to accomplish with the utterance. Thus an explicit and an implicit speech act have the same illocutionary force but have distinct locutions. A particular locution has a particular illocutionary force (counts as a specific speech act) if it meets the appropriateness conditions for that act.

Speech acts may be performed either **directly** or **indirectly.** Saying (*I promise that*) *I will return the book tomorrow,* directly promises that I will return the book tomorrow; a promise is used to perform a promise. However, clever critters that we are, we can perform one speech act with the intention of performing another. For example, we might say *That was a delicious meal* to our friends after they have had us over for dinner. Superficially, this is a representative, simply asserting that the meal was delicious. It can also be taken as a verdictive, giving a judgment on the meal. But most likely it will be taken as an expressive, a compliment on the quality of the meal.

We often use indirect speech acts when we wish to be polite. For example, we are more likely to say (1) *Can you give me a ride to the airport this weekend* than (2) *Give me a ride to the airport this weekend* or (3) *I want you to give me a ride to the airport this weekend.* We prefer (1) because it allows the addressee an out (*I'm sorry. I have an exam on Monday and haven't cracked the book yet.*). On the face of things, (1) appears to be a neutral question, a directive, merely a request for information. But it can, and very likely would, be interpreted as a polite directive, an indirect request for a ride.

2.3.5   Speakers' intended meanings

When in the course of ordinary conversation we speak about communication, we are apt to characterize the process as one in which our utterances "convey" our meanings. Our metaphor is one of a conduit, or perhaps a mail service. We package our thoughts in linguistic wrappings and our hearers at the other end of the conduit, unwrap them and extract the message. A slightly more sophisticated version of this same understanding of communication uses a cryptography metaphor in which a message sender encodes the message at one end, transmits it over some channel to a receiver, who then decodes it. Neither of these metaphors fully characterizes the activities of communicators.

To see why we do not, indeed cannot, merely package and unpackage messages, imagine a situation in which two students, David and Tammy, wonder whether they're going to have to suffer through a pop quiz in grammar class today:

[66] *David:* Do you think he'll give us a pop quiz today?

Tammy: Well, we haven't reached the end of the chapter yet.

David's question seems clear enough. He asks Tammy whether she thinks the teacher will give them a quiz today. However, Tammy's reply doesn't mention pop quizzes at all, but David (and the rest of us) would probably interpret it as indicating that Tammy doesn't believe that there will be a quiz today. How is it that Tammy's reply, which literally means "we haven't reached the end of the chapter yet," and thus seems hardly relevant, can be interpreted as an appropriate answer to David's question?

Suppose that Tammy believes, and believes that David believes (or at least can figure out from her remark), that the teacher only springs pop quizzes when the class has finished discussing a chapter. Then, with this belief as background, she can assume that David will figure out that she thinks that there will be no pop quiz today. David, for his part, will interpret her remark as intended as a reply to his question, and not just a random remark. Because David believes that Tammy intended her remark to be interpreted as a reply to his question, he looks for clues to its interpretation. If he assumes that people (in general) have some evidence for their beliefs, then he can interpret Tammy's remark as evidence for some belief that she holds. He can then figure out that she believes that there will be no pop quiz today.

The two crucial notions in this discussion are *intention* and *figuring out*. Hearers figure out (*infer*) the meanings which speakers intend them to figure out. Meanings therefore are not "conveyed" entirely by utterances. They cannot be obtained by a simple decoding process. Utterances (and their contexts) are merely clues to the meanings hidden away in the minds of speakers. The principles that guide us as we figure out speakers' intended meanings are the topic of the following section.

2.3.5.1 Implicatures

Imagine the following fragment of conversation:

[67] *Sam:* What time is it?

Pam: The mailman has just arrived.

Rather than simply assuming that Pam was being uncooperative and irrelevant in her reply, Sam uses the information she supplied to construct an answer to his question. Suppose that both Sam and Pam know that the mailman typically arrives at about 1:30 P.M. and that each knows that the other knows this. On the basis of this background knowledge, Sam can figure out that the time must be shortly after 1:30 P.M. He may also conclude that Pam must not know the exact time, that perhaps her watch is broken. However, nothing in her reply expresses time or indicates that she is or isn't in a position to tell him the time. So, how does Sam garner all this information from Pam's apparently irrelevant remark? What principles or assumptions about conversation guided her in constructing her reply and guided Sam in drawing his conclusions?

The philosopher Paul Grice attempted to answer these questions in some very influential work presented in the late 1960s. He proposed that conversation is one of many cooperative enterprises that people engage in and that it's governed by the very general assumption called the **Cooperative Principle (CP)**:

[68] Make your conversational contribution such as is required, at the stage at which it occurs, by the accepted purpose or direction of the talk-exchange in which you are engaged. (Grice, 1975)

Grice made this rather general principle more concrete and specific by adding four **maxims**:

[69] Maxim of **Quantity**:
   a. Make your contribution as informative as is required.
   b. Do not make your contribution more informative than is required.
[70] Maxim of **Quality**:
   Try to make your contribution one that is true, specifically:
   a. Do not say what you believe to be false.
   b. Do not say that for which you lack adequate evidence.
[71] Maxim of **Relation**:
   Be relevant.
[72] Maxim of **Manner**:
   a. Avoid obscurity of expression.
   b. Avoid ambiguity.
   c. Be brief.
   d. Be orderly.

These aren't moral strictures, or still less, descriptions of typical communication. We all know people who rattle on interminably, who get off the point, who lie, or who relate a sequence of events in any order but the one in which they occurred. Rather, the maxims are designed to express the assumptions which we generally make as we converse (and indeed, as we interpret any piece of language).

To see how these maxims work, let's revisit our conversation between Sam and Pam, [67]. Sam asks a question of Pam. Pam makes a remark immediately after. Sam assumes that she's being cooperative and in particular that she's abiding by the maxims. Only if he makes these initial assumptions, can Sam make sense of Pam's remark and interpret it as a reply to his question. He assumes that her remark is relevant to his question and isn't just the expression of a random thought. On the assumption that Pam has been relevant, Sam can examine her remark for clues as to how it constitutes an answer to the question. Given that her remark doesn't directly say anything about time, Sam can assume that she isn't in a position to say exactly what time it is, because if she were, she should have done so in order to abide by the maxims of quality and quantity. So Sam concludes that Pam is giving him the most truthful information for which she has evidence. She's also giving enough (and no more) information to enable Sam to work out the approximate time himself. The answer is also clear, unambiguous, brief, and orderly. So, by assuming that Pam is being cooperative and following the maxims, Sam can derive a considerable amount of information from her reply, which in turn is crafted in such a way as to allow him to do just this. That is, Pam's reply tells of the mailman's arrival. Sam can now activate his knowledge about the mailman's usual time of arrival and from that infer that the time must be about 1:30. Inferences like this, which are based on the meaning of an utterance, the Cooperative Principle and the maxims, and in some cases the context, are called **implicatures.**

As another example, let's examine expressions such as:

[73]   He ate some of the candy.

Typically, this sentence would be interpreted to implicate that he didn't eat all of the candy. Generally, upon hearing an expression containing *some,* we infer "not all." This implicature is based on the fact that *all* is stronger than *some* in that if I ate all of the candy, then I ate some of it: A proposition with *all* entails the same proposition in which *all* is replaced by *some;* e.g., [74a] entails [74b]. That is, if [74a] is true, then [74b] must be true too:

[74a]   I ate all of the candy.
  [b]   I ate some of the candy.

The maxims of quantity and quality essentially require us to make the strongest claims that we have reason to believe. So, if we say *He ate some of the candy,* our hearers will assume that this is the strongest claim we are in a position to make, and will conclude that we could not have made the stronger claim *He ate all of the candy.* They will conclude that he didn't eat all of the candy. In general, when a speaker makes a weaker claim in a situation in which a stronger claim would be relevant and no less straightforward to express, he implicates either that he knows the stronger claim to be untrue or at least that he doesn't have good reason to believe the stronger claim.

The "Be orderly" clause of the maxim of manner, [72d], prompts us to interpret the sequence of events in a narration as the sequence in which the events occurred in reality. For example, [75a] suggests that John got ill and then went to the doctor, whereas [75b] suggests the opposite order:

[75a]   John got ill and he went to the doctor.
  [b]   John went to the doctor and he got ill.

We interpret sentences such as these in this way even though *and* merely conjoins the two clauses without indicating any temporal order between them, as in:

[76]   Zelda is a doctor and Zubin is a lawyer.

And indeed, we can counter the temporal effects with a specific reference to the order:

[77]   John went to the doctor and he got ill, but in the usual order.

"Be orderly" also explains the oddity of [78b]:

[**78a**] Brando vaulted onto the Triumph and rode off into the sunset.
  [**b**]   ?Brando rode off into the sunset and vaulted onto the Triumph.

We expect the order in a narrative to mirror the real order, but an orderly interpretation of sentences like [78b] makes no sense.

2.3.6   Discourse and text analysis

We have seen that well-formed sentences meet requirements on a variety of levels—syntactic, semantic, and pragmatic. Texts and discourses are also thought of as having to meet analogous requirements. In folktales, for example, the events must occur in a particular order or the tale is defective; sonnets must fulfill particular rhyming and rhythm requirements; conversations are expected to be topically sensible; academic essays, papers, theses, and dissertations are expected to conform to the organizational requirements accepted or conventional in their fields. Teaching students how to write largely amounts to teaching the conventions of particular genres. Studies of text and discourse have focused a lot of attention on two aspects: **cohesion** and **coherence.**

Cohesion in texts is signaled by the expressions that writing teachers have traditionally called "transition devices." These are words or phrases that make explicit the temporal, spatial, and logical connections among sentences in a text. They include such words and phrases as *then, therefore, because,* and *as a result.* They also include such devices as coreferential expressions, deictics, pronominalization (and proverbalization), and ellipsis.

Especially noteworthy in this regard are expressions called **textual** (or **discourse**) **deictics.** For example, writers can refer to places in, or parts of a text relative to the point being currently read (the **textual deictic center**), by using expressions such as *above* or *below:*

[79]   We dealt with issues of deixis above, and deal below with issues of coherence.

Clearly, *above* and *below* refer to places in the text before and after the points at which these expressions occur in the text.

Demonstrative pronouns are often to be interpreted as textual deictics:

[80]   Jack: Have you heard this joke?
             (Tells joke.)
      Mack: That one was born before you were.

In Jack's question, *this* refers forward deictically to the joke; Mack's *that* refers back to it.

There is a crucial distinction to be drawn between discourse deictics and **anaphora**, another important device for creating cohesion in texts. Anaphoric expressions are coreferential with (i.e., refer to the same entities as) other expressions in a text. For example, the noun phrase *the armadillo* and the pronoun *it* are coreferential in:

[81]   *The armadillo* trudged slowly along the center stripe. *It* was entirely oblivious to the traffic that whizzed by on either side.

It is said to be an anaphor for the full noun phrase, which in turn is said to be its **antecedent.** In fact, it's only on the assumption that these two expressions are antecedent and anaphor (i.e., are coreferential) that the passage makes sense. Clearly, the antecedent/anaphor relation is a potent cohesive tie in a text.

The antecedent/anaphor relation is only one among a number of coreferential relationships, all of which involve lexical substitutions. For example, epithets may substitute for other noun phrases such as proper names:

[82]   *Oscar* got himself elected. *The rat* persuaded even the dead to vote for him.

Here *the rat* and *Oscar* refer to the same individual. Frequently, hypernyms (superordinate terms) substitute for hyponyms (subordinate terms). In the following, the superordinate term *animal* substitutes for the subordinate term *cat:*

[83]   *My cat* is a bit of a klutz. *The animal* can't walk along a mantlepiece without knocking everything off.

The assumption of coreferentiality between an antecedent and either an anaphor, an epithet, or a semantically related term is an important device for creating cohesion in texts.

A related study is that of **discourse coherence.** This examines the intuited, but not necessarily overtly indicated, meaning connections between parts of texts. In fact, many who study discourse coherence would argue that it's only by assuming coherence that the cohesive devices can be interpreted as such. We have tried to indicate this in our discussion of cohesion by saying such things as, "It's the assumption of coreferentiality that creates cohesion." Scholars are fond of creating texts which have plenty of cohesive ties but are semantically incoherent. The following passage illustrates this.

[84]   John was late. The station clock had struck nine. It was time for Susan to start work. She took the first essay from the pile. It was by Mary Jones. Mary had not been well for weeks. The doctor had told her to take a holiday. The problem was that she couldn't afford one. Living in London is now very expensive. All central government subsidies to the Greater London Council have been abolished. Paradoxically, this might be seen to follow from the premises of Libertarian Anarchism. The minor premise might be difficult for the reader to discern. Our theorem proving program does this using a "crossed-syllogism" technique.
(Blakemore, 1987: p. 108)

In this passage, each sentence is connected to the one adjacent to it by at least one cohesive device. Nonetheless, no one would regard the passage as a coherent text. The reason for this is that we cannot construct a meaning that encompasses the entire passage. We would be hard pressed to say what the topic of the piece might be, and so we couldn't give it a title.

Without a topic, a piece of text has no coherence, and providing a title, and thus a topic, for a text can make one that initially seemed incoherent and hard to interpret coherent and straightforward, as the following passage illustrates. Read it before you check its title/topic below, then compare how opaque it is on the first reading with how sensible it is on the second:

[85]   The procedure is actually quite simple. First you arrange things into different groups. Of course, one pile may be sufficient depending on how much there is to do. If you have to go somewhere else due to lack of facilities that is the next step, otherwise you are pretty well set. It is important not to overdo things. That is, it is better to do too few things at once than too many. In the short run this may not seem important but complications can easily arise. A mistake can be expensive as well. At first the whole procedure will seem complicated. Soon, however, it will become just another facet of life. It is difficult to foresee any end to the necessity for this task in the immediate future, but then one never can tell. After the procedure is completed one arranges the materials into different groups again. Then they can be put into their appropriate places. Eventually they will be used once more and the whole cycle will have to be repeated. However, that is part of life. (Bransford and Johnson, 1973: p. 400, quoted in Brown and Yule, 1983: p. 72)

Experimental subjects who were told that the topic of the passage was "washing clothes" understood and could recall aspects of the passage better than subjects who weren't told this.

In another experiment, Anderson et al. (1977) showed that a text will be interpreted according to the assumptions or interests brought to the task of interpreting it by its readers. Even individual words in the following passage can be interpreted differently by readers with different interests:

[86]   Every Saturday night, four good friends get together. When Jerry, Mike and Pat arrived, Karen was sitting in her living room writing some notes. She quickly gathered the cards and stood up to greet her friends at the door. They followed her into the living room but as usual they couldn't agree on exactly what to play. Karen's recorder filled the room with soft and pleasant music. Early in the evening, Mike noticed Pat's hand and the many diamonds. . . . (Quoted in Brown and Yule, 1983: p. 248)

Anderson and his colleagues found that female music education students interpreted the passage as a description of a musical evening. In contrast, a group of male weight-lifting students thought that the passage described people playing cards. Clearly, readers who interpret the passage as a description of a musical evening are likely to interpret *recorder* as a musical instrument and *play* as "play music," whereas those who interpret the passage as describing a card-playing evening may think *recorder* refers to a tape recorder and *play* to cardplaying.

Clearly, making sense of a text requires making some assumptions about what its topic is and what the speaker's intentions in uttering it are. These assumptions guide readers in deciding what individual words in the text refer to. They also guide us in deciding whether two expressions are, in fact, coreferential. While the cohesive devices may be important in helping to create coherence in texts, they are dependent, as coherence in general is, on readers' assumptions about such semantic characteristics of the text as its topic. It's these assumptions which create coherence, and they may do so without the aid of "transition devices," which are neither necessary nor sufficient to create textual coherence.

REFERENCES AND RESOURCES

Aitchison, J. 1987. *Words in the Mind: An Introduction to the Mental Lexicon.* Oxford: Blackwell.

Anderson, R. C., R. E. Reynolds, D. L. Schallert, and E. T. Goetz. 1977. "Framework for Comprehending Discourse." *American Educational Research Journal;* 14:367–381.

Blakemore, D. 1987. *Semantic Constraints on Relevance.* Oxford: Blackwell.

Blakemore, D. 1992. *Understanding Utterances.* Oxford: Blackwell.

Bransford J. D., and M. K. Johnson. 1973. "Considerations of Some Problems of Comprehension." In W. G. Chase, ed. *Visual Information Processing.* New York: Academic Press, 383–438.

Brown, G., and G. Yule. 1983. *Discourse Analysis.* Cambridge: Cambridge University Press.

Cruse, D. A. 1986. *Lexical Semantics.* Cambridge: Cambridge University Press.

Grice, H. P. 1975. "Logic and Conversation." In P. Cole and J. L. Morgan, eds. *Syntax and Semantics 3: Speech Acts.* New York: Academic Press, 42–58.

Landau, S. 1984. *Dictionaries: The Art and Craft of Lexicography.* New York: Charles Scribner's Sons.

Levinson, S. 1983. *Pragmatics.* Cambridge: Cambridge University Press.

9,000 Words: A Supplement to Webster's Third. 1983. Springfield, MA: Merriam Webster Co.

Room, A. 1981. *Room's Dictionary of Distinguishables.* Boston, MA: Routledge & Kegan Paul.

Searle, J. 1970. *Speech Acts.* Cambridge: Cambridge University Press.

12,000 Words: A Supplement to Webster's Third. 1986. Springfield, MA: Merriam Webster Co.

Webster's Third New International Dictionary. 1961. Springfield, MA: Merriam Webster Co.

GLOSSARY

Absolute (also called **"nongradable"**) **antonyms:** words such as *alive* and *dead* that indicate sharp boundaries in their semantic range; i.e., if one is alive, one isn't dead and vice versa. See **scalar antonyms.**

Anaphor: an expression (e.g., a pronoun) that refers to the same entity as some other expression in a text (its **antecedent**).

Antecedent: an expression (e.g., a noun phrase) sharing the same referent as an **anaphor.**

Antonyms: words with opposite meanings.

Appropriateness conditions (also called **"felicity conditions"**): contextual circumstances that must be present for an utterance to be a successful speech act.

Argument: elements semantically implied by the predicate of a proposition.

Cleft sentence: a sentence of the form *It was x that . . . .*, e.g., *It was his trip west that Oscar enjoyed.*

Coherence: the overall sense of topical relatedness of the parts of a text.

Cohesion: specific expressions in a text that contribute to **coherence.**

Commissives: speech acts which obligate a speaker to a course of action, including promises, threats, vows.

Component (also called **"feature"**): in semantics, a primitive unit of meaning that combines with other such units to form the meaning of individual words.

Context: the circumstances in which a sentence is uttered. See **linguistic context** and **situational context.**

Converses: antonyms that bear symmetrical relations to each other; e.g., *above/below.*

Cooperative Principle: a general principle of communication by which speakers make their conversational contribution fit the stage at which it occurs and the accepted purpose or direction of the talk exchange.

Declarations: speech acts which bring about states of affairs, including namings, firings, hirings, pardons, resignations.

Deictic (also called **"shifter"**): a linguistic expression that indicates deixis.

Deictic center: the setting of deixis assumed by speakers unless specified otherwise.

Deixis: the property of a linguistic expression whose reference changes with each occasion of its utterance.

Directives: speech acts which attempt to get the addressee to do something, including questions, requests, orders.

Discourse coherence: see **coherence.**

Entail: a semantic relationship between two sentences where, if (and only if) one is true, the other must also be true.

Essential condition: a prerequisite for a speech act whereby the speaker intends the utterance to have a certain force.

Existential quantifier: the logical symbol ($\exists$) attached to a proposition indicating that one argument is to be interpreted as "there exists at least one. . . ."

Expressives: speech acts which denote a speaker's psychological state or attitude, including apologies, compliments, greetings, thankings.

Factive predicate: a verb or adjective that presupposes the truth of its complement.

Feature: see **component.**

Felicity conditions: see **appropriateness conditions.**

Hyponym: a word which includes the meaning of a broader word; e.g., *rose* is a hyponym of *flower.* See **superordinate.**

Illocutionary act: the communicative goal that a speaker intends to accomplish with an utterance.

Implicatures (also called **"conversational implicatures"**): inferences based on the meaning of an utterance, the Cooperative Principle and the maxims and in some cases the context.

Lexical competence: the unconscious knowledge of the meanings and semantic relationships of the words in one's vocabulary.

Lexicon: (1) an individual's knowledge of vocabulary (= "mental lexicon") and (2) a linguistic model of the vocabulary of a language.

Linguistic context: the actual words and sentences that precede and follow an utterance.

Locution: the linguistic form of an utterance used in a speech act.

Manner: a communicative maxim that enjoins speakers to avoid obscurity and ambiguity and to be brief and orderly.

Maxim: a provision of the Cooperative Principle of communication.

Meronym: a word that is semantically related to another as its part; e.g., *elbow* is a meronym of *arm*.

Metaphoricity: a relationship between two senses of a word, in which one sense is a nonliteral (metaphorical) extension of the other.

Network: a set of semantic interrelationships among words in the lexicon.

Personal deixis: a deictic reference to speakers or addressees; usually centered on the speaker.

Polysemy: the semantic property of a word which has more than one sense.

Predicate: (1) in semantics, the central element of a proposition which determines the number and nature of its arguments and (2) in syntax, the part of a sentence excluding its subject.

Preparatory condition: a prerequisite for a speech act that expresses the contextual background required for that act.

Presupposition: in pragmatics, a proposition whose truth is assumed whether the presupposing sentence is true or false.

Primitive concept: a concept which cannot be analyzed into more basic concepts.

Primitive relations: relations of meaning among words which cannot be analyzed into more basic relations.

Proposition: a semantic structure, composed of a **predicate** and its **arguments,** that expresses the basic literal meaning of a sentence.

Propositional analysis: representing the meaning of a sentence as one or more propositions.

Propositional content condition: a prerequisite for a speech act whereby an utterance indicates the speech act intended and its content.

Pseudo-cleft sentence: a sentence of the form *what . . . is x,* e.g., *What Oscar enjoyed was his trip west.*

Quality: a communicative maxim that enjoins speakers to make their contribution one that is true and supported by appropriate evidence.

Quantifier: a logical expression added to propositions to indicate the ways in which arguments are interpreted. See **existential quantifier** and **universal quantifier.**

Quantity: a communicative maxim that enjoins speakers to make their contribution as informative as is required, not more or less so.

Reference: the connection between a linguistic expression (**referring expression**) and the extralinguistic entity that it applies to (referent).

Referring expressions: expressions that pick out things (people, places, objects, activities, qualities, relations, etc.) in the real world or in a fictional one.

Relation (also called "**relevance**"): a communicative maxim that enjoins speakers to make their contribution relevant to the topic of a discourse.

Representatives: speech acts which denote states of affairs, or at least speakers' purported beliefs about states of affairs, including assertions, descriptions, reports, statements.

Reversives: antonyms in which each indicates the reverse action or state of the other; e.g., *open/close.*

Scalar (also called "**gradable**") **antonyms:** antonyms that indicate dimensions on a scale; e.g., *strong/weak.* See **absolute antonyms.**

Selectional restriction: semantic limitations on how words can be combined in close grammatical relationships such as subject and predicate, verb and object, etc.

Semantic field: a group of words related by synonymy, meronymy, antonymy, etc.

Sense: in semantics, a clearly distinguishable meaning of a word.

Sincerity condition: a prerequisite for a speech act that states the beliefs, feelings, and intentions required of the speaker.

Situational context (also called "**extralinguistic context**"): the external setting that accompanies an utterance, including (1) objects in the immediate environment, (2) knowledge shared by speaker and hearer, and (3) level of formality.

Spatial deixis: a deictic reference to place, usually to the place where speaking occurs.

Speech act: a direct or indirect action carried out by the use of language under specific conditions. See **illocutionary act.**

Superordinate (also called "**hypernym**"): a word whose general meaning is included in the meaning of narrower words; e.g., *flower* is a superordinate of *rose, petunia,* etc. See **hyponym.**

Synonyms: in semantics, two or more words with the same meaning.

Temporal deixis: a deictic reference to time in an utterance, usually centered on the time of speaking.

Textual deixis: a deictic reference to a specific part of a discourse, e.g., a past or future part.

Truth conditions: the conditions that must be met for a sentence to be true.

Universal quantifier: the logical symbol (V) attached to a proposition to indicate that one of its arguments is to be interpreted with the meaning "all."

Variable: a part of a logical formula, usually indicated by the letters x, y, and z, which indicates an argument but without denoting any specific individuals.

Verdictives: speech acts which denote an assessment or judgment, including assessments, appraisals, judgments, verdicts.

PART TWO

Approaches to Grammar

KEY CONCEPTS

The structure of English
Form, function, and meaning

In Part Two, we examine in detail the structure of English, including its sound system, word formation, and grammar. Our approach synthesizes three approaches to the subject: traditional, American Structural, and Transformational-Generative. These three represent the dominant strains of linguistic study in the western world. Traditional grammar dates from antiquity and is still widely used in textbooks and other resources on language. American Structural grammar arose early in the twentieth century under the leadership of the linguist Leonard Bloomfield. Structuralism emphasizes objectivity and the empirical analysis of real-life data. Transformational-Generative linguistics developed around the middle of the century, a result of the work of the MIT scholar Noam Chomsky. Chomskyan linguistics emphasizes the role of theory in the study of language, the nature of language as a mental system, the almost mathematical orderliness of that system, and the possibility that such orderliness has its roots in universal human cognition.

THE STRUCTURE OF ENGLISH

Language is a system of great complexity. There are so many interconnections among its parts that any entrance into the system occurs at an arbitrary point and often presupposes knowledge—or at least an awareness—of other parts of the whole. The present overview will give you an initial glimpse at the overall system, as presented in this book. An outline of the structural topics we will discuss appears in Table 1.

TABLE 1   Overview of the Structure of English

I. The sounds of language (Chapter 3)
A. Phonetics
1. Articulatory characteristics of consonants
2. Articulatory characteristics of vowels
B. Phonology
1. Phonemes
2. Phonological rules

II. Words
A. Morphology (the internal structure of words): **Chapter 4**
B. Major parts of speech: **Chapter 5**
1. Nouns
2. Verbs
3. Adjectives
4. Adverbs
C. Minor parts of speech: **Chapter 6**
1. Pronouns
2. Auxiliary Verbs
3. Prepositions
4. Intensifiers
5. Conjunctions
6. Interjections

III. Phrases: Chapter 7
A. Grammatical functions
1. Subject
2. Predicate
3. Objects
4. Complements
5. Adjuncts
B. Types
1. Noun Phrase
2. Verb Phrase
3. Adjective Phrase
4. Adverb Phrase
5. Prepositional Phrase

IV. Clauses
A. Basic clause patterns: **Chapter 8**
B. Graphic representations of sentence structure: **Chapter 9**
1. The Reed-Kellogg system
2. Tree diagrams
C. Elaboration of basic sentence patterns: **Chapter 10**
D. Generative grammar: **Chapter 11**

Our coverage begins with the study of sounds—**phonetics** and **phonology** (Chapter 3). In later chapters, we will have occasion to refer to sounds as a background for understanding other aspects of language, including grammar, the difference between speech and writing, and language variation. Meaningless in themselves, sounds provide the building blocks for larger structures. The first such structure is the **morpheme,** the smallest element of meaning (Chapter 4). Morphemes are of various types and can be combined in many ways to make up the words of the language.

The discussion of major parts of speech (nouns, verbs, adjectives, and adverbs) examines these categories in various ways (Chapter 5). We begin with the traditional definitions of the category and consider some of the weaknesses of those definitions, drawing upon the distinctions, made later in this section, among form, function, and meaning. Traditional definitions are then supplemented with operational tests that will enable students to identify more effectively the categories of words. In addition, we discuss some of the main grammatical details of each category such as number for nouns and tense for verbs. Finally, we examine semantic characteristics associated with each part of speech.

The minor parts of speech (e.g., pronouns, auxiliary verbs, prepositions, etc.) are frequently occurring words in the language that bond together the major categories in a sentence (Chapter 6). Because they're relatively small in number, we can recognize the members of these classes through familiarity with (not memorization of!) lists of these elements. The frequent occurrence of these items corresponds to their important semantic and grammatical roles. We will thus examine notions such as gender, voice, aspect, and modality as they're signaled by words of these classes.

Moving to structures beyond the word-level, our study of phrases opens with a traditional definition of the phrase, examines its adequacy, and suggests one important modification—that a phrase can consist of a single word (Chapter 7). The rest of the chapter examines the major phrasal categories of English (noun, verb, adjective, adverb, and prepositional). As in the previous chapter, we distinguish carefully among phrasal forms, functions, and meanings.

Phrases combine with one another to create clauses, those structures consisting of a subject and a predicate. Chapter 8 introduces the eight basic patterns into which nearly all clauses in the language fall, as well as the elements of which they're composed. We again build on the formal, functional, and semantic perspectives of earlier chapters. Traditional semantic and function/discourse interpretations of the grammatical relations (subject, object, predicate) have some serious inadequacies. To remedy them, the chapter introduces thematic (semantic) roles such as agent, patient, instrument, etc. Using these roles, we can more fully appreciate the variety of meanings expressed by the grammatical functions.

The visual diagramming of sentences has played a part in grammatical study for over a century. Chapter 9 introduces two widely used systems of diagramming—the traditional functional (Reed/Kellogg) and the formal (tree diagram). Each approach is presented in a simple step-by-step manner. We also introduce the concept of phrase structure rules and discuss their relationship to structural trees and the ways in which the major grammatical relationships can be "read off" a tree diagram.

Chapter 10 leads the reader into some areas of greater complexity. Parallel with the discussion in Chapter 8 of basic clause patterns, this chapter examines complex and coordinated sentence types. We illustrate finite and nonfinite clause types. Our discussion is, again, both formal and functional.

Finally, Chapter 11 introduces the fundamentals of Transformational-Generative (TG) grammar. The presentation takes place in two stages. First, we introduce an earlier version of TG, based on Chomsky's *Aspects of the Theory of Syntax*. We introduce the concepts of deep and surface structure and the transformations that relate these two levels. This section explains several transformations, including particle movement, subject auxiliary inversion, topicalization, wh-movement, passive, *there* insertion, and imperative subject deletion. We also describe the discourse effects of many of these transformations.

The second, more advanced, part of Chapter 11 explores contemporary attempts by generative linguists to refine their model. We explore attempts to limit the number and the power of transformations and to account for universal properties of language. In this vein, we introduce current reformulations of generative grammar, particularly the **Government-Binding model** of Noam Chomsky. Here we focus on the attempt to view language in terms of several **modules** (subcomponents), each with a limited and precise role to play in language.

Each of the chapters in this section presupposes a clear grasp of preceding chapters. For your convenience, we have provided glossaries and numerous cross-references to allow you to make necessary connections.

FORM, FUNCTION, AND MEANING

Chapters 3 to 11 depend critically on the notions of **form** (AKA structure), **function** (AKA relation), and **meaning**. In each case, we provide linguistic examples drawn from parts of speech (word classes). This topic is developed in detail in Chapters 5 and 6.

Form

The notion of **form** refers to the essential observable components that make an object what it is. A toothbrush, for instance, has the formal features of a 5- to 6-

inch long, narrow handle with bristles at one end. Individual toothbrushes might have other formal characteristics such as color, stiffness of bristles, devices for massaging the gums, etc.; but only the two originally noted are necessary and sufficient conditions for something to be identified as a toothbrush. (**Necessary conditions** must be satisfied; **sufficient conditions** are the minimum number that must be satisfied.) As long as the necessary and sufficient conditions are met, no one would hesitate about the identity of the object. Of course, one might imagine an object that causes confusion about whether or not it's a toothbrush—e.g., a handle with water jets rather than bristles at the end, or a handle with bristles in the middle. However, any argument about whether such an object is or isn't a toothbrush will inevitably center around the main formal features of prototypical toothbrushes.

In grammar, you will often find that the criteria for prototypical analyses are simple and uncontroversial. Occasionally, however, their application will be indirect or even contrary to common analysis. This situation is part and parcel of grammatical analysis. At a general or abstract level, observations may apply broadly across the language. Concretely, you may encounter exceptions. But language is like that. Generalities exist. But so do exceptions. The generalities apply to the prototypical situations. (For a more thorough discussion of prototypes and their relation to language, see Appendix B at the end of Chapter 5.)

In the study of parts of speech, the form of a word comprises its observable properties. Its formal features include the following:

1. Actual and potential inflectional elements
2. Actually occurring derivational elements
3. Stress (voice emphasis)
4. Potential position in grammatical structures
5. Potential for grammatical operations such as movement, deletion (omission), or substitution

These features will serve as fundamental means for the identification of parts of speech. For instance, consider how we might assign the word *realize* to the class of verbs. First, it has the potential to accept inflectional endings typical of verbs: *realizes, realized, realizing.* It also ends in the verb-creating derivational ending *-ize.* The word can occur after other words commonly associated with verbs: *will realize, has realized, to realize,* etc. Finally, it can be replaced (along with its associated elements) by the form *do so,* as in *She tried to realize her ambitions and eventually she did so.*

Note that in this example not all of the criteria are useful. Stress tells us little about the class membership of *realize.* With words such as *con'vert* (verb) and *'convert* (noun), stress provides a useful clue.

Much of the skill involved in grammatical classification consists of the discovery of appropriate formal tests. As the list above suggests, one can begin with a generally useful set of criteria. But many arguments for grammatical classification remain to be made by insightful analysts. Consider, for example, the word *down* in the following sentences:

[1] I fell down the hill.
[2] I cut down the tree.

What part of speech is *down*? Is it one part of speech or two? There is no *right* answer apart from the arguments one can make on the basis of its grammatical behavior. Meaning is particularly unhelpful in this case since the word preserves its literal meaning in both cases. However, in sentences [1] and [2], *down* has different formal characteristics. In [1] it cannot be moved to the end of the sentence:

[3] *I fell the hill down.
      (* indicates ungrammatical with respect to the rules of competence)

Sentence [2], in contrast, allows movement, one of the formal features of language:

[4] I cut the tree down.

Another grammatical operation is substitution. What happens if, instead of *the tree,* we substitute the pronoun *it*? Sentence [2] emerges as [5]—with stress on *down*:

[5] *I cut down it.

Sentence [4] (= sentence [2] with movement) turns out as [6]—again, with stress on *down*:

[6] I cut it down.

Now perform the same substitution on sentences [1] and [3]:

[7a] ?I fell down it.   (= [1] with substitution)
   [b] *I fell it down.   (= [3] with substitution)

By formal criteria of movement and substitution, we can argue that *down* in sentences [1] and [2] cannot be classified as the same part of speech, even though the forms have the same spelling and meaning. We will leave open the question of which parts of speech we assign to *down* to until we reach Chapters 5 and 6.

Our analysis points out an important consequence of part-of-speech identification. When we include two words as members of the same category, we implicitly claim that they have important *formal* grammatical characteristics in common. Our classifications are thus valid and useful only insofar as they predict that words actually do share these characteristics.

EXERCISES   1. Consider sentences [i] to [iv]. Do they strengthen or weaken our analysis of *down* into two different grammatical forms? How do the examples do so?

>   [i]   Down the hill, I fell.
>   [ii]   *Down the tree, I cut.
>   [iii] It was down the hill that I fell.
>   [iv]   *It was down the tree that I cut.

2. Consider these two sentences:

>   [i]   I fell down the hill.
>   [ii]   I fell down.

Think of formal criteria such as those noted above that distinguish the two sentences, and thus the two instances of *down*. Is either of the two *downs* like the word in sentences [1] and [2]?

Our example not only illustrates the process of discovery that surrounds part-of-speech analysis on the basis of form, it also exemplifies several important principles:

1. Any word is potentially a member of more than one different part of speech.
2. The meaning of a word provides no reliable clue to its part of speech.
3. Distinguishing the formal properties of words is a necessary preliminary to assigning them to a class. In other words, you must learn to explore the ways in which a word works, being prepared for surprises and sometimes for a bit of complexity.
4. Formal criteria apply in different ways to different words. In the case of *down*, inflectional and derivational clues were unavailable—although, in fact, we should have looked for them more carefully. Had we done so, we would have noted that the word can sometimes be pluralized (as in *ups and downs*), though not in any of the sentences we examined (**I cut*

the tree downs). However, grammatical operations and sentence stress did provide useful data.

Function

The functional view of language, in contrast to the formal, doesn't ask the question "What is it?" but "How is it used?" Let's return to our toothbrush. Generally, one uses a toothbrush to clean one's teeth. This is its *primary function* or purpose. Notice, though, that function isn't a definitive feature in the identification of a toothbrush since many other objects have the same function: e.g., dental floss, water-powered cleaners, and instruments used by dentists. Moreover, you can use a toothbrush for numerous *secondary functions* besides its *primary* one—e.g., to clean objects such as eyeglasses, figurines, golf clubs, faucets, dials, etc. Regardless of its use, it's still a toothbrush by formal criteria.

In language, **function** designates the way in which a word or larger unit is used in a sentence; i.e., function expresses the **relationship** of the unit in question to other parts of the sentence. Also, most linguistic forms have a variety of functions, some of them primary, some secondary. Just as a toothbrush can have many uses, so can a part of speech. Let's take the noun *stone*. We can identify it as a noun by formal criteria, principally its ability to carry inflectional endings: *stones* (plural), *stone's* (possessive). Also, it can be preceded by noun identifiers such as *the* and *a*. On these bases, we can identify its functions:

[8a] A stone broke the window. (Function = subject)
 [b] I dropped the stone. (Function = direct object)
 [c] I slipped on a stone. (Function = object of preposition)

There are several more functions in language, but their number is limited. Table 2 identifies the main functions discussed in this text.

TABLE 2   Major Grammatical Functions

Subject	Indirect Object
Predicate	Complement
Direct Object	Modifier
Object of Preposition	Head

The distinction of subject and predicate separates a sentence into two parts. The sentences in [9] illustrate this division:

[9a] Jose—ran.
 [b] The aardvark—confronted the anteater.

[c] Wilbur—became angry.
[d] Waldo—is a nerd.

The distinction between subject and predicate is crucial to grammatical analysis. The subject, in traditional terms, identifies "something about which something is said." The predicate indicates "that which is said about the subject." Rhetorically, this distinction makes a good deal of sense. However, it doesn't serve as a grammatical criterion to divide the subject and the predicate. In fact, there is no foolproof criterion for making this distinction, especially when the sentence is complicated. In Chapter 8, we discuss ways to identify subjects and predicates.

Since the grammatical functions of direct object, object of a preposition, and complement are typical of noun phrases, we will postpone their discussion until the chapter on how noun phrases function within clauses (Chapter 8).

The modifier-head relation extends to many different parts of speech. Like the subject-predicate relationship, it rests on a largely intuitive sense, though some examples may help to clarify the nature of that intuition. Let's begin with some examples of modifier-head relations (the head word appears in italics):

[10a] reliable *source* (adjective—noun)
  [b] *something* strange (noun—adjective)
  [c] *ran* swiftly (verb—adverb)
  [d] cautiously *approached* (adverb—verb)
  [e] very *reliable* (intensifier—adjective)
  [f] very *cautiously* (intensifier—adverb)

A **head word** serves as the main element of the construction that contains it. A **modifier** is of secondary importance in the construction, serving to qualify the head. The head is thus the "syntactic center" of the construction and determines its grammatical category, e.g., NP, VP. If the head changes, other parts of a sentence containing the construction may be affected:

[11a] A reliable *source* is hard to find.
  [b] Reliable *sources* are hard to find.

The use of the singular *source* calls for an article (*a* or *the*) and a singular verb; the plural *sources* prohibits the use of *a* and requires a plural verb. *Reliable* has no effect on these changes. In some cases, e.g., [10c] and [10d], modifiers can appear either before or after the head. Finally, some words (such as *very* and *quite*) nearly always function as modifiers. As in much grammatical analysis, there is no single formal characteristic for a modifier-head relation. Each instance calls for the use of different principles.

Functions can also occur within functions, as in [12]:

[12]   [[very reliable] source]

In this case, we have two headwords, *reliable* and *source. Reliable* serves as the headword of the construction *very reliable* and *source* serves as the headword of the construction *very reliable source,* in which *very reliable* is analyzed as a single modifier. Our analysis can be represented clearly in a "tree diagram" format, as in [13]:

[13]

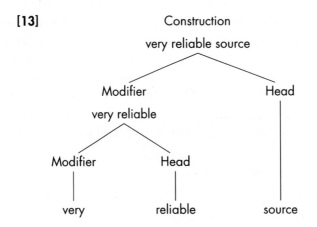

As we will observe later, tree diagrams are used also to represent layers of grammatical structure based on *formal* grounds. This mode of representation is, in fact, more common in modern linguistics than the use of functional trees. Thus the phrase above might be formally labeled as in [14]:

[14]

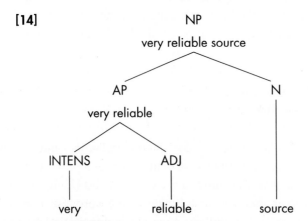

(NP = noun phrase; AP = adjective phrase; N = noun; ADJ = adjective; INTENS = intensifier)

We can "translate" the formal labels of [14] into the functional labels of [13] in a fairly simple way. We define a *head* of this NP as the noun (N) directly connected to NP. The AP to its left is a modifier. Within the AP, the adjective is the head and the form to its left is a modifier. Obviously, for more elaborate structures, our translations will be more complex. However, the general principles are the same. For instance, the headword will always determine the grammatical category of the phrase that it heads. Thus a phrase with a noun head will be a noun phrase; one with a verb head will be a verb phrase; and so on.

The position adopted in this book is that an initial formal identification of parts of speech and of phrase-types will provide students with a reliable basis to proceed to functional analysis. To illustrate this point, consider the word *stone* in the phrase *stone wall.* Is *stone* an adjective or a noun? If you consult the entry in a standard dictionary, you stand a good chance of finding it labeled as an adjective. Such a labeling would reflect a confusion between form and function. In English, *stone* is formally a noun: note *stones* and *stone's.* (It can also be a verb by other formal features: *stoned, stoning.*) But it doesn't accept adjective inflections for comparative and superlative: **stoner* and **stonest.* We thus argue that, in the phrase *stone wall,* the word *stone* is a noun that modifies another noun. This analysis clearly distinguishes formal and functional labels. In contrast, traditional grammars and dictionaries sometimes confuse the distinction by saying that *stone* is a noun used as an adjective. In our terminology, the phrase "noun used as an adjective" is illogical. Of course, adjectives often modify. However, that isn't their only function; and other parts of speech besides adjectives modify—including nouns. In recognition of this fact, grammars and dictionaries sometimes describe *stone* in *stone wall,* as an **attributive noun.** This label is perfectly consistent since attribution is one type of modification.

Meaning

The third perspective on grammar is that of semantics, or **meaning.** In this context, we include the meaning of words, phrases, and whole sentences. (See Chapter 2.) A simple example of lexical (word) meaning used in grammatical analysis is the familiar definition of a verb as a word that refers to "action or state of being." Another familiar example of attribution of semantic content to a grammatical construction is the traditional definition of a subject as the "doer of an action." Several chapters in this section will say more about such constructional meanings in regard to phrases, clauses, and entire sentences.

Our position in this book will be that the study of grammar can take place most successfully when built on a solid base of formal analysis. Thus in Chapters 5 and 6, we will identify parts of speech with no appeal to the meaning of the words under consideration. To do so, of course, doesn't imply that function and meaning are unimportant to language. Exactly the opposite is true, and we will include functional and semantic commentary on parts of speech and other grammatical forms. However, we will not use function or meaning as *criteria* for identification. As we proceed to phrases and clauses, we will—precisely because of our strong formal foundation—be able to make a more extensive inquiry into the functional and meaningful properties of grammar.

GLOSSARY

Attributive noun: see Chapter 5.

Form (general): the essential, observable properties of something that make it what it is.

Form (linguistic, applied to words): the word's observable characteristics, including actual and potential inflections, actual derivational endings, stress, potential position in grammatical structures, and potential for grammatical operations.

Function (general): the way in which something is used. See **relationship**.

Function (linguistic): the way in which a word or phrase is used in a sentence. Functions include Subject, Predicate, Direct Object, Indirect Object, Object of a Preposition, Complement, Adjunct, Modifier, Head, Auxiliary.

Government-Binding theory: see Chapter 11.

Head: see Chapter 5.

Meaning (linguistic): everything encompassed by semantics and pragmatics. See Chapter 2.

Modifier: see Chapter 5.

Module: see Chapter 11.

Morpheme: see Chapter 4.

Necessary conditions: conditions that must be satisfied for a definition to apply. See **sufficient conditions.**

Phonetics: see Chapter 3.

Phonology: see Chapter 3.

Relationship: a term that expresses the function of a word in a sentence.

Sufficient conditions: the minimum number of conditions that must be satisfied for a definition to apply. See **necessary conditions.**

3 PHONETICS AND PHONOLOGY

KEY CONCEPTS

Phonetics and phonology
Articulatory phonetics
Phonology

3.0 PHONETICS AND PHONOLOGY

Our earlier definition of language (Chapter 1) claimed that it is a system composed of rules and that its systematic nature suggested a set of subsystems or components. In this chapter, we sketch the components of English that deal with sounds. Phonetics and phonology provide the basis for an objective understanding of the spoken language. They're also useful for describing other aspects of the language, particularly word structure, grammar, semantics, and pragmatics. They can help us to understand the differences between spoken and written forms of the language. Finally, they provide us with a tool for describing the differences among varieties of the language.

We begin with **phonetics,** the attempt to record and describe the sounds of language objectively. Phonetics provides a valuable way of opening our eyes—and ears—to the many nuances of language that we take for granted. **Phonology,** in contrast, concerns itself with the ways in which a given language shapes sounds into distinctive categories of perception. Through phonology, we can begin to see the way in which language is rule-governed.

3.1 ARTICULATORY PHONETICS

We have three goals in this section. First, we introduce you to the ways in which the sounds of English are produced. Simultaneously, we introduce an alphabet which will allow us to refer unambiguously to individual sounds. Finally, we develop a system for classifying speech sounds on the basis of how they're produced.

The alphabet we introduce here uses many of the letters of the English alphabet, but their values are very restricted and there are no "silent" letters; every phonetic symbol represents an actual sound. In addition, no symbol represents more than one sound. (To make fine distinctions, phoneticians add special symbols, called **diacritics,** to the basic letters. Also, for languages other than English, further symbols have been devised.)

A word of caution. Most of the symbols we use here are the ordinary English alphabetic symbols. Remember that they have only a single pronunciation regardless of their context,

TABLE 3.1   Consonants of English

	Bilabial	Labio-dental	Inter-dental	Alveolar	Palatal	Velar	Glottal
Stop	p b m			t d n		k g ŋ	
Fricative		f v	θ ð	s z	š ž		h
Affricate					č ǰ		
Lateral				l			
Retroflex				r			

TABLE 3.2   Vowels of English

	Front		Central		Back
	i				u
High	I			U	
		e			o
Mid		ɛ	ə	ɔ	
Low		æ		ɑ	
	Diphthongs	ay	aw	ɔy	

and that the pronunciation may not be the one you expect. The major phonetic symbols for English appear in Tables 3.1 and 3.2. In the sections below, we describe the sounds represented by these symbols and how they're made.

Producing speech involves the **lungs**, the **larynx**, the **oral cavity**, and sometimes the **nasal cavity.** The sounds are produced by modulating the airflow from the lungs as it makes its way to the outside world. The air stream can be stopped or impeded. Each of these modulations will produce a distinct speech sound. In the oral cavity, the tongue, because of its remarkable flexibility, is the major modifier.

The vocal tract consists of a sound source (the **vocal cords/folds**) and two resonating chambers (the oral and nasal cavities). Figure 3.1 gives a pictorial rendering of the mouth. On the basis of how they are produced, we distinguish between consonants and vowels and deal with each class of sounds separately.

3.1.1   Consonants

Consonants include the sounds we represent as p, d, m, f, v, s, z, l, r, etc. in the ordinary alphabet. All **consonants** are produced either by entirely stopping the air stream coming from the lungs or at least by constricting the air stream enough that it's forced through an opening so narrow that a noisy friction is created.

We classify consonants according to three sets of characteristics: (1) **voicing**, (2) **place of articulation**, (3) **manner of articulation**, and (4) **nasality.**

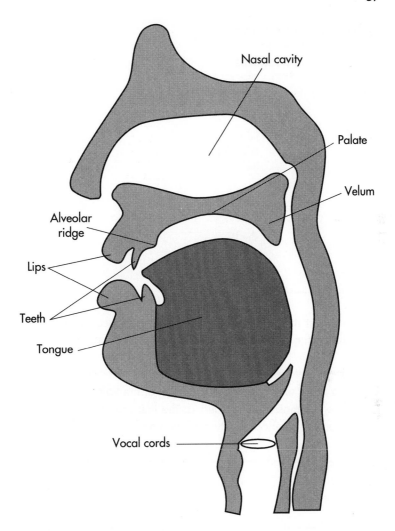

FIGURE 3.1   Vocal Apparatus

3.1.1.1   Voicing

Sounds produced with vibrating vocal cords (see Figure 3.1) are said to be **voiced.** Those produced without vocal cord vibration are referred to as **voiceless.** To become familiar with the difference between voiced and voiceless sounds, try this experiment. (Some people may prefer a private place to do it.) First, put your hands over your ears. Then produce the sound represented by the *f* of *feel* (just the *f*, don't include the following vowel). Continue the sound for a few seconds. Now switch to the sound represented by the *v* of *veal* (again, just the *v*). Again, continue the sound for a few seconds. As you produced the "f" sound there was no vocal cord vibration, but as you produced the "v" sound your vocal cords vibrated. Try the same exercises with the first sounds of the following words: *thigh, thy; sip, zip.* You should

TABLE 3.3   Voiced and
Voiceless
Consonants

Voiced	Voiceless
by [b]	pie [p]
my [m]	
vie [v]	fie [f]
thy [ð]	thigh [θ]
die [d]	tie [t]
nigh [n]	
zip [z]	sip [s]
guy [g]	kite [k]
gong [ŋ]	
beige [ž]	shy [š]
jive [ǰ]	chive [č]
lie [l]	
rye [r]	hat [h]

be able to feel the cords vibrate as you make the second sound of each pair. Table 3.3 distinguishes the voiced and voiceless consonants of English.

EXERCISE   Collect a set of examples in which each of the voiced and voiceless sounds listed in the two columns above occurs as the first sound of a word and also in the middle of words (specifically between two vowels), as in: [b] bird, rubbing; [p] pan, tapping.

3.1.1.2   Place of articulation

By **place of articulation** we mean the area in the mouth at which the consonantal closure or constriction occurs.

English uses only seven places of articulation (see Figure 3.1): **bilabial** (both lips); **labiodental** (bottom lip and top teeth); **interdental** (tongue tip protrudes between teeth); **alveolar** (bony ridge immediately behind the teeth); **alveopalatal** (the hard palate just behind the alveolar ridge); **velar** (soft palate); and **glottal** (vocal cords). Examples of each type appear in Table 3.4.

3.1.1.3   Manner of articulation

By **manner of articulation** we mean the kind of closure or constriction used in making the sound. We classify consonants according to five manners of articulation: **stops** (full stoppage of the air stream anywhere in the *oral* cavity from the vocal cords to the lips, as in [p], [b], [m]); **fricatives** (constriction of the air stream producing friction anywhere in the same area, as in [f], [v], [s], [z]); **affricates** (full stoppage of the air stream followed

TABLE 3.4   Places of Articulation

Bilabials
[p]	pie	cupping	cup
[b]	by	clubbing	cub
[m]	my	coming	come

Labiodentals
[f]	feel	coffin	puff
[v]	veal	coven	dove

Interdentals
[θ]	thigh	ether	mouth (noun)
[ð]	thy	either	mouth (verb)

Alveolars
[t]	tub	boating	boat
[d]	dub	boding	bode
[n]	nun	boning	bone
[s]	sip	fussy	grace
[z]	zip	fuzzy	graze
[l]	lip	teller	tale
[r]	rip	terror	tear

Alveopalatals
[š]	sure	vicious	rush
[ž]	jour (soupe du _)	vision	rouge
[č]	chin	catcher	etch
[ǰ]	gin	edger	edge

Velars
[k]	could	backer	tuck
[g]	good	bagger	tug
[ŋ]	—	banger	tongue

Glottal
[h]	hat	cahoots	—

immediately by constriction, as in [č], [ǰ]); **laterals** (the tongue touches the top of the mouth but the air is allowed to pass along one or both sides, as in [l]); and **retroflex** (the tongue is turned upward and backward, as in [r]). Table 3.5 summarizes the different manners of articulation.

EXERCISE   Collect a set of examples in which each of the sounds listed in Table 3.5 occurs as the last sound of a word and also in the middle of words (specifically between two vowels), as in: [ŋ] ring, ringing.

An articulatory description of any consonant must specify (at least) its place and manner of articulation, whether voiced or voiceless, and whether oral or nasal (i.e., with air

TABLE 3.5   Manners of Articulation

Stops			Affricates	
[p]	pad		[č]	chin
[t]	tad		[ǰ]	gin
[k]	cad			
[b]	bad		Lateral	
[d]	dad		[l]	laugh
[g]	gad			
[m]	mad		Retroflex	
[n]	Nat		[r]	retroflex
[ŋ]	tang			

Fricatives	
[f]	fie
[v]	vie
[θ]	thigh
[ð]	thy
[s]	Sue
[z]	zoo
[š]	shoe
[ž]	jus (au jus)
[h]	how

flowing through the nose). For example, [m] is made by stopping the air stream at the lips, is voiced, and is nasal. These features are represented as:

	[m]	[p]
Place	bilabial	bilabial
Manner	stop	stop
Voicing	voiced	voiceless
Nasality	nasal	oral

EXERCISE   For each of the following consonants, you should now be able to specify these four characteristics. Consult Tables 3.3 to 3.5.

	[p]	[t]	[k]	[b]	[d]
Place					
Manner					
Voicing					
Nasality					

	[g]	[n]	[ŋ]	[f]	[v]
Place					
Manner					
Voicing					
Nasality					

	[θ]	[ε]	[s]	[z]	[š]
Place					
Manner					
Voicing					
Nasality					
	[ž]	[č]	[ǰ]	[l]	[r]
Place					
Manner					
Voicing					
Nasality					

3.1.2   Vowels

Vowels include the sounds we ordinarily represent as a, e, i, o, u, as well as a number of others for which the ordinary alphabet has no unique symbols.

Vowels are distinguished from consonants in several ways. Consonants are produced by narrowing the oral tract enough to close it completely or to cause turbulence at the narrowest point. Vowels are produced with a smooth airflow through the oral tract. Also, vowels can be sung, whereas consonants cannot. In technical terms, vowels are thus more **sonorant** than consonants.

Differences in vowel quality are produced by changing the shape of the oral cavity. Characteristic vowel qualities are produced primarily by varying the height of the back or the front of the tongue in the mouth; second, by the configuration of the lips; third, by the tension of the musculature of the oral tract; and finally, by the length of time for which the vowel is maintained.

3.1.2.1   Tongue height

If you pronounce the words *beat* and *bat,* drawing out the vowels for as long as you need, observe that your mouth is considerably more open in pronouncing *bat* than in pronouncing *beat.* If this isn't obvious to you just by playing with these two words, look in a mirror as you produce them.

Once you've become accustomed to the relative openness of these two vowels, pronounce the word *bait* between the first two. Its degree of openness falls between *beat* and *bat,* so there is a continuous increase in mouth openness as you slip from one word to another. These degrees distinguish **high, mid,** and **low vowels.**

In this book, we will use the following symbols for this sequence of vowels:

[1]   beat   [i]   High
      bait   [e]   Mid
      bat   [æ]   Low

EXERCISE   Find ten words to illustrate each of the three vowels we distinguish in [1] above. Be clear about which symbol most accurately applies to each vowel.

3.1.2.2   Front versus back vowels

Now compare the vowel of *beat* with that of *boot*. Alternate the words, and then just the vowels. It will be more difficult this time to monitor the activities of your tongue as you shift from one of these to the other, but try anyway. You produce [i] with the front (*blade*) of your tongue raised toward your palate. If you draw in your breath as you make this vowel, you will feel the cold air against your palate. As you shift from [i] to the vowel of *boot*, represented phonetically as [u], you will find yourself raising the back of your tongue. (You will also find yourself pursing (**rounding**) your lips, but disregard this for the moment.) Because of the relative positions in the mouth at which these vowels are made, phoneticians call [i] and all the others in [1] **front vowels,** and [u] a **back vowel.**

Again, the back vowels, like the front series, descend from high through mid to low, in a continuous sequence. As you produce the series of vowels you'll find your mouth opening from *coot* to *cot*. We use the following symbols for back vowels:

[2]   coot   [u]   High
      coat   [o]   Mid
      cot   [a]   Low

EXERCISE   Find ten words to illustrate each of the three back vowels in [2]. Be clear about which symbol most accurately applies to each vowel.

We can represent these two series of vowels graphically in Table 3.6.

TABLE 3.6   Front and Back Vowels

	Front	Back
High	i	u
Mid	e	o
Low	æ	a

EXERCISE   Find another ten words to illustrate each of the vowels we distinguish in Table 3.6. Be clear about which symbol most accurately applies to each vowel.

3.1.2.3   Lip rounding

As you compared [i] and [u] you probably noticed that your lips changed shape as you shifted from the front vowel to the back one. Your lips were **rounded** as you produced [u]. They were **spread (unrounded)** as you produced [i]. As you moved through the series of back vowels you may also have noticed that lip rounding decreased as you moved from high to low. In fact, the amount of lip rounding on [a] is minimal. In English, only the back vowels are rounded, although languages such as French and German have front rounded vowels.

EXERCISE   Find ten pairs of words to illustrate lip rounding. The vowel of the first member of each pair should be rounded; the second member should be as similar as possible to the first but its vowel must not be rounded. Assign a phonetic symbol to each vowel.

3.1.2.4   Muscle tension

Now pronounce the pairs of words *heat* and *hit,* and *hoot* and *hood.* The vowels of *heat* and *hoot* are **tense.** That is, the musculature of the tongue and mouth is tighter. The vowels of *hit* and *hood* are **lax** in comparison. Table 3.7 identifies both types of vowels.

TABLE 3.7   Tense and Lax Vowels

Tense	Lax
heat [i]	hit [I]
hoot [u]	hood [U]
hate [e]	head [ɛ]
tote [o]	taught [ɔ]
	hat [æ]
	hot [a]

EXERCISES   1. Find ten words to illustrate each of the vowels we distinguish in the chart just above. Be clear about which symbol most accurately applies to each vowel.
   2. For each of the following vowels, indicate its height, position (front or back), tension, and lip configuration.

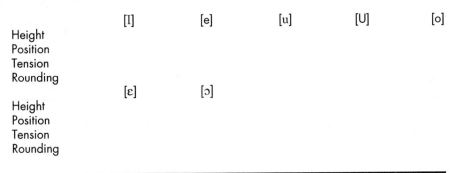

	[I]	[e]	[u]	[U]	[o]
Height					
Position					
Tension					
Rounding					

	[ɛ]	[ɔ]
Height		
Position		
Tension		
Rounding		

Besides these vowels, there is one other we must mention. This is the sound of the second vowel of *sofa* and *soda,* called **schwa** and written [ə]. This vowel is made farther forward than the back vowels and farther back than the front ones, hence it's **central.** In addition, [ə] is a mid, lax, unrounded vowel. It can be heard in both stressed and unstressed syllables, as in the word *above.*

EXERCISE   Find ten words to illustrate the vowel [ə]. Can you estimate how common this vowel is in English? What letters of the alphabet normally indicate this sound?

We can present the vowels as we presented the consonants, on a chart indicating their articulatory properties (see Table 3.8).

TABLE 3.8   English Vowels

		Front	Central	Back	
High	Tense	i		u	Back Rounded
	Lax	I		U	
Mid	Tense	e		o	
	Lax	ɛ	ə	ɔ	
Low		æ		a	Back Unrounded

3.1.2.5   Glides or semivowels

The two sounds [y], in *yet, boy, boyish,* and [w], in *wet, row,* and *rowing,* fall between true consonants and true vowels. They occur in the positions typical of consonants in English, i.e., at the beginnings and ends of syllables, but from an articulatory point of view, they don't involve either the degree of closure that characterizes other consonants or the degree of openness that is characteristic of true vowels. Because they're intermediate between these two main classes of sounds, the two sounds have been called **semivowels.** (They're also intermediate in **sonority** (i.e., resonance), being more sonorant than consonants but less so than vowels.) [y] is made by raising the middle of the tongue toward the hard palate, close to where the vowel [i] is made. [w] is made by raising the back of the tongue toward the velum and rounding the lips, much as in the production of [u]. [y] is referred to as a palatal **glide,** and [w] as a labiovelar glide.

EXERCISE   Find ten words to illustrate each of the glides [w] and [y].

One reason that these sounds are referred to as glides is that they may occur as the second member of the complex vowel sounds called diphthongs.

3.1.2.6   Diphthongs

We have approached vowels as if they were articulated by a specific configuration of the tongue, lips, and oral cavity, which was then held constant throughout their pronunciation. Some vowels are made like this, the **monophthongs;** others involve a change in the configuration of the mouth, the **diphthongs.**

The vowel sounds in the words *boy, by,* and *how* involve a change in the shape of the mouth as the vowel is being produced. The vowel of *boy* begins approximately with the mid back vowel [ɔ] and finishes with the palatal glide [y]. The vowel of *by* begins with approximately the low back vowel [ɑ] and finishes with [y]. The vowel of *how* begins with approximately [ɑ] and finishes with the labiovelar glide [w]. We represent these diphthongs, respectively, as [ɔy], [ɑy], and [ɑw].

The second set of English diphthongs isn't as clearly distinguished as the first, primarily because we tend to perceive them as simple vowels. However, in a precise (**narrow**) phonetic transcription, they must be represented as diphthongs. The two tense front vowels [i] and [e] are actually pronounced as [iy] and [ey], as you will notice if you listen carefully. The two tense back vowels also are diphthongized, but instead of ending in a front glide, they end in [w]. Thus the vowels in *boot* and *boat* are [uw] and [ow], respectively.

Because the front tense vowels end in the front glide [y] and the back tense vowels end in the back glide [w], we can predict which glide will occur with which vowel. We can express this pattern as a rule: *Tense vowels are diphthongized by the addition of a glide, and the frontness or backness of the glide is the same as the frontness or backness of the vowel.*

Diphthongization of these vowels is a feature of English rather than a universal feature of natural language. Other languages, notably Spanish and German, don't diphthongize their corresponding vowels. The tendency to diphthongize these vowels is one characteristic of the "foreign accent" that English speakers betray when they begin to learn these languages.

3.1.3 Syllables

It's a lot easier to count syllables than to give them a satisfactory definition. If the entire class were to count the syllables in this paragraph, there would be considerable agreement about the number, but probably not about where each syllable begins and ends. The fact that syllabic writing systems developed before alphabetic systems suggests that syllables are very easily perceived linguistic units. The fact that children seem to be able to associate symbols with syllables before they can associate symbols with phonetic segments also points to the importance of the syllable.

Every syllable ($) consists of at least a **nucleus (N)**. The nucleus may be preceded by an **onset (O)** and followed by a **coda (C)**; O and C may each consist of one or more consonants or glides. The nucleus and the coda together make up a unit called the **rhyme (R)**. Example [3] illustrates the schema using the word *then*:

[3]

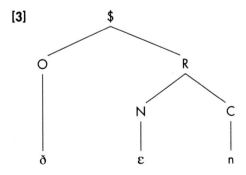

Usually, the nucleus is a vowel because vowels are high in sonority. (A glide or a consonant with a high sonority value, such as [l, r, m, n, ŋ] may also be a nucleus.) The sonority levels of the syllable thus rise from the onset (if there is one) up to the peak in the nucleus and fall off again in the coda. In this respect, the onset and coda are (almost) mirror images of each other.

The rhyme is so called because of its importance in rhyming, to which the onset is usually irrelevant, as the rhyming words in the following stanza show:

[4]   Piping down the valleys wild,
      Piping songs of pleasant glee,
      On a cloud I saw a child,
      And he laughing said to me:

          (William Blake, Introduction to *Songs of Innocence*)

The [w] of *wild* and the [č] of *child* are syllable onsets, which though different, don't affect Blake's rhyme. Likewise, with [gl] of *glee* and [m] of *me*.

In speech, syllables are combined into rhythmic units called feet, units which are also of considerable importance in scanning lines of poetry. Each **foot** consists of one **stressed** syllable (its energy peak) and one or two unstressed syllables. Feet are differentiated from each other by the number of unstressed (U) syllables they contain and by the position of the stressed (S) syllable. In [5], the stressed syllable of each sample word is italicized:

[5]   Iambic: [U S]   to*day*
      Trochaic: [S U]   *por*trait
      Anapestic: [U U S]   inter*vene*
      Dactylic: [S U U]   *per*sonal

In English, stressed syllables are more or less equally far apart in time; as a result, unstressed syllables may be articulated slower or faster, depending on the type of foot.

EXERCISE   In the stanza given in [4], identify each stressed syllable, determine the feet, and identify the kind of meter (iambic, trochaic, etc.) involved.

3.2 PHONOLOGY

Bloomfield (1933) defined **phonology** as "the study of *significant* speech sounds" (p. 78; emphasis in original). With this definition, he distinguishes phonology from phonetics, which can be characterized as the study of speech sounds as sounds without regard for their linguistic functions or status. The study of phonology necessarily "involves the consideration of meaning"; phonetics doesn't. In this section, we explore phonology and the basic unit of phonological analysis, the **phoneme**.

3.2.1 Phonemes

Not all differences in sound signal differences in meaning, so the question becomes, Which differences in sound do and which don't signal differences in meaning? For example, English speakers may freely pronounce the final stops of words such as *rot* in one or another of several ways. They may either release the stop with considerable breathiness (**aspiration**) or they may not release it at all. We represent these two possibilities with the diacritics, superscript [ʰ] or superscript [º], respectively; [ratʰ] and [ratº]. The important point here is that English speakers don't associate any difference in meaning with the difference in pronunciation of the final consonant. Both pronunciations represent "the same unit." They're interchangeable; i.e., they're in **free variation.** Substituting one of the sounds for the other doesn't affect the meaning represented.

Not all sounds in a language can be substituted one for another without affecting meaning. If we replace the [t] in [rat] with [d], then we get the sequence of sounds [rad], representing the word *rod,* quite distinct in meaning from *rot.* Clearly, English speakers treat the difference between [d] and [t] differently from the way they treat the difference between [tʰ] and [tº]. In the former case, the difference can signal a difference in meaning; in the latter, it cannot. Differences in sound which signal differences in meaning are said to be **distinctive** or **contrastive.** Differences which don't signal meaning differences are **nondistinctive, noncontrastive,** or **redundant.** One objective of phonology is to identify which differences are contrastive and which aren't.

Table 3.9 lists the phonemes of English. You will note that the symbols are graphically the same as those we used for phonetics. To distinguish phonology from phonetics, we enclose phonemes in *slanted brackets*—/ /—and use square brackets—[ ]—for phonetic notation.

As you have no doubt noticed, there are approximately forty phonemes of English (the number varies from variety to variety), while there are only twenty-six letters in the English alphabet. This is one of the reasons that the alphabet appears to fit the language so poorly. Another reason that the fit between English sounds and spellings is so poor is that the spelling system developed several centuries ago, and many major changes have occurred in the sound system since that time. While the sound system changed rapidly, the spelling system has been very conservative.

TABLE 3.9 English Phonemes

Consonants:	/p, t, k/
	/b, d, g/
	/m, n, ŋ/
	/f, θ, s, š, h/
	/v, ð, z, ž/
	/č, ǰ/
	/r, l/
Glides:	/w, y/
Vowels:	/i, I, e, ɛ, æ, ə, a, ɔ, o, U, u/
Diphthongs:	/ay, aw, ɔy/

EXERCISE   Compare the aspirated and unreleased pronunciations of the final stops in *stick* and *step*. Are they in free variation?

We noted above that [tʰ] and [t°] don't contrast with each other and that they represent "the same unit." We must now address the nature of the unit that these and other analogous sets of sounds represent. We call the unit represented by these two sounds the **phoneme** /t/ and say that [tʰ] and [t°] are **allophones** (nondistinctive variants) of that phoneme. We use / / to enclose phonemic and [ ] to enclose phonetic and allophonic entities.

EXERCISE   If you decided that the aspirated and unreleased pronunciations of the final stops of *stick* and *step* in the last exercise were in free variation, how do you interpret this in phoneme and allophone terms? Represent your interpretation using the notational conventions presented in the paragraph above.

The allophones of /t/ that we have so far mentioned are in free variation. Speakers of English can freely use either at the ends of words. However, not all allophones of a phoneme can be freely substituted for each other. Some are in **complementary distribution;** i.e., they occupy distinct positions (**environments**) in words. For instance, the English phoneme /t/ has a third allophone, [t], released but unaspirated. When /t/ occurs after /s/, as in the word *still* (/stIl/), it's pronounced [t]. If, however, /t/ is the first phoneme of a word, it's pronounced as its allophone [tʰ]. English speakers don't pronounce /t/ as [t] in word initial position or as [tʰ] after /s/. If we were to substitute one allophone for the other, e.g., to pronounce *still* as [stʰIl] or *till* as [tIl], our pronunciations wouldn't represent different words with distinct meanings. They would merely be odd and un-English pronunciations of the two words.

We can sum up our discussion of the allophones of /t/ as the following **phonological rule:** plain [t] occurs after /s/, at the beginning of stressed syllables [tʰ] occurs, and [t°] freely alternates with [tʰ] at the ends of words. See Figure 3.2. Statements such as these describe the **distribution** of the allophones of the phonemes of a language. One of our objectives in studying a language is to be able to make such distributional statements, i.e., to be able to specify the phonetic environments in which each allophone occurs.

FIGURE 3.2   Distribution of Allophones of the /t/ Phoneme

Environment	Stressed/syllable initial	After /s/	Ends of words
Allophone	[tʰ]	[t]	[tʰ] or [t°]

EXERCISE   Phonemes are most easily identified through **minimal pairs**—two words of different meaning that are phonetically the same except for one sound. Thus *pit* ([pIt]) and *bit* ([bIt]) make a minimal pair that shows that /p/ and /b/ are separate phonemes in English. For each pair of sounds below, identify a minimal pair that shows that they are different phonemes.

[k]—[g]	[θ]—[ð]	[a]—[ɔ]
[n]—[ŋ]	[w]—[y]	[ay]—[aw]
[f]—[s]	[i]—[ɪ]	[ay]—[ɔy]
[s]—[š]	[ɛ]—[æ]	

If we explore the allophones of other English phonemes, we can see how the phonemic concept explains native speakers' perceptions of sound. Nonphoneticians normally don't pay attention to the differences between allophones. For instance, the vowels of *cap* and *can* differ phonetically: that of *cap* is a plain [æ]; that of *can* is **nasalized,** represented by [æ̃]. (If you have trouble hearing the difference, try starting to say each word normally and then omit the final consonant.) The phoneme /æ/ thus has two allophones, [æ] and [æ̃].

EXERCISE Try your hand at distinguishing allophones of phonemes. Using the discussion above as a guide, see if you can describe the differences between the allophones of the designated phoneme in the example words.
a. /k/: kin, skin, sick
b. /ɛ/: bet, Ben
c. /e/: rate, raid
d. /ɛ/: bet, bed
e. /l/: lead, pull

3.2.2 Phonological rules

As we have seen above, a **phonological rule** is a general statement about the distribution of a phoneme's allophones, e.g., those of /t/. This definition is somewhat narrow, however, for there are other kinds of phonological rules.

The rule for the [tʰ] allophone of /t/ can be seen as adding the feature of **aspiration** ([ʰ]) to a voiceless stop in certain contexts. Such rules are referred to as **feature addition rules.** This rule adds the aspiration feature to the consonant.

The nasal pronunciation of the vowel of *can,* noted above, is due to the influence of the nasal consonant /n/. There is a rule which predicts that *any* vowel will be nasalized before a nasal consonant. This is a **feature changing rule.** In this case, it changes an oral sound to a nasal one.

In informal speech, as well as in Black English, the second of a pair of consonants at the end of a word gets deleted by a **segment deletion rule.** Thus words such as *frost* and *ask,* are pronounced as [fras] and [æs] when they occur before consonants (e.g., *Ask Bill*).

French adjectives which end in consonants routinely lose those consonants if the following word begins with a consonant: "small friend" *petit ami* [pɛtit ami] versus "small thing" *petit chose* [pɛti šoz].

Phonological rules may reverse the order of segments in words. In some dialects of English, the verb *ask* is pronounced as [æks], reversing [s] and [k]. Such a rule is called a **metathesis rule.**

Rules also change the relationships between segments and their neighbors. Some rules, such as the vowel nasalization rule, make a segment and its neighbor more alike. Such rules are called **assimilation rules.** Assimilation can be so thoroughgoing that two sounds can merge into one. For example, [t, d, s, z] are **palatalized**—i.e., pronounced as [č, ǰ, š, ž], respectively—when they occur at the ends of words and the next word begins with [y]. For example, *Did you?* is typically pronounced as [dĭ ǰ ə], where the [ǰ] results from the coalescence of [dy].

Through phonological rules we can demonstrate the orderliness of language. By putting information about general, predictable patterns into the phonological rules, we leave only that information which is unpredictable and idiosyncratic to be listed in the set of phonemes. We thereby minimize the number of basic units we need to posit, and also minimize the number of times any given piece of information is mentioned, thus simplifying the overall grammar or description of the language. For example, English has two series of vowels, those with and those without nasalization. If we merely listed all these vowels as belonging to the language, then we would have postulated far more basic units than we—as native speakers—really need, and we would have missed the generalization that the two series of vowels are really quite alike, one series being merely a predictable positional variant of the other. We capture this generalization by eliminating the series of nasalized vowels from our inventory of basic units and replacing it with the nasalization rule.

EXERCISES   Try your hand at stating phonological rules.

1. Consider the allophones that you discovered in the previous exercise and express their occurrence through rules.
2. Examine the *natural* pronunciation of the word *in* in the phrases below. Write each entire phrase phonemically. Then try to state a rule that accounts for the different pronunciations. What *type* of rule did you discover?
   a. In Bill's house
   b. In Ted's house
   c. In Greg's house

REFERENCES AND RESOURCES

Bloomfield, L. 1933. *Language.* London: Allen & Unwin.

Hogg, R., and C. B. McCully. 1987. *Metrical Phonology: A Course Book.* Cambridge: Cambridge University Press.

Ladefoged, P. 1982. *A Course in Phonetics.* 2d ed. New York: Harcourt, Brace, Jovanovich, Inc.

Lass, R. 1984. Phonology: *An Introduction to Basic Concepts.* Cambridge: Cambridge University Press.

GLOSSARY

Affricate: a sound produced with full stoppage of the air stream followed immediately by constriction.

Allophone: a nondistinctive phonetic variant of a phoneme.

Alveolar: a sound produced at the bony ridge behind the teeth.

Alveopalatal: a sound produced at the hard palate just behind the alveolar ridge.

Aspirated: a consonant sound released with a puff of air.

Assimilation rule: a phonological rule which makes a sound similar to a nearby sound; e.g., nasalization.

Back vowel: a vowel produced with the back of the tongue raised toward the soft palate.

Bilabial: a sound produced with constriction of both lips.

Broad phonetics: the attempt to record pronunciation without regard to noncontrastive details. See **narrow phonetics.**

Central: a vowel—e.g., [ə]—produced with the tongue raised at the center of the mouth rather than at the front or back.

Coda: the concluding part of a syllable; follows the nucleus.

Complementary distribution: the property of allophones that occupy distinct positions in words.

Consonant: a sound produced with complete or partial obstruction of the airflow through the mouth. See **vowel.**

Contrastive (also "**distinctive**"): sounds used in a language to signal differences of meaning.

Diacritics: phonetic symbols used to make fine distinctions of pronunciation; e.g., the [ʰ] of aspiration.

Diphthong: a vowel unit consisting of two elements, a nucleus and a glide. See **monophthong.**

Distinctive: see **contrastive.**

Distribution: specific circumstances (**environments**) in which a sound occurs; e.g., at the beginning, middle, or end of a word.

Environment: see **distribution.**

Feature addition/changing rule: a phonological rule that changes the pronunciation of a sound by adding or changing a phonetic feature such as aspiration or nasalization.

Foot: a rhythmic unit consisting of one stressed syllable and one to two unstressed syllables.

Free variation: a situation in which two sounds are interchangeable in a word with no effect on meaning.

Fricative: a sound produced with constriction of the air stream producing friction.

Front vowel: a vowel produced with the front of the tongue raised toward the hard palate.

Glides: see **semivowels.**

Glottal: a sound produced by constriction or stoppage at the vocal cords.

High vowel: a vowel pronounced with the mouth in least degree of openness. See **mid vowel** and **low vowel.**

Interdental: a sound produced with the tongue protruding between the teeth.

Labiodental: a sound produced with constriction between the bottom lip and top teeth.

Lateral: a sound produced with the tongue touching the top of the mouth with air allowed to pass along one or both sides, as in [l].

Lax: a sound produced with the musculature of the mouth relatively relaxed. See **tense.**

Low vowel: a vowel pronounced with the mouth in greatest degree of openness. See **high vowel** and **mid vowel.**

Manner of articulation: the kind of closure or constriction used in making a consonant sound.

Metathesis rule: the phonological rule that reverses the order of segments in words.

Mid vowel: a vowel pronounced with the mouth in moderate degree of openness. See **high vowel** and **low vowel.**

Minimal pair: two words of different meaning that are phonetically the same except for one sound; e.g., *pit* and *bit*.

Monophthong: a vowel unit consisting of a single segment held constant during its pronunciation. See **diphthong.**

Narrow phonetics: the attempt to record noncontrastive details of pronunciation. See **broad phonetics.**

Nasalized: articulated with air flowing through the nasal cavity.

Noncontrastive (also **"nondistinctive," "redundant"**): sounds not used in a language to signal different meanings.

Nucleus: the central part of a syllable, i.e., that segment with highest sonority.

Onset: the initial part of a syllable; precedes the nucleus.

Palatalized: a consonant which has been assimilated to a palatal sound.

Phoneme: a contrastive category of speech sounds in a language.

Phonetics (articulatory): the study of how sounds are produced.

Phonological rule: a general descriptive statement about the distribution of a phoneme's allophones and about other phonological processes.

Phonology: the study of the ways in which a given language shapes sounds into distinctive categories of perception and of its rules of pronunciation.

Place of articulation: the area in the mouth at which the consonantal closure or constriction occurs.

Retroflex: a sound produced with the tongue turned upward and backward, as in [r].

Rhyme: the nucleus and coda of a syllable.

Rounded: a vowel sound produced with the lips pursed. See **unrounded.**

Schwa: a midcentral unrounded vowel, represented as [ə].

Segment deletion rule: a phonological rule that eliminates a sound from pronunciation in a word or phrase.

Semivowel: sounds—e.g., [y] and [w]—that are intermediate in openness and sonority between consonants and vowels.

Sonorant: sounds produced with a smooth airflow, allowing for a high degree of voicing.

Sonority: overall loudness or resonance of a sound.

Stop: a sound produced with full stoppage of the air stream anywhere in the *oral* cavity from the vocal cords to the lips.

Stress: the degree of energy (emphasis) with which a sound or syllable is pronounced.

Tense: a sound produced with the musculature of the mouth relatively tight. See **lax.**

Unrounded: a vowel produced with lips flat. See **rounded.**

Velar: a sound produced with constriction at the soft palate.

Voiced: a sound produced with the vocal cords vibrating.

Voiceless: a sound produced with the vocal cords not vibrating.

Vowel: a sound produced with no obstruction of the air stream in the mouth. See **consonant.**

4 MORPHOLOGY AND WORD FORMATION

KEY CONCEPTS

Words and morphemes
Root, inflectional, and derivational morphemes
Morphemes, allomorphs, and morphs
Words
Inflectional morphology
Derivational morphology
Compounding
The internal structure of complex words
Classifying words by their morphological possibilities

4.0 WORDS AND MORPHEMES

In traditional grammar, words were the basic units of analysis. Grammarians classified words according to their parts of speech and identified and listed the forms that words could show up in. Although the matter is really very complex, we will assume for the sake of simplicity that we are all generally able to distinguish words from other linguistic units. It will be sufficient for our purposes here if we assume that words are the main units used for entries in dictionaries. In section 4.3, we will briefly describe some distinctive characteristics of words.

Words are potentially complex units, composed of even more basic units, called morphemes. A **morpheme** is the smallest meaningful part of a word; we will designate them in braces—{ }. For example, *sawed, sawn, sawing,* and *saws* can all be analyzed into the morphemes {saw} + {-ed}, {-n}, {-ing}, {-s}, respectively. None of these can be further divided into meaningful units and each occurs in many other words such as *looked, mown, coughing,* and *bakes.*

{Saw} can occur on its own; it doesn't have to be attached to anything else; it's a **free morpheme.** However, none of the other morphemes listed above is free. Each must be attached (**affixed**) to some other unit. Morphemes that must be attached are said to be **bound.**

Affixes are classified according to whether they're attached before or after the form to which they're added. **Prefixes** are attached before and **suffixes** after. The bound morphemes listed above are all suffixes; the {re-} of *resawn* is a prefix.

4.1 ROOT, INFLECTIONAL AND DERIVATIONAL MORPHEMES

Besides being bound or free, morphemes can also be classified as **root, inflectional,** or **derivational**. A **root morpheme** is the basic form to which other morphemes are attached. The morpheme {saw} is the root of *sawers*. {-er} is a **derivational suffix**, whose addition turns the verb into a noun (usually meaning one who performs the action denoted by the verb), and {-s} is an **inflectional** morpheme suffixed to nouns to indicate plurality.

4.2 MORPHEMES, ALLOMORPHS, AND MORPHS

The English plural morpheme {-s} can be expressed by three different but clearly related phonemic forms /s/, /z/, and /Iz/. These three have in common not only their meaning but also the fact that each contains an alveolar fricative phoneme. The three forms are in complementary distribution because it's possible to predict just where each occurs: /s/ after voiceless segments, /z/ after voiced, and /Iz/ after sibilants—/s/, /z/, /š/ /ž/, /č/, and /ǰ/. Given the functional and phonological similarities among the three forms and the fact that they're in complementary distribution, it's reasonable to view them as variants of a single entity. In parallel with phonology, we will refer to the entity of which the three are variant representations as a morpheme, and the variants as **allomorphs**. When we wish to refer to a minimal meaningful form merely as a form, we will use the term **morph**. Compare these terms and the concepts behind them with phoneme, allophone, and phone.

4.3 WORDS

Words are notoriously difficult entities to define in either universal or language-specific terms. Like most linguistic entities, they're Janus-like. They look in two directions—upward toward phrases and sentences and downward toward their constituent morphemes. This, however, only helps us understand words if we already understand how they're combined into larger units or divided into smaller ones, so we will briefly discuss several other criteria which have been proposed for identifying them.

One possible criterion is spelling: Words are spelled with spaces on either end. Unfortunately, this leads to inconsistent and unsatisfactory results. For instance, *cannot* is one word but *may not* is two; compounds (words composed of two words) are irregularly divided (cf. *influx, in-laws, goose flesh, low income* versus *low-income*).

Words in general tend to resist interruption; we cannot freely insert pieces into words as we do into sentences. We cannot, for example, separate the root of a word from its inflectional ending by inserting another word: **boy-fingerprint-s,* for *boys' fingerprints*. Sentences, in contrast, can be so interrupted. We can insert adverbs between subjects and predicates: *John quickly erased his fingerprints*. By definition, we can also insert the traditional interjections: *We will, I believe, have rain later today*.

In English, though by no means in all languages, the order of elements in words is quite fixed. Inflections, for example, are suffixed. We cannot reorder roots and inflections. At higher levels in the language, different orders of elements can differ in meaning: Compare *John kissed Mary* with *Mary kissed John*. But we don't contrast words with prefixed inflections and words whose inflections are suffixed. English doesn't contrast, for example, *piece+s* with *s+piece.*

In English too, it's specific individual words that select for certain inflections. Thus the word *child* is pluralized by adding {*-ren*}; *ox* by adding {*-en*}. So, if a form takes the {-en} plural, then it must be a word.

4.4 INFLECTIONAL MORPHOLOGY

English has only eight inflectional morphemes, as listed in Table 4.1. Because of its long and complex history, English has many irregular forms. Most grammar and writing textbooks contain long lists of exceptions. Even the regular inflections show historical traces. The *-en* form of the past participle appears as such only on a few relics such as *frozen* and *broken.* It appears as *-n* in words such as *thrown* and *drawn.* For most verbs, however, the past participle is identical in outward appearance to the past tense. One thousand years ago, past participles with an *-n* were the rule. Irregular forms of the plural include the internal vowel changes in *man/men* and *woman/women.* Some forms aren't even historically related; *went,* the past tense of *go,* historically was the past tense of *wend.* This sort of realignment is known as **suppletion.** Irregular forms demonstrate the abstract status of morphemes. Thus the word *men* represents (**realizes**) the two morphemes {man} and {-s}; *women* represents {woman} and {-s}; *went* represents {go} and {-ed}.

We will return to inflectional morphemes in Chapter 5, where we will use them to help us identify parts of speech.

EXERCISES   1. Can you think of a reliable way to distinguish the past tense and past participle of a verb, no matter if it's regular or irregular?
2. Check a reference grammar for further examples of irregular inflections.
3. From the following words, determine the three distinct pronunciations or allomorphs of the past tense morpheme {-ed}: *towed, sighed, tapped, tabbed, tossed, buzzed, raided.* Specify the phonological environment in which each allomorph occurs.

TABLE 4.1 English Inflectional Morphemes

Verbs:	-s	Third person singular present	(proves)
	-ed	Past tense	(proved)
	-en	Past participle	(has proven)
	-ing	Progressive aspect	(is proving)
Nouns:	-s	Plural	(the birds)
	-s	Genitive	(the bird's song)
Adjectives:	-er	Comparative	(older)
	-est	Superlative	(oldest)

4.5 DERIVATIONAL MORPHOLOGY

As we noted, **derivationally related forms** may differ from each other in belonging to different parts of speech, e.g., *saw* the noun and *saw* the verb.

[1a] This saw is too dull.
  [b] Don't saw that board.

Words belonging to different parts of speech take different inflections—e.g., {$_N$saw} + {$_{pl}$-s}; {$_V$saw} + {-ed}. Because derivationally related forms differ in category and consequently in the inflections they allow, and because the meanings of derivationally related pairs don't parallel each other as their forms do, derived forms are given their own entries in dictionaries. *Webster's New World Dictionary,* for instance, has separate entries for *generate* and *generation;* likewise for *compete* and *competence.* Look up these words and note how the meanings of *generation* and *competence* aren't entirely predictable from those of *generate* and *compete,* respectively.

Derivation can involve prefixing, as in *resaw;* suffixing as in *sawing, sawer,* and *sawable;* or no change at all (**conversion**), as in *saw* (verb) and *saw* (noun). It can also involve a change in the position of stress; compare *per'mit* (verb) with *'permit* (noun). Some verb and adjective pairs are also distinguished in this way: *per'fect* (verb) and *'perfect* (adj.).

In many instances, the addition of a derivational affix involves a change in the stress patterns with consequential changes in the pronunciations of the vowels, and sometimes also of the consonants. In other cases, the stress doesn't move, but the vowels and consonants change anyway. In most cases, an unstressed vowel is pronounced as schwa:

[2] 'telegraph   te'legraphy
      'regal   re'galia
      'tutor   tu'torial

In cases where the stress doesn't migrate, the vowel may change:

[3] di'vine   di'vinity
      pro'fane   pro'fanity
      se'rene   se'renity
      ap'pear   ap'parent

In some pairs, only a feature of the final consonant changes, usually the value of the voicing feature:

[4] advice   advise   /s/ → /z/
      belief   believe /f/ → /v/
      mouth   mouthe /θ/ → /ð/

In others, the addition of a suffix triggers a change in the final consonant of the root. Generally, an alveolar stop becomes a palatal fricative with the same voicing value:

[5] collide   collision /d/ → /ž/
     part   partial /t/ → /š/

In still others, we find suffixing, stress migration with vowel reduction to schwa, and change of consonant:

[6] ap'prove   appro'bation /v/ → /b/
     e'lectric   elec'tricity /k/ → /s/

A list of English derivational morphemes appears as Appendix A at the end of this chapter.

EXERCISE   Write each of the example words in [2] to [6] in a phonemic notation.

4.6 COMPOUNDING

The underlined words in [7] are created by combining *saw* with some other word, rather than with a bound morpheme.

[7a] A *sawmill* is a noisy place.
  [b] Every workshop should have a *chain saw*, a *table saw*, a *jigsaw*, a *hack saw*, and a *bucksaw*.
  [c] *Sawdust* is always a problem in a woodworker's workshop.
  [d] *Sawing-horses* are useful and easily made.

In ordinary English spelling, compounds are sometimes spelled as single words, as in some of the instances above; sometimes the parts are connected by a hyphen, as in *saw-toothed*; and sometimes they're spelled as two words, as in *coping saw*. Nonetheless, we are justified in classifying all such cases as compound words regardless of their conventional spelling for a variety of reasons.

First, the stress pattern of the compound word is usually different from the stress pattern in the phrase composed of the same words in the same order. Compare:

[8] | COMPOUND | PHRASE |
|---|---|
| 'White House | white 'house |
| 'funny-farm | funny 'farm |
| 'blackbird | black 'bird |

In the compounds, the main stress is on the first syllable; in the phrases, the main stress is on the last syllable. While this pattern doesn't apply to all compounds, it's so generally true that it provides a very useful test.

In many compounds, the order of the constituent words is different from that in the corresponding phrase:

[9] COMPOUND   PHRASE
     sawmill   mill for sawing
     sawing-horse   horse for sawing
     sawdust   dust from sawing

The meaning of the compound may differ to a greater or lesser degree from that of the corresponding phrase. A blackbird is a species of bird regardless of its color. A black bird is a bird which is black regardless of its species. So, because the meanings of a compound aren't always predictable from the meanings of its constituents, dictionaries provide individual entries for compounds but not (except rarely) for phrases. Generally, the meaning of a phrase is predictable from the meanings of its constituents, and so phrases need not be listed individually. (Indeed, because the number of possible phrases in a language is infinite, it's in principle impossible to list them all.)

There are a number of ways of approaching the study and classification of compound words, the most accessible of which is to classify them according to the part of speech of the compound and then subclassify them according to the parts of speech of its constituents. Table 4.2 is based on discussion in Bauer (1983).

EXERCISE   Categorize the words below, using Bauer's typology.

acid rain	agoraphobia	audiophile	bad-mouth
ballpark	double-quick	fallout	flat-out
free-associate	head-hunt	hovercraft	leadfree
machine readable	moonshine	offhand	open-endedly
overkill	overachieve	put-down	quick-change
software	solid-state	stop-go	ready-made
turnkey	uptight	wraparound	teach-in

An alternative approach is to classify compounds in terms of the semantic relationship between the compound and its head. The **head** of a compound is the constituent which is modified by the compound's other constituents. In English, heads of compounds are typically the rightmost constituent (excluding any derivational and inflectional suffixes). For example, in *high-rise* the head is *rise,* which is modified by *high.*

Using this approach, we distinguish three types of compounds: **endocentric, exocentric,** and **appositional.** An endocentric compound denotes something which is a subtype of whatever is denoted by the head. An *armchair* is a type of chair; a *breath test* is a kind of test.

An exocentric compound is understood as denoting a subtype of a category which isn't mentioned within the compound. A *pickpocket* is neither a kind of pocket nor a kind of pick; it's a kind of person. *Redneck* and *yellow jacket* are exocentric compounds for analogous reasons.

An appositional compound is understood as denoting an entity or property to which both constituents contribute equally. *Bittersweet* refers to a quality which is both bitter and

TABLE 4.2   English Compounds

1. **Compound nouns**
   a. Noun + Noun: bath towel; boyfriend; death blow
   b. Verb + Noun: pickpocket; breakfast
   c. Noun + Verb: nosebleed; sunshine
   d. Verb + Verb: make-believe
   e. Adjective + Noun: deep structure; fast-food
   f. Particle + Noun: in-crowd; downtown
   g. Adverb + Noun: now generation
   h. Verb + Particle: cop-out; dropout
   i. Phrase compounds: son-in-law
2. **Compound verbs**
   a. Noun + Verb: skydive
   b. Adjective + Verb: fine-tune
   c. Particle + Verb: overbook
   d. Adjective + Noun: brownbag
3. **Compound adjectives**
   a. Noun + Adjective: card-carrying; childproof
   b. Verb + Adjective: fail-safe
   c. Adjective + Adjective: open-ended
   d. Adverb + Adjective: cross-modal
   e. Particle + Adjective: overqualified
   f. Noun + Noun: coffee table
   g. Verb + Noun: roll-neck
   h. Adjective + Noun: red-brick; blue-collar
   i. Particle + Noun: in-depth
   j. Verb + Verb: go-go; make-believe
   k. Adjective/Adverb + Verb: high-rise
   l. Verb + Particle: see-through; towaway
4. **Compound adverbs**
   uptightly
   cross-modally
5. **Neoclassical compounds**
   astronaut
   hydroelectric
   mechanophobe

Source: Bauer, 1983.

sweet. It would be misleading to interpret bittersweet as merely a kind of sweetness, or merely a kind of bitterness. The elements seem to modify each other.

EXERCISE   Assign each of the compounds in the previous exercise to one or another of each type: endocentric, exocentric, appositional.

As a third (and final) possible mode of analyzing compounds, we briefly consider that mode used in the series of modern-traditional grammars prepared by Quirk et al. (1972,

TABLE 4.3 Underlying Syntactic Analysis of English Compounds

1. Subject and verb:
sunrise	the sun rises
beesting	the bee stings

2. Verb and object:
bloodtest	X tests blood
self-control	X controls self

3. Verb and adverbial:
swimming pool	X swims in a pool
adding machine	X adds with a machine

4. Subject and object:
windmill	the wind powers the mill
motorcycle	the motor powers the cycle

5. Subject and complement:
girlfriend	the friend is a girl
killer shark	the shark is a killer

1985) (see Table 4.3). In this method, the compounds are analyzed and classified according to the relationships which their constituents bear to each other when the meaning of the compound is expressed as a sentence.

EXERCISE Classify each of the following according to their underlying sentence meaning (see Table 4.3).

baby-sitter	X sits with the baby
catfish	the fish is like a cat
crybaby	the baby cries
dancing girl	the girl dances
darkroom	the room is dark
doorknob	the door has a knob
security officer	the officer controls security
sleepwalking	X walks in his sleep
storytelling	X tells stories
taxpayer	X pays taxes

4.7 THE INTERNAL STRUCTURE OF COMPLEX WORDS

Complex words (those of more than one morpheme) aren't merely unstructured sequences of morphemes. For example, the plural {-s} suffix on *dropouts* must be added to the entire compound *dropout,* not to *out* to which *drop* is then added. The reason for this is that the plural suffix may be attached to nouns but not to verbs or particles. *Drop* and *out* constitute a noun only *after* they have been brought together in the compound. We can use brackets with subscripts to represent these relations: [$_N$[$_N$[$_V$drop] [$_{Prt}$out]]s]. Alternatively, and equivalently, we can use tree diagrams to indicate the parts (**constituents**) of complex words and their structural relations:

[10]

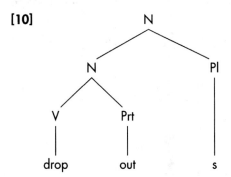

Consider another example: *unreadability.* We can analyze this entire word as [$_N$[$_{Adj}$un[$_{Adj}$[$_V$read]able]]ity], which translates into the following tree:

[11]

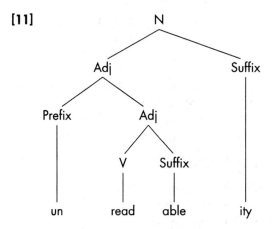

Let's consider this analysis more closely. The suffix {-able} attaches to verbs to create adjectives. Besides *readable* we have the adjectives *doable, manageable,* and *attachable,* derived from the verbs *read, do, manage,* and *attach,* respectively. We can represent this part of the word as [$_{Adj}$[$_V$read]able].

The prefix {un-} attaches to adjectives, basic or derived, meaning "not" or "the converse of." Compare *unwise, unfair, ungrateful,* and *uncomfortable* with *unreadable.* All can be glossed as not having the quality denoted by the adjective to which *un-* is attached: not comfortable, not fair, etc. This morpheme must be distinguished from the prefix {un$_2$-} meaning "to reverse the action," which can be attached to verbs (e.g., *untie*).

Un- cannot attach to *read,* although there is the word *unread,* pronounced [ənrɛd], not [ənrid], an adjective meaning "not read," derived from the past participle of *read.*

Consequently, in *unreadable, un-* must be attached to *readable* and not *-able* to *unread*. We will represent this part of the word as [$_{Adj}$un[$_{Adj}$[$_V$read]able]].

The suffix {-ity} attaches to adjectives to create abstract nouns. Consequently, it must be attached to the adjective *unreadable*. The structure of the entire word therefore must be [$_N$[$_{Adj}$un[$_{Adj}$[$_V$read]able]]ity], as specified above. In pronunciation, the morpheme {-able} will be assigned its allomorph /əbIl/, the same allomorph that appears in *ability*.

4.8 CLASSIFYING WORDS BY THEIR MORPHOLOGICAL POSSIBILITIES

Once the morphemes of a language have been identified, their allomorphs determined, and their distributions specified, we can use our analysis to assign the words of a language to parts of speech. For many words, inflections provide the main basis of this assignment.

Nouns can be identified as those words that can be inflected for plural, possessive, and possessive plural.

Verbs are words which can be inflected for third person singular present tense, past tense, past participle, and progressive. These forms are often referred to as the principal parts of the verb.

Adjectives are words which can be inflected for comparative and superlative.

Derivational regularities can also be used to classify words. We might, for example, classify as adverbs words derived from adjectives by the addition of the suffix *-ly*, e.g., *quickly*.

Classifying words on the basis of their internal morphological structure works only up to a point. There are lots of words that aren't internally complex and so cannot be classified without recourse to other types of criteria. For example, the preposition *to* has no internal morphological structure, and so cannot be assigned to a grammatical class on that basis. Likewise, adverbs such as *hard* or *fast* lack the characteristic *-ly* ending. It becomes necessary to use syntactic criteria to classify these and many other words. We consider in detail the principles which have been proposed for assigning words to parts of speech in Chapters 5 and 6.

EXERCISE   To appreciate the importance of a word's syntactic environment and of its inflectional and derivational morphemes in determining its part of speech, consider the following texts. (Try to read them aloud.) The first two should present no problems. The remainder should prove increasingly difficult and finally impossible.

1. 'Twas misty and the tiny doves
   did glide and glitter in the air.
2. 'Twas brillig and the slithy toves
   did gyre and gimble in the wabe.
3. 'Twas brillig and ut slithy toves
   did gyre and gimble in ut wabe.
4. 'Twas brillig agus ut slithy toves
   did gyre agus gimble in ut wabe.
5. 'Twas brillig agus ut slithy toves
   did gyre agus gimble er ut wabe.

6. Vi brillig agus ut slithy toves
   did gyre agus gimble er ut wabe.
7. Vi brillig agus ut slithy toven
   taw gyre agus gimble er ut wabe.
8. Taw vi gyre brillig agus ut
   toven slithy agus er wabe.

REFERENCES AND RESOURCES

Bauer, Laurie. 1983. *English Word-Formation.* Cambridge: Cambridge University Press.
————1988. *Introducing Linguistic Morphology.* Edinburgh: Edinburgh University Press.
Matthews, P. H. 1974. *Morphology: An Introduction of the Theory of Word Structure.* Cambridge: Cambridge University Press.
Quirk, Randolph, Sidney Greenbaum, Geoffrey Leech, and Jan Svartvik. 1972. *A Grammar of Contemporary English.* New York: Seminar Press.
————. 1985. *Comprehensive Grammar of the English Language.* London: Longman.
Spencer, A. 1991. *Morphological Theory: An Introduction to Word Structure in Generative Grammar.* Oxford: Blackwell.

GLOSSARY

Affix: to attach one morpheme to another morpheme.

Allomorph: a variant phonological representation of a morpheme.

Appositional compound: a compound word that denotes an entity or property to which both constituents contribute equally; e.g., *bittersweet* refers to a quality which is both bitter and sweet.

Auxiliary verb: see Chapter 6.

Bound morpheme: a morpheme that must be attached to another morpheme.

Compound: a word created by combining roots. See **appositional, endocentric,** and **exocentric.**

Constituent: a unified part of a construction (e.g., of a word, phrase, or sentence).

Conversion: see Chapter 5.

Derivation: a process of changing a word from one part of speech to another or from one subclass to another, typically by adding a prefix or a suffix.

Endocentric compound: a compound word that denotes a subtype of whatever is denoted by the head. An *armchair* is a type of chair; a *breath test* is a kind of test.

Exocentric compound: a compound word that denotes a subtype of a category which isn't mentioned within the compound; e.g., a *pickpocket* is neither a kind of pocket nor a kind of pick; it's a kind of person.

Free morpheme: a morpheme that need not be attached to another morpheme.

Head: the main constituent of a compound, which is modified by the compound's other constituents.

Inflectional morpheme: a bound morpheme that signals a grammatical function and meaning in a specific sentence; e.g., *-s* plural, *-ed* past tense, *-er/-est* comparative and superlative.

Morph: a minimal meaningful form.

Morpheme: the smallest meaningful part of a word.

Prefix: a bound morpheme attached before a root.

Realization: the representation of one or more abstract elements (e.g., morphemes) by concrete elements (e.g., sounds); e.g., *women* represents the morphemes {woman} + {$_{pl}$ -s}.

Root: the basic constituent of a word, to which other morphemes are attached.

Suffix: a bound morpheme attached after a root.

Suppletion: irregular inflectional forms of a word resulting from the combination of historically different sources; e.g., *go/went*.

APPENDIX A
English Derivational Morphemes
(Adapted from Bauer, 1983)

PREFIXES

Class/category changing

a-blaze	Adj < V
be-calm	V < Adj
be-friend	V < N
en-tomb	V < N

Class maintaining

Nouns
- mini-dress
- step-father
- mal-nutrition

Verbs
- de-escalate

Adjectives
- a-typical
- cis-lunar
- extra-sensory

Noun or Verb
- fore-tell
- fore-ground
- re-arrangement
- mis-lead
- mis-fortune

Noun or Adjective
- in-definite
- mid-morning
- mid-Victorian
- ex-president
- ex-orbital

Verb or Adjective
- circum-navigate
- circum-polar

Noun, Verb, or Adjective
- counter-culture
- counter-demonstrate
- counter-intuitive
- dis-information
- dis-ambiguate
- co-author
- inter-mix
- sub-let
- sub-conscious

SUFFIXES

Deriving Nouns

from Nouns

-dom	king-dom
-ess	lion-ess
-iana	Victor-iana
-er	Birch-er
-ette	kichen-ette
-hood	man-hood
-ism	absentee-ism
-let	stream-let
-ling	duck-ling
-scape	sea-scape
-ship	kin-ship

from Verbs

-ation	especially with -ize: categor-iz-ation
-ee	blackmail-ee
-ure	clos-ure
-al	arriv-al
-ary	dispens-ary
-er	kill-er
-ment	manage-ment

from Adjectives

-ity	divin-ity
-cy	excellen-cy
-ce	dependen-ce
-ness	good-ness
-dom	free-dom
-er	six-er
-hood	false-hood
-ist	social-ist
-th	warm-th

Deriving Verbs

from Nouns

-ify	metr-ify
-ize	Cambodian-ize

from Adjectives

-en	short-en

Deriving Adjectives

from Nouns

-al	education-al (allomorphs: -ial, -ual: presidential, habitual)
-esque	pictur-esque
-less	clue-less
-ate	passion-ate
-en	wood-en
-ese	Peking-ese

-ful	doubt-ful
-ic	algebra-ic
-ly	friend-ly
-ous	venom-ous
-y	catt-y

from Verbs

-able	believ-able
-less	count-less
-ant/-ent	absorb-ent
-atory	affirm-atory
-ful	resent-ful
-ive	generat-ive

from Adjectives

-ish	green-ish
-ly	good-ly

Deriving Adverbs

-ly	slow-ly
-ward(s)	in-ward(s)
-wise	length-wise

Miscellaneous

iff-y, upp-itty
down-er
in-ness, much-ness, such-ness, there-ness, why-ness
thus-ly

5 THE MAJOR PARTS OF SPEECH

KEY CONCEPTS

Word categories
Nouns
Verbs
Adjectives
Adverbs

5.0 WORD CATEGORIES

In this chapter and the next, we examine the individual parts of speech. This chapter covers nouns, verbs, adjectives, and adverbs, which contribute the major "content" to a message, and hence are sometimes called **content words,** as opposed to other parts of speech known as **function words** or **structure words.** As we will see in Chapter 6, function words express important meanings and are so grammatically crucial that nearly every sentence contains one or more of them. However, the content words allow language to relate to an infinite number of different topics.

In our presentation, we begin by noting the traditional description of each category and indicating whether it's semantic, functional, or—less commonly—formal. Next, we analyze some of the shortcomings of the traditional treatment and suggest more effective means of classifying the word type through formally based analytic tests. On this basis, we examine some of the major functions of the form in question, often integrating semantic characteristics. Each section concludes with a discussion of subclasses of the larger form class.

5.1 NOUNS

The traditional definition of a noun is a "word that names a person, place, or thing." By this definition, *Grover Cleveland, Pittsburgh,* and *typewriter* are nouns. This is a semantic definition. It echoes the Greek position that naming objects in the real world is the essential—and perhaps the original—role of language. For all its apparent simplicity, this definition immediately runs into problems. First, the criterion of person is suspect. *Shaw* is clearly the name of a person and thus a noun. However, the adjective *Shavian,* derived from the proper name—and still carrying its capitalization—might be construed as the name of characteristics of Shaw's plays. More disturbingly, *here* and *above* refer to places, although the former is an adverb and the latter a preposition or adverb. Of course, one might argue that the criterion of place applies only to proper nouns. However, many common nouns indicate places: *kitchen, church,* and *sky.* But the greatest equivocation in the standard definition lies in the use of the word "thing." The most straightforward use of the term is to designate a physical object. But not all nouns actually designate physical objects.

Many terms, such as *beauty, belief,* and *certainty,* don't designate things, but nonetheless, grammarians include them as nouns under the heading of **abstract nouns.** Many **concrete nouns** refer to collections of things, and so are designated as **collective nouns.** *cattle, congress,* and *trade.* Finally, a concrete noun such as *typewriter* names not a specific thing, but rather, a class of things, namely, the class of typewriters—any and all typewriters. To name a specific typewriter, we have to resort to expansions such as *the Olivetti on the table.*

One solution to the problem would involve listing all of the words that qualify as nouns. Such a list would no doubt be extremely complex, and yet it wouldn't tell us what a noun is or how to decide whether or not the next word to be added to the language is a noun. As the examples of *here* and *up* suggest, a word's status as noun depends not so much on external reality as on how the language (and its speakers collectively) treat it.

Clearly, purely semantic criteria for nouns will not provide reliable results. And no one has proposed a functional definition for nouns, perhaps because they occur in such a wide range of functions and because other parts of speech also occur in typically nominal functions. For more suitable analyses, we must consider the form of nouns.

5.1.1   Formal characteristics of nouns

We approach the classification of nouns, as for other parts of speech, through a series of formal tests. The tests will help students to determine parts of speech by using the native speaker intuitions that they already possess. Remember, though, that part-of-speech identification requires complex analysis; often, no single test will lead to a conclusive result.

ANALYTIC TEST 1.   *A word may be a noun if it ends or can end in the two noun inflections, plural and genitive.*

Regular noun inflections can be considered in both spoken and written forms, as shown in Table 5.1.

TABLE 5.1   Regular Noun Inflections

Plural:	phonemically /s/, /z/, or /ɪz/ graphically -s or -es
Genitive:	phonemically identical to plural graphically 's or s'

The vast majority of nouns will accept the s-plural. The exceptions are the small subclass of nouns that refer to animals (*deer, fish,* etc.), noncount nouns (*furniture, ice*), and irregular words (*child, man, woman*). A general principle of language is that irregularity tends to occur in the most frequently used items. As a result, teachers can assume that students are aware of many irregular forms (although the irregularities may change from dialect to dialect). Our tests apply to the majority of forms. One special caution on the genitive inflection is necessary, however. Although genitives occur on nearly all nouns, sometimes an alternative *of*-phrase sounds stylistically more natural; cf. *the cause of the argument* versus *the argument's cause.* In English, the inflected genitive is most comfortable with animate entities.

EXERCISES

1. Provide the plural and genitive forms of the following nouns: *insect, bug, hinge, solo, calf, surf, disease, foil, stuff, promise, crazy.* Consult a dictionary if you are uncertain. Some of the forms will sound odd. Why?
2. While *a cup of coffee* is perfectly grammatical **a coffee's cup* is odd. Think of other cases where the *'s* genitive and the *of-* phrase don't correspond. Do your examples have anything in common—particularly their semantic characteristics?

ANALYTIC TEST 2.   *A word may be a noun if it actually ends in a nominal derivational suffix.*

In English, if a word ends (in its dictionary form) in a derivational suffix, that suffix supplies a strong clue to the word's grammatical class. The derivational suffixes typical of nouns are contained in Table 5.2.

A common role of derivational forms in a language is to change words of one part of speech into another part. Thus the verb *tolerate* becomes the noun *tolerance;* likewise, the adjective *active* becomes the noun *activity.* Sometimes derivations will change a word to a different subclass of the same part of speech. Within nouns, for example, the suffix *-hood* will make the concrete noun *knight* into the abstract noun *knighthood.*

TABLE 5.2   Typical Noun-Forming Derivational Suffixes

Suffix	Example
-age	acreage, message
-ance/-ence	tolerance, adherence
-ard	drunkard
-cy	decency
-dom	freedom
-er/-or	teacher, actor
-ess	actress
-hood	knighthood
-ism	existentialism
-ist	existentialist
-ity	activity
-ment	amusement
-ness	truthfulness
-th	truth
-tion	adulation, fruition
-ude	gratitude

Derivational endings on nouns have some other noteworthy properties. First, noun derivations are frequently **suffixes;** i.e., they appear at the ends of words. Second, only the *final* derivational suffix on a word determines its part of speech. *Disestablishmentarianism* contains five suffixes; only the last, *-ism,* is relevant to its status as a noun. (Plural and possessive inflections may follow the derivational suffix without affecting test 2.) Finally, noun derivations can change an entire sentence to a noun phrase. Thus [1] can be changed to [2] when the verb *amuse* becomes the noun *amusement:*

[1]   The clown amused the children.
[2]   The clown's amusement of the children

The process by which a word (or group of words) becomes a noun (or noun phrase) is called **nominalization.**

EXERCISES   In some cases, you will not be able to make the changes called for below. Try to decide why this might be so.

1. Change the following verbs to nouns by adding derivational suffixes: *relate, emerge, block, train, strain, talk, wonder.*
2. Change the following adjectives to nouns via derivational suffixes: *rude, productive, healthy, satisfactory.*
3. Change the following sentences into noun phrases, using the process of nominalization.

    [i]   The true story gradually emerged.
    [ii] Werner inspected the package.
    [iii] Pamela enjoys bobsledding.

4. Change the following noun phrases to sentences by reversing the process of nominalization (i.e., by removing derivational suffixes).

    [i]   Manuel's toleration of teasing
    [ii] Manuel's tolerance of teasing
    [iii] The expectation of Helen that she would be rescued

A large number of verbs can undergo nominalization. Linguists describe such a situation by the term **productivity.** A process such as nominalization is productive if it applies freely to many items in its range. In addition, certain forms may be more productive than others. For example, *-ude* (as in *gratitude*) is unproductive as a suffix forming abstract nouns; in contrast, *-ness* (as in *gratefulness*) is relatively productive.

Derivational suffixes are less powerful than inflections as clues to nouns because of their limited productivity. Moreover, English possesses a process called **conversion** (also called **zero derivation, category change,** and **functional shift**), by which a word's grammatical category may be changed without the addition of a derivational suffix. Thus the verb *trade* has been nominalized to the noun *trade,* as illustrated by the ability of the latter to accept plurals and possessives. As a result of conversion, there will be many derived nouns that have no derivational endings. In addition, such forms will appear to students to possess the semantic characteristics associated with their original class. For instance, the noun *trade* will seem to name an action rather than a person, place, or thing. This fact further illustrates the danger of semantic definitions.

EXERCISE   The following words have undergone zero derivation to nouns: *rip-off, snap, wipe out, update.* For each, apply test 1 to demonstrate its membership in the noun class.

ANALYTIC TEST 3.   *A word may be a noun if it can occur alone after a word that typically precedes nouns.*

Nouns can be identified by the company they potentially keep. Words that can occur immediately before nouns are:

1. Articles: a, an (indefinite)
                    the (definite)
2. Genitives: my, our, your, his, her, its, genitive noun
                        phrases (e.g., *the big building's*)
3. Demonstratives: this, that, these, those
4. Quantifiers: some, any, all, no, every, numerals,
                        ordinals (e.g., *first, second,* etc.)
5. Most adjectives: good, subtle, ridiculous, etc.

Some of these forms—particularly demonstratives, quantifiers, and adjectives—can occur by themselves. It's their potential to precede a noun that is relevant here.

This test operates simply. Just take the word suspected to be a noun and place words from groups (1) to (5) immediately before it. If the combination is grammatical outside any larger context, the word is probably a noun. In [3], items with asterisks (denoting ungrammaticality) are *not* nouns; unmarked items are nouns:

[3a]   this defense
 [b]   *this defend
 [c]   my kitchen
 [d]   *my here
 [e]   this activity
 [f]   *this active
 [g]   no certainty
 [h]   *no certain
 [i]   a good beating
 [j]   *a good demanding
 [k]   my uncle's limousine
 [l]   *my uncle's luxurious

EXERCISE   Apply test 3 to the following words and determine whether or not they're nouns: *vaporize, force, colossal, quietly, graciousness, amplitude.* Identify any sources of difficulty that you have in applying the test. Afterwards supplement test 3 with tests 1 and 2.

5.1.2   Functional characteristics of nouns

Single nouns have one dominant function—that of the **head** of a noun phrase. All other functions traditionally associated with nouns (e.g., subject, direct and indirect object, object of a preposition, subject and object complement, etc.) are really the property of noun phrases within clauses. Hence we will postpone discussion of such functions until Chapter 8, which examines basic clause structure in detail.

Traditional grammars often define a phrase as (1) a group of words (2) which doesn't contain a verb and its subject and (3) which is used as a single part of speech. Condition (2) distinguishes a phrase from a clause and isn't at issue here. Conditions (1) and (3) highlight a paradox of phrases—they consist of more than one word but behave as one. The paradox can be resolved by a redefinition of the term **phrase** in the following way: *A phrase is a grammatically unified structure that consists of a headword and any words or phrases that modify or complement it.*

Putting aside the question of whether clauses also count as phrases, the main consequence of our new definition is that a phrase can consist of *only* one word, namely its head. It's also the headword, rather than modifiers or complements, that give phrases their names.

We will explore this notion of the phrase in Chapter 7. For the moment, though, we can illustrate it with reference to the noun phrase (which we will abbreviate as NP). Table 5.3 lists typical NP structures. (Remember that the term NP is formal and the terms **head, modifier,** and **complement** are functional.)

TABLE 5.3   Typical Noun Phrase Structures

Modifier(s)	Head	Modifiers/Complements
	horses	
the	horses	
the swift	horses	
several swift	horses	
large swift	horses	
	horses	in the pasture
	horses	that eat grass
	horses	running in the field
the	horses	in the pasture
the swift	horses	in the pasture
several swift	horses	running in the field
large swift	horses	running in the field
the	fact	that horses eat grass

Table 5.3 illustrates several important points about NPs. First, you will notice that (in English) modifiers may precede or follow the head noun. Also, both modifiers and complements can consist of several words of different grammatical types, including articles *(the)*, adjectives *(large, swift)*, prepositional phrases *(in the pasture)*, clauses *(that eat grass)*, and verbal phrases *(running in the field)*.

The NPs above, however, have a single constant core—a head noun. In its function as head of a NP, a noun determines important properties of the larger structure. First of all, it contributes the feature of number— singular or plural—to the NP. Thus *the swift horse* is singular and can be replaced by the pronouns *he, she,* or *it*. In contrast, *the swift horses* is plural and must be replaced by *they*. Gender, likewise, depends on the head noun, whenever that noun is gender-specific. So *the young man* will be replaced by *he* and *the young woman* by *she*. Of course, nouns that aren't gender-specific don't influence gender. The gender of *the young child* is indeterminate and can only be specified through modifiers, as in *the young female child*.

As we have just shown, pronouns may be used to provide evidence for the grammatical features of NPs. Let's examine this fact a bit further by noting a characteristic of single nouns in NPs. Consider the single noun *horses* in the sentence *Horses can run fast*. This word seems to be just a noun. However, we can substitute a pronoun for this noun, just as we substituted pronouns for NPs containing more than a single word: *They can run fast*. So it seems that pronouns substitute for an entire NP not just for a noun. If this is so, then we must conclude that an NP may consist of a single noun just as it may consist of a noun and its modifiers and complements. This supports our redefinition of phrases in general as consisting of a headword and its modifiers and complements.

5.1.3   Subclasses of nouns

One important subdivision of nouns is that between **mass** and **count** nouns. Semantically, mass nouns (also called **noncount**) are thought of as representing things in the world as if they were undifferentiated masses, whose parts aren't identified as discrete units *(rice, sugar, milk)*. Count nouns represent entities that can be individuated and counted *(typewriter, diskette, page)*. Moreover, mass nouns don't take the plural without undergoing a semantic shift. This shift changes the meaning of the noun to either *type of* (e.g., *the rices grown in China*) or *unit of* (e.g., *three milks*). Count nouns may also be preceded by *many*, while mass nouns are preceded by *much*.

Nouns also fall into **concrete** and **abstract** subclasses. Semantically, a concrete noun names an object that can be apprehended by any one of the five senses *(sneeze, floor, paper)*. An abstract noun names something that is apprehended by the mind *(goodness, idea)*. Formal differences include a tendency for abstract nouns to be noncount and to end in certain derivational suffixes (e.g., *-ness, -ity, -th, -ude*).

Collective nouns denote entities which are collections of individuals *(army, jury, the public, The United States)*. In American English, collective nouns normally take a singular verb (e.g., *The jury is out*), while in British English they take a plural (e.g., *The jury are out*). The American variety sometimes uses the plural to suggest lack of unity within the group (e.g., *The jury are divided*). Pronoun substitutes for collectives are also normally singular in American and plural in British.

Some grammars distinguish **proper nouns,** which refer to particular entities (*Thomas Jefferson, Denver, the Koran*) from **common nouns,** which refer to classes (*tissue, box, xylophone*). This semantic difference mainly affects capitalization since a noun phrase with a common noun head can also designate a single entity (e.g., *the box on the dresser*).

5.2 VERBS

Verbs can be subdivided into **main verbs** and **auxiliaries.** We will treat the various types of auxiliaries as function words in the next chapter, and so we will concentrate only on what traditional grammars call **main verbs,** i.e., those which may occur alone in a verb phrase. Traditional grammars typically define verbs semantically, i.e., as "words that designate actions (*kiss, run*), processes (*grow, change*), experiences (*know*), or states of being (*be, have*)."

As with most meaning-based criteria, the semantic definition above is somewhat misleading. For instance, nouns derived from verbs through zero derivation (e.g., *strike, kick, throw*) will maintain their verbal sense of action. Likewise, verbs derived from nouns—e.g., *man*—may appear to maintain whatever naming sense that they have. In addition, students occasionally classify as verbs, adjectives that suggest activity (e.g., *vigorous, playful, cruel*). Moreover, the notions of both activity and state conceal a variety of finer semantic distinctions that students don't always reliably associate with the general concepts. Table 5.4 identifies some of those semantic subtleties.

The distinction between action and state in Table 5.4 is somewhat arbitrary if based solely on semantic factors. For instance, does the verb *own* indicate an action or a state? Does the verb *smell* indicate a bodily feeling or a state? (Compare the sentences *I smelled the roses* and *The roses smelled sweet.*) There is, fortunately, at least one formal feature associated with the action-state distinction—the possibility of the progressive inflection. Typically, action

TABLE 5.4   Action and State Meanings of Verbs
(Adapted from Quirk and Greenbaum, 1973, section 3.35)

Action
a. Pure activities:
   i. throw, run, carry, (enduring physical activity)
   ii. strike, hit, jump (momentary physical activity)
   iii. say, ask, promise (verbal activity)
   iv. think, read, consider (mental activities)
b. Processes: become, thicken (= become thicker), improve (= become better)
c. Bodily feelings: ache, hear
d. Transitional events: arrive, fall, land

State
a. Pure states:
   love, fear, dislike (emotional states)
   suppose, know, doubt (intellectual states)
b. Relations: involve, deserve
c. Other: own, have, resemble

verbs allow the progressive *-ing* inflection; state verbs don't. Thus *own* is a state verb because *I am owning a farm* is ungrammatical. Since *I am smelling the roses* is grammatical, at least one sense of the verb *smell* is actional. But since *The roses are smelling sweet* is ungrammatical, another sense of *smell* is stative. This latter fact indicates another weakness in the traditional semantic definition of verbs: It doesn't recognize that the criteria apply to the individual meanings of a word. Since most common verbs have several dictionary definitions, the criteria may become quite disconcerting for a beginning student to apply.

EXERCISES

1. Classify the following verbs as action verbs or as state verbs; indicate the sub-type of each verb, according to Table 5.4. What difficulties did you experience in classifying these verbs semantically?

   cost   depart   approve   approve of   remember   remain

2. Look up the word *appear* in a good desk dictionary. How many different meanings does it have? Identify which of these meanings indicate action and which indicate state.

3. While the progressive occurs with action verbs, it doesn't always have the same meaning with each subtype. What differences of meaning can you see in the progressive verbs below? (*Hint:* compare progressive meanings to those of the simple present.)
   a. Our opinion of grammar is changing.
   b. The orchestra is playing a Beethoven symphony tonight.
   c. My head is aching.
   d. The plane is landing.

4. Which type of verb, action or state, can be used to give commands? Supply example sentences, both grammatical and ungrammatical, to support your answer.

Clearly, the semantics of verbs will only serve to confuse students, simply because their meaning is so extraordinarily complex. A far simpler approach employs formal considerations.

5.2.1 Formal characteristics of verbs

We must first distinguish between main verbs and auxiliary verbs. The main verb can appear by itself in a verb phrase; an auxiliary verb regularly appears only preceding a main verb. Consider sentences [4a] to [4d] below:

[4a] Harris made strudel.
 [b] Harris is making strudel.
 [c] Harris has been making strudel.
 [d] Harris may have been making strudel.

In each sentence, some form of *make* is the main verb. Notice that it cannot be removed from the sentence without producing an ungrammatical result (e.g., **Harris may have been strudel*). The main verb will always be the farthest to the right in any series of English verbs. Further, auxiliaries can be inverted in questions (e.g., *Can you go?*), while main verbs cannot (e.g., **Went you?*). In the next chapter, we will say more about the auxiliary verb; for the moment, however, we will concentrate on main verbs in simple sentences.

ANALYTIC TEST 4.   *A word may be a verb if it can take the four verb inflections:* **Vs, Ved, Ving, Ven.**

Like nouns, verbs have a limited potential for taking inflectional endings. English has four inflections for verbs:

1. Third person singular present tense (spelled -s or -es and pronounced /s/, /z/, or /ɪz/).
   We symbolize verbs with this inflection as *Vs*.
   For example, Harris bak**es** strudel regularly.
2. Past tense (in regular verbs, spelled -ed and pronounced /t/, /d/, or /əd/)
   We symbolize verbs with this inflection as *Ved*.
   For example, Harris bak**ed** strudel last night.
3. Ing-form (spelled -ing and pronounced /ɪŋ/.
   We symbolize verbs with this inflection as *Ving*.
   For example, Harris is bak**ing** strudel.

(Traditionally, Ving is sometimes called the **progressive** since it is often used to form the progressive verb structure, as in *is baking*. However, Ving also occurs in structures traditionally known as **gerunds.** Only the progressive use of *-ing* is regarded as an inflection. When *-ing* is attached to form a gerund, it is regarded as a derivational morpheme because its addition causes a change of part of speech.)

4. En-form (in regular verbs, spelled and pronounced identically to the past tense).
   We symbolize verbs with this inflection as *Ven*.
   For example, Harris has bak**ed**/eat**en** strudel.

(Traditionally, Ven has been called the **past participle** form of the verb. However, Ven can function in ways other than participial. In *The strudel was baked/eaten last night,* Ven functions as the head of the verb phrase.)

The ability to accept these inflections is sufficient to qualify a word as a verb in English. However, because of both zero derivation and identical spelling of certain derivational endings, it will always be necessary to confirm that a word *in a specific sentence* is actually a verb. Confirmation results from applying the analytic tests for other parts of speech. Consider [5] and [6]:

[5] Walter enjoyed working.
[6] The inner workings of the computer astounded us.

For verbs in actual sentences, we must rephrase our formal test for verbhood. *A word is a verb in a sentence if it actually ends in a verb inflection.* Clearly, *enjoyed* and *astounded* are verbs because they actually end in past tense inflection (Ved). But what about *working* and *workings*? We know intuitively that the -s inflection of *workings* isn't the present tense morpheme but, rather, the plural morpheme, which is pronounced the same as the present tense. *Workings* in [6] is therefore, by formal criteria, a noun. *Working* in [5], on the other hand, cannot be made plural:

[7]   *Walter enjoyed workings.

Working in sentence [5] is therefore, by formal criteria, a verb.

So valuable are tests based on inflections that some traditional grammar books, especially those used to teach non-native speakers, provide extensive lists of the **principal parts** of verbs. Rather than using inflections to identify verbs, however, these grammars often suggest that students memorize these vast lists. A sample of such a list appears as Table 5.5.

Grammarians sometimes use differing labels for the principal parts. The **stem** or **infinitive** form is the verb without any inflection—i.e., the form which you would look up in a dictionary. We will abbreviate this form simply as V. Ving, as already noted, is also called progressive because verbs inflected with -*ing* function as headwords of the progressive construction with the auxiliary verb *be* (e.g., *is starting*). Ven is also known as the past participle because verbs with -*en* endings often function as modifiers of nouns (e.g., *shrunken head*). Traditionally, the term **participle** is reserved for verbs that function as modifiers of nouns. We will continue to use our labels rather than the traditional ones because ours emphasize the primacy of form in the identification of parts of speech and allow a clear separation of form and function.

Table 5.5 also shows some important properties of verb inflections. First, certain inflections sometimes require changes in the spelling of the stem (e.g., *tries, hitting*). Phonologically, these words follow the regular patterns noted above. Second, for regular verbs—e.g., *start, clean, try*—the past tense and Ven forms are identical in sound and spelling. Irregular verbs—those which, for historical reasons, differ from the ordinary

TABLE 5.5   Principal Parts of Selected Verbs

V Stem Infinitive	Vs Present	Ved Past	Ving Ing-form Progressive	Ven En-form Past Participle
start	starts	started	starting	started
clean	cleans	cleaned	cleaning	cleaned
try	tries	tried	trying	tried
run	runs	ran	running	run
bring	brings	brought	bringing	brought
see	sees	saw	seeing	seen
throw	throws	threw	throwing	thrown
shrink	shrinks	shrank	shrinking	shrunk(en)
hit	hits	hit	hitting	hit

pattern—display a variety of inflectional differences, but only in the Ved and the Ven forms. Vs and Ving forms fit the ordinary pattern. Moreover, some irregular verbs, such as *bring* and *hit,* follow the same pattern as regular ones by having identical Ved and Ven forms. Besides varying among themselves in the formation of Ved and the Ven forms, irregular verbs sometimes have dialect variants. For instance, *shrink* has the alternate past *shrunk.* Although *shrank* resembles the historically older form of the verb, *shrunk* reflects a pressure in modern English to make irregulars more regular, especially by making the Ved and Ven forms identical. Indeed, the archaic *shrunken* is used in only a limited number of cases, such as *shrunken head. Shrunken* is also one of the few modern English verbs to preserve the *-en* spelling for the Ven form. (Others are *broken* and *frozen.*) Finally, irregular verbs often have regional and social variants that may be stigmatized, particularly in academic settings. Students have thus unfortunately been considered slow or ignorant if they used *dove* for *dived* or *drunk* as the past tense of *drink.* We discuss these issues in Chapter 13.

Enormous lists of principal parts of verbs may be useful for reference purposes or for non-native speakers, but they aren't a generally useful pedagogical tool; nor is the rote memorization of such lists anything but a mind-numbing form of trivia. Knowledge of the basic patterns discussed above, along with normal native-speaker intuition will allow any student to produce the principal parts of all common English verbs. For instance, the Ved form can be determined by placing the verb in a simple sentence beginning with the word *yesterday* (e.g., *Yesterday, I drank a gallon of grapefruit juice*). The Ven form can be quickly obtained by placing the verb in a simple sentence following the auxiliary *have* or *has.* (For example, *I have run two miles.*)

EXERCISES

1. Identify which of the words below are verbs, using as many of the inflectional criteria above as possible. Don't be surprised if, with a little ingenuity, you can turn other parts of speech into verbs. Such potential innovations attest to the power of conversion and to the uselessness of semantic definitions.

eraser	elbow	sense
fork	several	even
easy	always	up

2. Because of historical changes in English, formerly inflectional morphemes have come to be derivational morphemes that are pronounced the same as their inflectional counterparts. This change affects two forms. First, *-ing* has come to occur on nouns formed from verbs, as in *the grumblings of the sailors.* Note the possibility of pluralizing the *-ing* word and preceding it by *the.* Second, both *-ing* and *-en* have, in some words, become adjective endings, as in *more interesting remarks* and *very frozen pipes.* In this case, the preceding words *very* and *more* formally indicate an adjective. Consider the sentences below and make an argument that the italicized word is or isn't a verb.

   a. Frederick's constant *working* out in the gym

   b. The inner *workings* of a computer

   c. A *shrunken* head

   d. Juan's *penetrating* observations

ANALYTIC TEST 5.   *A word may be a verb if it actually begins or ends in a verbal derivational affix.*

A second formal clue to verb status is the actual presence of certain derivational elements. Typical verb derivational affixes appear in Table 5.6.

TABLE 5.6   Typical Derivational Verb Prefixes and Suffixes

Suffixes	Examples
-ify	magnify
-ize	canonize
-en	lighten

Prefixes	Examples
dis-	disappoint
un-	untie
mis-	misrepresent
mal-	malfunction
out-	outdistance
over-	overestimate
under-	underestimate
fore-	foresee
re-	reconsider
en-	enlighten
be-	belabor

Great care should be taken in using these derivational forms, and they should never be used separately from inflectional criteria. The main reason for this caution is that, in many instances, the same derivation may also be associated with a noun or adjective. For example, *dis-* occurs in the nouns *disappointment* and *distemper*. It appears in an adjective in *dissimilar* and *dissolute*. Moreover, students will occasionally analyze words as having derivations, particularly prefixes, where none in fact exists, e.g., *district* and *discipline*.

EXERCISES

1. For each word below, add, remove, or change a derivational affix to make it into a verb. Double-check your answer by using inflectional criteria.

   assassin (noun) tight (adjective) critical (adjective) alive (adjective) fat (noun, adjective) extermination (noun) harmony (noun)

2. Compare the words *untie* (verb) and *unfashionable* (adjective). Does the prefix *un-* have the same meaning in these two words? Which meaning occurs with verbs and which occurs with adjectives? Give examples of other verbs and adjectives beginning with *un-*. Does your earlier generalization hold true?

3. The words *district* and *discipline* show that the sequence of letters *d-i-s* doesn't always constitute a morpheme. (Analogous examples are **mis**sion, **mis**sile, **be**gin, and **re**trofit.) List five further instances where a sequence of letters identical to the *prefixes* in Table 5.6 aren't a morpheme. Then list three words in which each of the letter sequences identical to the *suffixes* in Table 5.6 aren't morphemes.

ANALYTIC TEST 6.   *A word may be a verb if it can be immediately preceded by words that typically precede verbs.*

Verbs have the potential to occur immediately following several classes of other words:

1. Auxiliaries (*be* and *have*)
2. Modals (*do, did, will, would, can, could, may, might, shall, should, must*)
3. *to* (infinitival)
4. *not*

It's important to use as many of these situations as possible. The reason for this stipulation is that most of the test words can appear before other parts of speech. As an example, let's ask whether *apply* and *eager* are verbs:

[8a]   I am applying.
 [b]   I have applied.
 [c]   I will/can/should apply.
 [d]   I want to apply.
 [e]   I did not apply.
[9a]   I am eager. (cf. *I am eagering)
 [b]   *I have eager/eagered.
 [c]   *I will/can/should eager.
 [d]   *I want to eager.
 [e]   *I did not eager.
 [f]   I am not eager.

These examples show that *apply* is a verb but that *eager* isn't. Note that *eager* did pass part of test 6, namely (1) and (4). Also, to apply the test, you must allow the inflections of the word under scrutiny to vary so as to fit the test sentences. Finally, one must make certain that the test sentences are appropriate. For instance, *to* can have a directional meaning, as in *We drove to Paris.* Confusing the preposition *to* with the infinitive *to* will lead to wrong results. The infinitival *to* in [8d] has no meaning; it serves only to mark a verb. (To make matters more complex, there is a third *to* that indicates purpose, as in *I drove to relieve tension.* In this sense, *to* can be followed by a verb.) Similarly, the word *not* may precede both an adjective and a verb, but only the *do not* or *did not* combination precedes a verb.

EXERCISE   Determine which of the words below are verbs. Write sentences (grammatical or ungrammatical) that support your analysis, showing the word in question preceded by the four types of function words.

tall   stretch   replace   playful   table

5.2.2   Functional characteristics of verbs

Main verbs have one function, that of head of the verb phrase (VP). As such, they are preceded by their auxiliaries (Chapter 6) and followed by their objects and complements (Chapter 8). As in the case of noun phrases, a VP may consist of a single word (e.g., *Harris* **left**).

5.2.3   Subclasses of verbs

Verbs are subdivided into **transitive, intransitive,** and **linking**. Transitive verbs (e.g., *see, arrest*), require a direct object, which takes the form of a following noun phrase (e.g., *The police arrested* **Steve Biko**). Intransitive verbs (e.g., *die*) don't require a direct object (e.g., *He died in custody*). Linking verbs (*be, become, seem*) must be followed by a **subject complement,** which may appear as either a noun phrase (e.g., *He is* **a nurse**) or an adjective phrase (e.g., *She is* **aware of the situation**). Traditional grammars often refer to the former as a predicate nominal and to the latter as a predicate adjective. In either case, with a linking verb, the subject and the complement both refer or apply to the same individual (*he—a nurse; she—aware of the situation*). (See Chapter 8.)

5.3   ADJECTIVES

While traditional grammars usually define nouns and verbs semantically, they often shift to functional criteria to characterize adjectives. Their definition of an adjective is "a word that modifies a noun or pronoun." While we might criticize this definition for changing from meaning to function, it's more appropriate to determine whether it leads to reasonably successful identification of adjectives by students of grammar. If it does, we might admit the hobgoblin of inconsistency as a necessary expedient.

The definition holds good in simple cases, such as *old shoes, offensive remark,* and *matters inconsequential,* though in the last case, students will have trouble recognizing the second word, rather than the first, as an adjective. But in each case, the adjective does modify a noun, which serves as the head of the phrase. However, other words can modify nouns that are clearly not adjectives. For instance, *stone* in *stone wall* is by formal criteria a noun and not an adjective (e.g., *stones* and *stone's*). Likewise, *the* in *the wall* shows none of the formal characteristics of adjectives, although it clearly modifies its head noun. In other words, the fact that a word modifies a noun doesn't provide sufficient reason to call it an adjective.

The definition suffers also because it's extended to functions that don't include modification. Note the words "or pronoun" in the definition. Clearly, an adjective cannot modify a pronoun in any of the examples below:

[10a]　*old them
　[b]　*offensive it
　[c]　*they inconsequential

To justify the inclusion of pronouns, grammarians refer to a different use of adjectives, as in sentences [11] and [12]:

[11]　The judge was late.
[12]　She was late.

In [11] and [12], the adjective *late* is called a **predicate adjective** or a **subject comple-ment.** But the use of these separate labels suggests—correctly—that such uses of adjectives are really not instances of modification at all, but rather, instances of complementation. (We will discuss this function shortly.) Any student who tries to relate such examples to clear cases of modification will become befuddled.

We will thus discard this misleading functional definition of adjectives and attempt to replace it with a more reliable one based on formal criteria.

5.3.1　Formal characteristics of adjectives

The major formal characteristic of an adjective is its ability to be compared.

ANALYTIC TEST 7a.　*A word may be an adjective if it allows comparison through the addition of the inflectional suffixes* **-er** *and* **-est.** *(Applies to short words.)*

ANALYTIC TEST 7b.　*A word may be an adjective if it allows comparison by being preceded by* **more** *and* **most.** *(Applies to longer words.)*

Comparison is a semantic change in adjectives that is regularly signaled by formal means. Uncompared forms are in the **positive degree;** compared forms occur in two further degrees, the **comparative** and the **superlative.**

A short adjective (one of one to two syllables) takes the *-er* and *-est* inflectional endings. Longer adjectives, including some two-syllable words such as *alone,* accept *more* and *most* as preceding words. In addition, adjectives may be preceded by a variety of degree words called **intensifiers:** *very, quite,* etc.

Positive	Comparative	Superlative
old	older	oldest
beautiful	more beautiful	most beautiful

EXERCISE   Using analytic tests 7a and 7b, identify which of the following words can be compared:

strong	strength	honest	retaliate
harsh	fashion	uncommon	local

While these criteria are very powerful, they don't work for all adjectives, especially scientific adjectives such as *nuclear* and *barometric.* Fortunately, a second type of test is available.

ANALYTIC TEST 8.   *A word may be an adjective if it actually ends in an adjectival derivational suffix.*

Remember that, as for nouns and verbs, the word must *end* with the adjective-forming suffix. Table 5.7 lists some of the major adjective suffixes in English.

**TABLE 5.7   Adjective Derivational
              Endings**

-ish	boorish, skittish
-al	comical, alphabetical
-ar	nuclear, circular
-ful	cheerful, careful
-some	winsome, awesome
-y	funny, uncanny
-ic	choleric, atmospheric
-able/-ible	debatable, sensible
-ing	interesting, amusing
-ed	disputed, concerned

EXERCISES   1. Extend the list of adjectival derivational endings. If you're in doubt about an
ending, consult a good desk dictionary or a reference grammar.
2. Which of the italicized words in the sentences below are adjectives? Justify
your answers by tests 7a, 7b, and 8.
   a. Your tie is *outlandish.*
   b. I have no *particular* doubts about your proposal.
   c. This chamber contains more *particular* matter than that one.
   d. Zubin is quite *stable.*
   e. *Some* dogs are mean.
3 The last two derivational suffixes in Table 5.7 are superficially identical to verb
forms in the present participle (Ving) and the past participle (Ven). Think of example sentences that the adjectives appear in; think of sentences in which the

verb forms appear. How can you differentiate the two? (We have noted that there is an ongoing historical process through which participles shift to adjectives. The process apparently occurs word by word. Can you identify any other verbs that are currently in the course of becoming adjectives?)

The tests we have provided eliminate from the list of adjectives many sorts of words that have been traditionally—and confusingly—included with this class. For instance, cardinal numerals such as *five* and ordinal numerals such as *fifth* cannot be called adjectives since we don't say **fiver* or **fivest* or **fifther* or **fifthest*. Similarly, we exclude: (1) the articles *the* and *a/an*; (2) the demonstratives *this, that, these,* and *those*; (3) indefinites, including quantifiers such as *all, no, every*; (4) possessive pronouns such as *my, your, their*; and (5) interrogative pronouns such as *what* and *which*. All of these forms regularly modify nouns. None of them is a true adjective.

To tests 7 and 8, we can add one further formal feature of adjectives, their position in a sentence. Adjectives tend to occur in relatively set locations. The two most common are: (1) between a determiner and a noun, and (2) after a verb of the *be-become-seem* type. We will discuss determiners in the next chapter. Briefly, this class includes words such as *a/an, the, this, that, some, every,* and *many*. Thus the italicized words in sentences [13a] to [13c] are adjectives:

[13a] The *recent* discovery of HG 116 . . .
  [b]   This *remarkable* discovery . . .
  [c]   Some *unnerving* developments . . .

Examples of adjectives that appear after *be-become-seem* verbs are:

[14a] I am *steadfast.*
  [b]   She grew *stubborn.*
  [c]   He appears *pig-headed.*

These tendencies aren't as strong as the analytic tests that we have examined since nonadjectives can appear in both positions. However, they may support the tests in doubtful cases.

5.3.2 Functions of adjectives

While adjectives often do modify nouns, they may also enter into a wider range of functions. We will illustrate below some of the more prominent of these functions.

Adjectives function as heads of **adjective phrases (AP)**. As such, they can be modified by only a small number of words, including *very, quite,* certain degree adverbs discussed in the next section, and prepositional phrases (e.g., *very careful, quite reasonable, thoroughly insane, unusual for its beauty*). Since APs most often appear as single adjectives, many grammarians ignore the difference between adjectives and APs.

Adjectives are modifiers of nouns typically when they occur before their noun head: e.g., *long walks.* Occasionally, they will follow the head noun, especially if the head is an indefinite word such as *something, anything, nothing,* etc.:

[15a]   I heard something *strange.*
  [b]   I haven't heard anything *new.*
  [c]   I see nothing *unusual.*

In addition, if the adjective is post-modified or complemented (e.g., [16b]), the AP of which it's the head will normally follow the head of the noun phrase in which it occurs:

[16a]   She is a *sensitive* person.
  [b]   She is a person *sensitive* to gender issues.

Modifiers of nouns typically are subject to a paraphrase test, in which the headword is followed by *who is* or *which is* and the adjective. For example:

[17a]   I heard something [which is] *strange.*
  [b]   She is a person [who is] *unusual* for her knowledge of astronomy.

Adjectives that directly modify nouns by preceding or following them are often called **attributive adjectives.**

Another common function of adjective phrases is **predicative.** Predicate adjectives occur after verbs in the *be-become-seem* type. We illustrated this function earlier in this chapter since it's one that adjectives share with nouns:

[18a]   Faust is *anxious.*
  [b]   Mephistopheles became *despondent.*
  [c]   Wagner seems *puzzled.*

A second function of adjective phrases is that of **object complement.** Examples are:

[19a]   We consider him *foolish.*
  [b]   Your attitude makes me *angry.*

Adjectival object complements are particularly common in certain set phrases, such as *make X clear.* Table 5.8 contains a sample of such set phrases.

A third function of adjective phrases is as the headword of a noun phrase. (We will have more to say about noun phrases in Chapter 7.) For the moment, consider the following sentence:

[20]   The poor are always with us.

TABLE 5.8 Adjectives as Object Complements (X = Direct Object)

cut X short	push X open
drain X dry	put X straight
keep X loose	set X right
leave X clean	shake X free
make X plain	wash X clean
pack X tight	

We might be tempted to say that *poor* is a noun since it's the head of a noun phrase *(the poor)* and since the noun phrase functions as the subject of the sentence. But a closer examination reveals that the word *poor* can be compared:

[21]   The poorest are always with us.

By our criteria, *poor* is thus an adjective.

EXERCISE   You might object that sentences [20] and [21] contain an "understood" noun that *poor* modifies—e.g., the noun *people*. To do so, of course, concedes the status of *poor* as an adjective. However, one might respond that the understood noun is purely fictitious. Suppose that you and I are experts at badminton. We observe two players who are clearly inept at the game, and I say to you, *The poor are always with us*. In this context, the understood subject of the sentence is *badminton players*. However, since the given sentence could be uttered in an infinite number of circumstances, it would have an infinite number of understood nouns. Rather than reducing the grammar of the sentence to contextual absurdity, it's more reasonable to say that it has only one subject, which isn't "understood" but which actually appears. That subject is *the poor*, a noun phrase whose headword is the adjective *poor*. We have noted earlier, however, that nouns function as the heads of noun phrases. The question arises then: Can adjectives function as heads of noun phrases? How would you answer this question? In framing your answer, consider the following, indicating your judgments of grammaticality:
a. the honestly poor
b. the very poor
c. the extremely poor
d. the especially poor
e. the dirty poor
f. the extreme poor
g. the normal poor
h. the honest poor

5.3.3 Subclasses of adjectives.

Traditional grammarians employ a set of distinctions that we will not adopt because some of the subcategories are based on a confusion of form and function. For purposes of completeness, we list these distinctions here but treat the forms elsewhere. **Descriptive adjectives** are those adjectives that satisfy the analytic tests in section 5.3.1. Like nouns, this group is sometimes subdivided into **common** (e.g., *honest, alive*) and **proper** (e.g., *Atlantic, Indian*). Proper descriptive adjectives normally don't allow comparison, although they regularly end in the derivational suffixes typical of adjectives.

Aside from descriptive adjectives, traditional grammars recognize as adjectives other forms which aren't formally adjectives but simply modifiers of nouns. Throughout this section, we have tried to justify their exclusion from the adjective category. Table 5.9 identifies some of these subclasses, each of which confuses a word's part of speech with its function.

The attempt to classify such a disparate group of structures as adjectives destroys the possibility of any simple unified system of parts of speech. In our approach, none of these categories exists. Instead, we would call the members of Table 5.9 "noun as modifier," "pronoun as modifier," "article as modifier," "phrase as modifier," etc.

TABLE 5.9 Traditional Subclasses of Adjectives

Noun as Adjective	*Easter* bonnet
Pronoun as Adjective	*this* situation
Adverb as Adjective	*far* South
Possessive Adjective	*someone's* lunchbox
Demonstrative Adjective	*such* effrontery
Interrogative Adjective	*Whose* signature is this?
Relative Adjective	the person *whom* I will help
Numeral Adjective	*five* guesses
Article Adjective	*the* truth
Phrase as Adjective	members *in good standing*
Adjective Clause	anyone *who desires an education*

5.4 ADVERBS

The traditional definition of an adverb is "a word used to modify a verb, an adjective, or another adverb." This definition is clearly functional and actually represents the typical functions of adverbs fairly well. As usual, though, exceptions exist. For instance, we have argued that *poor* in *The poor are always with us* is an adjective. Since *the* modifies an adjective, by our definition we would be forced to call *the* an adverb. No grammarian would ever agree to such a preposterous assignment. *The* is an article, even though it seems to modify an adjective. Nor is it clear that adverbs are as restricted in their scope of modification as the definition suggests. In sentence [22]:

[22] Frankly, I don't like calamari.

the adverb *frankly* doesn't modify *like* but, rather, denotes the speaker's degree of candidness in uttering the sentence.

EXERCISE   To what extent do the italicized adverbs below conform to the traditional definition?
  a. Atwood writes *clearly*.
  b. *Clearly*, Atwood wrote the letter.
  c. This sample is *obviously* atypical.
  d. *Obviously*, this sample is atypical.
  e. Belinda smiled *hopefully*.
  f. *Hopefully*, Belinda will bring some refreshments.

While most grammarians agree that adverbs nearly always function as modifiers, they're hard put in such cases to identify exactly *what* element in the sentence or discourse the adverb actually modifies. In most cases, grammarians ritually attach adverbs to verb heads, unless there is compelling reason to do otherwise.

Our approach here will again begin with a formal characterization of adverbs. We will then proceed to a functional division of adverbs into **sentence modifiers** and **adjuncts**. Finally, we will indicate some of the traditional semantic categories of adverbs.

5.4.1   Formal characteristics of adverbs

In their inflectional characteristics, adverbs are nearly indistinguishable from adjectives. Hence we recycle the formal criteria of 7a and 7b as:

ANALYTIC TEST 9a.   *A word may be an adverb if it undergoes comparison by the addition of the suffixes* **-er** *and* **-est**. *(Applies to short words.)*

ANALYTIC TEST 9b.   *A word may be an adverb if it undergoes comparison by being preceded by* **more** *and* **most**. *(Applies to longer words.)*

Criterion 9a, in fact, rarely applies since the language contains few one-syllable adverbs. *Hard* and *fast*—but not *soft* or *slow*—are examples. One such form, *well,* has irregular comparative and superlative forms, *better* and *best*. Colloquially, words such as *quick* are inflected for the comparative:

[23]   She threw it quicker than anyone expected.

Such usages, though, are usually regarded as prescriptively incorrect, the form *more quickly* being preferred. In general, test 9b serves as the norm of acceptable comparison of adverbs:

[24a]   She threw it *more quickly* than anyone expected.
  [b]   That is *most often* the case.

Derivational tests also apply to adverbs, though there are only a few adverbial suffixes.

ANALYTIC TEST 10.   *A word may be an adverb if it actually ends in an adverbial derivational suffix.*

The typical adverbial suffixes are listed in Table 5.10.

TABLE 5.10   Adverbial Derivational Endings

-ly	quickly, frequently, awkwardly
-wise	lengthwise, otherwise
-ward	homeward

Aside from a handful of derivational suffixes, it may seem difficult to distinguish between adjectives and adverbs. In practice, however, it's usually not difficult to tell them apart because of their positions in sentences.

ANALYTIC TEST 11a.   *Adverbs don't occur in the positions typically occupied by adjectives.*

ANALYTIC TEST 11b.   *Adverbs tend to be relatively movable in a sentence.*

Let's use the adjective *frequent* and its matching adverb form *frequently* as an example of these criteria. As we have seen, adjectives can occur between determiners and nouns or after *be-become-seem* verbs, as in [25] and [26]:

[25]   Harriet was a frequent visitor.
[26]   Harriet's visits were frequent.

Adverbs in these positions sound odd:

[27]   *Harriet was a frequently visitor.
[28]   *Harriet's visits were frequently.

The sentences below show the results of applying test 11b:

[29a]   Harriet was a frequent visitor.
 [b]   *Frequent, Harriet was a visitor.
 [c]   *Harriet was frequent a visitor.
 [d]   *Harriet was a visitor frequent.
 [e]   Frequently, Harriet was a visitor.
 [f]   Harriet was frequently a visitor.
 [g]   Harriet was a visitor frequently.

The portability of adverbs in sentences isn't arbitrary; they tend to occur in three positions: (1) at the beginning of a sentence, (2) at the end of a sentence, and (3) in a verb group. Due to restrictions on particular adverbs, not all adverbs will occur in all three positions:

[30a]   I will *never* leave you.
  [b]   **Never* I will leave you.
  [c]   *Never* will I leave you.
  [d]   ?I will leave you *never*.

5.4.2   Functions of adverbs

Adverbs serve as heads of **adverb phrases (AdvP).** Like adjectives, however, they accept only a few preceding modifiers (mainly *more/most, very,* and *quite*) and a limited range of following prepositional phrases (e.g., *more rapidly than a speeding locomotive*). Again, since most adverbs are unmodified, many grammarians include among their functions those that properly apply to AdvPs.

Adverbs and adverb phrases seem almost exclusively to modify. But what do they modify? Our position here will be to distinguish one subclass of adverbs that clearly modify the sentence and another that modify, in some general sense, the verb group or verb phrase. The first function is the **sentence modifier;** the second is the **adjunct.**

Sentence modifiers have two major functions. They can indicate a speaker's evaluation of the truth of the sentence as in [31a], or of what the sentence refers to, as in [31b] and [31c]:

[31a]   *Apparently/obviously/clearly,* Wonkers is a schizo.
  [b]   *Frankly/honestly,* my dear, I don't give a damn.
  [c]   *Luckily/fortunately,* I regained control of the car.

Sentence modifiers can also connect one clause or part of a clause with another, as in [32a] to [32c]:

[32a]   The paramedics arrived and *eventually* Oscar was stabilized.
  [b]   Summer arrived; *however,* the weather remained poor.
  [c]   He gambled away his inheritance, and *consequently* had to work for a living.

The class of expressions referred to as "transition devices" by composition teachers includes such connective adverbs. All adverbs besides sentence modifiers are adjuncts.

EXERCISE   The use of the word *hopefully* is often chastised in prescriptive circles, specifically in sentences such as *Hopefully, my paycheck will arrive soon.* Check the usage labels on this word in a current dictionary. What reasons support the disapproval of this word? What does the word mean? Is it an adverb or some other part of speech? What kind of adverb is it? How does it differ grammatically or semantically from other adverbs in its class?

5.4.3 Subcategories of adverbs

Adverbs are often classified semantically in terms of time, place, manner, frequency, and degree. Table 5.11 illustrates these meanings.

TABLE 5.11   Semantic Classes of Adverbs

Meaning	Examples
Time	today, yesterday, now, then
Place	here, there
Manner	well, slowly, convincingly, quietly
Frequency	often, regularly
Degree	completely, thoroughly, absolutely

These categories are worth remembering since most of them also apply to prepositions, to be considered in Chapter 6. In addition, some of these adverbs (e.g., *then, there*) serve as substitutes for prepositional phrases.

Our analysis of adverbs eliminates the traditional inclusion in this class of certain words that modify adjectives or other adverbs. Such words occur in the examples below:

[33a] *very* old
  [b] *quite* frequently
  [c] *only* occasionally

Traditionally, these words are often lumped together with **degree adverbs.** We will classify these words in Chapter 6 as **intensifiers.**

EXERCISE   Apply analytic tests 9 to 11 to demonstrate that the italicized words in [33] aren't adverbs.

REFERENCES AND RESOURCES

Celce-Murcia, Marianne, and Diane Larsen-Freeman. 1983. *The Grammar Book: An ESL/EFL Teacher's Course.* Rowley, MA: Newbury House Publishers, Inc.

Fries, Charles Carpenter. 1940. *American English Grammar.* New York: Appleton-Century-Crofts, Inc.

———. 1952. *The Structure of English.* New York: Harcourt, Brace & World, Inc.

Quirk, Randolph, and Sidney Greenbaum. 1973. *A Concise Grammar of Contemporary English.* New York: Harcourt Brace Jovanovich, Inc.

Quirk, Randolph, Sidney Greenbaum, Geoffrey Leech, and Jan Svartik. 1972. *A Grammar of Contemporary English.* London: Longman.

Radford, Andrew. 1988. *Transformational Grammar.* Cambridge: Cambridge University Press.

Sledd, James. 1959. *A Short Introduction to English Grammar.* Glenview, IL: Scott, Foresman and Company.

GLOSSARY

Abstract noun: a noun that denotes entities apprehended by the mind; e.g., *truth, belief.* See **concrete noun.**

Adjective phrase: a phrase with an adjective as its head. See Chapter 7.

Adjunct: a modifier within a verb phrase.

Adverb phrase: a phrase with an adverb as its head. See Chapter 7.

Attributive adjective: a function of an adjective (phrase) which precedes (or occasionally follows) its head noun. See **predicate adjective.**

Auxiliary verb (also called "**helping verb**"): verbs such as *be, have,* and *can,* which indicate aspect, voice, or modality.

Category change: see **conversion.**

Collective noun: a noun that denotes groups of individuals (*army, jury, the public, The United States*).

Common noun: a noun which refers to classes rather than to specific individuals; e.g., *tissue, box, xylophone.* See **proper noun.**

Comparative: a degree of an adjective or adverb, signaled by *-er* or *more.* See **superlative.**

Complement: see Chapter 10.

Concrete noun: a noun that denotes an entity that can be apprehended by any one of the five senses; e.g., *sneeze, floor, paper.* See **abstract noun.**

Content word: words (nouns, verbs, adjectives, and adverbs) which express the major information of a sentence. See **function word.**

Conversion (also called "**zero derivation**," "**category change**," and "**functional shift**"): a derivational process in which no derivational morpheme is added to a word.

Count noun: a noun that represents entities that can be counted, and hence can be made plural; e.g., *typewriter, diskette, page.* See **mass noun.**

Degree adverb: see **intensifier** (Chapter 6).

Descriptive adjective: any adjective that meets the formal requirements for adjectives.

Function word (also called "**structure word**"): see Chapter 6.

Functional shift: see **conversion.**

Gerund: in traditional grammar, a verb phrase that functions as a subject or object. See Chapter 10.

Head: the main grammatical word of a phrase, which determines the category of the phrase. See **modifier.**

Infinitive: (1) a form of a verb without any inflection—i.e., the form which one would look up in a dictionary; e.g., *eat.* Abbreviated as V. (2) The same form of a verb when preceded by *to;* e.g., *to eat.* See Chapter 10.

Intensifier: see Chapter 6.

Intransitive verb: a verb that doesn't accept a **direct object.** See Chapter 8.

Linking verb: a verb that is followed by a **subject complement.** See Chapter 8.

Main verb: the head of a verb phrase or predicate. See **auxiliary verb** (Chapter 6).

Mass noun (also called "**noncount**"): a noun thought of as representing things in the world as undifferentiated masses, whose parts aren't identified as discrete individuals (*rice, sugar, milk*). See **count noun.**

Modifier: a secondary element of a phrase which qualifies its head but doesn't determine the grammatical category of the phrase. See **head.**

Nominalization: the process by which a word (or group of words) becomes a noun (or noun phrase), often through the addition of a derivational suffix.

Noncount noun: see **mass noun.**

Noun phrase: a phrase whose head is a noun. See Chapter 7.

Object complement: see Chapter 8.

Participle: (a) the Ving or Ven inflectional form of a verb. (b) In traditional grammar, a verb form that modifies a noun. See Chapter 10.

Past participle: the Ven inflectional form of a verb.

Phrase: a grammatically unified structure consisting of a head word and any words or phrases that modify or complement the head word. See Chapter 7.

Positive degree: the degree of adjective or adverb that isn't compared. See **comparative** and **superlative.**

Predicate adjective: an adjective (phrase) that appears after the verbs *be, become, seem,* etc. See **subject complement.**

Principal part: a list of the infinitive and inflectional forms of a verb: V, Vs, Ving, Ved, and Ven.

Productivity: a characteristic of a linguistic process, e.g., nominalization, that applies freely to items in its range.

Progressive (also called "**present participle**"): a verb form indicated by *be* + Ving. See Chapter 6.

Proper noun: a noun that refers to individual entities; e.g., *Thomas Jefferson, Denver, the Koran.* See **common noun.**

Sentence modifier: the function of adverbs that describe either (1) the speaker's manner of presenting information in a sentence or (2) the speaker's judgment about the truth of the sentence.

Stem: see **infinitive.**

Structure word: see **function word.**

Subject complement: the function of an adjective phrase or noun phrase after verbs such as *be, become,* and *seem.* See Chapter 8.

Suffix: see Chapter 4.

Superlative: the degree of an adjective or adverb, signaled by *-est* or *most.*

Transitive verb: a verb that requires a direct object. See Chapter 8.

Verb phrase: a phrase whose head is a verb.

Zero derivation: see **conversion.**

APPENDIX B
Prototypes

Perhaps the greatest frustration of students—and teachers—of grammar is the discovery that seemingly clear and airtight definitions fail to work smoothly in all cases. We argued in our chapter on parts of speech that one source of this difficulty is the faulty status of definitions, e.g., those that determine parts of speech on the basis of their meaning or function. Our system replaces such definitions with a set of *formal conditions* pertaining to morphological (inflectional and derivational) and syntactic (positional) characteristics of words. As some of our exercises demonstrate, not all conditions will apply in all cases. For instance, the condition that nouns can be made plural might seem to rule out as nouns words such as *cattle* and *furniture*. On the other hand, these words can accept the possessive, as in *the cattle's thirst* and *the furniture's delivery*. Moreover, the *-ure* morpheme is typical to nouns: *armature, ligature, caricature,* and *signature.* However, other words besides nouns appear to end in the *-ure* morpheme: *pure* (adjective), *mature* (adjective or verb), and *insure* (verb). In other words, we seem to find cases where our conditions (1) fail to apply to all members of a parts-of-speech class and (2) apply to words outside the class that the conditions specify.

Two natural reactions to this situation are possible. One response would simply ignore the anomalies and present the conditions as absolutes. This approach would demand that conditions should be both *necessary* and *sufficient.* (They would be necessary because they would *all* have to apply; they would be sufficient because no other conditions—e.g., meaning—are needed.) This course has the serious disadvantage of creating a head-on collision with reality. It's practically impossible for a teacher to focus students' attention only on examples that meet all of the conditions. Indeed, to do so would deny students the flexibility they need to extend grammatical knowledge beyond the limited confines in which it was presented to them. A second response would give up the entire enterprise of defining parts of speech as too haphazard to be worth doing. The drawback of this approach is that it fails to teach students anything about language, except perhaps that language is chaotic.

As you might suspect, we view both of these extreme positions as fundamentally wrong—wrong about the nature of language and wrong about the way in which language should be studied. Let's now examine why.

Let's begin with two exercises. (These make excellent party games.) First, ask a group of your friends to make a list of ten birds. Second, show them the pictures in Figure 5.1 and ask them to identify which is a cup, which is a bowl, and which is a vase.

If you tally your list of birds, you will find that certain names appear early on many lists (e.g., eagle, robin, sparrow), while others appear later (e.g., owl, crow). Also, some names will appear on almost all lists, while others (e.g., chicken, penguin,

FIGURE 5.1   A Series of Cuplike Objects (Source: Labov 1973: 354. Reprinted by permission of Georgetown University Press.)

ostrich) will appear less frequently. Your cup-bowl-vase survey will likewise show some general consensus but much disagreement about where the borderlines should be drawn among the objects.

The next step is to ask your subjects *why* they made their choices. On the bird exercise, they will probably mention such conditions as having feathers, being capable of flight, and laying eggs. On the vessel exercise, they might rest their cases on such features as relation of height to width and having versus lacking a handle. In both experiments, however, you will notice several things: (1) in clear cases, all of the conditions apply; (2) sometimes in marginal cases, some but not all conditions apply; and (3) sometimes in marginal cases, the conditions conflict. For example, robins have feathers, fly, and lay eggs, while chickens typically don't fly, or at least don't fly long distances; penguins and ostriches don't fly at all. In the case of cups, bowls, and vases, a high and narrow object with no handle will probably be considered a vase; an object with an equal height and size with a handle might be called a cup; and an object that is wider than high with no handle will likely be called a bowl. But take any different combination of these features and the issue will immediately become clouded. What do you call a high and narrow object that has a handle? What if you put flowers into it? If you put flowers into a soupbowl, does it become a vase?

While our experiment deals with the real world, it's also an exercise in language. It tells us a good deal about how words relate to reality. When we use expressions like *bird* or *cup,* we group together objects not so much on the basis of rigid characteristics, but on a set of criteria or conditions that we use somewhat flexibly. In this way, we group together objects on the basis of what the philosopher Ludwig Wittgenstein has called "family resemblances." You might envision, then, a target, with some objects close to the bull's eye—those entities that are clearly bowls or birds. Those entities that fall close to the center of the target are called *prototypes.* They possess all or most of the features typical of our conception of the entity. Toward the periphery of the target lie entities that are less "bowly" or "birdy," according to how many of the conditions they meet. In language also, the boundaries between the application of words may be "fuzzy." That is, one may occasionally have trouble deciding whether to call a given object a bowl or a vase.

Of course, not all conditions have equal importance. Some are *essential;* their lack disqualifies something from being an instance of a category. For instance, a bird must lay eggs rather than producing live babies. On the other extreme, some conditions are *excluded;* they must *not* be present. A bowl, for example, cannot be flat. In the middle of the extremes lie other conditions. *Expected* conditions are associated with normal or typical characteristics, such as flight for birds and handles for cups. Lack of such features—e.g., a penguin or a cup with its handle broken off—may serve to make the object an atypical or defective member of its class, without disqualifying it from membership altogether. Some conditions are merely *possible;* they result from common associations of the object. For example, birds commonly eat worms and cups often are used to drink warm beverages. Yet one would hardly be surprised at a bird that ate only seeds or at a cup used for holding pencils. Finally, certain conditions are *unlikely,* although not strictly impossible. A 500-pound bird or a cup with a 50-gallon capacity might strain the imagination but would hardly lead us into doubt about the name of the object (Cruse, 1986).

We thus seem to identify objects on the basis of their resemblance to certain prototypes—an object which we consider a very typical member of the category. In other words, prototypes share all of the necessary and expected conditions, perhaps some of the possible ones, and none of the excluded or unlikely ones.

How does the notion of prototypes relate to grammar? Well, labels such as "noun" and "verb" have much the same status as "bird" and "cup." We can state a set of conditions—inflectional, derivational, syntactic—that allow us to classify words (rather than objects) in a relatively consistent and logical fashion. However, cases arise when not all of the conditions apply. That is, certain nouns may be less "nouny" than others. Nevertheless, nouns demonstrate a family resemblance to one another because they share many characteristics. Of course, you can expect to encounter words that cause difficulties since the borders of the noun category are fuzzy. For instance, consider the following words that end in -ing: *interesting, meeting, singing*. Let's consider the condition of taking the plural morpheme, along with the related feature of appearing in the noun slot *two* . . . . We can thus immediately eliminate *interesting* (**two interestings*) and *sing* (**two sings*); likewise, we can immediately qualify *meeting* as a noun (*two meetings*). *Singing* raises some problems: Is *two singings* grammatical? Speakers will vary in how they answer this question, indicating that the expression lies on the border of the noun category. Note, however, the variation has no impact on the force of the conditions. Even someone who accepts the phrase as grammatical will readily agree that it isn't a typical use of the word *singing*. Thus we might conclude that the capacity to be made plural is an expected—though not essential—condition for nouns.

You might object that the notion of prototypes leads to linguistic anarchy. Perhaps there are no essential conditions. Moreover, if standards are flexible, aren't we in danger of measuring with a rubber ruler? This reaction, however initially reasonable, has no real justification. In fact, our position allows the maintenance of analytic standards without reducing grammar to legalistic rigidity.

For one thing, English itself is grammatically flexible. The prevalence of conversion from one part of speech to another with no derivational marker provides one clear example. There is no reason in English why any word cannot be converted to another part of speech, at least in restricted contexts, as the following suggests:

[1a] *Ifs, ands,* or *buts* (Subordinating and coordinating conjunctions as nouns)
  [b] *Whys* and *wherefores* (Interrogatives as nouns)
  [c] *But* me no *buts.* (Coordinator as verb and noun)

What we see here are instances of *linguistic creativity,* the ability to make infinite use of finite linguistic resources. Of course, creativity need not stretch the limits of a language, but often it does so. Nor does creativity limit itself to English. It's characteristic of all languages. It would seem, then, that our descriptive resources should fit the subject that we wish to describe. Prototypical thinking provides just this adjustment of analytic tools to language. Pedagogically, it doesn't require an abandonment of standards, but rather, an adjustment of one's attitude toward them—a change that demands that one consider individual cases on their own merits rather than by adhering to mechanical procedures.

This may sound somewhat abstract. What practical consequences arise from the fact that not all criteria apply to every word in a class? One result is the existence of a set of *subclasses;* e.g., those nouns that cannot be made plural (e.g., *furniture, cattle, independence*). Those that cannot be made plural constitute the subclass of noncount (mass) nouns; others are count nouns. Too often, teachers present grammatical categories to their students as simple classes. Students need to recognize that large categories consist of smaller categories. Since the variability of conditions on classes allow us to define subclasses, the prototypical status of the conditions is of practical importance.

A second consequence of prototypes is that they allow us to see similarities between categories. For instance, it encourages us to ask questions like, How is a noun like a verb? Perhaps this question seems initially illogical. But is it? Suppose we distinguish two subclasses of verbs—transitive and intransitive—on the formal basis of their ability to be followed by a noun phrase, as in [2a] and [2b]:

[2a]   The Broncos defeated the Jets.
 [b]   The rabbit disappeared.

In [2a], the word *defeat,* inflected for past tense, is clearly a verb and is transitive because of the noun phrase *the Jets.* In sentence [2b], *disappeared* is likewise a verb but is intransitive since it cannot be followed by a noun phrase, as [3a] and [3b] show:

[3a]   *The rabbit disappeared itself.
 [b]   *The magician disappeared the rabbit.

Corresponding to the verbs in [2], we can cite nouns that resemble them:

[4a]   The Broncos' defeat of the Jets
 [b]   The rabbit's disappearance

Example [4a], you will notice, contains the noun *defeat* (it can be made plural), which has been converted from a verb and has in its genitive phrase an expression (*The Broncos'*), which corresponds to the subject of the verb *defeat* in [2a]. Likewise, the fully derived noun *disappearance* in [4b] corresponds to the verb *disappear* in [2b]. However, just as the verb *disappear* cannot accept an object, the noun *disappear* cannot take an *of*-phrase complement. This fact is supported by the ungrammaticality of [5a] and [5b]. (Compare to [3a] and [3b].)

[5a]   *The rabbit's disappearance of itself.
 [b]   *The magician's disappearance of the rabbit.

In other words, nouns have restrictions that closely parallel those of transitivity on verbs.

The facts of English grammar thus suggest that the rigid separation of parts of speech conceals a potentially rich network of similarities among categories, similarities that might prove interesting for teachers of writing. A prototype approach encourages one to explore, rather than ignore possible connections between categories.

Summary

We have seen that prototypes and family resemblances account for the ways in which we identify and name objects in the world. The same use of standard models and conditions holds true for our identification of parts of speech. Far from loosening our definitional power, prototypical thinking calls for a recognition of grammatical subclasses and encourages one to discover unsuspected similarities among word classes.

REFERENCES AND RESOURCES

Aitchison, Jean. 1987. *Words in the Mind.* Oxford: Blackwell.

Cruse, D. A. 1986. *Lexical Semantics.* Cambridge: Cambridge University Press.

Hurford, James R., and Brendan Heasley. 1983. *Semantics: A Course Book.* Cambridge: Cambridge University Press.

Jackendoff, Ray. 1983. *Semantics and Cognition.* Cambridge, MA: MIT Press.

Labov, William. 1973. "The Boundaries of Words and Their Meanings." In C.-J. N. Bailey and R. W. Shuy, eds., *New Ways of Analyzing Variation in English.* Vol. 1. Washington, DC: Georgetown University Press, 340–373.

6 MINOR PARTS OF SPEECH

KEY CONCEPTS

Function words
Pronouns
Wh-words
Articles
Auxiliary verbs
Prepositions
Intensifiers
Conjunctions
Other minor parts of speech

6.0 FUNCTION WORDS

Aside from the major parts of speech—noun, verb, adjective, adverb—there are many minor classes. Their number varies according to the level of detail of a particular analysis; more important is the clarity with which classes are distinguished. Our approach in the previous chapter has rather strictly narrowed the members of the major parts of speech. As a result, the number of minor parts of speech will increase. This consequence is acceptable, though, since it permits the criteria for major classes to operate in a straightforward way.

Moreover, the minor form classes can be defined easily by listing their members. We will distinguish about a dozen of these classes, and the largest of them has only about fifty members. Students can readily become familiar with such words through experience, without any recourse to memorization.

Minor word classes have several properties in common. First, they tend not to alter the basic content of a sentence. For this reason, they have sometimes been called **function words,** in contrast to the major parts of speech, called **content words.** Content words bear the main semantic burden in communication. They're the words that you would use to send a telegram: *Broke: send money.* Minor words, in contrast, signal relatively subtle shades of meaning, obvious information, or redundant grammatical information: *I am broke; will you please send some money.* Members of minor word classes occur more frequently than members of major classes. All of the fifty most common words in English are function words; they account for about 60 percent of words used in speech and 45 percent of those used in writing. Although sometimes used to dramatize the sorry state of English, this statistic is as true of Henry James's prose as of the most pedestrian discourse. The reason is that minor words form the necessary cement to hold together the bricks of content, whether those bricks are laid by the brilliant or the dull. Their frequency results from their importance for integrating content words into the organization of sentences. For this reason, minor words are sometimes referred to as **structure words.**

In presenting the minor word classes, we will proceed mainly by listing their members. Where necessary, we will also note semantic, functional, and formal characteristics. Except for pronouns, the formal properties of these items don't (in English) include inflectional or derivational marking. Rather, they emerge from the items' ability to combine with other words, phrases, or sentences. For instance, *after* is a preposition because it can combine with a noun phrase, as in *after the announcement.* The combination of a preposition and its following noun phrase is called a **prepositional phrase.** We will examine this and other phrases in the next chapter. Since minor class members can enter into several different combinations, they will sometimes, like content words, be members of more than one class. For example, when *after* is followed by both a noun phrase and a verb phrase (i.e., a clause), it's a **subordinating adverbial conjunction.** *After* has this formal status in *After the announcement appeared, we received many phone calls.*

6.1 PRONOUNS

The standard definition of the pronoun is "a word used in place of one or more nouns." Let's test the adequacy of this definition by examining some examples:

[1a] Jonathan felt sorry for Jeremy, so *he* repaired *his* bike for *him.*
 [b] Because *he* wanted to sell *it*, Jonathan repaired *his* bike.
 [c] Jonathan repaired *his* bike.
 [d] Jonathan and Jeremy repaired *their* bikes.

The standard definition is a formal one since you can easily test it by replacing each one of the pronouns with either *Jonathan* or *Jeremy.* The replacement test is usually presented with some related terminology. The noun(s) that the pronoun replaces is the pronoun's **antecedent.** Literally, this term means "going before," and in most cases, the antecedent precedes the pronoun. (Sentence [1b] shows that the antecedent can sometimes follow its pronoun.) In English, pronouns show *agreement* with their antecedent in person, number, and gender. All of the sentences above illustrate agreement. *Jonathan* and *Jeremy* are each third person, singular, and masculine, and thus select the pronouns *he, his,* or *him.* Both the pronoun and its antecedent refer to the same entity in the real world; this is the relation of **coreference.** Incidentally, the actual reference (and antecedent) of a pronoun may depend on context and on our expectations of the world. In sentence [1a], we assume that feeling sorry for a person would lead one to repair that person's bike, not one's own. Moreover, the examples in [1] have another interpretation, by which they don't designate either Jonathan or Jeremy, but rather two other individuals in the context.

Returning to our original definition, we can observe one further point. Sentence [1d] shows how a pronoun may replace more than one noun. The definition is somewhat misleading, however, since it suggests that pronouns substitute merely for *lists* of nouns. As sentence [2] indicates, pronouns substitute for more than lists:

[2] All of the members of the class elected Juan as their representative.

What does *their* replace? Certainly not a list of nouns. In fact, the phrase *all of the members of the class* contains only two nouns. This phrase, as we saw in Chapter 5, is a **noun phrase,** a group of words that has a single noun (in this case, *members*) as its headword. As a result, the standard definition of a pronoun must be amended to read "a noun or noun phrase." This reformulation is not airtight, though. If we tried to replace the noun *members* in sentence [2] with a pronoun, sentence [3] would result:

[3]   *All of the their of the class elected Juan as their representative.

So pronouns apparently replace nouns only when there are no other words in the noun phrase; otherwise, they replace the entire noun phrase. But emending the definition to take account of this fact adds needless complexity. In the next chapter, we will allow a minimal noun phrase to consist of a single head noun. Anticipating this description, we can simply define a **pronoun** as "a word that replaces a noun phrase."

This definition applies most readily to the third person pronouns *he, she, it,* and *they.* While *I, you,* etc. might be taken as substitutes for noun phrases like *the speaker,* and *the addressee,* respectively, this expedient seems unnatural. For the first and second persons, a more appropriate description might be: "a minimal expression referring to the speaker or addressee."

English contains several different types of pronouns. We will list each type below and comment on their basic characteristics.

6.1.1   Personal pronouns

Table 6.1 identifies the categories of personal pronouns.

TABLE 6.1   Personal Pronouns

Person	Case		Singular		Plural
First	Nominative		I		we
	Accusative		me		us
	Genitive		my		our
			mine		ours
Second	Nominative		you		you
	Accusative		you		you
	Genitive		your		your
			yours		yours

		Gender			
		Masc.	**Fem.**	**Neut.**	
Third	Nominative	he	she	it	they
	Accusative	him	her	it	them
	Genitive	his	her	its	their
		his	hers	its	theirs

6.1.1.1 Person and number of personal pronouns

As Table 6.1 indicates, the personal pronouns represent categories of person, number, case, and gender. Number simply distinguishes singular (one) from plural (more than one). The pronoun forms *I, you, he/she/it,* represent distinctions within the category **person.** Person differentiates between speakers (first person: *I, we*), addressees (second person: *you*), and entities that are neither speaker nor addressee (third person: *she, he, it, they*).

The pronoun system of English reflects an inflectional variety that hints at the morphological complexity of the language a millennium ago. For instance, Old English had pronouns that referred specifically to two people (called "dual" pronouns), thereby creating a three-way number distinction.

Standard English is unusual among languages in that it makes no distinction in the personal pronouns between second person singular and plural. Many nonstandard dialects do differentiate singular and plural, e.g., by adding either the ordinary nominal plural ending *-s: youse,* or by adding *all: you-all* or *y'all.*

Many languages have different forms for second person singular and plural. German has *du* (informal singular) and *ihr* (informal plural), Spanish *tu* (informal singular) and *vosotros* (informal plural), French *tu* (singular) and *vous* (plural). In French, the distinction does double duty. It can indicate not only the ordinary person and number distinction but also certain aspects of the relationship between an individual speaker and addessee(s), most notably their relative social statuses and the degree of intimacy between them. Thus the French singular pronoun *tu* may be used by an adult to a child. The child would normally use *vous* to the adult. *Tu* can be used between people who are relatively friendly or familiar with each other. *Vous* would be used among people who aren't on friendly or familiar terms, or in formal situations. The other languages have other pronouns with which to indicate analogous social distinctions. German uses *Sie* as a polite or formal second person pronoun. Except for the fact that it's written with an initial capital letter, it's formally identical to the third person plural pronoun, *sie.* Spanish uses *usted* as a polite second person singular form, and *ustedes* as a polite second person plural form. The dimensions of status and familiarity have been extensively discussed by linguists and anthropologists under the terms **power** and **solidarity,** respectively, which we discuss again in Chapter 13.

The person distinction is required also to account for certain alternations in verb form, most obviously in the present tense, singular forms of the verb *be*: first person *am;* second person *are;* third person *is.* Other verbs make a person distinction only in the third person singular of the present tense, indicated by the ending *-s: gives.* No other verb form is marked for person: *I/you/we/they give.* Modal auxiliary verbs, e.g., *can,* don't indicate person.

6.1.1.2 Case of personal pronouns

English masculine and feminine pronouns come in three different forms: *he, him, his; she, her, hers.* These different forms are said to represent different **case forms** of the pronouns. The case distinction is necessary too for the description of certain English noun forms. Which form of a pronoun or noun we use depends on the relation of that word to other parts of the sentence: We use *he* and *she* when the pronoun is a subject; *him* and *her* if it's the object of a verb or a preposition; and *his* and either *her* or *hers* if they modify or complement a noun or pronoun. We will use the traditional names to refer to these cases: *he/she* are in the

nominative case; *him/her* are in the **accusative** (AKA **objective**) case; and *hers/his* are in the **genitive.**

English also differentiates other pronouns according to case. Thus *I, you, we,* and *they* are all nominative; *me, you, us,* and *them* are all accusative; and *my, mine, your, yours, our, ours, their,* and *theirs* are all genitive.

You will no doubt have noticed that there are two genitive forms of certain pronouns, such as *my* and *mine.* The forms corresponding to *my* (*your, our, their*) are used when the nouns they modify occurs immediately after them. Otherwise, we use the other genitive forms: e.g., *That is my horse,* as opposed to *That horse is mine.* The former are sometimes referred to misleadingly as **possessive adjectives,** as they occur before the nouns they modify in the positions typical of attributive adjectives. The latter are often distinguished as **possessive pronouns** because they appear to replace nouns or noun phrases, e.g., compare *That bike is mine* with *That is my bike.*

English nouns functioning as subjects don't differ in form from nouns functioning as objects, and so we don't distinguish between nominative and accusative cases for nouns. Grammarians occasionally refer to the nominative/accusative form of nouns as the **common case.** English does, however, distinguish between common case and genitive nouns. The genitive is indicated in written English as *'s: Bill* versus *Bill's.* Nouns, of course, don't have two genitive forms parallel to the pronouns.

EXERCISE   Why don't nouns have two genitive forms like the pronouns? (Hint: Compare the endings on genitive nouns and pronouns.)

Earlier forms of English, the classical languages such as Latin and Greek, and modern languages such as Finnish, have much more elaborate case distinctions than modern English. Table 6.2 provides a list of traditional case names and some of their functions.

Many languages require case markings on parts of speech besides nouns and pronouns. Modern German, for instance, makes case differentiations on both articles and adjectives.

A pronoun may function as the head of a noun phrase, as our revised definition suggests. Genitives may function as either the head of a noun phrase, as in [4a], or a modifier of a noun, as in [4b]:

[4a]   Give me mine/ours/yours/his/hers/theirs.
 [b]   She gave me my/our/your/his/her/their evaluations.

**TABLE 6.2   Traditional Case Names
and Functions**

Name	Function
Nominative	subject
Accusative	object
Genitive	possessive, partitive
Dative	recipient, beneficiary
Ablative	place from where
Vocative	addressee

As these sentences demonstrate, personal pronouns have different forms to differentiate headwords from modifiers. (A genitive NP—e.g., *Mary's* in *Mary's success*—is a full NP.)

Incidentally, we use the Latinate term **genitive** rather than the common English label **possessive** to emphasize the fact that such forms of pronouns don't necessarily indicate possession. For instance, *her performance* doesn't designate a performance that she owns, but rather, one that she gives.

6.1.1.3   Gender of personal pronouns

The pronoun system of English distinguishes three **genders:** *masculine* (forms of *he*), *feminine* (forms of *she*), and *neuter* (not "neutral"; forms of *it*), distinguished primarily according to the nature of the objects they refer to. Masculine pronouns refer to males, primarily human males; feminine pronouns refer to females, again, primarily human females; and neuter pronouns refer either to entities which are nonanimate, and consequently aren't differentiated according to sex, or to nonhuman animals. Infants whose sex is unknown are also occasionally referred to by neuter pronouns. A system in which the gender of a word depends on characteristics of its referent is called a **natural gender** system.

Other languages, such as French, German, Italian, Spanish, and Gaelic, have **grammatical gender** systems. The choice of gender is not dependent on characteristics of a word's referent; rather, words are assigned to gender classes according to formal linguistic criteria. In Italian and Spanish, for example, words ending in *-a* are typically feminine; in German, words ending in *-chen* are typically neuter. However, many words in these languages are assigned to gender classes somewhat arbitrarily, and so when learning a word, one must also learn its gender. Also, in these languages the gender system is reflected not only in the pronouns but in nouns and adjectives too. In Spanish, a noun and any articles or adjectives modifying it must agree in gender; if the noun is masculine, then any article or adjective must be masculine (e.g., *el libro blanco,* lit. the book white, "the white book"). If the noun is feminine, its modifiers must also be feminine (e.g., *la casa blanca,* lit. the house white, "the white house").

In recent years, the English gender system has given rise to much discussion of the issue of sexism in language and the need to develop forms that are sex-neutral. It's impossible in standard English not to refer to the sex of a human referent when choosing a personal pronoun regardless of whether the person's sex is relevant or even known or knowable. For example, compare the sentences: *Every doctor works hard for her patients* and *Every doctor works hard for his patients.* The first suggests that all doctors are women; the second that they are all men. Clearly, neither is true. Traditional prescriptive grammars have required that the pronoun after quantifiers such as *every* be masculine—and in general, that the **generic pronoun** be the masculine one. Many people find this norm to be objectionable and would like to find expressions which wouldn't give any indication of the referent's sex for use in situations where sex is irrelevant. Growing numbers of organizations require that their publications be sex-neutral. We return to this topic in Chapter 13.

EXERCISES   1. In the passage below
   a. Identify all the personal pronouns.
   b. Specify the antecedent of each pronoun.

Hercules was the strongest man on earth and he had the supreme self-confidence magnificent physical strength gives. He considered himself on an equality with the gods—and with some reason. They needed his help to conquer the Giants. In the final victory of the Olympians over the brutish sons of Earth, Hercules' arrows played an important part. He treated the gods accordingly. Once when the priestess at Delphi gave no response to the question he asked, he seized the tripod she sat on and declared that he would carry it off and have an oracle of his own. Apollo, of course, would not put up with this, but Hercules was perfectly willing to fight him and Zeus had to intervene. The quarrel was easily settled, however. Hercules was quite good-natured about it. He did not want to quarrel with Apollo, he only wanted an answer from his oracle. If Apollo would give it the matter was settled as far as he was concerned. Apollo on his side, facing this undaunted person, felt an admiration for his boldness and made his priestess deliver the response.

(From Edith Hamilton, *Mythology*)

2. You will notice from the previous exercise that (a) all of the pronouns in the passage are in the third person and (b) they all have a clear antecedent in the passage. Consider now first and second person pronouns. Is it possible for them to have a verbal antecedent or do they always refer to some entity outside the sentence? (A word with this latter property is called **deictic.** See Chapter 2.) Try to think of examples to support your position. How does your analysis affect our definition of pronouns?)

6.1.2 Demonstrative pronouns

English contains only four **demonstrative** pronouns; they appear in Table 6.3.

TABLE 6.3 Demonstrative Pronouns

Singular	Plural
this	these
that	those

Demonstrative pronouns have the effect of "pointing out" entities, often for the purpose of contrast or of selection:

[5a] Press *this* button, not *that* one.
 [b] I'll take one of *these* and one of *those*.

As the examples suggest, speakers often accompany demonstratives with pointing gestures. As we noted in Chapter 2, these forms are sometimes called **deictics**, after a Greek word meaning "to point." In written prose, of course, gestures aren't available, so writers must take care to make the referents of the pronouns clear:

[6]   Harry told Mabel that Maude had written the letter. This is typical.

What is typical? Harry's telling Mabel? Harry's telling anyone? Maude's writing letters?
    Like personal pronouns, demonstratives have two potential functions, as heads and as modifiers, though there is no differentiation of form:

[7a]   *That* is a serious mistake. (Head)
 [b]   *That* mistake is serious. (Modifier)

6.1.3   Reflexive and intensive pronouns

Reflexive and **intensive** pronouns end in the morpheme -*self* (or -*selves*); they have the same forms, as shown in Table 6.4.

TABLE 6.4   Reflexive/Intensive Pronouns

Person	Singular	Plural
First	myself	ourselves
Second	yourself	yourselves
Third	himself	
	herself	themselves
	itself	

    In spite of their identity of form, these two types of pronouns are easily distinguished. The reflexive pronoun functions only as an object; the intensive functions only as a modifier:

[8a]   Adelaide hurt *herself.*
 [b]   Adelaide bought *herself* a new Lamborghini.

In [8], *Adelaide* functions as the head of the subject noun phrase; *herself* functions as the head of either the direct [8a] or indirect [8b] object noun phrase. The pronouns and their antecedents are in different noun phrases.
    An intensive pronoun normally occurs *within* the noun phrase of its antecedent, typically following and modifying the antecedent directly:

[9]   Adelaide *herself* completed the audit.

The intensive pronoun also has a related form in which the pronoun is moved away from its antecedent (which it still modifies):

[10]   Adelaide completed the audit *herself.*

(Sentences [9] and [10] differ slightly in meaning. Can you describe the difference?) Sentences with reflexives cannot be related as [9] and [10] are. In other words, sentence [8] cannot be transformed to become [11] without significantly changing its meaning:

[11]   *Adelaide herself hurt.

6.1.4   Indefinite pronouns

Indefinite pronouns constitute a loose category of words brought together traditionally by the semantic fact that they don't refer to a specific person, place, thing, or idea. The common indefinites are listed in Table 6.5.

TABLE 6.5   Indefinite Pronouns (1 = head or modifier; 2 = head only)

all (1)	another (1)	any (1)
anybody (2)	anyone (2)	both (1)
each (1)	either (1)	everybody (2)
everyone (2)	few (1)	many (1)
most (1)	neither (1)	nobody (2)
none (2)	no one, or noone (2)	others (2)
one (2)	other (1)	somebody (2)
several (1)	some (1)	
someone (2)	such (1)	

Occasionally, students will misapply the semantic definition and label as indefinites generic nouns such as *people,* collective nouns such as *group* or *crowd,* and abstract nouns such as *concern* or *beauty.* Formally, indefinite pronouns have little if anything in common. They are a "leftover" class to which pronouns that fit in no other category are relegated. The general semantic notion that unifies a majority of indefinities is that of "quantity," e.g., *all, many, no,* etc. For this reason, such members of Table 6.5 are sometimes assigned to a separate class called **quantifiers.**

Indefinites have a limited range of functions, acting only as heads or modifiers. The range of individual words is indicated in Table 6.5.

EXERCISE   Select any five indefinites labeled as (1) in Table 6.5. For each, give an example where the pronoun is used (a) as a head and (b) as a modifier.

6.2   WH-WORDS

English contains an important set of words that enter into a wide range of constructions. In traditional grammars, they're called **interrogative** (or **relative**) pronouns. These forms are usually distinguished by the constructions in which they function, but there is little formal reason to separate them. We thus list them as a single group in Table 6.6. We will explain briefly the range of their functions here and go into more detail in later chapters.

TABLE 6.6   Wh-Words

who	whom	which
what	whose	when
where	why	whether
how		

Some of the words in Table 6.6 are traditionally called pronouns. Because of our emphasis on form, we will not use this label. Some of the members of the group function as pronouns in certain constructions but not in others. To call them pronouns on this limited basis confuses form with function.

The label **wh-word** is a mnemonic that clearly applies to all members of the class except *how*. Nevertheless, this form deserves inclusion on the basis of its grammatical behavior.

Wh-words occur in three distinct functions:

1. Introducing information questions
2. Introducing relatives
3. Introducing noun clauses

To illustrate these functions, we will select three wh-words: *who, which,* and *where*. We will also indicate cases where these words can occur as headwords and as modifiers.

An **information question** requests that the hearer respond with some information beyond a mere "yes" or "no." These questions appear with all wh-words. In this role, wh-words are traditionally called **interrogative pronouns**:

[12a]   *Who* invented the telescope? (Head)
  [b]   *Which* do you want? (Head)
  [c]   *Which* donut do you want? (Modifier)
  [d]   *Where* did she find that hat? (Head)

Wh-words also introduce **relative clauses.** In the next chapter, we will see how relative clauses occur as a part of a noun phrase that follows the head noun. Most wh-words can introduce relatives:

[13a]   Anyone [*who* wants a ticket] should call Herman.
  [b]   The book [*which* you requested] is out of print.
  [c]   The locale [*where* the movie is set] is fictional.
  [d]   The person [*who* called you] left no message.

Finally, wh-words serve to introduce **noun clauses**, which are entire clauses that function as if they were noun phrases. (For this reason, the entire clause can often be replaced by a simpler noun phrase or by a pronoun.)

[14a] I don't know [*who* can get you a leash that big].
  [b] Tell me [*which* tranquilizer is the strongest].
  [c] Kong didn't say [*where* he dropped those banana peels].

Among the wh-words we can detect a second gender system at work in English: *who* refers to humans; *which* refers to nonhumans.

EXERCISES
1. Select three wh-words not used in the illustrations above. Provide sentences to show how each word can occur as an interrogative, a relative, or a noun-clause introducer.
2. Which wh-words cannot introduce relative clauses?

6.3. ARTICLES

The last minor class associated with nouns contains only two words: the indefinite article *a(n)* and the definite article *the:*

[15a] a visitor
  [b] the United Nations

Articles always function as modifiers of the head noun in a noun phrase.

While articles are easily recognized and have a single function, their meaning is quite complex. First, they signal **definiteness**. *The* used definitely indicates the assumption that a reader/hearer can identify the entity referred to by the NP. *A(n)* makes the contrary assumption. Contrast [16a] and [16b]:

[16a] I saw the movie. (= hearer knows which one)
  [b] I saw a movie. (= hearer doesn't know which one)

For this reason, the indefinite article is normally used to introduce a new person or topic into a discourse:

[17a] Once upon a time, there was a bear named Grizzwold.
  [b] ?Once upon the time, there was the bear named Grizzwold.

A second meaning associated with articles is that of **referentiality**. A **referring NP** denotes a *particular* entity or set of entities. An **attributive** (nonreferring) NP provides a description but doesn't refer to any particular individual. Anyone or anything that fits the description will do. Attributive NPs can often be paraphrased by *whoever . . . , whatever . . . ,* or *any . . . :*

[18a] I saw the elephants at the zoo. (Referential and Definite)
  [b] The next caller will win a vacation to Miami. (Attributive and Definite: = whoever is the next caller)
  [c] I want an elephant. Its name is Big Bob. (Referential and Indefinite)
  [d] I want an elephant. Any pink one will be fine. (Attributive and Indefinite.)

Finally, articles can have **specific** or **generic** meaning. **Generic** reference designates an entire class (i.e., category, set) of entities. A **specific** reference designates particular members of a class:

[19a] The cat is asleep. (Specific and Definite)
  [b] The cats are asleep. (Specific and Definite)
  [c] Cats are skilled predators. (Generic and Indefinite)
  [d] The cat is a skilled predator. (Generic and Definite)
  [e] A cat is a skilled predator. (Generic and Indefinite)

EXERCISE Identify each italicized expression as (1) definite or indefinite, (2) referential or attributive, and (3) generic or specific. Notice where ambiguities arise.
  a. I need *a sandwich.*
  b. I need *a part for my car.*
  c. Alice appreciates *the elephant.*
  d. *The president's detractors* must be insane.

6.4 AUXILIARY VERBS

In this section, we discuss verb forms that we mentioned in passing in Chapter 5, the **auxiliary verbs**. These forms are never used without a main verb, except elliptically. There are few auxiliaries in the language, but each of them plays several important semantic roles.

6.4.1 Modality and mood

A common, perhaps typical way to express future time in English is to use the auxiliary verb *will: I will leave immediately.* However, the position in the sentence occupied by *will* could be filled with any one of several other modal verbs (*will, would; shall, should; may, might; can, could; must*). We can reasonably view the *-d/t* at the end of the second member of each pair as a variant of the past tense inflection *-ed.* This allows us to view each pair (excluding *must*) as composed of a present and a past tense form.

Besides occupying the same sentential position, these verbs express related concepts. These concepts include notions such as (1) **necessity,** either logical or social: *He must arrive by 10* p.m.; (2) **possibility,** logical or social: *He may leave the room;* (3) **ability:** *He can do long division in his head;* or (4) **intention,** either definite or conditional: *I will/would/shall/ should write another ten pages today.* What these modal concepts all have in common is that they indicate the speaker's judgment or beliefs about the truth of the sentence.

Intimately connected to modal notions are notions of **mood.** Traditional grammarians distinguished four moods: **declarative** (or **indicative**), **interrogative, imperative,** and **subjunctive.** The last of these is only marginally relevant to English, although very important in other languages. These forms indicate what we might call the **interactional force** of the sentence. Traditionally, declarative sentences were viewed as expressing assertions, interrogatives as expressing questions, and imperatives as expressing orders or requests. However, we will use these four terms to distinguish among and identify sentence forms, rather than sentence functions.

In **declarative sentences,** the subject precedes the predicate and any auxiliary verbs it may contain: *John will have to leave early in the morning.*

Interrogative sentences come in two types: **yes-no questions** and **wh-** or **information questions.** In yes-no questions the first auxiliary verb (of the main clause) appears to the left of the subject: *Could I possibly borrow your Maserati to take my poodle to the vet?* In simple wh-questions, the first auxiliary verb appears to the left of the subject, and a wh-word such as *who, when, where,* etc. appears to the left of the auxiliary: *How could he possibly ask such a ridiculous question?*

An **imperative sentence** typically is missing its subject: *Get out!* The missing subject is usually interpreted as *you,* singular or plural.

The typical uses of these sentence types are given in Table 6.7 below.

However, it's important to remember that there is no one-to-one correlation between sentence type or form and the uses to which it may be put. For instance, sentences in declarative form may be used to ask questions; sentences in interrogative form need not be interpreted as asking questions (e.g., rhetorical questions). In this book, when we use the terms declarative, indicative, interrogative, and imperative, we will be referring to sentence forms. When we wish to refer to sentence functions, we will use terms such as those on the right in Table 6.7.

The subjunctive is, as we have mentioned, somewhat marginal in English. It's required to distinguish between the forms in: *I insist that he **leave** tomorrow morning* and *I believe that he **leaves** tomorrow morning.* In the first (subjunctive) sentence, the verb has no ending, whereas in the second, the verb has the ordinary indicative third person ending *-s.* Another

TABLE 6.7   Mood: Typical Form-Function Correspondences

Form	Function
Declarative	asserting
Interrogative	questioning
Imperative	ordering, requesting

context in which third person singular verbs don't have the expected ending is in wishful formulas such as: *Long live the queen.* These too can be viewed as subjunctives.

There are two other sentence types which are frequently categorized as subjunctive. The first involves a contrary-to-fact conditional clause, typically introduced by *if*: *If I were a rich man, ...* When the verb of the if-clause is *be*, it takes the form *were* in the past tense in formal styles. Otherwise (in informal styles, in other tenses, or with other verbs), the verb form is the ordinary indicative: *If I am successful, . . .; If he falls, ...*

The final type of sentence usually categorized as subjunctive expresses wishes such as: *May he rest in peace.* Because these sentences typically include a modal verb such as *may,* they're clearly distinguishable as modal subjunctives. However, the subjunctive category is based on Greek and Latin verbal inflections, and so was a more homogeneous formal category in those languages than it is in English. As learners of French, Spanish, and Italian (as in the example below) know, it's an important inflectional category in those languages, where, just as in modern English, its most usual occurrence is in subordinate complements to certain verbs and other elements such as negation: *Voglio che tu vada (subj.) a casa.* ("I want you to go home.") If the verb in the subordinate clause were in the indicative mood, it would be *vai.*

6.4.2 Aspect

The category of **aspect** allows us to distinguish among the [a], [b], and [c] forms in [20] and between [21a] and [21b]:

[20]   When we arrived,
  [a]   he made sandwiches.
  [b]   he was making sandwiches.
  [c]   he had made sandwiches.
[21a]   He cycled to work.
  [b]   He used to cycle to work.

We will refer to the sentence form illustrated in [20b] as the **progressive aspect.** Characteristically, it consists of a form of the verb *be* followed by a verb ending in *-ing.* Sentences like [20c] are said to be in the **perfect aspect,** characterized by a form of *have* followed by a past participle (verb + *-en*). Sentence [21b] illustrates the **habitual aspect,** indicated by the expression *used to* followed by an infinitival verb. The auxiliaries *be* and *have* of the progressive and perfect aspects can be either past or present tense. These aspects can occur together in sentences:

[22]   He has been making sandwiches for over an hour.
[23]   He used to be writing a book.

Sentence [22] combines perfect and progressive; sentence [23] combines habitual and progressive.

Tenses and modals can also combine with the progressive and perfect aspects. Sentence [24] is past perfect progressive; sentence [25] is present perfect progressive, with a modal:

[24] He had been making sandwiches when we arrived.
[25] He may have been making bombs for all we know.

While tense links the situation represented by a sentence with the time at which it is uttered, aspect represents features of the temporal structure of the situation. The progressive aspect characterizes an event as ongoing, as enduring for a period of time, but which isn't considered permanent, and which may or may not be complete at the end of the period. The perfect indicates that a situation that obtained in the past is still relevant at some later time. If the sentence is a present perfect (e.g., *I have lived here for seven years*), the relevant time is the time of utterance. If the sentence is a past perfect (e.g., *I had met him several times by 1992*), the relevant time is prior to the time of utterance and may be specified by an adverb. *1992* has this function in the current example. The habitual aspect indicates that a situation obtained for such an extended period of time in the past that it can be taken as a characteristic of the entire period. We explore the complexities involved in interpreting these forms in more detail below.

6.4.2.1   Progressive aspect

We begin by illustrating the three features of the interpretation of the progressive aspect. The form indicates that the event is viewed as involving a period rather than merely a point of time:

[26] The jet changed direction.
[27] The jet is changing direction.

The first of these two sentences is neutral as to whether the change of direction is sudden or gradual. The second sentence characterizes the change of direction as taking time. How much time isn't at issue.

The situation represented in the progressive aspect is viewed as temporary rather than permanent, as illustrated in [28] and [29]:

[28] I live with my parents.
[29] I am living with my parents.

The progressive sentence is readily compatible with a continuation like: *while my own house is being rebuilt*. The simple present is not quite so natural with that continuation.

The progressive suggests that the situation it represents is not necessarily complete, as [30] and [31] show:

[30] The man died.
[31] The man was dying.

The latter sentence is compatible with a continuation which indicates that the dying process was never completed: *but we managed to save his life*; the former isn't.

The progressive occurs frequently when one event is represented as occurring during another:

[32]   When the police arrived, the burglar was leaving by the rear window.

It's also interpreted as the repetition of an action when the verb it's associated with is one which represents events as taking only a point of time. Compare the following:

[33]   John is hitting his carpet.
[34]   John is beating his carpet.

Hit is understood as taking only a point of time; *beat* as requiring a period. So the first implies that John repeatedly hits his carpet; the second doesn't necessarily imply repeated beatings, just continuous activity.

The final issue we raise in regard to the progressive is that of the classes of verbs that can occur in this aspect. We noted in Chapter 5 that all verbs except those which refer to states or conditions can appear as progressives. Thus verbs representing events, whether momentary (*hit, wink*), transitional (*arrive, leave*), activity (*drink, type*), or process (*grow, widen*) occur with the progressive. State verbs, which include verbs of inert perception (*hear, see*), of inert cognition (*know, understand*), and of having and being (*be, contain, own*) aren't compatible with the progressive.

There are, however, certain state verbs that appear to be exceptions to this generalization. One can say, for example, *John is being silly*. When we view sentences such as this from the perspective we have developed, we can see that it really isn't particularly exceptional. Compare it to *John is silly*. The latter sentence suggests that silliness is a more or less permanent or typical characteristic of John, whereas the former suggests merely that while John is currently silly, he isn't necessarily typically so. Moreover, if we were to paraphrase the former sentence, we would probably use a verb such as *act: John is acting silly*. So it appears that *be* in this kind of sentence is interpreted as an activity rather than a state verb. We saw this kind of subcategorization of words earlier in our discussion of mass and count nouns.

EXERCISE   For each sentence, indicate the meaning of the progressive by selecting the appropriate choice in parentheses. (One of these sentences raises questions about the generalizations above. Can you find it?)
   a. The plane is taxiing. (raises/doesn't raise the question of whether the action takes time)
   b. I watch television. (is/isn't compatible with continuation "while my clothes are drying")
   c. I was watching television. (is/isn't compatible with continuation "while my clothes were drying")
   d. I am earning $4.75 an hour. (suggests permanence/impermanence)
   e. (1) As the beast advanced, (2) the hikers were planning their escape route. [action of (1) is contained in (2)/action of (2) is contained in (1)]
   f. Sarah was jumping well at the meet. (implies repeated jumping/continuous activity)
   g. You're being a ninny. (implies that you're a temporary/permanent ninny)

6.4.2.2 Perfect aspect

The perfect aspect represents an earlier situation as being relevant at a later time. Situations that continue right up to the time of reference can be viewed in this way:

[35] I have been a taxpayer since 1970.
[36] By 1985 I had been a taxpayer for 15 long years.

In [35], the time of reference is the time at which the sentence is uttered; in [36], it's 1985. Both sentences imply that the condition of being a taxpayer continued up to the reference time.

The situation need not be a state or condition. When the verb represents an event, the sentence may represent a repeated series of events. This usually requires an appropriate adverbial phrase:

[37] We have visited Norway every July for 50 years.

The relevance of the situation represented by the sentence need not be as clear as the continuation of the situation itself. *We have visited Norway* suggests that we made at least one visit during the period leading up to the time of utterance. The situation may also be interpreted as an event which resulted in a state which continued to the time of reference. *The bus has stopped* implies that the bus is now stopped, just as *Mother has arrived* implies that mother is now here.

The relevant time span can also be interpreted as shortly before the reference time, or recently:

[38] I had (just) finished another paper by then.
[39] Have you seen my spectacles (recently)?

EXERCISES 1. Identify what is implied by the use of the perfect in each sentence.
    a. Mary has played tennis for 17 years.
    b. Mary has played tennis.
    c. Mary has just played tennis.
    d. Martin has given a Groundhog Day party for 17 years.
  2. Why is the following interchange odd?

    Zeke: Have you cooked dinner?
    Clem: Yes, about 17 years ago.

(What happens if you add *ever* or *yet* to Zeke's question?)

6.4.2.3 Habitual aspect

The habitual aspect represents states or habits that are characteristic of an entire period. The English habitual with *used to* is generally understood as indicating a situation which obtained in the past: *We used to have five cats; We used to drive to work every morning.* However, these sentences don't strictly entail that these situations no longer hold. We could add to either of these sentences the continuation: . . . *and, in fact, we still do.*

6.4.3 Voice

English, like all languages, provides the means to express essentially the same idea in several distinct ways. In this section, we will discuss two of those ways, traditionally distinguished as the **active voice** (*The president gave this speech before*) and the **passive voice** (*This speech was given by the president before*).

There are certain systematic correspondences and differences between the active and passive forms of a sentence. The passive subject corresponds to the active object, and the active subject corresponds to the phrase governed by *by* in the passive. Whereas the active sentence may contain only a single verb, the passive requires an auxiliary form of *be* followed by the past (or passive) participle form of the main verb (verb + *-en*). These correspondences are shown in Figure 6.1 below.

There are certain restrictions on the relationship between active and passive sentences. For example, in English only transitive verbs have passive forms. Other languages, such as German and Dutch, allow the creation of passive sentences from intransitive verbs, e.g., *Es wurde getanzt* ("There was dancing"; lit. It was danced). Some verbs, even though transitive, may appear only in active sentences:

[40a] He weighs 175 pounds.
  [b] *175 pounds are weighed by him. (Note the change in meaning.)

Other verbs appear only in passive sentences:

[41a] He is rumored to be looking for a new job.
  [b] *They rumor him to be looking for a new job.

The passive allows the entire *by* phrase to be omitted; such structures are said to be **truncated:**

[42] This speech was given before.

Traditionally, active and passive sentences have been understood as distinct perspectives on an event. The active presents the event from the point of view of the agent or doer, whereas the passive presents it from the point of view of an entity affected in the event. This

FIGURE 6.1 Active-Passive Correspondences

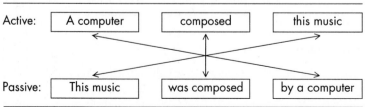

distinction is based on the traditional assumption that subjects represent doers and objects represent affected entities. The difference in perspective has led many commentators and teachers of writing to argue that passive sentences are less vigorous than their active counterparts, and because truncation omits reference to the entity who actually performs in an event or is responsible for it, they argue that passives are more vague and irresponsible than actives. For these and other reasons, they suggest that passives should be used sparingly if at all. The passive has, in fact, occasionally been referred to as an error.

Our view is that both passive and active (and a broad range of other sentence types) allow English users to tailor the form in which an idea is expressed to its specific context. To view passives as errors and to attempt to eliminate them from one's writing is simply to impoverish the resources available to the writer. We will have more to say about the grammar of passives in Chapters 8 and 11 and about their appropriate uses in Chapter 14.

6.5 PREPOSITIONS

Prepositions are important to English because they form phrases that play a wide range of grammatical roles. In other languages—and in earlier stages of English—prepositions may play a less significant role because their jobs are carried out by inflectional endings. Prepositions also express many of the major semantic relations that unite members of a sentence in a meaningful whole. It's thus important for teachers and students to become familiar with the approximately fifty members of this class. The common prepositions appear in Table 6.8.

In spite of the significance of prepositions, standard grammars often assign them a rather vague definition, such as "a word that shows the relation of a noun or pronoun to some other word in a sentence" (Warriner and Griffith, 1965: p. 16). The key word in this definition is "relation." Relations signaled by prepositions, as just noted, are both grammatical (e.g., modifier of noun or verb) and semantic (e.g., recipient, benefactive). This double role of prepositions will often provide important clues to the structure of sentences.

Grammatically, prepositions are formally recognizable by the fact that they're usually followed by a noun phrase:

[43a] *of* my toe
  [b] *to* Tangiers
  [c] *beneath* contempt

TABLE 6.8 Single-Word Prepositions

about	above	across	after	against
along	amid(st)	among	around	astride
at	before	behind	below	beneath
beside(s)	between	beyond	but (= except)	by
concerning	down	during	except	from
in	inside	into	like	of
on	onto	out	outside	over
since	through	throughout	till	to
toward	under	underneath	until	unto
up	upon	with	within	without

Although the majority of prepositions are followed by noun phrases, two apparent exceptions must be noted—questions and wh-clauses:

[44a] What did you call *about?*
  [b] She asked what you called *about.*
  [c] The lamp which you called *about* has been sold.

In these cases, the following NPs (*what* and *which*) have moved elsewhere in the sentence, and in fact, they precede their prepositions. In a sense, the preposition has been abandoned by the following NP; for this reason, we call such a case **preposition stranding**. The stranding of prepositions is sometimes criticized in prescriptive circles, but in many cases, unstranded prepositions sound either stilted or downright ungrammatical:

[45a] About what did you call?
  [b] *She asked about what you called.
  [c] The lamp about which you called has been sold.

Aside from their behavior in such cases, though, prepositions are formally very simple.

In functional terms, a preposition associated with a noun phrase will function as the *head of a prepositional phrase*. Its associated noun phrase will be called the *object of the preposition*.

Before examining the semantics of prepositions, we should mention one further formal complexity—the tendency of prepositions to enter into complex frozen expressions that resemble idioms; such cases appear in Table 6.9.

The structure of these multiword prepositions falls into two patterns: (1) preposition + noun + preposition (P + N + P; e.g., *by means of, in case of*) and (2) miscellaneous word + preposition (X + P; e.g., *according to, because of*). It would, of course, be possible to view such expressions, particularly the P + N + P type, as simply combinations of two prepositional phrases; however, most speakers perceive them as a logical unity. We will not take a hard-and-fast position on this issue, but simply note, as do most grammars, the presence of such constructions.

TABLE 6.9 Multiword Prepositions

according to	along with
apart from	as for
as to	because of
by dint of	by means of
by reason of	by virtue of
by way of	except for
in accord(ance) with	in addition to
in case of	in compliance with
in consequence of	in consideration of
in opposition to	in place of
in regard to	inside of
in spite of	instead of
on account of	out of
round about	with reference to
with regard to	with respect to

EXERCISE   Consider the following expressions. In each group, where would you draw a line between an idiomatic multiword preposition and a series of two prepositional phrases? On what grounds would you draw your line?
a. on behalf of
b. on account of
c. on grounds of
d. on the grounds of
e. on the face of (two meanings)
f. *on the behalf of
g. *on the account of
h. *on face of

The semantics of prepositions covers a wide range of meanings. Traditional categories, along with some typical examples, are given in Table 6.10 below.

The most obvious feature of prepositions is the variety of lexical meanings that many of them can have. What meanings of *around* and *beneath* occur in sentences [46] and [47]?

[46a]   They walked *around* the statue.
  [b]   I'll return *around* 5:00.
[47a]   Horace stood *beneath* the Balancing Rock.
  [b]   Horace is *beneath* contempt.

This variety of meanings sometimes creates confusion for students, particularly those who simplistically associate certain structures with prepositions. For instance, the indirect object construction is sometimes associated with paraphrases using the prepositions *to* and *for*. However, this semantic relation emerges only when *to* has a recipient meaning and *for* has a beneficiary meaning. In other words, the sentences in [48a] and [48b] can be rephrased as sentences with indirect objects [48c] and [48d]; those in [49a] and [49b] cannot, as shown by the ungrammaticality of [49c] and [49d]:

[48a]   I offered a dozen widgets to Hickle.
  [b]   I made an artificial earlobe for Hickle.
  [c]   I offered Hickle a dozen widgets.
  [d]   I made Hickle an artificial earlobe.

TABLE 6.10   Semantic Types of Prepositions

Place (Locative):	above, around, at, behind, beneath, between
Time (Temporal):	about, after, at, during, for, since
Manner:	with (exit *with a flourish*)
Accompaniment:	with (went *with Flora*)
Instrument (Means):	by, with (open it *with a knife*)
Recipient:	to (gave it *to Lucy*)
Beneficiary:	for (did it *for Lucy*)
Miscellaneous:	of, about, but, like, without

[49a] I sent Hickle to the lake.
  [b] I made an artificial earlobe for $3000.
  [c] *I sent the lake Hickle.
  [d] *I made $3000 an artificial earlobe.

Two other potential problems for students derive from the ability of many of these words to occur as **particles** [50a] and as modifiers of verbs [50b]:

[50a] I called my sister up.
  [b] I looked up.

In the Introduction to Part Two, we pondered some of the complexities of the word *down*. The sentences that we examined are repeated below for ease of reference:

[51a] I fell down the hill.
  [b] I cut down the tree.
  [c] I cut the tree down.
  [d] *I fell the hill down.

In both [51a] and [51b] *down* appears before the NP. However, in [51c], *down* appears after the NP, even though in [51d] it cannot. This difference in behavior suggests that *down* may represent two different parts of speech in these sentences. Semantically, we sense an idiomatic unity in *cut down* that we don't sense in *fell down*. In fact, *cut down* could be replaced by one word: *toppled* or *felled*. On formal and semantic grounds, then, *down* seems to represent different parts of speech [51a] and [51b]. Our tests show *down* in [51a] behaving like a typical preposition. For *down* in [51b], we have no ready-made traditional label. In such sentences, we will call it a **particle**, using a term recently adopted by linguists.
Next, consider the word *down* in the sentences below:

[52a] I fell down the hill.
  [b] I fell down.

Assuming in [52a] that *down* is a true preposition, we note in [52b] that formally *down* is neither followed by a noun phrase nor has been stranded since no noun phrase that could be construed as its object occurs elsewhere in the sentence. Moreover, we don't infer in [52b] that I fell down some inclined place—any more than we understand that some object did or didn't cause me to fall. Since we cannot apply any test of movability to the right that helped us to identify particles, we have no justification for calling *down* in [52b] a particle. Must we then invent a new part of speech? The answer is *yes*—unless we can fit the word into some other existing part of speech. Can you think of a candidate for the word *down*? Consider sentences [53a] to [53d]:

[53a] Harriet visited often.
  [b] Often, Harriet visited.
  [c] I fell down.
  [d] Down I fell.

These sentences provide evidence that *down* in [52b] and [53c] is an adverb since it answers to criterion 11b, that of relative movability. In practice, we would like to have more support of our analysis than this, but sometimes we don't have that luxury.

We should note, however, the semantic motivation for the tendency of prepositions to blend with adverbs. If you turn back to our discussion of adverbs, you will notice that the meanings expressed by adverbs (e.g., time, place, and manner) partially coincide with those of prepositions. This tendency for parts of speech to overlap in meaning is just one more reason to prefer an analysis that separates them on the basis of form.

6.6 INTENSIFIERS

Our earlier discussion of adjectives and adverbs made reference to a class of words specifically associated with them. This class includes words like *more, most, very, quite, rather, somewhat,* and a few others. Traditional grammars often call such words *degree adverbs,* as if they were ordinary adverbs—like *extremely* and *thoroughly*—that happen to indicate the meaning of degree. If you consider the criteria for adverbs that we suggested earlier, you will quickly realize that the words we have listed as intensifiers—even though they do indicate degree—don't share the formal characteristics of adverbs. For instance, intensifiers cannot occur in the comparative or superlative constructions; nor can they be preceded by each other:

[54a] *morer
　[b] *mostest
　[c] *more quite
　[d] *most rather
　[e] *very quite
　[f] *rather very

In contrast, standard degree adverbs (e.g., *extremely* and *thoroughly*) do admit these possibilities:

[55a] more extremely
　[b] very extremely
　[c] very thoroughly
　[d] rather thoroughly
　[e] extremely thoroughly

We will thus refer to the members of this small class of words as **intensifiers** rather than as adverbs.

6.7 CONJUNCTIONS

The word **conjunction** indicates the major role of these words, namely, to join (*junction*) together (*con-*) two or more grammatical elements—called **conjuncts.** The difference between **coordinating** and **subordinating conjunctions** reflects the differing grammatical status of the conjuncts that are united.

6.7.1 Coordinating conjunctions

The major one- and two-word **coordinating conjunctions** appear in Table 6.11. Since multiword coordinators require their members to align themselves (relate together) with their conjuncts, they're often called **correlative conjunctions**:

[56a] Jack *and* Jill ran up the hill. (Single)
  [b]   *Both* Jack *and* Jill ran up the hill. (Correlative)

TABLE 6.11 Coordinating Conjunctions

Single-word Coordinating Conjunctions

and	for
but	so
or	nor

Multiword Coordinating Conjunctions
(Correlative)
both . . . and
not only . . . but (also)
either . . . or
whether . . . or
neither . . . nor

The units connected by coordinators may be of any size—word, phrase, clause, or sentence. We show some typical instances below.

Two words

[57a] Tarzan and Jane [got married] (Nouns)
  [b]   wrote and sang [the song] (Verbs)
  [c]   can and will (Modals)
  [d]   eager and willing (Adjectives)
  [e]   wildly and frantically (Adverbs)
  [f]   he and she (Personal Pronouns)
  [g]   this and that (Demonstrative pronouns)
  [h]   any and all (Indefinites)
  [i]   who and why (Wh-words)
  [j]   in and about (Prepositions)

Two phrases

[58a]   many readers and some literary critics (Noun Phrases)
   [b]   may disagree and often have disagreed (Verb Phrases)
   [c]   extremely old and completely dilapidated (Adjective Phrases)
   [d]   very boldly and amazingly often (Adverbial Phrases)
   [e]   of the people and for the people (Prepositional Phrases)

Two clauses

[59a]   who comes early and who brings a camera (Relative Clauses)
   [b]   that I am right and that you are wrong (Noun Clauses)
   [c]   after the game ended and before the cleanup crew arrived (Adverbial Clauses)

Two sentences

[60]   Lou admitted his mistake and Bud forgave him.

Generally, the two conjuncts will be of the same type (i.e., noun and noun, verb phrase and verb phrase, relative clause and relative clause). However, in some instances, formally unlike structures may be conjoined, as in [61].

[61]   quietly and without leaving a trace (Adverb and Prepositional Phrase)

Such cases are relatively uncommon; moreover, the two unlike conjuncts must be functionally and semantically similar. (Thus sentence [61] conjoins two modifiers that indicate Manner.)

Apparent cases where coordinators appear to connect unlike units arise when ellipsis occurs, as in [62]:

[62]   Lou admitted his mistake, but Bud didn't (do so).

In such examples, however, the difference in conjuncts is illusory, for the second conjunct can be reconstructed as a structure formally comparable to the first, as sentence [63] indicates:

[63]   Lou admitted his mistake but Bud didn't admit his mistake.

6.7.2   Subordinating conjunctions

Subordinating conjunctions, as the name suggests, differ from coordinators by connecting structures of unequal grammatical status. In subordination, one of the structures is grammatically superior or dominant, and the other is grammatically inferior or subordinate.

In every case, the subordinate structure is the one introduced by the subordinating conjunction.

A second difference between coordinating and subordinating conjunctions is that the latter have a restricted range, being able to connect *clauses only*. Thus a structure introduced by a subordinating conjunction will be a subordinate clause. (It's possible, of course, for one clause to be subordinate to a clause that is itself subordinate, but we will not concern ourselves with this complication here.)

We will investigate subordinate clauses more fully in Chapter 10. For the moment, we will simply mention the three types of subordinate clauses and identify the conjunctions that may introduce them.

The three main types of subordinate clauses are **adverbial, nominal,** and **relative**.

6.7.2.1   Adverbial conjunctions

Adverbial clauses, as adverbs often do, function as modifiers of verbs or sentences. They're introduced by a group of words that we will call **subordinating adverbial conjunctions (SACs).** Table 6.12 lists the main SACs.

Table 6.12 groups SACs semantically, in a way that makes clear their overlap with adverbs. As we have just seen, prepositions also overlap with adverbs; so it should come as no surprise that prepositions have affinities with SACs. These affinities are more than semantic. Several items of Table 6.12 also appear on the list of prepositions (Table 6.8). Because of this overlap, students may experience difficulties in telling a preposition from a SAC—and a prepositional phrase from an adverbial clause. A simple way to keep the two clear is to remember that a preposition only occurs in construction with a following noun phrase. Let's consider an example:

[64a]   I left after the party.
 [b]   I left after the party was over.

In [64a], *after* is followed only by a noun phrase (*the party*), and so must be a preposition. In [64b], it's followed by both a noun phrase (*the party*) and a verb phrase (*is over*) that

TABLE 6.12   Subordinating Adverbial Conjunctions

Time:	after, as, as long as, as soon as, before, just as, now that, since, until, till, when, whenever, while
Place:	where, wherever
Manner:	as, as if, as though
Reason or cause:	as, because, inasmuch as, since
Result:	so . . . that, so that, such . . . that
Comparison:	as, as . . . as, just as, so . . . as, than
Purpose:	in order that, lest, so, so that, that
Condition:	as long as, if, on (the) condition that, provided, provided that, unless
Concession:	although, even if, even though, though, whereas, while

together constitute a clause; this *after* is a SAC. We can confirm our formal analysis further by moving the group of words *after the party:*

[65a] After the party, I left.
  [b] *After the party, I left was over.

Since phrases often move as a unit, the prepositional phrase in [64a] can be relocated at the front of the sentence, as in [65a]. But in [64b], *after the party* cannot be moved, as [65b] shows. Thus it must not be a complete phrase. In fact, the real unified structure in [64b] is *after the party was over,* as sentence [66] shows:

[66] After the party was over, I left.

6.7.2.2 Nominal conjunctions

Nominal clauses function as noun phrases typically function—i.e., as subjects, objects, and complements. When they do so, they will be introduced by a certain set of subordinating conjunctions. That set of conjunctions includes most of the wh-words listed in Table 6.6 along with the word *that.* Thus once you know the wh-words, you don't need to learn a separate list of nominal subordinating conjunctions. To illustrate, note the sentences in [67]:

[67a] I don't know [*who(m)* I should call].
  [b] [*What* you don't know] might hurt you.
  [c] [*Why* Zangooli fled] isn't clear.
  [d] I suspect [*that* he was wanted by the police].

To assure yourself that the clauses truly have a nominal function, replace them with the pronouns *it* or *that.*

6.7.2.3 Relative conjunctions

Relative clauses function as modifiers of the nouns that they follow. Typically, they're introduced by members of the wh-word class, discussed above (traditionally called **relative pronouns**), and by the word *that.* Examples of relative structures appear below:

[68a] Anyone [*who* knows the answer] will receive a prize.
  [b] The cat [*that* caught the mouse] was jubilant.
  [c] The reason [*why* she left] wasn't clear.
  [d] I anticipate the day [*when* the world will be at peace].

6.7.2.4 Complexities of subordinating conjunctions

Subordinating conjunctions have several properties that make them more complicated than this basic presentation suggests. One that deserves mention is the tendency of subordinating conjunctions to be omitted from sentences where their presence is easily inferred. Examples from each type occur in [69].

[69a]   I am so tired [. . . . I could sleep on a bed of nails].
        (SAC: *that*)
  [b]   Everyone said [. . . . they had a good time].
        (Nominal: *that*)
  [c]   The reason [. . . . she left] wasn't clear.
        (Relative: *why*)

6.7.2.5   A note on the word *that*

Grammatically, *that* is particularly troublesome in English, largely because it belongs to at least four different parts of speech. First, it can be a demonstrative pronoun that functions as either a modifier (e.g., **That** *answer is correct*) or the head of a noun phrase (e.g., **That** *is correct*). Second, it can introduce a relative clause (e.g., *The answer* **that** *she gave was correct*). Third, *that* can act as a noun clause connector (e.g., *I said* **that** *the answer was correct*). Fourth, it can appear as part of a subordinating adverbial conjunction indicating either result or purpose. (For example, *The answer was so persuasive* **that** *it astounded us all. The answer was phrased so* **that** *it would confuse everyone.*)

So, how can you determine which class *that* belongs to in a particular sentence? One useful test is that of substitution. If you can substitute *it* for *that,* you have a headword demonstrative; if you can substitute *the,* you have a modifying demonstrative; if you can substitute *who* or *which* for *that,* it introduces a relative clause. If you cannot make any of these replacements, you have either a noun-clause connector or a SAC. Distinguishing the SAC is very simple since it occurs normally with the word *so* either next to it or nearby.

6.8   OTHER MINOR PARTS OF SPEECH

While our catalog of parts of speech includes nearly all words in English, we should ask whether other categories might be identified. There is no reason in principle to believe that we have discovered all the parts of speech, any more than to believe that we have discovered all the moons of Saturn. Certainly, we would expect to find other parts of speech if we dealt with languages other than English. Japanese, for instance, has words similar to our prepositions, except that they follow rather than precede their associated noun phrases. Thus English *of a book* would be rendered in Japanese as *hon ni* (lit. *book of*). Because of their position in relation to their nouns, these Japanese words are often called **postpositions.**

Those familiar with traditional grammar will also recall one part of speech that we haven't mentioned, the **interjection.** This class includes words such as *shucks, darn, gee, wow,* and a host of saltier expressions. Usually, a grammar will list the tamer interjections and let the matter drop.

Interjections have some interesting grammatical properties. First, they aren't grammatically connected to other sentence parts, and consequently, are typically separated from the remainder of the sentence by commas. They typically indicate speakers' attitudes or feelings about what they're expressing (e.g., *Well, our budget deficit isn't as large as that of the Evil Empire*).

Individual expressions also have certain unusual properties. *Darn,* for example, enters into a variety of constructions:

[70a]   Darn it!
  [b]   That darn cat!
  [c]   I don't give a darn.

In [70a], *darn* seems to act like a verb expressing a wish of damnation (*darn,* of course, is a euphemism for *damn*). However, such literal meanings are rarely intended since even atheists can use such expressions. In [70b], *darn* seems to modify *cat,* although it isn't an adjective by formal criteria: **That darner cat, *that darnest cat, *that very darn cat.* Sentence [70c] suggests that *darn* could be a noun, although unfortunately we are unable to give more than one of them: No matter how bad things get, the word cannot be pluralized.

Aside from interjections, we have already seen one important way in which new parts of speech may emerge. That is, they may be distinguished from other classes of which they were thought to be normal members. For instance, we separated intensifiers from the category of adverbs and particles from prepositions. In highlighting a group of words, the grammarian attempts to direct our attention to a set of formal, functional, or semantic similarities and differences. As a result, some categories will be particular to a specific analysis rather than to English grammar in general. The practice of reclassifying words is, in fact, relatively common, especially as one discovers more about language. Studying parts of speech mirrors the study of ecological characteristics of plants and animals in nature, so it shouldn't be surprising that, as we learn more about a particular species, we discover unexpected similarities between it and other apparently unrelated species. Thus, if prepositions and adverbs aren't as distinct as we once thought, our discovery of this fact derives from our closer observation of their verbal ecology.

REFERENCES AND RESOURCES

Celce-Murcia, Marianne, and Diane Larsen-Freeman. 1983. *The Grammar Book: An ESL/EFL Teacher's Course.* Rowley, MA: Newbury House Publishers, Inc.

Fries, Charles Carpenter. 1940. *American English Grammar.* New York: Appleton-Century-Crofts, Inc.

———. 1952. *The Structure of English.* New York: Harcourt, Brace & World, Inc.

Hamilton, Edith. 1940. *Mythology.* Boston: Little, Brown & Company.

Jackson, Howard. 1990. *Grammar and Meaning.* London: Longman.

Quirk, Randolph, Sidney Greenbaum, Geoffrey Leech, and Jan Svartik. 1972. *A Grammar of Contemporary English.* New York: Seminar Press.

Quirk, Randolph, and Sidney Greenbaum. 1973. *A Concise Grammar of Contemporary English.* New York: Harcourt Brace Jovanovich, Inc.

Radford, Andrew. 1988. *Transformational Grammar.* Cambridge: Cambridge University Press.

Sledd, James. 1959. *A Short Introduction to English Grammar.* Glenview, IL: Scott, Foresman and Company.

Warriner, John E., and Francis Griffith. 1965 (1951). *English Grammar and Composition: Complete Course.* Revised ed. New York: Harcourt, Brace & World, Inc.

GLOSSARY

Accusative (also called **"objective"**): a case of nouns associated with functions of direct object and object of a preposition.

Active: a voice of a verb phrase, expressed without *be* + Ven. See **passive.**

Adverbial clause: a clause that begins with a subordinating adverbial conjunction and typically modifies a verb or an entire sentence.

Antecedent: see Chapter 2.

Aspect: a category of a verb phrase signaled by inflection, auxiliary verbs, and other constructions; e.g., progressive, perfect, habitual.

Attributive noun phrase: an NP that provides a description but doesn't refer to any particular individual. See **referring noun phrase.**

Case form: one of the inflectional variants of a noun, pronoun, adjective, or (in some languages) article.

Common case: the uninflected form of English nouns found in subject and object functions.

Conjunct: a grammatical element connected by a coordinating or subordinating conjunction to another grammatical element.

Conjunction: a function word that joins grammatical elements as either coordinate to each other or one subordinate to the other.

Content word: see Chapter 5.

Coordinating conjunction: a function word such as *and, but, or,* etc. that connects elements as grammatically equal. See **subordinating conjunction.**

Coreference: the property of noun phrases denoting the same entity; applied to a pronoun and its antecedent or to two noun phrases.

Correlative conjunction: a multiple-word coordinating conjunction; e.g., *both . . . and, either . . . or.*

Declarative (also called **"indicative"**): in traditional grammar, the mood of a sentence used to make an assertion.

Definiteness: the property of some NPs (and the (pro)nouns and articles they contain), which denote a speaker's assumption that their referent can be identified. See **indefiniteness.**

Degree adverb: see **intensifier.**

Deictic: see Chapter 2.

Demonstrative: the deictic words *this, that, these,* and *those.*

Function words (also called **"structure words"**): words such as prepositions, auxiliaries, and articles that are used frequently in a language to signal recurrent semantic and grammatical information.

Gender: the linguistic category distinguishing entities as masculine, feminine, and neuter; signaled by pronouns and suffixes. Languages other than English may signal gender by adjective inflection, articles, verb agreement, etc.

Generic: the property of an article whereby it designates an entire class. See **specific.**

Generic pronoun: a pronoun that makes no gender distinction; e.g., *one.*

Genitive: the case of nouns signaled by *'s* and *s'*.

Genitive pronoun: a pronoun of the form *my, our, your, his, her, its, their,* etc., which modifies a noun.

Grammatical gender: gender assigned to words on the basis of formal linguistic criteria. See **gender, natural gender.**

Imperative: in traditional grammar, the mood of a sentence used to give a command.

Indefiniteness: the property of some NPs (and the (pro)nouns and articles they contain), which denote a speaker's assumption that their referent cannot be specifically identified. See **definiteness.**

Indicative: see **declarative.**

Information question: a question, introduced by a wh-word, requesting information rather than a yes-no response. See **yes-no question.**

Intensifier: a function word (typically, *more, most, very, quite, rather,* and *somewhat*) used to modify an adjective or an adverb.

Intensive pronoun: a pronoun ending in *-self* or *-selves* that ordinarily occurs within the noun phrase of its antecedent, following and modifying the antecedent directly; e.g., *I* **myself** *did it.* See **reflexive pronoun.**

Interactional force: the function of a sentence in a discourse to make assertions, ask questions, express orders, etc.

Interjection: a word, often not grammatically integrated with a sentence, that expresses an emotional response of the speaker; e.g., *Ouch!, Wow!*

Interrogative: in traditional grammar, the mood of a sentence used to ask a question.

Interrogative pronoun: a wh-word used in a sentence to ask a question.

Mood: in traditional grammar, the category indicating whether a sentence makes an assertion, asks a question, expresses an order, etc.

Natural gender: gender assigned to a word on the basis of biological characteristics of the object it refers to. See **gender, grammatical gender.**

Nominal clause (also called "**noun clause**"): a subordinate clause that functions as subject, object, or complement. See **adverbial clause** and **relative clause.**

Nominative: the case associated with the subject function.

Noun phrase: see Chapter 5.

Noun clause: see **nominal clause.**

Objective: see **accusative.**

Particle: a function word closely associated with a verb but separable from it; e.g., *call* **up** *my sister/call my sister* **up.**

Passive: a voice of a verb phrase, expressed by the form *be* + Ven.

Perfect: an aspect of a verb phrase, expressed by *have* + Ven.

Person: grammatical category distinguishing the speaker (first person), addressee (second person), and entity spoken about (third person).

Possessive: see **genitive.**

Possessive adjective: in traditional grammar, a term used for pronouns such as *my* that modify nouns.

Possessive pronoun: a pronoun such as *mine* that replaces a noun phrase. See **genitive pronoun, pronoun.**

Postposition: a word analogous to a preposition, but appearing after its object NP; appears in Japanese and Old English, but not in modern English.

Power: see Chapter 13.

Preposition: a function word that serves as the head of a prepositional phrase; e.g., *in, on, with, of.*

Preposition stranding: ending a clause or sentence with a preposition whose object has been moved.

Prepositional phrase: a phrase that consists of a preposition and a noun phrase. See Chapter 7.

Progressive: an aspect of a verb phrase signaled by *be* + Ving.

Pronoun: a word (e.g., *he, she, it*) that replaces a noun phrase, representing such grammatical categories as person, number, gender, and case.

Quantifier: see Chapter 2.

Referring noun phrase: an NP that denotes a particular entity or set of entities. See **attributive noun phrase.**

Reference: see Chapter 2.

Reflexive pronoun: a pronoun ending in *-self* or *-selves* that functions as the head of an NP; e.g., *I hurt* **myself.** See **intensive pronoun.**

Relative clause: a subordinate clause that follows and modifies a head noun; often introduced by a wh-word or *that.* See Chapter 10.

Relative pronoun: in traditional grammar, a wh-word or *that* introducing a relative clause.

Solidarity: see Chapter 13.

Specific: the property of articles whereby they designate particular members of a class. See **generic.**

Structure words: see **function words.**

Subjunctive: in traditional grammar, the mood of a sentence used to indicate wishes, contrary-to-fact conditions, probability, possibility, etc.

Subordinating conjunction: a function word such as *if, when, because, that, who,* etc. that connects two clauses, making one of secondary grammatical status, specifically a modifier or a complement.

Subordinating adverbial conjunction: a conjunction such as *when, if, because,* etc. that introduces a subordinate adverbial clause.

Truncated passive: a passive sentence without a *by*-phrase.

Wh-question (also called "**information question**"): a question that begins with a wh-word and asks for some sort of information as a response. See **yes-no question.**

Wh-word: a function word such as *who, why, which* that introduces questions, relative clauses, and nominal clauses.

Yes-no question: a question that can be appropriately answered with *yes* or *no.* See **wh-question.**

7 PHRASES

7.0 FROM WORDS TO PHRASES

You have probably noticed that our discussion of parts of speech in the last chapter led us to consider phrasal categories. Although traditional grammars often treat word classes apart from their role in larger structures, it's really not possible to do so. For one thing, we cannot study a word's functions without viewing it in a larger setting. Another reason is that single words can make up phrases. For instance, a noun phrase can contain a single noun—its head. Likewise, a verb phrase can contain a single verb.

The word "syntax," in its root sense, means "arranging together." The *-tax* root is the same one as in *tactics*. *Syn* means "with" or "together." Syntax concerns the combining of words into phrases and sentences. In identifying parts of speech, we are really abstracting from observations made about words in sentences. Nearly all dictionaries specify whether a word is a verb, a noun, a preposition, etc. But lexicographers (those who write dictionaries) make their identifications largely by examining words in sentence contexts according to the principles developed in the previous two chapters.

As we examine phrases, then, we begin the study of how words relate to each other syntactically in larger structures. In later chapters, we will examine the ways in which phrases form clauses and clauses form sentences. Our discussion will treat the five major types of phrase in English:

1. Noun Phrase (NP)
2. Verb Phrase (VP)
3. Adjective Phrase (AP)
4. Adverb Phrase (AdvP)
5. Prepositional Phrase (PP)

We will discuss each of the five types in a similar way. First, we will examine their basic structure; then, where appropriate, we will explore some of the complexities associated with the phrase. Whenever such complexities lead us to topics considered in a later chapter, we will provide a brief commentary and then defer fuller treatment to the later time.

Our distinction of form, function, and meaning will continue to apply. As will become clear, phrases are most simply summarized in functional terms. Using a functional formula as a base, we will illustrate the range of formal items (primarily the parts of speech) that can satisfy these functions. Thus, where form dominated the previous chapter, the role of function will now come into balance. This balance is possible only because of our insistence on the prior importance of form in identifying parts of speech.

7.1   DEFINITION OF *PHRASE*

The traditional definition of a **phrase** calls it "a group of words that does not contain a verb and its subject and is used as a single part of speech."

This definition contains three defining characteristics: (1) a group of words, (2) the lack of a subject and predicate, and (3) its use as a single part of speech. Our treatment of the phrase differs from the traditional one. To see why we need to alter the definition, let's consider it in more detail.

Provision 2 of the definition is designed to distinguish phrases from clauses. (A clause has both a subject and a predicate.) This stipulation, while useful, does lapse into circularity by defining phrases and clauses in terms of each other. We will try to identify phrases without appealing crucially to larger structures.

Provisions 1 and 3 of the definition present an apparent paradox: A phrase is more than one word that behaves as if it were one word. The idea is fairly simple. We can observe sentences of two words, such as [1]:

[1]   Birds fly.

The single word *birds* can be replaced by a group of words such as *most of the members of the genus avis* without making any change in the grammar of the rest of the sentence:

[2]   Most of the members of the genus avis fly.

So, in spite of the different numbers of words, *birds* and its verbose paraphrase can be used alike. The term *use* should alert us to a key syntactic notion—that of **function.** Our definition, then, suggests that single words and certain groups of words function alike. In the examples, both units function as the subject of the sentence. So we might say that a subject can consist of either a noun or a phrase equivalent to a noun—i.e., a **noun phrase (NP).** If we were to examine other functions, we would be led to say that functions such as direct objects, indirect objects, and objects of prepositions contain either single nouns or noun phrases.

While the definition thus captures an essential property of nouns and noun phrases, there is one flaw: It's redundant. It turns out that nearly any time we use the term "noun phrase" in syntax, we will need to add the provision that a single noun will do as well. That is, anything a noun phrase can do, a single noun can do. To remove the need for repetition of this fact, we made in the last chapter one simple change in the definition of a noun phrase:

A noun phrase includes either a single noun or a group of words that functions like a single noun. In other words, a noun phrase can be one word long.

We will extend this discussion to all phrases and make the following assumption: *Any phrase may be* one or more *words long*. In this way, we can dismiss provision 1 from the traditional definition. This practice is common in contemporary syntax. Doing so makes the study of grammar simpler, although it can confuse students who aren't aware of the practice.

One consequence of our change is that it appears to make any single word into a phrase and thus to destroy the distinction between words and phrases that the traditional definition maintains clearly. In fact, this problem doesn't arise, for we will define only five phrase types in the language, each of which will have only a certain range of parts of speech that normally function as phrasal heads.

Moreover, the traditional distinction between word and phrase is, as we have shown for noun phrases, artificially rigid. So another reason for relating words and phrases is that we can now speak of a word such as *cabbage* as either a noun or a noun phrase. This flexibility is sometimes useful:

[3a] Fooster ate cabbage.
  [b] Fooster ate the cabbage.

One of our tests for a noun phrase is that it can be replaced by a pronoun. Sentences [3c] and [3d] illustrate that in [3a] *cabbage* is a noun phrase, but in [3b] it isn't:

[3c] Fooster ate it.
  [d] *Fooster ate the it.

What is the noun phrase in [3b]? The replacement test shows that it's *the cabbage*:

[3e] Fooster ate it. *(it = the cabbage)*

So the noun *cabbage* is both a noun and a noun phrase in [3a]; in [3b], it's only a (head) noun—not a noun phrase.

In considering word classes, we examined the most important ones first. In this chapter, we will present the three *least* important types first—prepositional, adjective, and adverb. The reason for this seemingly backwards approach is that the two major phrase types—noun phrases and verb phrases—often include the minor types as subparts.

7.2 THE PREPOSITIONAL PHRASE (PP)

The functional formula for a prepositional phrase is:

[4] Head + Object

The formal version of the PP is equally simple:

[5] Preposition + Noun Phrase

A **Prepositional Phrase (PP)** consists of a preposition followed by a noun phrase. Noun phrases are discussed in more detail later in this chapter. All you really need to know now is the list of single- and multiword prepositions presented in the last chapter. Prepositional phrases are relatively uniform constructions: Spot a preposition and the NP that immediately follows it and you're on fairly certain ground. However, you should recall that some apparent prepositions are actually particles and that others may be subordinating adverbial conjunctions. Examples of typical prepositional phrases appear below:

[6a] on the waterfront
  [b] of human bondage
  [c] with malice toward none
  [d] beyond the blue horizon
  [e] from the halls of Montezuma

It may seem odd to treat a preposition as the head of a phrase, but traditional grammar may have persuaded us to regard the preposition as insignificant. In fact, prepositions express meanings that encompass the entire range of key semantic relations in a sentence. Another sign of the importance of prepositional phrases is their ability to appear in so many structures—e.g., within noun phrases, verb phrases, and adjective phrases.

The second part of the PP is its **object,** a noun phrase. This terminology also suggests the central role of the preposition within its phrase. Just as verbs govern direct and indirect object NPs, prepositions also take object NPs.

EXERCISES   1. In the sentences below, draw brackets around the prepositional phrases. Circle each preposition and underline its NP object. Be sure to note where PPs contain other (embedded) PPs. Can prepositions take objects besides NPs?
   a. I put the dynamite in a safe place.
   b. In Warden's house, smoking isn't allowed.
   c. I thank you from the bottom of my heart.
   d. After all of his warnings about the dangers of smoking, Benjy consumed a cut of meat loaded with an exorbitant amount of cholesterol.
   e. Oscar resigned in the face of increasing evidence of his association with companies dealing in stocks acquired through questionable means.
   f. Hilary peeked from behind a tree.
   2. From the discussion above, identify the ideas that show how a preposition is the head of its phrase. Consider also how the following sentences add further support for this claim:
   a. Sheila hit the ball almost into the parking lot.
   b. Werner spilled oil all over his new jacket.

Try to think of other sentences similar to these. How do they call for a revision of our functional and formal formulas for PPs?

7.3   THE ADJECTIVE PHRASE (AP)

In keeping with our definition of a phrase, the headword of an **Adjective Phrase (AP)** is an adjective. An AP often contains only a single word, the head adjective; but the complete functional possibilities are more extensive:

[7]   (Intensifier) + Head + (Complement)

Let's consider each possibility (APs are italicized):

[8a]   *impertinent* questions (Head alone)
 [b]   *very impertinent* questions (Intensifier + Head)
 [c]   *unaware of any wrongdoing* (Head + Complement)
 [d]   *unaware that everyone had confessed* (Head + Complement)
 [e]   *afraid to make any move* (Head + Complement)
 [f]   *quite unaware of any wrongdoing* (Intensifier + Head + Complement)

The head alone possibility [8a] occurs when an adjective appears alone in any of its functions. According to our notion of phrases, this form is both an adjective and an adjective phrase.

The intensifier function can be played by formal **intensifiers** and by **degree adverbs** (see Chapter 6). Table 7.1 lists some illustrative forms.

TABLE 7.1   Typical Intensifiers and Degree Adverbs

very	somewhat
quite	reasonably
rather	particularly
too	extremely
more	terrifically
most	unbelievably
only	extraordinarily

Complements of adjectives are of three formal types: prepositional phrases [8c] and [8f]; noun clauses [8d]—clauses beginning with the conjunction *that;* and infinitive verbal phrases [8e]—verbal phrases beginning with *to.* In other words, an adjective phrase doesn't always end with the head adjective; it may contain further grammatical structure. As you become more acquainted with adjectives, you will realize that only some adjectives take complements—particularly those that semantically refer to mental or emotional states, e.g., *aware, afraid, sorry, disappointed, astonished, hopeful, sad.*

EXERCISE   Draw brackets around each AP, then underline the head adjective. Don't forget to use formal criteria to check that the word you underline actually is an adjective.
a. All of the seriously undernourished animals were isolated.
b. I was very impressed with your presentation.

c. Mindy was completely unaware of his ability to dance.
d. The reasons for his sudden resignation eluded even the most astute observers in the company.
e. Afraid of hand-to-hand combat, Reginald purchased a large squirt gun.

7.4   THE ADVERB PHRASE (AdvP)

Phrases with adverbs as headwords, **Adverb Phrases (AdvPs)**, contain a head adverb and an (optional) intensifier drawn from the same limited class illustrated in Table 7.1.
    The functional formula is thus:

[9]   (Intensifier) + Head

Examples are as follows:

[10a]   quickly (Head alone)
   [b]   very quickly (Intensifier + Head)

As we noted for single adverbs (i.e., adverb phrases with head alone), adverb phrases are relatively movable within a sentence.

EXERCISE   Draw brackets around each adverbial phrase in the sentences below. Then underline the head adverb. Some sentences will raise problems. Try to explain what the problems are and to resolve them by formal criteria.
a. They surrendered peacefully.
b. Quite often, I go to movies by myself.
c. Esmiralda acted awfully strangely.
d. Slowly but surely, we edged down the mountain.
e. She somewhat reluctantly returned home a week early.
f. They went along reluctantly.

7.5   THE NOUN PHRASE (NP)

We begin our discussion of the major phrase types with the **Noun Phrase (NP)** because it enters so extensively into the composition of the verb phrase. After identifying the basic functional formula for NPs, we will then illustrate the simple ways in which these functions can be played by various parts of speech. Finally, we examine more complex constructions, particularly those that use more elaborated forms and those that employ a large number of simple forms to build up extended NPs.
    The NP functional formula has three parts:

[11]   (Premodifier*)   Head   (Postmodifier*)

(Asterisks denote elements that may appear more than once.)

The NP formula states that a noun phrase must contain a headword but need not contain anything else. (Thus we allow for a single-word NP.) If the NP has more elements than the head, it may contain one or more premodifiers (which precede the head) and/or one or more postmodifiers (which follow the head). The formula thus abbreviates several possibilities:

[12a]   Head
  [b]   Premodifiers(s) + Head
  [c]   Head + Postmodifier(s)
  [d]   Premodifiers(s) + Head + Postmodifiers(s)

7.5.1 Simple noun phrases: Head alone

Single-word NPs will always consist of a headword which is a noun or pronoun. Table 7.2 illustrates the possibilities; italics indicate the NPs.

TABLE 7.2   Single-Word Noun Phrases

Form of Head	Example
Noun	*Wombats* are playful.
	Cabbage is nutritious.
Personal pronoun (subject/object)	They saw *her.*
Personal pronoun (genitive)	*Mine* are chartreuse.
Indefinite pronoun	*None* was/were found.
Wh-word	*Who* placed the call?

Notice that personal pronouns often serve as heads, particularly the subject and object forms. Genitive, indefinites, and wh-words may be either heads, as shown above, or premodifiers.

7.5.2 Simple noun phrases: Premodifier + Head

Simple NPs can also contain a head preceded by a single-word premodifier, as Table 7.3 illustrates.

The range of premodifiers of noun heads is large, including nearly all of the parts of speech, at least in some form. The items in Table 7.3 present the basic possibilities. The only somewhat difficult case in the table is the **noun modifier,** i.e., the case where a noun phrase modifies a head noun, as in *metal plates*. Remember that for formal reasons *metal* isn't an

TABLE 7.3   Simple Premodifiers

Form of Premodifier	Example
Article	[*The* wombats] escaped.
Demonstrative pronoun	[*That* vase] is valuable.
Genitive pronoun	[*Her* serve] is powerful.
Indefinite pronoun	[*Some* survivors] remained.
Wh-word	[*Which* lobster] do you want?
Numeral	[*Seven* boxes] fell.
Ordinal	[*Second* thoughts] entered our minds.
Noun (phrase)	[*Metal* plates] shielded the instruments.

adjective—i.e., it cannot be compared or intensified: *metaler, *more metal, *very metal. Noun modifiers appear frequently when one speaks of a material out of which something is made, but the semantic range of such constructions is extensive:

[13a] railroad crossing
  [b] wire cutter
  [c] elevator operator
  [d] relativity theory
  [e] Sunday newspaper
  [f] culture shock

EXERCISES
1. Try to describe the semantic relations between the head noun and its NP modifier in each of the constructions in [13].
2. What do writing handbooks say about the use of noun modifiers? Examine a piece of real-life prose, identifying various types of premodifiers. Can you distinguish different writing styles according to their variety of premodifiers?

7.5.3   Simple noun phrases: Head + Prepositional Phrase

Most of the simple premodifiers above contain one word. The least complex postmodifier—and by far the most common—is the prepositional phrase (PP). You will recall that PPs consist of a preposition and a noun phrase. So this simple postmodification will have the structure: N + PP. Examples appear in [14]:

[14a] songs about rebellion
  [b] clocks on the wall
  [c] walks with my mother
  [d] arguments about abortion
  [e] reasons for my hesitation
  [f] sources of concern

One useful test for a NP of this form is the general one for NPs: It can be replaced by a personal pronoun. For instance, you could replace all of the expressions in [14] by the word *they*. We call this the **Pronoun-substitution (Pro-sub) Test.** To see its value, consider [15]:

[15a] Woody admired the picture on the wall.
   [b] Woody put the picture on the wall.

Assume that *the picture on the wall* in [15a] is a NP that contains a head and a PP postmodifier. Using our Pro-sub Test, we arrive at [16a]. The assumption that *on the wall* isn't a postmodifier leads, by our test, to the ungrammatical [16b]—assuming that Woody isn't suspended on the wall:

[16a] Woody admired it.
   [b] *Woody admired it on the wall.

Now assume that *the picture on the wall* in [15b] is a single NP. The Pro-sub Test thus yields [17a]. The contrary assumption that *on the wall* isn't a part of the NP in [15b] leads to [17b].

[17a] *Woody put it
   [b] Woody put it on the wall.

The pattern of grammaticality leads to the conclusion that [15a] contains an NP made up of a head with a PP postmodifier. Sentence [15b] contains the simpler NP *the picture*.
   If you're getting the hang of argument by grammaticality judgment, you might object that, in fact, [16b] is perfectly grammatical, in the sense of [18]:

[18] Woody admired it when it was hanging on the wall but not [when it was hanging] on the ceiling.

There is no syntactic reason why we wouldn't hang pictures on the ceiling. We may prefer a picture thus placed to one in more traditional locations. Moreover, even the pragmatically improbable interpretation where Woody hangs from the wall is at least imaginable. So the Pro-sub Test isn't absolutely conclusive, at least in this instance.
   Other tests are available to help us determine whether a sequence of noun + prepositional phrase is a noun phrase. One such device is the **Wh-question Test.** By this test, you replace the sequence under analysis by an appropriate question word and turn the sentence into a question. Assume both possible analyses—i.e., the sequence of words is and isn't a unified NP.
   Let's apply this test to [15a] and [15b]. In [15a], assume first that *the picture on the wall* is a unified NP. Replacing the sequence with the wh-word *what* leads to [19]:

[19] What did Woody admire?

On the contrary assumption, we arrive at [20], which is grammatical, although under the interpretation [18]:

[20]   What did Woody admire on the wall?

Finally, the unity of *the picture on the wall* is shown by [21], which is ungrammatical, unless one construes it as an abbreviation for *what thing on the wall:*

[21]   *What on the wall did Woody admire?

Now let's turn to [15b]. Assume that the sequence *the picture on the wall* is unified. The result is [22]:

[22]   *What did Woody put?

The contrary assumption, that the sequence of words constitutes two phrases rather than just one, leads us to replace only *the picture* with *what:*

[23]   What did Woody put on the wall?

Again, the Wh-question Test shows that in [15b] *the picture* and *on the wall* aren't part of the same phrase, let alone of the same NP. If you found [21] grammatical by the same logic that you applied in [18], then you should still remain unconvinced that *on the wall* is a postmodifier in [15a].

But don't give up on tests. Another one—the **Passive Test** is also helpful in most cases. We have already examined the passive construction in Chapter 6. Here we give a thumbnail sketch as a reminder. To form a passive, take a nonpassive (i.e., active) sentence and perform the following changes: (1) take the active subject and place it to the right of the verb and precede it with the preposition *by,* (2) take the active direct object and make it the subject, (3) add the auxiliary *be* to the verb with the tense of the active verb, and (4) change the active verb to its Ven form.

Apply these changes to [15a], assuming first that *the picture on the wall* is a unified NP. The result is [24]:

[24]   The picture on the wall was admired by Woody.

Next make the contrary assumption that *on the wall* isn't unified with *the picture* in a NP. The result is [25]:

[25]   *The picture was admired on the wall by Woody.

The same test applied to [15b] yields [26a] and [26b].

[26a]   *The picture on the wall was put by Woody.
  [b]   The picture was put on the wall by Woody.

At this point, we have still not shown a separation between *the picture* and *on the wall* in [15a] when interpreted as in [18]. Let's try another test for NPs, the **Topicalization Test.** Simply move the item in question to the front of the sentence, omitting it in its original position. For [15a], we find the following results (boldface indicates extra emphasis):

[27a]   The **picture** on the wall Woody admired.
[b]   *The **picture** Woody admired on the wall.

You can try this test for sentence [15b] on your own.

There is also a paraphrase test for a noun head + PP. If you can insert the words *which is/was* or *that is/was* between the noun head and the PP, the construction is probably of the head + postmodifier type. We call this the **Whiz Test** (*wh* comes from *which; iz* comes from the pronunciation of *is*). Applying this test to [15a] and [15b], we end up with the paraphrases [28a] and [28b], respectively:

[28a]   Woody admired the picture which was on the wall.
[b]   *Woody put the picture which was on the wall.

Thus we can conclude that *the picture on the wall* in [15b] is clearly not a single NP containing a head noun and a following PP. In [15a], the same words may or may not be part of a single NP, depending on the interpretation of the sentence. We have spent a great deal of time in what might seem to be a trivial issue, but in fact, it's of critical importance. Our tests demonstrate aspects of the process of **grammatical reasoning**—the use of formal tests, the need for several such tests, the consideration of multiple hypotheses, and the role of grammaticality judgments. A further dividend is that our tests will apply to just about any question pertaining to NPs, not just the single issue of nouns and following PPs.

7.5.4 Multiple and phrasal premodifiers

Our examples so far have provided only single-word premodifiers. In fact, premodifiers can be multiple, as the examples in [29] show:

[29a]   the two culprits (Article + Numeral)
[b]   those metal plates (Demonstrative + Noun Modifier)
[c]   several other candidates (Two Indefinites)
[d]   one such oddity (Numeral + Indefinite)
[e]   a second chance (Article + Ordinal)

Multiple one-word premodifiers cause little trouble for students. More complicated, however, are the cases where prenominal modifiers consist of phrases. Table 7.4 presents the major types.

TABLE 7.4 Phrasal Premodifiers

Form of Premodifier	Example
Genitive NP (GenNP)	[*My friend's* hobby] is knitting.
Adjective Phrase (AP)	[*Very old* memories] return easily.
Verbal Phrase (VblP)	[*Carelessly organized* meetings] annoy everyone.

As premodifiers, phrases can be expanded further, adding greater complexity to the structure. Moreover, genitive NPs and APs readily combine with other structures to create heavily premodified NPs:

[30a] [*All my friends'* hobbies] are interesting. (GenNP with internal quantifier and genitive pronoun)
   [b] [*All my friends' very old* plates] (Three premodifiers: quantifier; GenNP with possessive premodifier; AP with intensifier)
   [c] [*Those very old counterfeiting* plates] belonged to Capone. (Three premodifiers: demonstrative; AP with intensifier; verbal phrase)

We will consider verbal phrases later in this chapter.

Genitive NPs raise two further issues of complexity. First, they're closely related to postmodifiers that use a prepositional phrase headed by *of*. Compare the following:

[31a] my friend's hobbies
   [b] the hobbies of my friend
   [c] my friend's house
   [d] the house of my friend
   [e] the house of the friend that I met in Palo Alto
   [f] the birth of a daughter
   [g] a daughter's birth
   [h] the home of the brave
   [i] ?the brave's home
   [j] ?the braves' home
   [k] a cup of soup
   [l] *a soup's cup

These examples indicate that the choice of genitive NP versus *of*-PP depends on various factors, including whether the entity in the genitive is or isn't human, and the length of the *of*-PP [31e]. A further influence is whether the genitive NP indicates true possession or some other semantic relation between the head noun and its modifier [31f] to [31l]. While native speakers aren't likely to have trouble with such complexities, nonnative students may encounter serious difficulties with this construction.

In addition, genitive NPs themselves contain an NP. When one structure contains another structure, we say that the second structure is *embedded* in the first. The NP *Harry's sister's paintings* contains a genitive NP within a genitive NP. In other words, *Harry's* is embedded within *Harry's sister's,* which in turn is embedded in *Harry's sister's paintings*. This structure is represented in [32]:

[32]

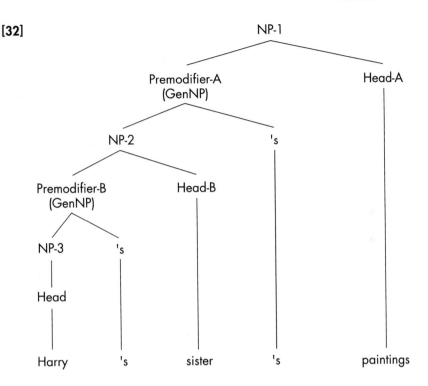

The diagram in [32] presents a very important lesson about grammatical organization, that of embedding. **Embedding** is a feature of linguistic structure in which one function (or form) is inserted into another function (or form). To put it another way, functions can contain other functions; forms can contain other forms. An understanding of the principle of embedding is critical to analysis of grammatical structures with any significant degree of complexity. Let's illustrate this fact with diagram [32]. NP-1 (*Harry's sister's paintings*) consists of a premodifier of the form GenNP (*Harry's sister's*) and a head (*paintings*). That GenNP in turn consists of a full NP (NP-2), along with the genitive inflection *'s*. In other words, the form NP-2 is contained in the form NP-1. Then, because NP-2 is a noun phrase, it too can be expanded functionally; it contains a premodifier (*Harry's*) and a head (*sister*). Finally, premodifier-B contains a single noun head (*Harry*), the *'s,* and no premodifiers.

There is nothing to stop us at this point. Under NP-3, we could have chosen a premodifier with a possessive pronoun and a noun modifier to give us *my uncle Harry's sister's paintings.* We could even have selected another GenNP under NP-3, in which case we might have gotten *Harry's cousin's sister's paintings.* In fact, we could go on forever—into infinity—producing ever longer and more genealogically bizarre series of structures: *Harry's aunt's cousin's son's granddaughter's niece's sister's stepchild's friend's paintings.*

Embedding enables language to be infinite in the number and length of the sentences it can create. Fortunately, speakers never come anywhere near to infinity, although occasionally writers such as Dylan Thomas, Henry James, and William Faulkner toy with the possibilities. As you progress through this book, you will see the pervasiveness of embedding.

EXERCISE Draw brackets around each NP and underline the headword. Using Tables 7.3 and 7.4, identify the type of each premodifier.
a. We noticed several suspicious details.
b. My best friend's parents gave his younger sister a European tour as a graduation present.
c. Three false alarms were mysteriously turned in during the following night.

7.5.5 Complex noun phrases: The range of postmodifiers

As complicated as possessives are, we easily recognize the infrequency of expressions such as *Harry's sister's paintings*. Much more common—and much more complex—are the various sorts of phrases and clauses that follow head nouns. We have already examined the prepositional phrase, probably the simplest postmodifier. Yet even this innocent construction raises the specter of mind-boggling expansions. Like possessive NPs, prepositional phrases contain NPs, which can contain prepositional phrases that contain other NPs that can contain a PP . . . all the way to the linguistic loony bin. In case you have doubts, consider the NP in [33]:

[33] the book in the drawer of the desk in the office of the leader of the rebellion against the oppression of readers of tales of adventures on far planets of the galaxy

Complexity arises, however, not merely because the language allows the multiple embedding of the same structure. It also—and more typically—comes about because of the potential for various sorts of postmodifiers, each more structurally involved than the premodifiers. We will treat these structures more fully in later chapters. For the present, we introduce the major types of postmodifiers in Table 7.5 and comment briefly on them.

We have seen **Adjective Phrases (APs)** that function as premodifiers. Such constructions tend to be brief—one or two words if the adjective isn't coordinated. However, some adjectives, like nouns, can appear with their own postmodifiers. (In the example in Table 7.5, *of kumquats* is a PP that complements *fond;* since that PP contains an NP, expansions like [33] are possible.) APs with postmodifiers almost always occur in the postmodifier position of NPs. Postmodifying APs also tend to allow the Whiz Test: *Anyone who is fond of kumquats.*

TABLE 7.5 Complex Postmodifiers

Type of Postmodifier	Example
Adjective Phrase (AP)	[Anyone *fond of kumquats*] should buy this recipe book.
Appositive NP (AppNP)	[His nominee, *an infamous scoundrel,*] is unlikely to be elected.
Verbal Phrase (VblP)	[The contestant *guessing the title*] will win a vacation in Tahiti.
	[The person *seated at the president's right*] is her bodyguard.
	[The player *to watch*] is Tzrdsky.
Relative Clause	[The contestant [*who guesses the title*] will win a trip to Tahiti.
Noun Complement Clause	The realization [*that his hair was false*] amused the audience.

Appositive Noun Phrases (AppNPs) are NPs that occur as "parenthetical asides" after their head noun. They're usually blocked off in writing by surrounding commas (dashes are also possible). In speech, they're surrounded by audible pause and often a fall in voice pitch, as if to mirror the aside spoken by a stage actor. Grammarians also observe that the appositive NP has the same referent as the rest of the NP. Thus in Table 7.5 *his nominee* and *an infamous scoundrel* designate the same individual. Since appositives can be expanded just like any other NP, they allow for infinite embedding. Sentence [34] suggests the possibilities:

[34] His nominee, an infamous scoundrel with principles learned from years of service in one of the most corrupt political machines ever devised by the devious minds that have blemished history, is unlikely to be elected.

Verbal Phrases (VblPs) will be dealt with further in the next section under the heading of participles and infinitives. Like adjective phrases, short VblPs precede noun heads. VblPs, however, may be relatively long because they may possess their own range of objects, complements, and modifiers. In such cases, they follow the head noun within a noun phrase. In general, short modifiers tend to precede head nouns and longer ones tend to follow them.

Relative clauses will be discussed in Chapter 10. These clauses usually begin with a wh-word or *that*.

Noun complement clauses will also be discussed in Chapter 10. These clauses usually begin with the word *that*, which has no grammatical function other than to connect the clause to the noun head. (The noun-clause connector *that* cannot be replaced by *who/m* or *which*.)

EXERCISES
1. Draw brackets around each NP and underline the headword. Using Tables 7.3, 7.4, and 7.5, indicate the type of each premodifier and postmodifier.
   a. The squirrel that Bonzo, my pet chimp, chased became quite flustered.
   b. Some friends of Boris gave him a box filled with his favorite candy as a going-away present.
   c. Alvin set the goldfish bowl near the window.
   d. The cat near the window is Salome.
   e. I saw the cat near the window.
      (Ambiguous: Analyze two different ways.)
   f. Don't go out in the midday sun.
   g. The witnesses at the scene noticed a stranger who drove away in a red station wagon full of flowers.
2. In many cases, roughly the same information can be expressed as either a premodifier of a noun or its postmodifier. Consider the following NPs:
   a. a teacher of English from Canada
   b. a teacher from Canada of English
   c. an English teacher from Canada
   d. a Canadian teacher of English
   e. a Canadian English teacher

      f. a teacher of English and (of) French
      g. a teacher of English and from Canada
      h. a teacher from Canada and of English

Put an asterisk before any NP above that you find ungrammatical.
Identify which NPs are ambiguous and state their different interpretations.
Identify which pairs (triples, quadruples, etc.) of NPs are synonymous. Assume that
      a person from Canada is a Canadian.

Based on your observations above, what differences can you see between *of*-post-
modifiers of nouns and other PP postmodifiers? What similarities can you see?
What other sentences can you concoct that shed light on these issues?

7.5.6   Complex noun phrases: Coordination

Perhaps on the principle that too much of a good thing is impossible, English bestows on
us the possibility of repeating NPs twice, thrice, even—you guessed it—an infinite number
of times. Coordinated NPs will be joined by a coordinate conjunction, usually *and* or *or,* as
in [35]:

[35] *My sister* and/or *her best friend* will deliver the letter.

Such structures are relatively simple to deal with—except for one problem. Consider the
famous ambiguous sentence [36].

[36] Old men and women will be served first.

Who will be served first? Old men and all women? Old men and old women? The answer
seems to depend on whether the premodifying adjective *old* applies to *men* only or to the
conjunction of *men and women.* To differentiate between these possibilities, we must allow
not only full NPs to coordinate but also heads of NPs. We can analyze the ambiguity
diagrammatically as in [37].

[37a]

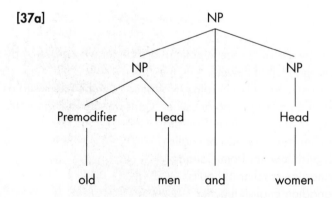

[37b]

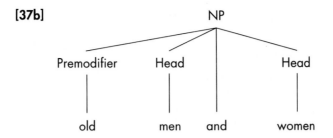

Diagram [37a] represents the situation where *old* modifies only *men*, the NP boundary serving as a limit on its scope. In [37b], *old* modifies *men and women*. In general, if a modifier applies to two conjoined nouns, the structure is a "doubleheader" like [37b]. If it applies only to the first noun, we have conjoined NPs. In short, adjectives have the power to modify only within their NP.

7.6   THE VERB PHRASE (VP)

The verb phrase has a verb as its head. As before, we begin with the functional formula for VPs and then examine the forms that can satisfy that function:

[38]   VP functional formula

(Auxiliary*) + Head + (Object(s)/Complement) + (Modifier*)

This formula states that a VP must contain a headword, optionally preceded by one or more auxiliaries and optionally followed by any of its object(s), complement, and modifier(s). You will recall from Chapter 5 that only intransitive verbs don't require an object and that modifiers are optional. The possibilities are thus:

Head
Auxiliary(ies) + Head
Head + Object(s)/Complement
Head + Modifier(s)
Combinations of the above

7.6.1   Simple verb phrases: Head alone

Single-word VPs always consist of a headword that is a verb:

[39a]   Hector *walks*.
  [b]   All of the employees *agree*.
  [c]   The lemmings *followed*.

In traditional grammar, the terms **main verb** and **simple predicate** sometimes are used for the headword of the VP.

7.6.2   Verb phrases: Auxiliaries and Head

In the previous two chapters, we distinguished between head or main verbs (sometimes called **lexical verbs**) and auxiliary verbs. The discussion primarily concerned head verbs. However, heads often occur in the company of other verbs, called **helping verbs, auxiliaries,** or simply **AUX,** some of whose functions we described in Chapter 6.

The major auxiliary verbs in English are *have, be,* and *do.* (We leave to chapter 8 the discussion of the **modal auxiliaries** *will, would, can, could, shall, should, may, might,* and *must*). The forms of *have, be,* and *do* are illustrated in [40]:

[40a]   The zombies *departed* from Hector's house. (Head alone)
   [b]   Hector *is acting* strangely. (be + Head Verb)
   [c]   Hector *has* never *looked* at me like that. (have + Head Verb)
   [d]   Hector *does* not *eat* vegetables. (do + Head Verb)
   [e]   Hector *has been consorting* with the zombies. (have + be + Head Verb)

As these examples show, a (noncompound) VP will contain one head verb; in English, auxiliaries always precede (occur to the left of) the main verb. Occasionally, the auxiliaries may be separated from the verb, through either interruption (e.g., *has never looked* in [40c]) or inversion (e.g., *Has* Hector *seen* Oswald?). Let's examine these auxiliaries in more detail.

Have is the auxiliary associated with the perfect aspect. It can accept all of the four potential inflections of a main verb:

[41a]   have sung
   [b]   has sung
   [c]   had sung
   [d]   having sung

These examples also demonstrate that *have* can be followed by a verb (whether another auxiliary or a main verb) in the past participle form, which we have abbreviated Ven. So our formula for auxiliary *have* will be:

[42]   HAVE   +   Ven

|
have
has   sung
had
having

One word of caution: *Have* may also serve as a head verb. If a single instance of *have* appears, it's a head: *I* **have** *a cold.* If two instances of *have* occur, the first is an auxiliary, as in *I* **have had** *a cold for two weeks,* and the second is the head verb.

Be is the auxiliary associated with the progressive aspect. It occurs in almost all of the forms possible for the verb *be:*

[43a] be singing
 [b] am singing
 [c] is singing
 [d] are singing
 [e] was singing
 [f] were singing
 [g] been singing

Whichever verb follows progressive *be* assumes its present participle form, Ving. Our formula is thus:

[44] BE + Ving

be
am
is
are   singing
was
were
been

When we combine this formula with that for *have* + Ven, the result preserves the general pattern we have observed. That is: (1) *have* precedes *be;* (2) the verb immediately to the right of *have* occurs as a Ven, whether that verb is a full lexical verb or another auxiliary; (3) the verb immediately to the right of progressive *be* occurs as Ving:

[45] HAVE and BE
      HAVE + Ven
                  BE + Ving
                          Main Verb

      have   been   singing
      has
      had

(To interpret the scheme above, imagine the two formulas as forming a series of steps, with the last part of one formula appearing above the first part of the next formula, until the head verb is reached. The actual verb structure results from reading each column vertically; e.g., the base form of *have* is *have;* the Ven form of *be* is *been;* and the Ving form of *sing* is *singing.*)

Like *have, be* may serve as a main verb, as in *Wiggles* **is** *a friendly boa.* When two instances of *be* occur, the same generalization holds—the first is an auxiliary (as in *Wiggles* **is** *being affectionate*) and the second is a head verb.

The auxiliary *be* is a bit more complex because it also occurs in the passive. This form is illustrated in the following:

[46a] be sung
  [b]   is sung
  [c]   are sung
  [d]   was sung
  [e]   were sung
  [f]   being sung
  [g]   been sung

As you will notice, the verb that follows passive *be* is in the past participle form (Ven). The formula for the passive verb group is thus:

[47] BE + Ven

    be
    is   sung
    etc.

Can this passive form occur with the progressive *be?* Sentence [48] shows that it can:

[48] That song is being sung poorly.

Sentence [48] also shows that the passive *be* follows the progressive *be.* We can represent the verb phrase in [48] as:

[49] BE + Ving
          BE + Ven
               Main Verb

    is   being sung

Finally, we can combine all of the auxiliaries above into a single VP. Can you think of what such a VP might be? Let's look at it formulaically:

[50] HAVE + Ven
           BE + Ving
               BE + Ven
                   Main Verb

    has   been   being sung

To imagine this ungainly VP in a sentence, consider [51], which implies either the singing of one extremely long song or repetitious performances of the same song.

[51] That song has been being sung for hours, and I'm sick of it.

Do, the last auxiliary, is something of an exception, as the sentences below suggest:

[52a] Jason does not/doesn't sing.
  [b] Does Jason sing?
  [c] *Jason may do sing.
  [d] *Jason do may sing.
  [e] *Jason is doing sing.
  [f] *Jason does be singing.
  [g] *Jason has done sing.
  [h] *Jason does have sing.
  [i] *Jason is done sing.
  [j] *Jason does be sung.

What can we learn from this odd pattern of sentences? First, when *do* occurs with a main verb, that verb is in its base (V) form. So we can posit the formula:

[53]   DO +   V

       | |

       do   sing
       does
       did

Second, *do* cannot occur with any of the other auxiliaries, either before or after them. Third, *do* occurs (1) when the main verb is negated by *not* or *n't* or (2) in a question.

Finally, we must observe that the auxiliary *do* differs from the **pro-verb phrase** *do.* Consider, for example, sentence [54]:

[54] Did-1 she do-2 so too?

In this example, *Did-1* is an auxiliary, while *do-2* acts as a pro-verb phrase, an expression that substitutes for a verb phrase.

One handy test for VPs is the **Do-so Test.** One simple application of this test is to substitute *do so* for the VP (with appropriate change of tense):

[55a] The Zombies *did so.* (= [40a])
  [b] Hector is *doing so.* (= [40b])
  [c] Hector has never *done so.* (= [40c])
  [d] Hector does not *do so.* (= [40d])
  [e] Hector has been *doing so.* (= [40e])

In another version of the test, the sentence in question is coordinated with one similar to it; in this case, the elements reverse to form *so do:*

[56a]   Hector juggles and *so does* Zenobia.
  [b]   All of the employees agree and *so does* their supervisor.
  [c]   The lemmings jumped and *so did* the zoologists.

In short, the expressions *do so* and *so do* replace a VP, including its objects, complement, and modifiers, but excluding its auxiliaries.

EXERCISE   In the sentences below, draw brackets around the main verb and any auxiliaries. Draw formulas similar to those used in the preceding section to describe the structure of the auxiliaries + verb.
a. I have bought all my textbooks for next semester.
b. I don't have a cent to my name.
c. Sylvia hasn't been doing much work lately.
d. Of course, we're being ironic.
e. Zelda was congratulated for her good work.
f. The job has been completed.

7.6.3   Verb phrases: Head + Objects(s)/Complement

A phrase that obligatorily follows a verb head is called an **object** or **complement**. These terms are roughly convertible, although tradition has attached the word "object" to some constructions and "complement" to others. The reasons for the variation are obscure. The label "object" dimly suggests the goal or purpose of the verb head, although neither of these semantic labels applies to every structure so labeled. The term "complement" suggests the notion of completing (hence the spelling) the verb in some way. This label also isn't a reliable clue to structure. Table 7.6 lists the main types of objects and complements.

A quick inspection of Table 7.6 will reveal that noun phrases can serve any object or complement function and that adjective phrases can also act in complement functions.

An important grammatical notion associated with the direct object is that of **transitivity**. A **transitive verb** takes a direct object; an **intransitive verb** doesn't. Thus the

TABLE 7.6   Objects and Complements of Verbs

Type	Example
Direct Object	The Vikings demanded [*tribute.* (NP)]
Indirect Object	Waldo gave [*his sister* (NP)] a dictionary.
Subject Complement	Freud was [*a prude.* (NP)]
	Freud was [*prudish.* (AP)]
Object Complement	I consider Jung [*a quack.* (NP)]/[*unreliable.* (AP)]
Complement Clause	I think [*that Freud was a prude.* (S)]

sentences [57a] to [57d] contain transitive verbs and those in [58a] to [58d] contain intransitive verbs. The direct objects in [57] are italicized:

[57a] Moriarty eluded *Sherlock.*
  [b] Everyone avoided *me.*
  [c] Sarah gave him *some good advice.*
  [d] I consider *Jung* a quack/unreliable.

[58a] We walked.
  [b] Smoke rises.
  [c] Harrison confessed.
  [d] Everyone in the room laughed.

In English, a large number of verbs can be either transitive or intransitive, sometimes with a considerable difference of meaning:

[59a] The fire smoked.
  [b] Shelley smoked.
  [c] Shelley smoked the salmon.

Thus whether such verbs are transitive or intransitive can only be determined by their use in an actual VP. One simple test is that an intransitive verb can potentially end a sentence, as in [58].

Two structures require not one but two phrases to follow the verb. The indirect object construction (e.g., [57c]) typically calls for a direct object also. Verbs that enter into such constructions are called **bitransitive** or **ditransitive**. The object complement construction (e.g., [57d]) requires a direct object preceding the complement. We deal in more detail with these constructions in Chapter 8.

7.6.4 Verb phrases: Head + Modifier(s)

To distinguish them from modifiers of nouns, modifiers of verbs often have special names such as **adverbial** and **adjunct**. Formally, modifiers are of only four types, as indicated in Table 7.7.

TABLE 7.7 Modifiers of Verbs

Type of Modifier	Example
Adverb Phrase	We left *(very) early.*
Prepositional Phrase	We stayed *in Helsinki.*
Adverbial Clause	We left *after it started to snow.*
Noun Phrase	We walked *a great deal.*

Adverbial clauses begin with the subordinating adverbial conjunctions mentioned in the preceding chapter. Like single adverbs, the phrasal and clausal modifiers are somewhat movable in the sentence:

[60a]   *Very early,* we left.
   [b]   *After it began to snow,* we left.

Sometimes a short (one- or two-word) adverbial will appear within the VP:

[61a]   We *very often* eat out.
   [b]   She has *very often* donated her legal services.

Noun phrase adverbials may be confused with direct objects. However, they will never become the subject of a corresponding passive sentence:

[62a]   *A great deal was walked by us.
   [b]   We walked a great deal.

Example [62a] is ungrammatical because *a great deal* isn't the true direct object.

The adverbials that modify verbs can be grouped semantically according to the semantic roles that they express. The most common appear in Table 7.8.

TABLE 7.8   Semantic Roles of Adverbials

Semantic Role	Examples
Time	He left *early.*
	We left *on Monday.*
	I'll leave *when the cows come home.*
Place	She stopped *there.*
	She relaxed *on the sofa.*
	She stopped *where the victim was found.*
Manner	The troup exited *gracefully.*
	The troup exited *with grace.*
Reason	He left *out of spite.*
	He left *because he was miffed.*
Purpose	He left *to milk the cow.*

EXERCISE   Draw brackets around each VP in the sentences below. Underline the headword and indicate the type of object, complement, or modifier accompanying the headword.
   a. Angela offered the job to her former rival.
   b. Angela offered Archie the job.
   c. We left for Austin in the morning.

d. In the morning, we left San Antonio for Austin.
e. Your proposal seems quite reasonable.
f. Zelda gets angry whenever Scott calls her a "pixie."
g. Eat this if you dare.

7.6.5   Complex verb phrases: Combinations of functions

Although we have illustrated separately each of the functions accompanying the verb head, the options in the formula stated at the beginning of this section allow for more than one function to appear with the verb. Consider, for example, the sentences in [63]:

[63a]   She *has been speaking for three hours.*
        (Auxiliaries + Head + PP-Modifier)

[b]   Scott *offered Zelda a ride since her car was out of gas.*
        (Head + Indirect Object + Direct Object + Adverbial Clause Modifier)

[c]   Hortense *never becomes angry with Heathcliff.*
        (Adverb Phrase + Head + AP-Subject Complement)

[d]   The remains *will be shipped to Cleveland on Wednesday.*
        (Auxiliaries + Head + PP-Modifier + PP-Modifier)

7.6.6   Verbal phrases (VblPs)

Verb phrases have one prominent purpose in life: to function as predicates along with subjects and thus to form clauses. That single role is a powerful one, but it would be a shame if such a linguistic marvel as a verb phrase would have no other use in the language. In fact, English has arranged for verb phrases to serve a much wider variety of functions—though at a small cost.

Traditional grammarians regularly distinguish these varied extended functions as **verbals.** However, this label suggests that we are dealing with properties of single verbs. In fact, the functions are filled by phrases. For this reason, we will call the structures that enter into such functions **verbal phrases** (VblPs). Whenever we use the term *verbals,* then it's shorthand for verbal phrases. Traditionally, the verbal phrases include **participles, gerunds,** and **infinitives.**

We identified verbs in the previous chapter by their ability to accept a tense marker. However, a verbal phrase is a verb phrase without tense and modals. The grammatical term **nonfinite** encapsulates this restriction. **Finite** verbs are thought to be "limited" by the presence of tense. (*Finis* in Latin means "limit or boundary.") Those VPs without tense are "unlimited" or nonfinite. Aside from this minor formal restriction—and a few others—VblPs look like other VPs: They have perfect, progressive, and passive auxiliaries, objects, complements, and modifiers.

One might also extend the notion of being unlimited to the range of functions into which the VblPs enter. While their functions aren't totally unrestricted, they can act as modifiers (premodifiers, postmodifiers, adverbial modifiers) or can substitute for noun phrases. We will explore these possibilities in detail.

7.6.6.1   Participles

Someone once defined a participle as "an irregular follower of a guru." That, however, isn't its grammatical definition. Traditional grammars call it a "verblike adjective." This definition has two flaws. First, it suggests that a participle is a single word—specifically an adjective—when actually it's a phrase that often includes several constructions within itself. Second, the definition confuses form and function. A better definition is the following:

[64]   A participle is a verbal phrase whose first verb is Ving or Ven; it functions as a premodifier or a postmodifier of a noun head.

By calling it a verbal phrase, we indicate that the participle lacks tense and modal but may include other auxiliaries, objects, complements, and modifiers. We also identify an important formal property of the participle, the use of Ving or Ven at the beginning. Finally, we specify precisely the functions of the participle without confusing it with adjectives.

Let's illustrate our definition. The forms characteristic of the participial verb group appear in Table 7.9. The relevant Ving or Ven represents either the head verb or the auxiliary, whichever occurs first.

TABLE 7.9   Forms of Participles

	Ving	Ven	Have + Ven
Active	freezing	frozen	having frozen
Passive	being frozen		having been frozen

Note: In traditional grammar, the Ving column in Table 7.9 is designated *present participle;* the Ven column is the *past participle; have + Ven* is known as the *perfect participle.* Such labels shouldn't be considered as tense forms. The labels have no consistent time implications. We give them here to enable you to recognize traditional terminology, but we will not use them any further.

The major functions of participles are illustrated below:

[65a]   A *cheerfully singing* bird is a delight. (Premodifier in NP)
  [b]   A tablet *inscribed with cuneiform* was discovered. (Postmodifier in NP)
  [c]   The old road, *winding beside the stream,* brought back fond memories. (Appositive Postmodifier in NP)

These examples also illustrate some of the possible constructions that accompany the head verb in the participial phrase: an adverb phrase in [65a] and PPs in [65b] and [65c]. Ving forms appear in [65a] and [65c]; [65b] has a Ven form. As usual, a short modifier precedes a noun head, as in [65a], while a long modifier follows it, as in [65b]. One unusual function appears here that is often associated with participial use; the appositive postmodifier in [65c] is a parenthetical aside, like the appositive NPs mentioned earlier in this chapter.

Occasionally, participles will cause problems for students because of their historical tendency to turn into full-blown adjectives. The completion of this change is apparent when the word becomes subject to comparison and intensification:

[66a]   Pope's metaphors are *more interesting* than Dryden's.
   [b]   I find Dryden's use of litotes *quite fascinating*.

7.6.6.2   Gerunds

The traditional definition of a gerund is a "verblike noun." This characterization has exactly the same flaws as the traditional definition of participles. Our definition is:

[67]   A gerund is a verbal phrase whose first verb is Ving; it functions in the range of NPs.

Formally, gerunds resemble participles, except that they cannot have a verb head with Ven. They can, however, express passive voice through the *be + Ven*. Only four verb groups are possible for gerunds; these are listed in Table 7.10.

TABLE 7.10   Forms of Gerunds

	Ving	Have + Ven
Active	praising	having praised
Passive	being praised	having been praised

The functions of the gerund are as extensive as those of the NP:

[68a]   *Running a biathlon* demands perfect conditioning. (Subject)
   [b]   I enjoy *running in the park*. (Direct Object)
   [c]   You must give *running* your undivided attention. (Indirect Object)
   [d]   A healthful exercise is *running to the ice cream parlor*. (Subject Complement)
   [e]   The importance of *her having run the marathon in record time* is hard to estimate. (Object of a Preposition)
   [f]   Do you call your limp jogging *running*? (Object Complement)
   [g]   His one skill, *running backward*, doesn't compensate for his many faults. (Appositive in NP)

We leave it to you to identify the various auxiliaries, objects, complements, and modifiers in the VblPs of [68]. Likewise, you should try the Pronoun-substitution Test to determine which gerund VblPs it identifies.

Like participles, gerunds are subject to historical change, turning into regular nouns over time. Such changes are completed when the noun can be pluralized, as in [69]:

[69]   The commission's *findings* were disputed.

7.6.6.3   Infinitives

The word **infinitive** is used by grammarians in two ways. First, it refers to the basic form of verb as it would appear if you looked it up in an English dictionary. (Dictionaries of other languages may use different basic forms.) A second definition is "a verb, usually preceded by *to*, that is used as a noun or modifier." Rephrasing this traditional definition to recognize infinitives as phrases and to remove the confusion of form and function, we define an infinitive as follows:

[70]   An infinitive is a verbal phrase, usually beginning with *to*, that functions in the range of noun phrases, or as a modifier or complement.

Formally, the regular appearance of *to* is the most reliable clue to the presence of an infinitive. The auxiliary forms allow six different versions, as listed in Table 7.11.

TABLE 7.11   Forms of Infinitives

	to + V	to + have Ven	to + Be Ving	to + Have + Be Ving
Active	to sing	to have sung	to be singing	to have been singing
Passive	to be sung	to have been sung		

The relatively large number of forms is really not troublesome since most of the time only the simpler forms occur. It is the extensive set of functions that makes the infinitive so complex—as well as so useful. Let's look at each type of function.

The nominal range of infinitives is typified in [71]:

[71a]   *To steal from the poor* is inexcusable. (Subject)
  [b]   I hate *to eat breakfast*. (Direct Object)
  [c]   It is inexcusable *to steal from the poor*. (Extraposed Subject)
  [d]   I consider it impossible *to do any better*. (Extraposed Direct Object)
  [e]   My ambition is *to retire in Tahiti*. (Subject Complement)
  [f]   I have one ambition, *to retire in Tahiti*. (Appositive)

As we would expect, infinitives have the same range of objects (note [71b]) and modifiers (note [71a]) as any verbal phrase. Likewise, it isn't surprising that as nominals they normally respond to the Pronoun-substitution Test:

[71g]   *It* is inexcusable.
  [h]   I hate *it*.

However, there are some idiosyncrasies. Infinitives will not appear as indirect objects or as objects of prepositions. In addition, they have the ability to be moved from the normal subject position (e.g., [71c]) and from a direct object position when the direct object is followed by an object complement (as in [71d]), where *impossible* is an object complement. In both cases, the infinitive is relocated to the end of the clause and replaced by *it*. This movement is called **extraposition** (literally, "placing outside"—i.e., placing the infinitive outside the normal structure of the clause). The moved infinitive is said to be *extraposed* (or *delayed*). The pronoun *it* is sometimes called an **expletive** or **dummy** element. The usefulness of extraposition is easy to see. English tends to place long or complicated structures toward the end of a clause after the basic grammatical business (i.e., subject, predicate, and objects) has been transacted. Extraposition keeps the subject and direct object position from getting cluttered with the extra structure that the infinitive brings with it. To see this, try [71c] and [71d] without extraposition:

[72a] *To steal from the poor* is inexcusable. (= [71c])
  [b] *I consider *to do any better* impossible. (= [71d])

Sentence [72a] is grammatical, though slightly cumbersome—and would be more so if the infinitive phrase were longer. Example [72b] is odd to the point of ungrammaticality.

The presentation above concentrates on the basic nominal roles of the infinitive. We might also consider some other details. For instance, the word *for* can be associated with the construction in certain instances:

[73] I consider it impossible *for* Zelda *to* do any better.

The infinitive in [73] overtly expresses the infinitive's **logical subject. A logical subject** is a word or phrase implied as the subject of a VP. Frequently, the logical subject of infinitives isn't expressed. For instance, the logical subject in [72a] is the implicit *anyone*. In *for-to* constructions, the logical subject *is* expressed. Certain regional varieties, as well as older forms of the language, allow *for-to* structures without a logical subject:

[74] Swing low, sweet chariot, coming *for to* carry me home.

The sentences of [75] illustrate a few final complexities of infinitives.

[75a] She let *me drive.*
  [b] The board considers *him to have disgraced himself.*
  [c] *Osgood* was asked *to leave.*
  [d] Edgar ordered *Monty to wash his car.*
  [e] Edgar promised *Monty to wash his car.*

Sentence [75a] shows that the marker *to* need not appear. Sentences [75b] to [75e] demonstrate that the logical subject of the infinitive may be expressed even without *for*. This possibility is determined by the verb of the clause that contains the infinitive. Contrast [75d] with [76]:

[76] *Edgar agreed Monty to wash his car.

Sentence [75c] illustrates that an expressed logical subject can undergo passivization and be moved outside the infinitive. Finally, [75d] and [75e] raise questions about the logical subject. In [75d], Monty will wash the car; in [75e], Edgar will do so. Again, the verb of the clause containing the infinitive determines which NP in the sentence will be interpreted as the logical subject of the infinitive. We return to this issue in Chapter 11.

The nonnominal functions of infinitives (as modifiers or complements) are less troublesome in spite of the fact that infinitives can modify several types of heads:

[77a] The articles *to be sold* include one of Ravel's manuscripts. (Postmodifier of Noun in NP)

[b] We were anxious *to leave*. (Complement of Head Adjective in Adjective Phrase)

[c] *To get to Reno*, you have to drive across the desert. (Adverbial Modifier of Verb)

[d] *To tell the truth*, verbals are flaky. (Sentence Modifier)

The status of *to be sold* in [77a] is clear because of the Whiz Test: *the articles which are to be sold*. The adjective complement of [77b] occurs—like many other complements—with heads that denote mental or emotional states. The adverbial use in [77c] is restricted to the expression of purpose and is usually paraphrasable by *in order to*. Like many adverbials, it's somewhat mobile:

[78] You have to drive across the desert *to get to Reno*.

The sentence modifier function in [77d] is set off from the rest of the sentence by a pause. Semantically, such functions resemble sentence modifying adverbs such as *truthfully*, which remark on a speaker's evaluation of an utterance.

EXERCISE Draw brackets around each VblP. Indicate (1) whether it is a participle, a gerund, or an infinitive; (2) its internal structure—i.e., its auxiliaries, objects, complements, and modifiers; and (3) its function within the larger sentence.
a. Winning against Roger is a difficult feat to accomplish.
b. Taking a different route, we discovered a promising fishing spot.
c. I would advise against your taking a different route.
d. To be perfectly honest, I'm tired of fishing.

REFERENCES AND RESOURCES

Brown, Keith, and Jim Miller. 1991. *Syntax: A Linguistic Introduction to Sentence Structure*. 2d ed. London: Harper Collins Academic.
Greenbaum, Sidney, and Randolph Quirk. 1990. *A Student's Grammar of the English Language*. London: Longman.
Liles, Bruce. 1987. *A Basic Grammar of Modern English*. 2d ed. Englewood Cliffs, NJ: Prentice-Hall, Inc.

GLOSSARY

Adjective phrase: see Chapter 5.

Adjunct: see **adverbial**.

Adverb phrase: see Chapter 5.

Adverbial (also called "**adjunct**"): a modifier of a verb.

Appositive noun phrase: a noun phrase that occurs as a "parenthetical aside" after its head noun.

Auxiliary verb (also called "**AUX**" or "**helping verb**"): see Chapter 6.

Bitransitive (also called "**ditransitive**"): a verb phrase having two objects.

Complement: a phrase (e.g., subject complement and object complement) that obligatorily follows and "completes" certain types of verbs. See **object** and Chapter 8.

Degree adverb: see Chapter 6.

Ditransitive: see **bitransitive**.

Do-so Test: a substitution test used to identify a verb phrase.

Dummy: see **expletive**.

Embed: to include one structure inside another structure.

Expletive (also called "**dummy**"): a meaningless form that has a grammatical function, sometimes marking the position of a moved element.

Extraposition: a movement of a structure to the end of its clause, marking its original position with the expletive *it*.

Finite: the property of a clause that has a verb marked for tense. See **nonfinite**.

Function: see Introduction to Part Two.

Gerund: see Chapter 5 and Chapter 10.

Grammatical reasoning: the process of analyzing grammatical structure by calling upon formal tests, hypothesis formation, and grammaticality judgments.

Helping verb: see **auxiliary verb**, Chapter 6.

Infinitive: see Chapter 5 and Chapter 10.

Intensifier: see Chapter 6.

Intransitive verb: see Chapter 5 and Chapter 8.

Lexical verb (also called "**main verb**" and "**simple predicate**"): the head, i.e., nonauxiliary, verb of a verb phrase.

Logical subject: in traditional grammar, a word or phrase referring to either the Agent of an action or the understood subject of a sentence.

Main verb: see **lexical verb**.

Modal auxiliary: one of the following auxiliaries: *will, would, can, could, shall, should, may, might,* and *must*.

Nonfinite: the property of a clause that lacks a verb marked for tense. See **finite**.

Noun complement clause: see **complement** and Chapter 10.

Noun modifier: a noun phrase that modifies a head noun.

Noun phrase: see Chapter 6.

Object: a phrase (e.g., direct object, indirect object, object of preposition) that obligatorily follows certain types of words. See **complement** and Chapter 8.

Object of a preposition: a noun phrase following a preposition in a prepositional phrase.

Participle: see Chapter 5.

Passive test: a test used to identify the direct object of an active clause by making it passive.

Phrase: a grammatically unified group of words containing a headword.

Postmodifier: the function of various structures that follow the head of a noun phrase. See **premodifier.**

Premodifier: the function of various structures that precede the head of a noun phrase.

Prepositional phrase: a phrase consisting of a preposition and a noun phrase, with the preposition as the head of the phrase.

Pro-verb phrase: a form that replaces a verb phrase.

Pronoun-substitution (Pro-sub) test: a test used to identify a noun phrase by substituting a pronoun for it.

Simple predicate: see **lexical verb.**

Topicalization test: a test used to determine whether a structure is a phrase by moving it to the beginning of its sentence.

Transitive verb: see Chapter 5 and Chapter 8.

Verb phrase: a phrase with a verb as its headword.

Verbal: a traditional grammatical term that includes participles, gerunds, and infinitives.

Verbal phrase (VblP): a verb phrase that functions in ways other than as a predicate of a clause; includes participle, gerund, and infinitive phrases.

Wh-question test: a test to identify a noun phrase by replacing it with a wh-question word and then recasting the sentence that contains it as a question.

Whiz test: a test to identify a noun phrase with a head + postmodifier structure by inserting *who* or *which* plus a form of the verb *be* after the supposed headword.

8 BASIC CLAUSE PATTERNS

8.0 CLAUSES AND CLAUSE PATTERNS

Until now we have examined the grammar of English in bits and pieces. In this chapter, we put these pieces together into the basic grammatical structure of language—the **clause.** Clauses are basic for several reasons. First, you need only one of them to make a sentence. Second, in actual communication, shorter utterances are usually reconstructed and understood by reference to clauses. For instance, *Over here* might be understood as *I'm over here* or *Shine the light over here.* The grammatical importance of clauses probably reflects the fact that the clause most directly represents the most fundamental structure of meaning—the proposition (a concept discussed more fully in Chapter 2). For the present, we will proceed on the assumption that the sense of "clausehood" is intuitive, based on our competence as native speakers and perhaps on our status as human makers of meaning. As such, it isn't something that can be taught or needs to be.

In this chapter, we will first examine the internal structure of clauses. Next we discuss the subject function, which appears in every clause. We will illustrate the use of formal characteristics to identify the subject of a clause and then discuss the **thematic** or **semantic roles** subjects may play. The main part of the chapter will provide details on eight major clause patterns in the language.

8.1 ELEMENTS OF THE CLAUSE

The basic structure of a clause is very simple:

[1]   A clause is a grammatical unit which contains a **subject** and a **predicate.**

That's all. No more than a subject and a predicate is needed. No less than a subject and a predicate will do. This definition thus includes as clauses all of the structures in [2]. (Subjects are italicized, predicates underlined.)

[2a] *Birds*—twittered.
 [b] *All the birds of the neighborhood*—congregated in the venerable elms in the park.
 [c] that *no one*—approves of the decision
 [d] which *I*—lost
 [e] whenever *the phone*—rings

In contrast, the structures in [3] aren't clauses:

[3a] twittered
 [b] all the birds of the neighborhood
 [c] approves of the decision
 [d] over here
 [e] when in the course of human events

The fact that a group of words has a certain length or can be understood in some context is inadequate to define a clause. Example [3b] for example, contains more words than [2a], [2d], and [2e]. Likewise, *Over here* can be understood if one imagines a context.

This isn't to say that it will always be clear whether a structure contains a subject and a predicate. We may debate, for instance, whether *her to stay* in [4] represents a subject-predicate relationship:

[4] We asked her to stay.

Some grammarians argue that *her* in sentences like [4] is a "logical" subject of the verb *stay*. We will consider such issues in a later chapter. For the present, let's assume rather narrowly that subjects must be more than "logical." That is, they must appear overtly in the spoken utterance or in the words on a page.

This assumption has an important consequence. Traditional grammarians occasionally appeal to "understood" elements in clauses. Thus imperatives such as *Eat your kumquats!* are said to possess an understood subject, *you*. For the hardheaded surface grammarian, such elements have as much reality as the ghost of your Uncle Cecil. As we progress from surface to deep grammar in later chapters, we will demonstrate that things can be invisible without being ghosts. But for the time being, we want you to adopt the skeptic's perspective: If you can't see it, it isn't there.

Clause patterns provide the basic skeletons of English sentences. Full sentences consist of clause patterns either minimally or extensively developed, through expansion of their component phrases and through the inclusion of more than one clause. When you can perceive the presence of clauses, you will be able to move in two directions: toward larger sentence structures and toward the smaller units of phrases and words. In fact, it would have been possible for us to present English grammar by starting with the clause and working "downward" to these lower units. Rather than such a "top-down" presentation, however, we have opted for a modified "bottom-up" exposition, in deference to the traditional manner of exposition of the subject.

In the following pages, we will consider first the subject function, in a way that will apply to all clause patterns. We will indicate the fundamental forms of subjects and then their meanings, stated in terms of **thematic roles.**

We will then turn to the various types of predicates, pointing out their functional and formal characteristics. Since different patterns have differing types of objects and complements, we will describe each pattern in a way that expands slightly on the simple subject + predicate division. In particular, we will examine:

1. The functional categories of each pattern
2. The formal realization(s) of the pattern
3. Some typical examples of each pattern
4. The semantics of the head verb
5. The form and meaning of the objects and complements within the verb phrase
6. Selected details of each pattern

8.2   SUBJECTS

The traditional definition of subject is a "what the sentence is about" (AKA the **topic** of the sentence). A traditional grammarian would say that sentence [5] is about *Oscar:*

[5]   Oscar willed Elmer his worm farm.

It says that Oscar willed his worm farm to Elmer. Predicates, from a traditional point of view, complete a sentence by saying something about its subject. This function is sometimes referred to as the *comment* of the sentence.

Subjects tend to refer to entities which are assumed to be already familiar to the hearer; they often represent what has been variously referred to as "known," "old," or "given" information. Predicates generally contain the "new" information in a sentence. The traditional definition of subject is neither formal, functional, nor semantic. Rather, it defines a subject in terms of how the sentence in which it appears relates to the ongoing play of meaning in a discourse.

There are, however, two problems with the traditional definition: (1) it doesn't hold true in all circumstances and (2) it distracts us from grammar into discourse. The traditional definition doesn't hold true because in many sentences the topic is referred to by phrases other than the subject:

[6]   As for Elmer, I don't know who's dating him these days.

In [6], given the appropriate context, we might argue that the topic is the person, Elmer, although *Elmer* isn't the subject.

In addition, the topical characterization of subjects leads us away from grammatical considerations. This distraction is particularly serious when we look at clauses outside the main clause of a sentence, as in [7]:

[7]   Whenever you feel like raking those leaves, go ahead and do it, because I won't rake them.

What is the topic of this sentence? Raking the leaves? If so, it isn't a subject. If only subjects can qualify as topics, then either *you* or *I* or both must be its topics. Can a sentence have two topics? The traditional definition doesn't say. Is every subject a topic? The traditional definition doesn't say. If every subject isn't a topic, how do you identify the topic? The traditional definition doesn't say. In short, one cannot identify topics of sentences out of context, and when we examine sentences in context, the topics may well turn out not to be subjects. Thus the traditional discourse-based criterion for establishing a grammatical category reflects a mistaken notion of grammatical criteria. Moreover, it just doesn't work.

EXERCISE   *Using the traditional definition of subject,* identify the subjects of the following sentences.
   a. It rained yesterday.
   b. There will be more rain tomorrow.
   c. No one understands me.
   d. Advantage was taken of the loophole by the cabinet ministers.
   e. It is clear that power breeds corruption.
   f. Who was it who first said "What, me worry"?
   g. One usually takes a long time to recover from a back injury.
   h. Oscar closed the door.
   i. Amanda helped herself to the nectarines.

   What kinds of problems did you run into?

8.2.1   Identifying a subject

We present in this section a formal characterization of the subject to replace the definition based on discourse function. We can provide a more accurate and more general characterization by using the position, agreement patterns, and case markings of subjects in clauses. Consider the following sentences:

[8a]   I am at home.
   [b]   You are at home.
   [c]   He/she/it is at home.
   [d]   We/you/they are at home.

The main verb of each of these sentences is a form of the verb *be*. The subjects of these sentences are the pronouns *I, you,* etc., that occur to the left of the verb. So one characteristic of a subject (in English) is that it's typically (1) a NP which (2) occurs *before* the verb of its sentence.

EXERCISE   *Using only the characteristic of subjects given just above,* identify the subject of each of the following sentences.

a. It is clear that chicanery is everywhere.
b. There is/are a number of rhetorical problems here.
c. As for TV bloopers, they should be left on the cutting room floor.
d. Bill, with great skill and daring, quickly extricated himself from the web of intrigue.
e. Many deer are killed on the roads each year.
f. In spite of his stature, Tom Thumb ran for election to high office.
g. Rarely have I been so disgusted.

What problems did you run into, and how did you resolve them?

Notice now that as we change the subject, we also change the form of the verb in the sentences in [8]. Thus *I* goes with *am; we/you/they* with *are; he/she/it* with *is*. When two (or more) parts of a sentence are mutually dependent in this way (when one is altered, the other must also be altered) they're said to **agree** with each other.

Notice too that in order to create grammatical sentences, our subjects *must* agree with their verbs. If they don't, the resulting strings of words aren't well-formed (standard) English sentences:

[9a]   *I is at home.
 [b]   *We/you/they am at home.
 [c]   *He/she/it are at home.

(Example [9a] occurs in some varieties as the regular, typical form, and is therefore grammatical in those varieties.)

The verb *be* is the most morphologically complex verb in English. It has far more forms than other verbs, and so shows the agreement between subject and verb most clearly. But this agreement pattern can be seen also in ordinary verbs, although to a considerably lesser degree:

[10a]   I/we/you/they/Bill and Molly like rutabagas.
 [b]   He/she/it/Fred likes rutabagas.

Ordinary verbs have only two forms in the present tense, one that ends in *-s* and another that has no ending. The *-s* form occurs with third person, singular subjects. The uninflected form occurs with all other subjects. So, in general, English subjects must agree with their verbs, as well as occur before them.

We can use these characteristics of subjects to determine just which of several phrases in a sentence is the subject. Suppose, for example, that we had a sentence in the past tense with several NPs in it, and we wished to decide just which one was the subject. Now the *-s* marker doesn't occur in the past tense. There are no verbs of the form **likeds* in English, so to observe the agreement pattern, we must change the verb to the present tense. Then we can systematically change the several NPs in the sentence and observe whether we must also change the verb. When we find the one (and there will be only one) that forces us to change the verb in order to create a grammatical sentence, we will have found the subject of the sentence. Consider:

[11]   I sent you a rose.

Change [11] to the present tense:

[12]   I send you a rose.

Remember that only a third person singular subject requires the -s ending on the verb. Note that *a rose* is third person. If *a rose* were the subject, the verb would be *sends*. Therefore *a rose* isn't the subject. *You* isn't a third person singular, but if we change it to *her,* we still don't have to change the verb. However, if we change the pronoun *I* to *he,* we must then change the verb to *sends* to maintain grammaticality:

[13]   He sends you a rose.

We can conclude that *he* is the subject of [13]; *I* the subject of [12]; and *I* the subject of [11].

EXERCISE   *Using only subject-verb agreement,* identify the subject in each of the following sentences.
a. We left early.
b. We saw the dawn.
c. The gasoline cost us a fortune.
d. There are several cookies in the box.
e. It was raining.
f. It upset Willard that Cindy hated grammar.

What problems did you encounter? How did you solve them?

Another way to determine the subject of a sentence is to replace all of its NPs with pronouns. The NP that can only be replaced by a pronoun in the **nominative** form will be the subject. Thus:

[14]   The man handed the child to the girl.

When we replace each NP with an appropriate pronoun, we get:

[15]   He handed him to her.

The only nominative pronoun is *he,* so *the man* must be the subject of [14].

EXERCISE   *Using only the case of pronouns,* identify the subject of each of the following sentences.
a. Mary had a little lamb.
b. Its fleece was white as snow.
c. Only silly people like nursery rhymes.
d. There are deep truths in this document.
e. It was Mary that locked us out.
f. It is raining.

What problems did you encounter? How did you solve them?

It's important to have a variety of ways of identifying subjects because it's not always easy to identify them in a specific sentence since sentences may obscure the relationship. For example, other NPs besides those which are subjects may occur first in a sentence.

[16] Bill, Fred likes.

This is called a **topicalized** sentence. The first NP *Bill* isn't the subject, as we can see by substituting pronouns:

[17] Him, he likes.

By this test *Fred* is the subject. *Fred* is also the subject by our other test—agreement. If we replace *Fred* by a first person form, we are forced to change the verb to *like*. This doesn't happen if we change *Bill* to a first person form:

[18a] Bill, I like.
  [b] *Bill, I likes.
[19a] Me, Fred likes.
  [b] *Me, Fred like.

EXERCISE   For each of the following sentences, identify its subject.
a. An afternoon nap is a must.
b. My bookstore just ran out of comics.
c. In the beginning, there was chaos.
d. Things aren't any better now.
e. Bill seems to have gone ahead.
f. Margaret has been awarded a fellowship.
g. There is a house in New Orleans.
h. It was a blast.
i. It was Jack that built the house.

What criteria did you use in each case? What problems did you encounter? How did you solve them?

8.3   THEMATIC/SEMANTIC ROLES

Now that we have developed ways to formally identify the subject of a clause let's examine another traditional definition of subject: The subject represents the doer of the action. This characterization sometimes helps:

[20a]   *The eagle* swallowed a trout.
  [b]   *Jesse* dismissed her campaign manager.
  [c]   *Abercrombie* embezzled $1,000,000.

However, as a general characterization of the subject, it will not do. We saw in Chapter 5 that not all verbs denote actions. For example, *be, belong, become, seem, ache, know,* and *own* denote states. How then can we use the definition to identify the subjects in [21]?

[21a]   *That sculpture* belongs to the Art Institute.
  [b]   *Egworm* seems moody today.
  [c]   *My sinuses* ache.
  [d]   *Who* owns the earth?

The situation is even more complex than this, as even verbs denoting actions may have subjects that don't denote the doer of that action (assuming that a doer is a person or at least an animate entity):

[22a]   *The keys* opened the door.
  [b]   *Fred* received a letter from the IRS.
  [c]   *The storm* knocked out the power lines.
  [d]   *The heavy oaken door* opened silently.

In this section, we define a set of terms developed by linguists to describe the **semantic** or **thematic** roles of subjects, as well as of objects and other phrases in clauses.
Consider the sentences:

[23a]   John broke the windshield.
  [b]   John approached Mary.

John is the subject of both sentences, and in traditional grammar would have been defined as the "doer" of the actions of breaking the windshield or approaching Mary. Glossing the subject in this way is an attempt to provide a general statement of the semantic relation between the subject and the verb in an indefinite number of sentences. Modern grammarians have attempted to give a more precise characterization of this relationship. They would say that *John* is the **Agent** of these two sentences. Agents are defined as *the animate instigators of the action denoted by the verb.*
The term *Agent* contrasts with other terms in a set of thematic roles that may be assigned to subjects and other grammatical relations. Compare the sentences of [23] with [24]:

[24]   The hail broke the windshield.

In [24], *the hail* cannot be the Agent of the action denoted by the verb. This is because hail is inanimate, and so cannot be agentive by our definition. We will refer to *the inanimate cause of an event* as the **Force**.

To insist that Agents be animate isn't to play a mere terminological game lacking empirical consequences. To appreciate the difference between Agent and Force in sentences [23] and [24], consider what happens when we add adverbs of willfulness to the sentences:

[25a] John deliberately broke the windshield.
  [b] John deliberately approached Mary.
  [26] *The hail deliberately broke the windshield.

Sentences [25a] and [25b] are perfectly innocuous sentences requiring no special interpretation. Sentence [26], on the other hand, can only be interpreted if we personify hail.

Consider now:

[27] John is in the kitchen.

In [27], *John* although animate is in no sense the "doer" or the instigator of an action, and therefore isn't an Agent. We will refer to the thematic relationship that *John* bears in [27] as the **Theme** of the sentence. Theme is *the NP referring to the entity whose movement, existence, location, or state is predicated.* For example, the italicized phrases below are Themes:

[28a] *The balloon* floated into the sky.
  [b] *The king* is in his counting house.
  [c] *Elves* no longer exist.
  [d] *Frederika* is very tall.

The movement or location may be metaphoricical:

[29a] *Harold* went from bad to worse.
  [b] *Susan* is in a foul mood.
  [c] *Leslie* weighs 145 pounds.

Consider now the roles played by the italicized noun phrases in:

[30] *John* is currently in *Turkey* walking along the *Dardanelles* on his way from *Pakistan* to *Malta.*

Here *John* is the Theme, as its referent is the entity whose movement is in question; *Turkey* is his **Location**; *the Dardanelles* are his **Path**; *Pakistan* is his **Source**, and *Malta* is his **Goal**.

The Path role is played by *the NP referring to the route along which something moves.* For example:

[31] We left by *the rear entrance.*

The Location role is played by *the phrase that designates the place or state at or in which something is at a particular time*. For example:

[32] John is in *bed*/in *Boston*/in *a foul humor*/in *his evening wear*.

The Source role is played by *the phrase indicating the location from which something has moved*:

[33] We took the candy from *the baby*.

The Goal role is played by *the phrase that indicates the place or state to which something moves*:

[34] We sent it to *the Pentagon*.
[35]   SOURCE   GOAL
        John went from *New York* to *New Orleans*.
                       his bed   *his bath*
                       silly   *serious*

Other thematic roles include:

Experiencer: *the animate entity inwardly or psychologically affected by the event or state:*

[36a] *Henry* knows all the answers.
  [b] *We* all feel the pain of loneliness occasionally.

Patient: *the animate entity physically affected by the state or event:*

[37a] The speeding car struck *Bill* a glancing blow.
  [b] The surgeons operated on *her* for several hours.

Instrument: *the object (usually inanimate) with which an act is accomplished:*

[38a] John opened the door with *the crowbar*.
  [b] *The crowbar* opened the door.

Recipient: *the animate being who is the (intended) receiver of the Theme:*

[39a] Some students give *teachers* gifts.
  [b] *Teachers* sometimes get gifts from their students.

Benefactive: *the animate being affected (positively or negatively) by the occurrence denoted by the verb:*

[40a] I cut the grass for *my grandmother*.
  [b] I baked *Sandy* a birthday cake.

Effected/Factitive: *the entity that comes into existence by virtue of the event denoted by the verb:*

[41] Frankenstein created *a monster*.

Attribute: *a status, property, or characteristic ascribed to some entity:*

[42a]   Bull Winkle is *the game warden.*
  [b]   The people elected William Clinton *President of the United States.*

Game Warden is a status ascribed to Bull Winkle by virtue of the state of being denoted by *is* in [42a], and *President of the United States* is attributed to *William Clinton* by virtue of the franchise in [42b].

Empty/Expletive: *a phrase which neither refers to an entity nor denotes an attribute:*

[43a]   *It* is snowing.
  [b]   *It* is late.
  [c]   I would appreciate *it* if you turned down the music.
  [d]   *There* are a number of issues to be considered.

Typically, NPs with Empty semantic roles are either *it* or *there*. Because they're semantically vacuous, these NPs cannot sensibly be questioned:

[44a]   *What is snowing?
  [b]   *What is late?
  [c]   *What would I appreciate if you turned down the music?
  [d]   *Where/what are a number of issues to be considered?

Let's look now at the kinds of thematic or semantic roles that subjects can play. Subjects can play most, if not all, of the roles that we have mentioned:

[45a]   *The horse* bucked the rider. (Agent)
  [b]   *The rider* felt the pain. (Experiencer)
  [c]   *He* underwent a heart transplant. (Patient)
  [d]   *Fred* is the strongest candidate. (Theme)
  [e]   *The keys* open the strongbox. (Instrument)
  [f]   *Fred* got a birthday kiss from his mom. (Recipient)
  [g]   *Fido* had his hair cut. (Benefactive)
  [h]   *Man* evolved from the apes. (Factitive)
  [i]   *Texas* is where the best hot sauce comes from. (Source)
  [j]   *Colorado* is where we're going. (Goal)
  [k]   *Spain* is where the rain falls. (Location)
  [l]   *The storm* knocked out the phone lines. (Force)
  [m]   *It* is raining. (Empty)

EXERCISE   Identify the semantic/thematic role of the subject in each of the following sentences.
  a. Macmillan gave his wife a ring.
  b. The ring was delivered by a liveried messenger.

c. It had been crafted by a skilled goldsmith.
d. Lightning causes forest fires.
e. Carelessness causes injuries.
f. Plastic is derived from petroleum.
g. There are only a few good tickets left.
h. This project cost me a great deal of time.

What problems did you encounter? How did you solve them?

The preceding discussion should make it clear how misleading it is to define the subject in terms of only a single role, that of Agent or "doer of an action." The exercise should give you an indication of how to assign the roles in specific instances.

As we progress through the various sentence patterns, we will take the subject for granted, except for instances where its form or thematic role helps us to understand the pattern.

8.4 AUXILIARY VERBS

Before dealing with the various basic clause patterns, we must discuss a characteristic that all patterns have in common—their capacity to include **auxiliary verbs** such as *be, have,* and the modal verbs *can, could, may, might, shall, should, will, would,* and *must.* As we noted in Chapter 6, these occur before the main verb of the clause:

[46a] Bill may/must/might leave.
 [b]   Bill is leaving.
 [c]   Bill has left.
 [d]   *Bill left has.

The modal verbs are followed by a verb in its infinitival form; the progressive *be* is followed by a verb ending in *-ing;* and the perfective *have* is followed by a verb in its past participial form.

The passive *be* must be mentioned here too. Unlike the progressive *be,* it's followed by a past participle:

[47] Bill was followed by the FBI.

A clause may contain several auxiliary verbs:

[48] Bill may have been being followed by the FBI.

But they will always occur in the order:

[49] (Modal) (Perfective *have*) (Progressive *be*) (Passive *be*)

Each auxiliary is enclosed in parentheses because each is optional. This allows for clauses that contain from zero to four auxiliary verbs.

Although the order of auxiliary verbs is invariant with respect to each other, the position of the first auxiliary verb with respect to the subject of its clause depends on the type of clause involved. In indicative clauses, it occurs between the subject and the verb phrase. In interrogatives, the first auxiliary is placed to the left of the subject. Compare the indicative [a] and interrogative [b] clauses in the pairs below:

[50a] Bill must leave.
 [b] Must Bill leave?
[51a] Bill is leaving.
 [b] Is Bill leaving?
[52a] Bill has left.
 [b] Has Bill left?
[53a] The postcard was mailed yesterday.
 [b] Was the postcard mailed yesterday?
[54a] Bill should have been being followed by the FBI.
 [b] Should Bill have been being followed by the FBI?

Because the placement of the first auxiliary verb is affected by whether its clause is interrogative or indicative, we place it in a special phrase, which we call **AUX**, for auxiliary. Because every clause may include an auxiliary verb, we include AUX in all the formal patterns that we present below. We will deal in more depth with the placement of multiple auxiliaries in Chapter 11.

8.5 BASIC CLAUSE PATTERNS

The basic clause patterns differ from each other by virtue of the type of main verb included in their verb phrases. The verb types are differentiated from each other by virtue of what functions and phrases they require to be present or absent in the VP.

8.5.1 Basic clause pattern 1: Intransitive

The simplest clause pattern corresponds to the functional formula in [55]:

[55] Basic clause pattern 1.

Subject Verb Head

Formally, this pattern contains an NP with a VP whose head verb is intransitive. (We abbreviate this verb as Vi.) The clause may contain no objects or complements. Formally, pattern 1 is:

[56] NP AUX [$_{VP}$Vi]

Examples of this pattern are:

[57a] A swarm of locusts appeared.
  [b] A swarm of locusts appeared on the horizon.
  [c] Edgar spoke.
  [d] Edgar spoke eloquently.
  [e] Edgar spoke to the crowd.
  [f] Edgar spoke eloquently to the crowd.
  [g] Edgar spoke eloquently to the crowd after the protest march.
  [h] Edgar spoke eloquently to the crowd after the protest march had concluded.

The greater length and complexity of some of these sentences don't arise from changes in the basic clause pattern of the simpler examples, but rather, they arise from choices in auxiliaries and modifiers. Modifiers in the VP and auxiliaries have no effect on the basic pattern. This fact holds true even when, as in [57h], the modifier itself is a clause. The modifying clause naturally has its own pattern—here also pattern 1; but as a modifier, it's irrelevant to the pattern of the clause that contains it.

8.5.2 Basic clause pattern 2: Simple transitive

In Chapter 7 we distinguished intransitive verbs by their ability to end sentences. Most of us are loquacious enough to need more than a subject and a single verb to convey an idea. The remaining clause patterns indicate a wealth of resources for expanding fundamental structures, through either objects or complements.

Pattern 2 has the functional structure [58], corresponding to the form [59]:

[58] Basic clause pattern 2

Subject   Verb Head   Direct Object

[59] NP   AUX   [$_{VP}$Vt   NP]

As is the case for all verbs that have an object, the head verb is transitive, indicated as Vt. The objects are italicized in the following examples of pattern 2:

[60a] Adam likes *ribs*.
  [b] Eve enjoys *apples*.
  [c] The snake held *a particularly luscious Granny Smith*.
  [d] Occasionally, Adam would accept *small appealing gifts* from Eve.
  [e] Adam likes *those who offer something for nothing*.

Regardless of the complexity of the direct object NP in [60a] to [60e], these sentences still represent pattern 2.

A convenient test for this pattern is to replace the NPs with appropriate pronouns. The result will be something like:

[61] He/she/it/they—Verb—him/her/it/them

The nominative pronouns replace the subject NP; the accusative pronouns replace the object. By this test, sentences [60a] and [60e] both reduce to *He likes them*. As in the case of the intransitive pattern, modifiers and auxiliaries don't affect the basic pattern.

Another test of "objecthood" is based on the fact that many clauses of pattern 2 may be passivized. In particular, the Passive Test distinguishes pattern 2 clauses from pattern 3. Objects may frequently be passivized; complements can never be. The [62a] and [63a] clauses below are the active counterparts of the passive [62b] and [63b] clauses:

[62a] The entire family can enjoy nature movies.
  [b] Nature movies can be enjoyed by the entire family.
[63a] Multinational corporations exploit the poorer countries.
  [b] The poorer countries are exploited by multinational corporations.

The subject of the passive clause corresponds to the object of the active. You should convince yourself that this is the case by applying the tests for "subjecthood" we developed earlier to the first NP in each of the passive clauses above.

As a final remark on objects, note that most of the thematic roles available to subjects are available also to objects. Objects may be interpreted in a wide range of ways other than the traditional "entity affected by the action of the verb."

EXERCISE Identify the thematic role of the object in each of the following sentences:
  a. Bill moved the table.
  b. Bill made the table.
  c. The divorce upset him.
  d. The doctor stitched the wound.
  e. We use a word processor for our work.
  f. The fund drive benefited the local radio station.
  g. We left the room.
  h. We approached the border.
  i. We skied the mountain trails.
  j. We would appreciate it greatly if you would leave.

What problems did you encounter? How did you solve them?

8.5.3 Basic clause pattern 3: Subject complement

The subject complement construction resembles the direct object pattern in having three basic elements. The main difference between the two lies in the nature of the head verb and the semantic relations it creates. The functional pattern is:

[64] Basic clause pattern 3.

  Subject Verb Head Subject Complement

The pattern is slightly complicated by the fact that two different forms can act as subject complement: a noun phrase or an adjective phrase. The italicized phrases in [65] and [66] illustrate NP and AP complements, respectively:

[65a] Mary became *a doctor.*
  [b] You are *a nuisance who ought to be barred from the pool.*
  [c] He proved *a success at ice-carving.*
[66a] Mary became *famous.*
  [b] I am *quite aware of her foibles.*
  [c] He proved *unwilling to cooperate with my attorney.*

To state pattern 3 formally, we need two formulas:

[67a] NP   AUX   [$_{VP}$V   NP]
  [b] NP   AUX   [$_{VP}$V   AP]

NP complements are sometimes called **predicate nominals** or **predicative nominatives.** AP complements are sometimes referred to as **predicate adjectives.** The subject complement can be viewed as a class with two subclasses, NP and AP.

We can collapse the two formulas [67a] and [67b] into a single expression by enclosing NP and AP in curly brackets, {}, which indicate that no more than one line within them may be chosen at a time:

[67c] NP   AUX   [$_{VP}$V $\left\{ \begin{matrix} NP \\ AP \end{matrix} \right\}$]

In the case of subject complements, form plays a limiting role. In particular, it restricts the function to NPs and APs; thus the prepositional phrase following the verb in [68] is a modifier of the VP, not a subject complement:

[68] I am in the kitchen.

A pattern which is helpful in distinguishing subject complements from objects and modifiers is the number agreement that occurs with the subject NP. If we make the subject NP plural, we must also make the subject complement NP plural. Compare [65a] with:

[69a] Mary and Terry became doctors.
  [b] *Mary and Terry became doctor.
  [c] *Mary became doctors.

This test doesn't work for AP subject complements because APs aren't marked for number in English.

Other than this, semantics influences the determination of a subject complement. First, the subject and the subject complement must apply to the same entity. This is often indicated by assigning the subject and the complement the same subscript:

[70] Mary$_i$ is a doctor$_i$.

Thus *Mary* and *a doctor* apply to the same individual. As we noted above, we designate the thematic role of the complement as Attribute. The subject complement denotes either a permanent or a temporary status, characteristic, or property, of the subject. This conception of the function will allow you to distinguish pattern 3 from pattern 2, where the NP following the verb group doesn't ascribe a characteristic to the subject:

[71]   Mary visited a doctor.

Of course, the entire VP assigns a characteristic (of visiting a doctor) to Mary, but our test applies only to the structure after the verb. In [71], we are referring to two distinct individuals; in [70], we refer only to one.

Semantics also enters into the identification of subject complements because of the nature of the head verb. We can describe the basic verb meaning in the subject complement function as BE/BECOME. These are the primitive notions of state and change of state. (Don't confuse this difference with stative and dynamic meanings of verbs.) Such verbs are often referred to as **linking verbs.** We list some of them in Table 8.1.

However, nearly all of these verbs may have meanings other than BE or BECOME. When they have those other meanings, they don't take a subject complement. In the following pairs of examples, the [a] clauses contain subject complements, and the [b] clauses represent some other pattern:

[72a]   Hoolihan appeared weak.
   [b]   Hoolihan appeared. (Pattern 1)
[73a]   Boris felt sorry.
   [b]   Boris felt pain. (Pattern 2)
[74a]   Newton proved unreliable.
   [b]   Newton proved the theorem. (Pattern 2)
[75a]   The milk turned sour.
   [b]   Osgood turned away. (Pattern 1)

As we noted in the previous section, we can use the Passive Test to distinguish between VPs containing subject complements and those containing direct objects. We can often passivize a direct object but never a subject complement:

[76a]   Einstein proved the better physicist.
   [b]   *The better physicist was proved by Einstein.
[77a]   Einstein proved the equation.
   [b]   The equation was proved by Einstein.

TABLE 8.1   Linking Verbs

be (am, is, are, was, were, be, being, been)			
appear	become	feel	get
go	grow	look	make
prove	seem	smell	sound
taste	turn		

8.5.4   Clause pattern 4: Object complement

The next two clause patterns add one more function to pattern 2: Subject - Verb Head - Direct Object. This part of the pattern remains intact, but the function of object complement is added to it to create pattern 4. The functional formula for pattern 4 is:

[78]   Basic clause pattern 4

   Subject   Verb Head   Direct Object   Object Complement

Object complements are similar to subject complements in four respects. First, an object complement may be formally expressed as either an NP or an AP, italicized in:

[79a]   I consider Elvira *a weirdo.*
   [b]   We proclaimed her *our champion.*
   [c]   She painted the room *a ghastly color.*
[80a]   I consider Elvira *weird.*
   [b]   We found her *guilty.*
   [c]   She painted the room *mauve.*

The two formal patterns corresponding to [78] are [81a] and [81b], which we can abbreviate as [81c]:

[81a]   NP   AUX $[_{VP}$V   NP   NP]
   [b]   NP   AUX $[_{VP}$V   NP   AP]

   [c]   NP   AUX $[_{VP}$V   NP $\begin{Bmatrix} NP \\ AP \end{Bmatrix}$]

The second feature common to subject and object complements is that in both an NP complement must agree with its antecedent (the subject or the object):

[82]   I consider Elvira and Elvis weirdos.

Here again, because English APs cannot be marked for plural, there can be no agreement between an AP object complement and the direct object of its clause.

To see the third parallel with subject complements, we must observe the semantic relation between the direct object and its complement. If you consider carefully the sentences in [79] and [80], you will notice that the semantic relations between the object and its complement are BE and BECOME. In [79c], the room becomes a ghastly color. Here again, we will say that the thematic role associated with the complement is that of Attribute.

The final similarity between subject and object complements is that the complement phrase and the subject or object to which it's semantically linked refer to a single entity. We indicate this by identically subscripting the object and the complement:

[83a]   NP   AUX $[_{VP}$V   NP$_i$ NP$_i$]
   [b]   NP   AUX $[_{VP}$V   NP$_i$ AP$_i$]

Object complements have one further defining trait—the meaning of the head verb. Examine Table 8.2 to see if you can identify any semantic common denominators.

TABLE 8.2   Typical Object Complement Verbs

appoint	call	choose	consider	
declare	designate	elect	find	
imagine	make	name	paint	prove

The two semantic classes which unite most of these words are CONSIDER TO BE (*consider, imagine, think*) and CAUSE TO BECOME (most of the others), illustrated by the examples in [84] and [85], respectively:

[84a] We find his conclusion ridiculous.
  [b] They called each other liars.
[85a] The president named him Secretary of the Bubblegum Department.
  [b] The children painted all the walls kelly green.

However, object complement verbs (like subject complement verbs) have a variety of meanings, not all of them compatible with object complements. The [a] version of each pair below contains an object complement; the [b] versions contain the same verb in a different pattern.

[86a] We declared Woople the winner.
  [b] We declared a holiday. (Pattern 2)
[87a] Scott and Zelda painted the town red.
  [b] Scott and Zelda painted the door. (Pattern 2)
[88a] His false predictions proved Weskin a hoax.
  [b] His false predictions proved Weskin's undoing. (Pattern 3)

Finally, there are many idiomatic constructions that involve an AP object complement. Some of these appear in Table 8.3, where X denotes a variable direct object. As will be clear, nearly all these expressions indicate the notion of BECOMING.

TABLE 8.3   Idiomatic Object Complement Expressions

cut the story short	cut X short
drain X dry	leave X clean
make X clear	make X plain
make X possible	pack X tight
push X open	put X straight
shake X free	

8.5.5   Basic clause pattern 5: Indirect object

This basic clause pattern also involves a head verb followed by two functions:

[89]   Subject   Verb Head   Indirect Object   Direct Object

As the formula indicates, the last two functions occur in order: first, the indirect object (IO), and second, the direct object (DO). (Recall that in pattern 4 the DO appeared *immediately after* the verb head.) Formally, both objects are typically NPs. The formal version of pattern 5 is:

[90]   NP   AUX   [_{VP}V   NP   NP]

In each of the following examples the IO is italicized:

[91a]   Willard gave *me* the roses.
  [b]   The eighteenth century brought *England* great prosperity.
  [c]   She paid *her creditors* a part of the debt.
  [d]   Oscar made *his friend* a beautiful desk.

In both patterns 4 and 5, a verb may be followed by two NPs. These two structures can be readily distinguished. In pattern 4, the two NPs refer to a single entity; in pattern 5, each NP refers to a separate entity.

Again, semantics plays a role in the pattern, in both the nature of the verb and the thematic role of the indirect object. The verb has the prototypical meaning of GIVING or of BENEFITING. In [91a] and [91c], the notion of *giving* is clear; [91b] and [91d] illustrate the meaning of *benefiting*. On these semantic grounds, we can identify certain verbs that take indirect objects. We list a typical sample in Table 8.4.

The list in Table 8.4 may be a bit misleading for several reasons. First, most of the verbs commonly occur in patterns that don't have explicit indirect objects:

[92a]   Allison asked a profound question. (Pattern 2)
  [b]   Walpole refused. (Pattern 1)
  [c]   Finkle made a successful legislator. (Pattern 3)
  [d]   We made Portnoy our representative. (Pattern 4)

TABLE 8.4   Some Indirect Object Verbs

allow	ask	assign	bequeath	bring
buy	deny	forbid	forgive	grant
hand	leave	lend	make	owe
pardon	pay	refund	refuse	remit
sell	send	show	sing	spare
teach	tell	throw	write	

Second, many verbs that are not on the list can be understood as having a Beneficiary, especially if they refer to some type of production [93a] or acquisition [93b]:

[93a] Wanda baked Phyllis a birthday cake.
  [b] Jack fetched Jill a pail of water.

Third, the action denoted by the verb may involve something which isn't literally "transferred" to a recipient, nor is it always beneficial:

[94] Roscoe gave Morgentherp a sound thrashing.

Since the meaning of verbs is so flexible, it's more illuminating to consider the thematic roles assigned to the noun phrases in this pattern. First, the subject is likely to instigate the action as an Agent or a Force:

[95a] Anderson bought us a souvenir. (Agent)
  [b] The accident taught us a bitter lesson. (Force)

Indirect objects tend to be Recipients or Benefactives; direct objects tend to be Themes. But this is just a tendency, not an absolute restriction. In [96], for example, the subject is an Agent, the direct object a Factitive, and the indirect object is a Source:

[96] They asked me an unanswerable question.

Second, we assume that pattern 5 is an outgrowth of pattern 2, which possesses only a direct object. The indirect object is in a sense a luxury—a piece of information added to this stable pattern when need arises in communication. The addition of an extra object alerts the hearer to devise a relevant role for the extra NP. What could that role be? Well, agents don't act in isolation or without motives. And those motives often involve other human beings—at least in prototypical situations. The indirect object provides clues about the motivation for an act by some agent. With a Force subject, it identifies the entities affected by the Force. We can often reduce these relations to Beneficiary or Recipient, but real-life connections will very likely exceed these bounds.

There is a relatively reliable test for distinguishing pattern 4 from pattern 5 constructions. We will call this the **Dative Test**. (*Dative* is the Latinate term for the case of indirect objects.) Pattern 5 clauses can generally be paraphrased by a clause pattern in which the order of the two object NPs is reversed and a preposition is inserted before the second (corresponding to the IO). *To* usually indicates Recipient; *for* usually indicates Beneficiary. The sentences in [97] paraphrase a selection of those above:

[97a] Willard gave roses to me.
  [b] The eighteenth century brought great prosperity to England.
  [c] She paid a part of her debt to her creditors.
  [d] Warthog built some kitchen shelves for his aunt.
  [e] Wanda baked a birthday cake for Phyllis.
  [f] Anderson bought a souvenir for us.

One drawback of the Dative Test is that it doesn't distinguish between the Recipient and Goal meanings of the preposition *to*. Only the former is relevant in this context, so [98] reflects pattern 2 with a verb modifier, not pattern 5:

[98a]   Anderson sent the children to the lake.
  [b]   *Anderson sent the lake the children.

Also, the test will not work with certain fixed indirect object constructions:

[99a]   It cost me a fortune.
  [b]   *It cost a fortune to/for me.
  [c]   He gave me a ring. (Ambiguous)
  [d]   He gave a ring to me. (Unambiguous)

The object complement construction has no such paraphrase:

[100]   *We elected president to/for him.

Moreover, we can apply passive to the IO in pattern 5 clauses, just as we can to the DO in pattern 4:

[101]   I was given the roses by Warthog.

Some varieties of English even allow the DO of pattern 5 clauses to be passivized:

[102]   The roses were given me by Warthog.

The second NP in the VP of pattern 4 clauses cannot be passivized:

[103]   *President was elected him by the voters.

A final restriction on this pattern is that the direct object NP may not be a pronoun:

[104a]   Wanda baked Phyllis the cake.
  [b]   *Wanda baked Phyllis it.

8.5.6   Basic clause pattern 6: Recipient/Benefactive

Like patterns 3, 4, and 5, this basic clause pattern includes a head verb followed by two functions:

[105]   Subject Verb Head Direct Object Recipient/Benefactive

The formal version of pattern 6 is:

[106]   NP AUX [$_{VP}$V NP PP]

Examples of this pattern include:

[107a] Willard gave the roses to Amanda.
  [b] The eighteenth century brought great prosperity to England.
  [c] Oscar baked a birthday cake for Amanda.
  [d] Oscar pulled the weeds for his friends.

The meanings and thematic roles represented by this pattern are similar but not identical to those represented by pattern 5. As a result, many traditional and school grammars refer to the NP expressing the Recipient or Benefactive as an IO. From a formal point of view, this NP is the object of the preposition that governs it, so in keeping with our formalist assumptions, we will restrict the term *indirect object* to the NP that occurs directly after the verb and before the DO in the sentences of pattern 5.

The two patterns cannot be viewed simply as variants of each other, as we noted in our discussion of pattern 5. That is, we cannot always rephrase a sentence in one pattern as a sentence in the other pattern. Such substitutions may either change the meaning or result in ungrammaticality. In particular, if the direct object of a pattern 6 sentence is a pronoun, as in [108a], then rephrasing the sentence as a pattern 5 results in an ungrammatical sentence like [108b]:

[108a] We made it for Oscar.
  [b] *We made Oscar it.

Sentences such as [109a] are ambiguous. They can describe a telephone call or a gift of a ring. However, their pattern 6 counterparts can only describe a gift-giving:

[109a] Oscar gave Amanda a ring.
  [b] Oscar gave a ring to Amanda.

8.5.7 Basic clause pattern 7: Location

Here again, we are dealing with sentences in which the verb implies two functions in the verb phrase:

[110] Subject Verb Head Direct Object Location

whose formal characterization is:

[111] NP AUX $[_{VP}$V NP $\left\{ \begin{matrix} PP \\ AdvP \end{matrix} \right\}$]

Here the second function in the verb phrase can be represented as either a PP or an AdvP. For example:

[112a] Oscar put his bicycle *in the laundry room.*
  [b] Oscar put his bicycle *away.*

Sentences of this pattern cannot be rephrased as sentences of pattern 5:

[113]   *Oscar put the laundry room his bicycle.

However, the fact that adverbs can move around relatively freely in English sentences does allow us to say:

[114]   Oscar put away his bicycle.

Sentences of this type shouldn't be confused with sentences of pattern 5.

8.5.8   Basic clause pattern 8: Passive

We have mentioned the passive construction a number of times in this and other chapters, and although it's not usually regarded as a basic sentence pattern from a grammatical point of view, it's of such importance that we will discuss it again here. First, we give its functional formula:

[115]   Subject   Be   Verb head   (Agentive phrase)

Passive sentences include some form of the verb *be* followed by a verb in its past participle form. They may include an agentive (*by*) phrase. Formally, they consist of:

[116]   NP   AUX   [$_{VP}$V + en   (PP)]

For example:

[117a]   The children were fed by the baby-sitter.
   [b]   The pretzels were eaten by the mice.
   [c]   The children were fed.
   [d]   The pretzels were eaten.

As a general rule, passive sentences have active counterparts, although a missing agentive phrase may have to be expressed as an indefinite pronoun:

[118a]   The baby-sitter fed the children
   [b]   The mice ate the pretzels.
   [c]   Someone fed the children.
   [d]   Someone/something ate the pretzels.

The active subject corresponds to the NP in the passive *by*-phrase and the passive subject corresponds to either a direct or an indirect object in the active:

[119a]   The package was sent to Amanda.
   [b]   Amanda was sent the package.

or occasionally to the object of a preposition:

[120] My bed has been slept in.

Style manuals and many school grammars and composition textbooks advise students to avoid the passive. However, some research has demonstrated that student writers use the passive less often than expert writers (Garvey and Lindstrom, 1989). It would appear therefore that what students need to learn is how to use the passive appropriately, a piece of advice that applies to all sentence types. There are two major traditional objections to passives. First, they're alleged to be deceitful: They can and often do omit reference to the agent responsible for an event. Second, because they begin with an NP whose thematic role isn't an Agent, they're alleged to be "weak."

In response to the first objection, we say that omitting pieces of sentences isn't something that only passives can do. Many if not all sentence types can. So in this regard, writers need to decide just what information must be presented and what can be omitted from a text. This is a matter of audience, not of grammar.

To the second objection, most languages of the world have constructions that correspond to the English passive. It would be most unlikely for these constructions to have developed and been retained if they weren't of considerable value. What they do is allow essentially the same information as that represented in the active to be reordered. In fact, languages generally include many constructions that allow information to be reordered. In English alone, we have at least the following:

[121a] The mice ate the pretzels. (Active)
   [b] The pretzels were eaten by the mice. (Passive)
   [c] The pretzels, the mice ate. (Topicalization)
   [d] What ate the pretzels were the mice. (Wh-cleft)
   [e] What the mice ate were the pretzels. (Wh-cleft)
   [f] It was the mice that ate the pretzels. (It-cleft)
   [g] It was the pretzels that the mice ate. (It-cleft)

The order in which information is deployed in a sentence depends on a number of factors, including whether it's already familiar to the audience, whether it's topical, and whether the speaker/writer wishes to give it special prominence. Each of the constructions illustrated above has its own idiosyncratic textual effects, and so must be used in appropriate contexts.

Before leaving these clause patterns, we should briefly discuss just why we regard them as basic. First, they're all simple sentences; i.e., none of them includes another clause within it. Second, they can all be elaborated by the addition of various types of optional modifiers, such as adverbial phrases. Third, and most important, each pattern reflects the class of verb that heads its verb phrase. In particular, each pattern reflects the thematic roles assigned by the verb to the phrases (if any) in the predicate. Each pattern also reflects the formal requirements imposed by its head verb. Some verbs require two NPs, some an NP and a PP, and some nothing at all. Thus verbs impose both thematic (semantic) and formal requirements on sentences.

REFERENCES AND RESOURCES

Brown, Keith, and Jim Miller. 1991. *Syntax: A Linguistic Introduction to Sentence Structure.* 2d ed. London: Harper Collins Academic.

Celce-Murcia, Marianne, and Diane Larsen-Freeman. 1983. *The Grammar Book: An ESL/EFL Teacher's Course.* Rowley, MA: Newbury House.

Fries, Charles Carpenter. 1952. *The Structure of English.* New York: Harcourt, Brace & World, Inc.

Garvey, James J., and David H. Lindstrom, 1989. "Pro's Prose Meets Writer's Workbench." *Computers and Composition* 6(2), 81–109.

Jackson, Howard. 1990. *Grammar and Meaning: A Semantic Approach to English Grammar.* London: Longman.

Greenbaum, Sidney, and Randolph Quirk. 1990. *A Student's Grammar of the English Language.* London: Longman.

Liles, Bruce. 1987. *A Basic Grammar of Modern English.* 2d ed. Englewood Cliffs, NJ: Prentice-Hall, Inc.

GLOSSARY

Agent: the thematic role that indicates the animate instigator of an action.

Agree: a grammatical relationship where the form of one element (e.g., a subject) varies with the form of another element (e.g., a verb).

Attribute: the thematic role that indicates the status, property, or characteristic ascribed to some entity.

AUX: abbreviation for **auxiliary verb.** See Chapter 6 and Chapter 7.

Benefactive: the thematic role that indicates an animate being affected positively or negatively.

Clause: a grammatical unit that contains a subject and a predicate.

Dative Test: a test used to identify a pattern 5 clause by using a *to* or *for* paraphrase.

Effected (also called "factitive"): the thematic role that indicates the entity that comes into existence by virtue of an event.

Empty/expletive: the thematic role assigned to a phrase which neither refers to an entity nor denotes an attribute.

Experiencer: the thematic role that indicates the animate entity inwardly or psychologically affected by an event or state.

Factitive: see **effected.**

Force: the thematic role that indicates the inanimate cause of an event.

Goal: the thematic role that indicates the place or state to which something moves.

Instrument: the thematic role that indicates the object (usually inanimate) with which an act is accomplished.

Linking verb: a verb, such as *be* or *become,* that serves as the main verb in basic clause pattern 3.

Location: the thematic role that indicates the place or state at or in which something is at a particular time.

Nominative: see Chapter 6.

Object complement: the grammatical function of a noun phrase or adjective phrase that follows a direct object, agrees with it grammatically, and has the same reference.

Path: the thematic role that indicates the route along which something moves.

Patient: the thematic role that indicates the animate entity physically affected by the state or event.

Predicate: the grammatical function of the verb phrase of a clause. See **subject.**

Predicate nominal (also called **"predicate nominative"**): the syntactic function of a noun phrase that follows a linking verb.

Predicate adjective: the syntactic function of an adjective phrase that follows a linking verb.

Recipient: the thematic role that indicates the animate being who is the (intended) receiver of the Theme.

Semantic role: see **thematic role.**

Source: the thematic role that indicates the location from which something has moved.

Subject: the grammatical function of the noun phrase which agrees with the verb in a clause. See **predicate.**

Subject complement: the grammatical function that includes **predicate nominal** and **predicate adjective.**

Thematic role: a semantic relation between a noun phrase and a verb, noun, or preposition in a clause.

Theme: the thematic role that indicates the entity whose movement, existence, location, or state is predicated by a verb.

Topic: a phrase that designates the entity that a sentence is about.

Topicalized: see Chapter 7.

9 GRAPHIC REPRESENTATIONS OF SENTENCE ELEMENTS

KEY CONCEPTS

Visualizing function and structure
Functional diagramming
Formal diagramming

9.0 VISUALIZING FUNCTION AND STRUCTURE

In the previous chapter, we explained grammatical constructions and their complexity using only words. Sometimes, though, students have difficulty relating to purely verbal accounts of structure. This is one reason why many systems of syntax have developed graphic devices—diagrams—to present their analyses. There are several diagramming systems available, more than any teacher would ever need. But in practice, two methods of diagramming provide all of the graphic equipment a teacher needs. Not surprisingly, one system is based on function, the other on form.

9.1 FUNCTIONAL DIAGRAMMING

The diagramming system that is most familiar in traditional grammar is actually fairly recent, dating back only to the end of the nineteenth century. In a text entitled *Higher Lessons in English,* Alonzo Reed and Brainerd Kellogg (1877) sketched what they called a means to understand "the natural development of the sentence (v)." By this they meant to distinguish their approach from one that began with the atoms of grammar—the parts of speech—and which often would "disregard the higher unities, without which details are scarcely intelligible (vi)." Their system has influenced the teaching of grammar until the present. We will thus refer to this system as Reed-Kellogg diagramming, RK for short.

RK is based almost exclusively on function rather than on form or meaning. As we have seen, phrases are most easily described in terms of simple functional formulas; so RK is particularly useful in revealing the phrase and clause levels of language. In contrast, parts of speech are given only scant attention. Most grammar books present the Reed-Kellogg system through a set of examples. While compact, this manner of explanation ignores more general principles that the system uses. As we go along, we will point out some of these principles.

9.1.1 Subjects and predicates

The key functional structure is that of subject and predicate. For each clause, the subject appears next to the predicate on a horizontal line, separated by a vertical line that bisects the horizontal one. Thus the sentences of [1] appear diagrammatically as [2]:

[1a] Cork floats.
 [b] Zelda may have arrived.

[2a] <u>Cork</u> | <u>floats</u>   [b] <u>Zelda</u> | <u>may have arrived</u>

Let's introduce some terminology. The actual printed sentence, as in [1], we call simply "the sentence"; the diagrammed sentence in [2] we call "the diagram." The line that contains the subject and predicate (and other major functions) we call the **baseline.** All baselines are horizontal, but not all horizontal lines are baselines.

Capitalization isn't important, although this aspect of the sentence is usually preserved—unlike punctuation, which isn't indicated. The word listed as subject will always be the **head** of the subject NP (what traditional grammars call the *simple subject*). In the predicate position, there will be listed (1) the head of the predicate VP (called the *simple predicate*) and (2) any auxiliaries that happen to occur in the sentence.

The principle behind this practice is that baselines are reserved for clauses and clauselike structures. Not all horizontal lines indicate bases, but bases are always clearly distinguishable by both their length and the fact that they contain the bisecting vertical subject-predicate stroke. A key element of Reed and Kellogg's program is the development of one's sense of "higher unities." Baselines are crucial elements of those unities.

9.1.2 Objects and complements

The RK system follows almost exactly our portrayal of the basic clause patterns in the previous chapter. Each pattern has a distinct formation. The direct object (pattern 2) is placed after the verb separated from it by a nonbisecting vertical line. Sentence [3] thus appears as [4].

[3] Barbi disdains mink.

[4] <u>Barbi</u> | <u>disdains</u> | <u>mink</u>

The graphic representation of the subject complement (pattern 3) resembles that of the direct object, except that it's separated from the verb by a line slanted back toward the subject. This line suggests the semantic assignment of an attribute to the subject. The sentences in [5] come out as [6]:

[5a] Napoleon became emperor.
  [b] Beethoven was furious.

[6a] Napoleon | became \ emperor **[b]** Beethoven | was \ furious

As we noted, parts of speech aren't directly distinguished in the RK system. So the fact that *emperor* is a noun/noun phrase while the fact that *furious* is an adjective/adjective phrase isn't expressly pointed out in the diagram.

The object complement construction (pattern 4) follows the analogy just established. The diagram is set up as for a simple direct object; then the object complement immediately follows it on the baseline, separated by a slanting line. This line suggests the semantic assignment of an attribute to the direct object. The sentences in [7] result in the diagrams in [8].

[7a] We chose her president.
  [b] We consider her trustworthy.

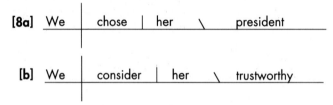

[8a] We | chose | her \ president

  [b] We | consider | her \ trustworthy

Again, whether the object complement is a noun phrase or an adjective phrase isn't indicated.

Indirect object constructions (pattern 5) are a bit more complex since they require material off the baseline. The subject, the verb (with its auxiliaries), and the direct object are represented as in pattern 2. Then the indirect object is attached under the verb by an angled line. The indirect object appears on the horizontal part of the angle; nothing appears on the slanted part of the angle. Examples [9] and [10] illustrate the formation:

[9] Alethia offered Caesar flowers.

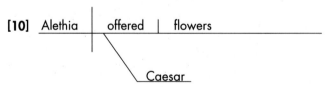

[10] Alethia | offered | flowers

          Caesar

This diagram deserves closer examination. By locating the indirect object off the baseline, the RK system appears to relegate it to a secondary status, as will become clear shortly. The placement of the structure under the verb is also significant; it suggests a close affinity between the indirect object and the verb.

EXERCISE   Diagram the following sentences.
1. The contract elapsed.
2. Greg caught the ball.
3. Cian offered Ray a lucrative contract.
4. The coach considers Brian her best forward.
5. Gineen was selected.

For the most part, Reed and Kellogg offer no distinct representation for the passive pattern. Instead, this pattern falls under the heading of some of the other structures in the system. On one hand, this failure to distinguish passives is a drawback in the system since it glosses over an important difference in grammatical structure. On the other hand, passives do have many functional resemblances to nonpassives.

EXERCISE   Diagram the following passive sentences.
1. The ball was dropped.
2. The ball was dropped by the quarterback.
3. We were given playoff tickets.
4. Playoff tickets were given to the kids.
5. This bed was slept in by Martha Washington.

9.1.3 Modifiers

The RK system has a general principle for modifiers: Put them on a slanted line under their headword. This principle encompasses much of the rest of the RK system. It allows one to represent a wide range of different formal types of modifiers, including articles, possessives, ordinals, adjective phrases, adverb phrases, prepositional phrases, and more.

Consider, first of all, the **premodifiers** in a noun phrase. Sentence [11] contains a selection of them:

[11a] Those three old stone buildings crumbled.
  [b] those = demonstrative
  [c] three = numeral
  [d] old = head of AP
  [e] stone = noun modifier

In the diagram of [11], these formal distinctions are leveled:

[12] buildings ǀ crumbled

Adjective phrases may be modified by an intensifier (e.g., *very*, *more*, and *quite*). When APs appear in diagrams, their modifiers accompany them on slanted lines:

[13a] Those buildings are very old.
  [b] The very old buildings crumbled.

[14a]

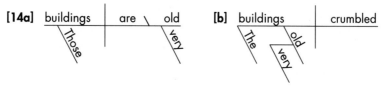

Textbooks vary as to how modifiers of modifiers are represented graphically. Diagram [14b] is one possibility. However, all variations adhere to the slanted-line convention.

Adverb phrases follow similar principles since they're normally treated as modifiers. Examples [15] and [16] suggest the pattern:

[15] Obviously, they seldom proceeded very carefully.

[16]

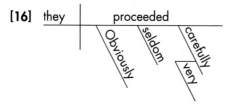

Examples [15] and [16] also illustrate the procedure when a head has two or more modifiers. One simply writes them on slanted lines in the order in which they appear in the sentence. However, adverb phrases are almost invariably placed under the main verb, whether they appear initially or later in the clause. Intensifiers within adverb phrases are treated similarly to those in adjective phrases.

Prepositional phrases have a distinct shape, but one related to the modification structure. PPs appear on angles, with the preposition on the slanted part and the object of the preposition on the horizontal line. (This is another case where the horizontal line isn't a baseline.) PPs, of course, can function variously as modifiers of nouns, verbs, and adjectives. Examples [17] and [18] provide illustrations of these possibilities:

[17a] The clock on the wall stopped. (Postmodifier of Noun)
  [b] Whizbang walked on coals. (Modifier of Verb)
  [c] Alethia offered flowers to Caesar. (Modifier of Verb)
  [d] I am fond of truffles. (Complement of Adjective)

[18a]

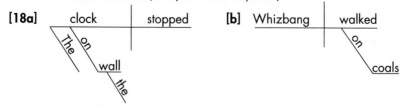

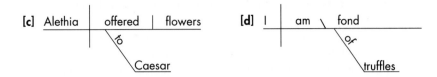

You will notice that diagram [18c] resembles the indirect object diagram in [10], except that the former lacks the preposition *to*. This similarity results from the attempt in the RK system to suggest the paraphrase relation between sentences with indirect objects and those with prepositional phrases headed by *to* and *for*.

9.1.4 Coordination

One final device in the RK graphic system is used to represent coordination. The basic principle is to place the conjoined phrases on parallel lines, joined by an angle. The conjunction is written between the two elements it connects.

Some simple instances appear in [19] and [20]. The types of structures coordinated appear in parentheses:

[19a] Willard cried but Wanda laughed. (Clauses)
[b] Oscar and his friend arrived late. (Subjects)
[c] Mary danced, sang, and played the trumpet. (Verb Phrases)
[d] I was both elated and embarrassed. (Subject Complements)

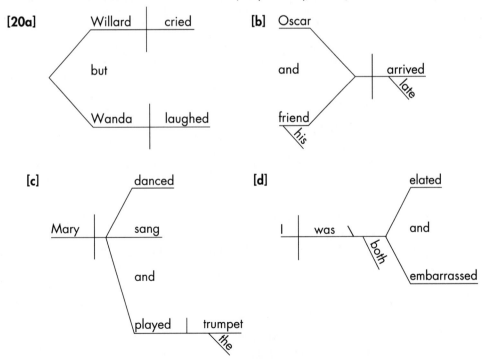

If you examine these diagrams carefully, you will note several important details. The angle points in the direction that most effectively integrates it with the rest of the diagram. In three of our examples, this direction is leftward. However, the rightward direction is used in [20b] to indicate that the conjoined subject shares a common predicate. Also, within the parallel lines of the conjunction, each conjoined structure is represented in the form it would take if it were not conjoined. So in [20a], the two clauses are further analyzed as separate subjects and predicates. In [20b], *his* modifies only *friends,* not *Oscar.* In [20c], *the trumpet* is the direct object only of *played.* When a word applies to both conjoined elements, it's placed on a line common to the parallels. So in [20d], *both* modifies *elated and embarrassed.*

Because of the power of coordination—as well as of many other structures that allow embedding—the equipment discussed here will enable you to diagram an infinitely long sentence. You are advised not to do so, however, for the sake of your sanity. Even moderately complicated sentences can create major difficulties and challenge students' sense of graphic aesthetics. For this reason, it's normally advisable to use diagrams only on relatively simple sentences. The RK system does provide apparatus for diagramming much more complex sentences, such as those considered in Chapter 10. For a more complete version of the RK mechanics, see Emery (1961).

9.1.5　Nonbasic sentences: Imperatives and questions

The RK system is concrete, in that every word of the sentence appears in the diagram. Two departures from concreteness arise, however, in the treatment of (1) understood elements and (2) word order. We shall see in Chapter 11 that the analysis of a sentence often requires a highly abstract representation. So the discussion here will provide a glimpse of more advanced approaches to sentence structure.

Imperative sentences share the basic sentence patterns of statements, except that they lack a subject. Traditional grammars usually assert (without support) that the subject of imperatives is the understood pronoun *you.* The RK system recognizes this element, putting it into the subject slot enclosed in parentheses. Thus [21] is diagrammed as [22]:

[21]　Scratch my back.

[22]

In fact, RK puts any understood element in parentheses. However, it recognizes very few such elements.

The system is somewhat more abstract in regard to word order. We have already seen that adverbial modifiers are located under the verb regardless of where they occur in the sentence. Questions also undergo rearrangement in diagrams. We distinguish between two types of questions—yes-no questions [23a] and wh-questions [23b]:

[23a]　Does Bertha play golf?
　[b]　What does Bertha play?

In both types of questions, an auxiliary verb, e.g., *does*, is inverted with the subject. In wh-questions, the wh-word appears in front of the inverted auxiliary. In [23b], then, *What* is the direct object of *play*, just as it is in [23a]. In a RK diagram, word order is *normalized*; i.e., the sentence is diagrammed as if it were a statement:

[24a]	Bertha	does play	golf		[b]	Bertha	does play	what

In both diagrams, the auxiliary occurs next to its verb. In [24b], the NP *what* appears in the position that indicates its function as a direct object.

9.2 FORMAL DIAGRAMS

Transformational-Generative (TG) linguists (see Chapter 11) emphasize the primacy of linguistic form. As a result, their graphic representations are stated in formal terms. The general term for such graphics is **constituent analysis.** A **construction** is a formally unified whole; it contains parts called **constituents.** Since each constituent/part may itself contain parts, it's possible to represent a construction in terms of vertical layers as well as a string of words. Functional diagrams, of course, do provide a rough indication of vertical and horizontal dimensions. In formal diagrams, however, the two dimensions are precisely, clearly, and completely depicted.

9.2.1 Formal diagrams of basic clause patterns

Let's begin with an example. Sentence [25] corresponds to clause pattern 1 in the previous chapter. (Remember that *Edgar* represents a complete noun phrase and *spoke* a full verb phrase.)

[25] Edgar spoke.

Clause pattern 1 consists functionally of Subject + Predicate. The subject is *Edgar* and the predicate *spoke*. Formally, pattern 1 is represented as NP + VP. A formal diagram for this much of [25] appears as [26]:

[26]

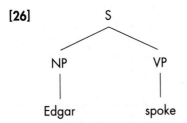

This simple graphic is called a **tree diagram.** It's based on a metaphor which views a sentence as having a quasi-botanical organization. **S**, the highest part, is called the **root** of the tree. (For those with a normal sense of perspective, the tree will appear to be upside down, but that doesn't seem to bother linguists.) Each part of diagram [26] can be identified by appropriate terminology. Each **node label** (**S, NP, VP**) abbreviates a formal category: **S** stands for sentence/clause, **NP** for noun phrase, and **VP** for verb phrase. The lines that connect the labels are called **branches.** Places where the lines/branches end are called **nodes.** In [26], grammatical labels—or words—appear at nodes. So [26] contains three labels, two words, five nodes, and four branches.

The relation between nodes can also be stated with precision. The relation of **domination** describes the connection between a higher node in the tree and one that it branches down to by a consistently downward path. In [26], S dominates NP and VP because you can get from S to NP or VP by going downward only. NP doesn't dominate VP because getting to VP from NP would involve an upward path on a branch. If you can get from one node to another by going downward by only one branch, the higher node *immediately dominates* the lower one. In [26], S both dominates and immediately dominates NP and VP. Conversely, NP and VP are immediately dominated by S. Two nodes immediately dominated by the same node are called **sisters.** In [26], NP and VP are sisters.

One important feature distinguishes formal from functional diagramming. While the functional method relies on the analytic intuitions of students to create diagrams, the formal method can be reduced to a simple set of rules or instructions about how to form a diagram. (These rules are descriptive, not prescriptive.) We can, for instance, write an instruction for a person (or a computer) to form the basic tree for sentence [25]. The first instruction would look like [27]:

[27]   S → NP   VP

We read this formula in the following way: Write the symbol S. Underneath it write the symbols NP and VP, in that order. Connect NP and VP to S by lines (branches). Rule [27] is often glossed as "S consists of NP   VP." In general, for any rule, the single symbol to the left of the arrow is rewritten as one or more symbols to the right of the arrow. Since this rule describes the structure of phrases (the sentence being considered the largest phrase), it's widely known as a **phrase structure rule.**

The formal treatment of diagramming would be very trivial if we considered it as purely mechanical. However, by introducing the view that diagrams result from rules, we have made a dramatic revision of traditional grammar. For by stating rules, we make a claim about the nature of language, not just about the structure of a particular sentence. The gist of the revision lies in this claim: When we state rules, we aren't merely telling you how to analyze sentences, we are making *general statements about the structure of English.* Thus the rule in [27] claims that every clause in English consists—at least in some abstract way—of an NP followed by a VP. This, in fact, is exactly the claim that appears in the formal part of pattern 1. Moreover, the formula in [27] holds not only for pattern 1 but for *every* pattern in the language since every pattern contains an NP and a VP.

EXERCISE   To what extent can the Reed-Kellogg system be expressed as a set of rules? What would the rules look like? To what extent does the RK system make general claims about the structure of English sentences?

We can take one further step from our formal diagram. We can "read" the functions of NP and VP from the diagram. That is, we can identify the subject of the clause as *the NP immediately dominated by S*. The predicate of the clause is *the VP immediately dominated by S*. Note that this correlation of form and function is a one-way street. Given the functions, we cannot automatically identify a form because many forms may represent a single function. (See, for instance, the earlier discussion of subject complements and object complements.)

There is, however, one way in which rule [27] is incomplete. Consider sentence [28]:

[28] Edgar will speak.

This sentence appears to conform to pattern 1. Likewise, it would be diagrammed functionally as [29]:

[29]   Edgar | will speak

By representing *will* as a part of the predicate, the functional diagram ignores the important question of the status of the form *will* and, more broadly, of the status of auxiliary verbs in general. Indeed, it's an open question as to whether auxiliaries are a part of the predicate (or its formal analogue, the VP). For the present, we will not make such an assumption, but instead, consider auxiliaries as at least partially distinct from the verb phrase. As a consequence, we restate our initial phrase structure rule [27] as [30]:

[30] S → NP   Aux   VP

In [30], **Aux** includes at least the first auxiliary verb. But the interpretation of the rule is unchanged. It tells us to analyze clauses (or simple sentences) as having three essential elements that occur, at some abstract level, in the order specified.

While basic sentence patterns all contain an NP, an Aux, and a VP, they may differ according to the constituency of their VPs. For instance, pattern 2 introduces a direct object, as in [31]:

[31] Adam likes ribs.

You will recall that we differentiated clause patterns on the basis of the differences of various types of VPs. In pattern 2, a head verb is followed by a direct object. In formal terms, a verb is followed by an NP. We represent these observations as diagram [32]:

[32]

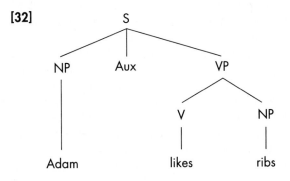

This diagram illustrates an important characteristic of grammatical structure noted earlier—that of levels of structure. In syntax, constructions can contain other constructions—i.e., forms may contain other forms and functions can contain other functions. Diagram [32] clearly illustrates this principle. The form S contains three forms, NP, Aux, and VP. (For ease of exposition, we have left Aux blank.) VP contains two forms—V and NP.

The terminology of formal diagramming also represents this layering of structure. S dominates NP, VP, V, and NP since we can get to any of these four nodes by going down from S. However, VP is more intimately related to V and the NP that it dominates because VP *immediately* dominates them. We can describe a grammatical category (such as VP) in terms of what it contains by specifying what it immediately dominates.

We can illustrate this observation further by examining clause pattern 3. An example of this pattern appears in [33].

[33] Mary may become famous.

Pattern 3 contains functionally a subject and a predicate that contains a subject complement. Formally, this pattern boils down to an NP, Aux, and VP, where the VP contains either an NP or an AP. Since sentence [33] happens to contain an AP, we can analyze it as [34]:

[34]

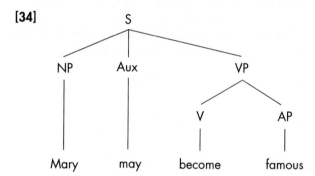

Our diagram likewise indicates a layering of structure similar to that of pattern 2.

We have seen that the pattern underlying the highest part of a tree can be represented as a rule. Lower levels of the tree can also be represented as rules, as in [35].

[35] $VP \rightarrow V \ (\begin{Bmatrix} NP \\ AP \end{Bmatrix})$

The phrase structure rule in [35] makes a general statement about an indefinite number of VPs in English. It indicates that a VP will contain a verb and, following the verb, the VP may also contain either an NP, an AP, or nothing at all.

Rule [35] allows for patterns 1, 2, and 3, thus providing a useful abbreviation for them. To see how this is so, you need to understand how parentheses and braces work within phrase structure rules. Both indicate optional elements. *Parentheses* indicate that elements within them may or may not be chosen; i.e., there may be something or nothing. *Braces* (also called *curly brackets*) indicate that one of the lines of the elements enclosed by the braces must appear; i.e., you must choose something. (*Note:* Parentheses and braces appear only in the rules, not in the trees themselves.)

Rule [35] produces pattern 1 when nothing is chosen from within the parentheses. Exercising the option within the parentheses, we may choose either the top line—NP—or the bottom line—AP. Choosing NP yields either pattern 2 or 3, depending on the verb. Choosing AP yields pattern 3.

For the present, we will not delve into patterns 4 and 5 since they raise further complications that are not relevant to elementary formal diagramming.

Also, you should be aware that while the general format of formal diagramming is well-accepted, the details may vary from system to system. Variation results from many causes, ranging from ease of presentation to disagreement about how to analyze a given construction. Variation in analysis is a fact of life that linguists, teachers, and students must learn to live with.

9.2.2   Formal diagrams of noun phrases

Let's now look at ways of diagramming smaller constructions within a sentence. In this and following sections, we will consider noun phrases, prepositional phrases, adjective phrases, and adverb phrases.

We have seen that NPs can appear in three places within patterns 1, 2, and 3, functioning as subject, direct object, and subject complement. In addition, NPs may function as objects of prepositions, indirect objects, and object complements. Such a versatile structure thus deserves some close attention. For now, we present a simplified version of NP diagrams, glossing over the variety of possible pre- and postmodifiers.

You will recall from Chapter 7 that NPs have the simple functional structure of [36]:

[36]   (Premodifier*)   Head   (Postmodifier*)

The formal picture is more complicated. Functional representations often conceal the variety of premodifiers and postmodifiers. Let's begin to explore this variety.

In the simplest case, an NP contains only a (head) noun:

[37]   NP
           |
           N
           |
          Elmo

So we begin with the phrase structure rule [38]:

[38]   NP → N

Pronouns, however, may also serve as heads. (**Pro** is an abbreviation for pronoun, including, personal, possessive, indefinite, and wh- versions.)

[39]   NP
        |
        Pro
        |
        he

To allow our rule to express both possibilities, we use curly brackets, indicating that the headword may be either a noun or a pronoun, but not both.

[40]   NP → $\begin{Bmatrix} N \\ Pro \end{Bmatrix}$

While [40] suffices for single-word NPs, what about premodifiers? Table 7.3 identifies several formal types of premodifiers. Some of them can occur only once in the premodifier position. (In other words, the choice of one excludes the choice of any other.) Example [41] illustrates some of the possibilities and restrictions:

[41a]   the wombats (Article)
  [b]   that vase (Demonstrative)
  [c]   her serve (Genitive Pronoun)
  [d]   some survivors (Indefinite Pronoun)
  [e]   which lobster (Wh Pronoun)
  [f]   *the that vase
  [g]   *her some survivors
  [h]   *the her serve
  [i]   *which the wombats
  [j]   *the which wombats

The fact that these items exclude each other suggests that they form a general class, of which only one member may appear as the premodifier. We will call this the **determiner (Det)** class. We can now expand our rule to [42]:

[42]   NP → (Det) $\begin{Bmatrix} N \\ Pro \end{Bmatrix}$

Rule [42] invokes both kinds of choices noted earlier. The parenthetical option indicates the presence or absence of a determiner, allowing for one- or two-word NPs. The braces allow for the choice of either a noun or a pronoun. So the right-hand side of [42] abbreviates the following possibilities:

[43a]   N
  [b]   Det N
  [c]   Pro
  [d]   Det Pro

Rule [42] thus creates the diagrams below:

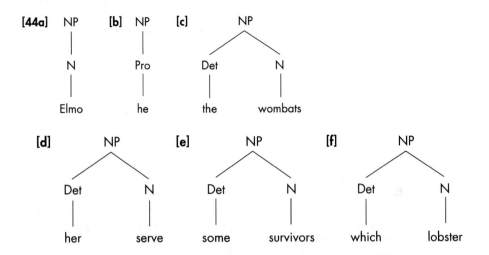

These diagrams and the rule that creates them are basically sound, except for two problems. First, the rule doesn't do justice to the variety of forms that can serve as determiners. We could revise rule [42] to name the possibilities, using curly brackets within the parentheses. To do so, however, erases the label **determiner** and thus obscures the generalization that the forms are members of a single class. To preserve their commonality, we can add another rule that indicates the membership of Det:

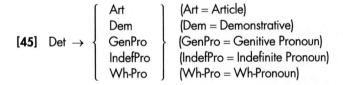

[45] Det → { Art / Dem / GenPro / IndefPro / Wh-Pro }

(Art = Article)
(Dem = Demonstrative)
(GenPro = Genitive Pronoun)
(IndefPro = Indefinite Pronoun)
(Wh-Pro = Wh-Pronoun)

Rule [45] simply lists the members of the determiner class.

The second problem created by rule [42] is that it allows for some ungrammatical structures:

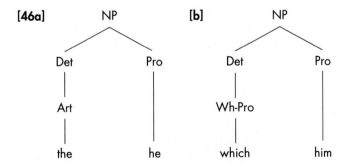

These problems arise because of the combination of a determiner and a pronoun. We observed that pronouns don't occur after determiners in English. Yet our rules suggests that they do. Which is right, English or the grammarian? You guessed it—English, of course. So we have to revise our rule to avoid allowing pronouns and determiners to co-occur.

The solution again involves the use of braces and parentheses, the two devices that allow us to represent choice in rules. We don't change the interpretation of parentheses or braces; we merely restate the rule in such a way as to express the general statement that determiners cannot occur directly before pronouns. The result is [47]:

$$\text{[47]} \quad NP \rightarrow \begin{Bmatrix} \text{(Det)} \;\; N \\ \text{Pro} \end{Bmatrix}$$

This time we have combined braces and parentheses. The braces say that we have two preliminary choices—the top line or the bottom line. If we select the bottom line, we are allowed only a pronoun—no determiner. In this way, the rule forces us to choose only the grammatical possibilities for NPs. When a rule is stated so that it represents a generalization about a language (here, the fact that determiners and pronouns cannot co-occur in English), we say that the rule *captures a generalization*. A major reason for stating the rules of a language is to represent the general patterns of the language accurately.

We haven't, of course, exhausted the range of NP premodifiers. However, we will not go into further detail here because it would add unnecessary complexity. Rather, we turn now to postmodifiers in NPs.

The simplest postmodifier in a NP is a prepositional phrase (PP). Consider the NPs in [48]:

[48a]   books on the shelf
  [b]   the source of conflict
  [c]   which book about crayfish
  [d]   *she on the shelf
  [e]   *the it of conflict
  [f]   *which it on crayfish

These examples lead to several observations. First, PPs occur after the head noun. Second, PPs may or may not occur regardless of whether the NP contains a premodifier. Third, PPs cannot co-occur with pronouns regardless of whether or not the pronoun is preceded by a determiner. Representing this observation requires a further modification of rule [47]:

$$\text{[49]} \quad NP \rightarrow \begin{Bmatrix} \text{(Det)} \;\; N \;\; \text{(PP)} \\ \text{Pro} \end{Bmatrix}$$

By placing PP on the top line within the braces, we allow it to be selected only if the NP has a headword that isn't a pronoun. So the grammatical sentences of [48] can be represented as:

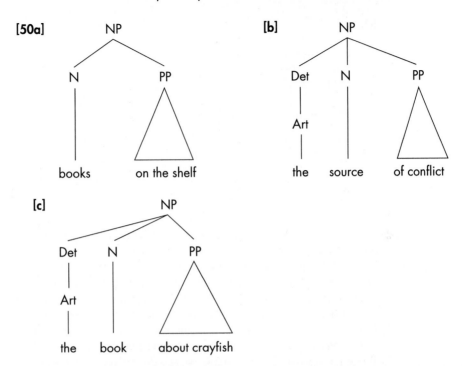

Again, rule [49] works fairly well, except that it doesn't tell us anything about the internal structure of the PPs. We can easily represent that structure as [51]:

[51]   PP → P   NP

In short, a prepositional phrase consists of a preposition followed by a noun phrase. We can now expand the diagrams in [50] to represent the internal structure of the PP:

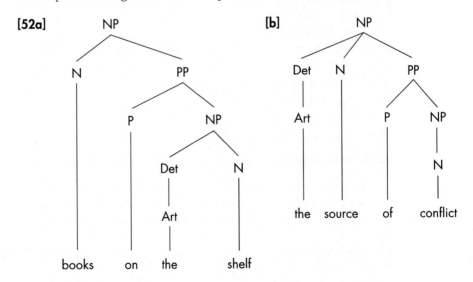

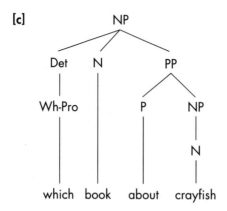

[c]

which book about crayfish

Diagram [52a] illustrates a property of language that we have referred to many times—the fact that constructions can contain other constructions. In this case, an NP contains a PP, which contains another NP. That is, structures can be **embedded** within other structures. The possibility of embedding structures within each other means that the rules are recursive, and can therefore generate an infinite number of structures, each of which may be infinitely long. For instance, there is no reason why the NP within the PP should consist only of the noun *crayfish*. It might just as well contain a noun followed by another PP, and so on ad infinitum. While you might get tired and confused adding PPs, the language itself doesn't prevent you from doing so, nor do our rules. Our recursive rules reflect this creative aspect of our linguistic competence.

EXERCISES
1. Draw a formal diagram for each of the following NPs.
   a. a student of physics
   b. his notebook
   c. any reason for a party
   d. whose notebook
   e. the reason for that
2. Explain why our rules so far don't generate the following NPs.
   a. *she on the shelf
   b. *any it of conflict
   c. *her which of that
   d. what (as in "What do you want?")
   e. Osgood's notebook

Given these examples, how would you change the NP rules?

3. Provide sentences that illustrate the *potential* infinity of sentences created by rules [49] and [51]. The sentences don't have to be infinitely long.

Earlier in this chapter, we briefly examined some of the objects and complements of the VP. In an earlier chapter, we saw that VPs could be accompanied by modifiers, particularly adverb phrases and prepositional phrases. The examples of [53] illustrate this:

[53a] fell often
  [b] fell in the well
  [c] fell in the well very often

To diagram these sentences, we must revise the VP rule:

[54] VP → V $\begin{Bmatrix} NP \\ AP \end{Bmatrix}$ (PP*) (AdvP*)

Rule [54] expresses the generalization that a VP may optionally contain one or more modifiers. (* after a category label in a phrase structure rule means "one or more.")

To finish this description of modifiers, we must add a rule for adverb phrases. Since we know that such phrases typically contain only a head adverb and an optional intensifier, we state the rules as:

[55] AdvP → (Intens) Adv

Using rules [54] and [55], we can generate the following trees:

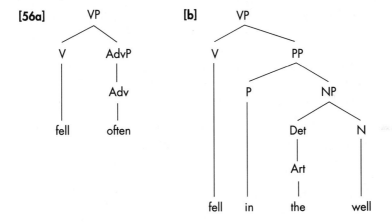

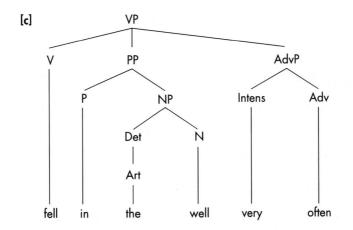

Adjective phrases (APs) are the only major phrasal category remaining for us to deal with here. APs can occur within VPs, as in [57]:

[57] Clyde is fond of anchovies.

APs, like all other phrases, contain a headword of its phrasal category; like adverb phrases they can contain an intensifier, and like NPs they may contain a PP. These observations are captured in rule [58]:

[58] AP → (Intens)   Adj   (PP)

Sentence [57] can therefore be diagrammed as:

[59]

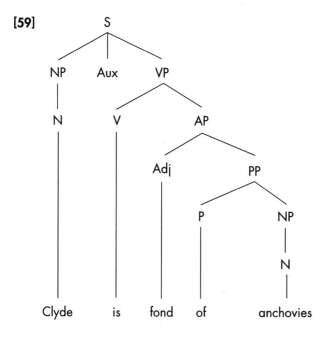

9.3   CONCLUSION

We conclude with a list of the phrase structure rules that we have finally arrived at in this chapter.

$$S \rightarrow NP \quad Aux \quad VP$$

$$VP \rightarrow V \quad \left\{ \begin{matrix} NP \\ AP \end{matrix} \right\} \quad (PP*) \quad (AdvP*)$$

$$NP \rightarrow \left\{ \begin{matrix} (Det) \ N \ (PP) \\ Pro \end{matrix} \right\}$$

$$Det \rightarrow \begin{cases} Art \\ Dem \\ GenPro \\ Indef\ Pro \\ Wh\text{-}Pro \end{cases}$$

$$PP \rightarrow P \quad NP$$

$$AdvP \rightarrow (Intens) \quad Adv$$

$$AP \rightarrow (Intens) \quad Adj \quad (PP)$$

REFERENCES AND RESOURCES

Emery, Donald W. 1961. *Sentence Analysis.* New York: Holt Rinehart and Winston, Inc.
Reed, Alonzo, and Brainerd Kellogg. 1877. *Higher Lessons in English.* New York: J. J. Little & Co.

GLOSSARY

Adjective phrase: see Chapters 5 and 7.

Aux: a label in a tree diagram for an auxiliary verb. See Chapter 6.

Baseline: the main horizontal line in the Reed-Kellogg system reserved for main and subordinate clauses.

Branch: a line in a tree diagram that connects one node to another.

Constituent: a grammatically unified part of a construction.

Constituent analysis: the analysis of larger grammatical units into their smaller parts.

Construction: a grammatically unified group of words composed of smaller parts. See **constituent.**

Det: abbreviation for **determiner.**

Determiner: a class of elements (e.g., *the, which*) that precede a head noun in a noun phrase.

Domination: the relation between a higher node in a tree and a lower one that it branches to by a consistently downward path.

Embedding: see **embed,** Chapter 7.

GenPro: abbreviation for **genitive pronoun.** See Chapter 6.

Head: see Chapter 5.

IndefPro: abbreviation for **indefinite pronoun.** See Chapter 6.

Intens: abbreviation for **intensifier.** See Chapter 6.

Node: a place in a tree diagram where a line (branch) ends; often assigned a grammatical label such as NP, Det, Adj, etc.

Node label: a symbol assigned to a node to indicate the grammatical category of the word or phrase dominated by that node.

Phrase structure rule (also called "**rewrite rule**"): a rule that describes the formal structure of sentences and their constituents; determines the construction of tree diagrams for sentences.

Premodifier: see Chapter 7.

Pro: abbreviation for **pronoun.** See Chapter 6.

Rewrite rule: see **phrase structure rule.**

Root: the topmost node of a tree diagram, usually labelled as S (sentence).

Sisters: two or more nodes immediately dominated by the same node.

Tree diagram: a graphic representation of the constituent structure of a sentence; defined by phrase structure rules.

Wh-Pro: see Chapter 6 (**wh-word**).

10 ELABORATIONS OF BASIC SENTENCE PATTERNS

KEY CONCEPTS

Clauses and sentences
Phrases and clauses
Finite and nonfinite clauses
Main and subordinate clauses
Types of subordinate clauses
Functions of subordinate clauses
Coordination

10.0 CLAUSES AND SENTENCES

In Chapter 8, we dealt with simple sentences. **Simple sentences** contain only one clause—i.e., a single subject (NP) accompanied by a single predicate (VP). In this chapter, we will examine elaborations of simple sentences, i.e., what are called **complex** and **compound** sentences. Complex sentences have more than one clause, and at least one of those clauses is included, or **embedded,** as a subject, object, or modifier, inside another clause. The clause which includes all subordinate clauses in a sentence is called the **main clause.** Embedded clauses are often called **subordinate clauses.** Compound sentences are composed of two or more clauses, none of which is subordinate to another. These clauses are connected by coordinating conjunctions. We will touch briefly on compound sentences later in this chapter, but mainly we will focus on complex sentences. We make our usual distinction between form and function and begin this discussion by developing three important distinctions—between **phrases** and **clauses,** between **finite** and **nonfinite** clauses, and between **main** and **subordinate** clauses.

10.1 PHRASES AND CLAUSES

We defined a *phrase* in Chapter 7 as a group of one or more words that combine to create a unified grammatical structure, e.g., an NP, a VP, a PP, etc. Phrases are subject to substitution tests such as pronoun-replacement for NPs. *Clauses are combinations of two phrases, specifically an NP and a VP, that are grammatically and semantically related to each other.* The two main relationships between clauses are equality (giving rise to coordination) and inequality (giving rise to subordination). This chapter will concentrate on subordination.

Let's begin by examining the sentences in [1]. The subordinate clauses are enclosed in square brackets:

[1a] Edgar (NP) loves Angela (VP).
  [b] Amos (NP) says [that Edgar (NP) loves Angela (VP)] (VP).
  [c] Wanda (NP) knows the person [who (NP) loves Angela (VP)] (VP).
  [d] Wanda (NP) left [because Edgar (NP) loves Angela (VP)] (VP).

Sentence [1a] is a simple sentence, with only one clause. The others have more than one clause. In [1b], the dominant clause, called the **main, independent,** or **matrix clause**, is "Amos says X." X marks the spot where the subordinate clause is inserted (i.e., embedded). In [1c], the bracketed clause *who loves Angela* modifies *the person*. In [1d], the bracketed clause *because Edgar loves Angela* modifies the main clause as an adverbial of reason.

From these examples you can learn two things about subordination. First, subordinated structures often have a fairly clear introductory word, a **subordinating conjunction.** In [1b], *that* is such a word; [1c] uses *who*; [1d] uses *because*. We will learn more about such words below. For now, only the fact that such words may occur in subordinate clauses is important. The second lesson is that a subordinate clause, *as a whole,* has a function within the clause that contains it. In [1b], the clause serves as a direct object; in [1c], the clause is a postmodifier of the head noun *person;* in [1d], the clause is an adverbial modifier of *left*. In speaking of clauses, we don't need to introduce a whole new set of grammatical functions. The familiar ones will, for the most part, be sufficient.

Just as we have varied from the traditional definition of the phrase by allowing it to contain only one member, linguists vary from the traditional definition of the clause. We define a **clause** as a grammatically unified structure that either actually or potentially contains a subject (NP) and a predicate (VP). By this definition, the bracketed structures in [1] as well as in [2] are clauses:

[2a] We watched [Osgood (NP) make the pizza (VP)].
  [b] [My mother (NP) being at sea (VP)], my brother served as witness.
  [c] [Zelda's (NP) giving Scott the memo (VP)] caused a commotion.

Sentence [2a] contains the (main) clause *We watched X* and the subordinate *Osgood make the pizza*. The main clause of [2b] is *My brother served as witness,* while the subordinate structure is *My mother being at sea.* Sentence [2c] has the structure *X caused a commotion* as a main clause, with the subordinate clause being *Zelda's giving Scott the memo.* The examples in [2] show that subordinate clauses don't always have an explicit introducer. Also, they may have considerable variety in their internal formal makeup. For example, the NP of [2c] is formally a genitive NP modifying a verb with an *-ing* suffix. Finally, the X-element indicates the position from which the subordinate clauses derive their grammatical functions in the clause that contains them. Thus in [2c], the bracketed clause functions as the subject of the main clause.

Our definition of clauses indicates that clauses may contain not only an actual but also a *potential subject.* The examples in [1] and [2] have all contained actual subjects. But subjects may be implied; i.e., they may be present at only an abstract level. The sentences in [3] illustrate this possibility:

[3a]   I expect [to run through the park].
  [b]   [Running through the park], Brian met an old friend.
  [c]   [Running through the park] is encouraged.

Sentence [3a] might be paraphrased as *I expect [I (NP) will run through the park (VP)]*, where the bracketed subordinate clause has its abstract subject NP restored. Likewise, the subordinate clause in [3b] can be reconstructed as *[Brian was running through the park]*, and that of [3c] as *[anyone running through the park]*. We thus extend the definition of a clause to a further level of abstraction, where the subject is only implicitly rather than directly stated.

On a less abstract level, you should note that subordinate clauses, whether or not they have an explicit subject NP, will *always* contain a verb phrase. For this reason, they will have the complete range of sentence patterns that we explored in Chapter 8. Here again, there is really nothing new; the familiar patterns are simply recycled to new grammatical circumstances. To illustrate this point, consider some of the subordinate clauses in [4], with attention to the italicized elements:

[4a]   Amos said [that Edgar loves *Angela*]. (Direct Object = Pattern 2)
  [b]   [Zelda's giving *Scott* the memo] caused a commotion. (Indirect Object = Pattern 5)
  [c]   [Running through the park] is encouraged. (Intransitive = Pattern 1)

10.2   FINITE AND NONFINITE CLAUSES

Consider the formal differences between the italicized clauses in the following sentences:

[5a]   We think *the ghost appears at midnight.*
  [b]   We want *the ghost to appear at midnight.*

We can see that both are clauses since each has a subject NP *(the ghost)* and a VP *(appear/s at midnight)*. However, the italicized clause in [5a] is a **finite clause**; it's in the present tense and its subject agrees with its verb. We could even include a modal in the clause:

[6]   We think *the ghost will appear at midnight.*

In contrast, the **nonfinite clause** in [5b] doesn't allow for agreement or modals:

[7a]   *We want the ghost to *appears* at midnight.
  [b]   *We want the ghost *will* appear at midnight.

By the term *finite,* then, we mean that a clause is *limited by a present or past tense inflection or by modal auxiliaries.* (The word *finis* in Latin means "limit or boundary.") An easy way to spot a finite clause is to look at the first verb in the VP; if it's in the present or past tense, or if it's a modal, then the clause is finite. Otherwise it's nonfinite.

Nonfinite clauses aren't inflected for present or past tense. As we have seen above in [3a] to [3c], their subjects are sometimes absent; and when they're present, as in [7a], subject and verb cannot be marked for agreement. Example [7b] shows that we cannot include a modal in nonfinite constructions.

10.3 MAIN AND SUBORDINATE CLAUSES

Because one clause can be included (embedded) in another, a given sentence may have any number of clauses:

[8a]   She said something (One Clause)
  [b]   She said [that I don't know anything]. (Two Clauses)
  [c]   She said [that I don't know [what I want]]. (Three Clauses)
  [d]   She said [that I don't know [what I want [Bill to do]]]. (Four Clauses)
  [e]   She said [that I don't know [what I want [[Bill to do] [when he gets there]]]]. (Five Clauses)
  [f]   etc. to infinity

The main clause is the one which isn't embedded in any other clause. In all of the sentences of [8], *She said X* is the main clause. All of the other clauses are subordinate. However, you should realize that not all subordinate clauses are directly subordinate to the main clause— they may instead be subordinate to *other subordinate clauses*. To see this point a bit more clearly, consider the graphic representation of [8e] in [9]:

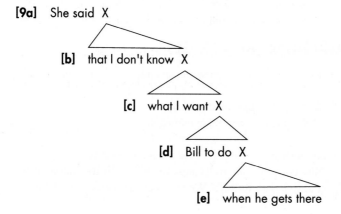

[9a]   She said X

  [b]   that I don't know X

  [c]   what I want X

  [d]   Bill to do X

  [e]   when he gets there

Of these five clauses, only clause [9a] is a main clause; the others are subordinate. Clause [9b] is subordinate to the main clause. Clause [9c] is subordinate to [9b], [9d] to [9c], and [9e] to [9d]. Of the five, only one clause is nonfinite—[9d]; all of the others are finite because they contain a verb with a present or past tense inflection. While a subordinate clause may be *either* finite or nonfinite, a main clause will *always* be finite.

10.4 TYPES OF SUBORDINATE CLAUSES

Clauses have both formal and functional properties. In section 10.5, we will explore these characteristics in detail. In this section, we will mainly provide a schematic sketch of basic formal properties of subordinate clauses as a quick reference. Read over Tables 10.1, 10.2,

TABLE 10.1   Types of Clauses

Finite	Nonfinite
1. Adverbial	1. Reduced Adverbial
2. Relative	2. Reduced Relative
3. Noun	3. Gerund
	4. Infinitive

TABLE 10.2   Types of Finite Clauses

1. Adverbial Clause
   Introducer: subordinating conjunctions—See section 10.5.1
   Function of introducer within adverbial clause: none
   Function of adverbial clause within higher clause: modifier of verb; occasionally, modifier of adjective/adverb in a result clause (*so X that . . .*)
2. Relative Clause (Adjective Clause)
   Introducer(s): wh-word *who, whom, which, whose;* complementizer *that* (may be omitted, except when subject); occasionally, *when* and *where*
   Function of wh-words within higher clause: common NP functions; *when* and *where* indicate adverbial functions
   Function of relative clause within higher clause: postmodifier of noun head
3. Noun Clause
   Introducer: unstressed complementizer *that* (may be omitted); wh-word in indirect questions
   Function of introducer within noun clause: *that*—none; wh-word—common NP functions
   Function of noun clause within higher clause: common NP functions

and 10.3 to prepare yourself for the more detailed discussion to come. Don't try to memorize the tables.

Finite clauses are of three types: Adverbial, Noun, and Relative. Table 10.2 identifies three characteristics of each type. First, we indicate the typical introducer; then the function of that introducer *within* the subordinate clause; and finally, the function of the *entire* subordinate clause within the higher clause. These points will receive further attention later in this chapter.

Nonfinite clauses come in four varieties, each of which has several formal variations and a range of functions. This variation is summarized in Table 10.3. Nonfinite clauses don't reliably have an introducer, although the infinitive has the marker *to* in many cases.

To reduce complications later in the chapter, we will briefly discuss some further formal characteristics of nonfinite clauses.

TABLE 10.3   Types of Nonfinite Clauses

Type	Subtypes	Function
1. Reduced Adverbial	SubConj + Ving/Ven	Modifier of Verb
2. Gerund	simple Ving Poss + Ving	NP Range
3. Reduced Relative	simple with subject	Modifier of Noun
4. Infinitive	simple V to + V	NP Range OR
	subject + to + V	Modifier of Verb OR
	for + subject + to + V subject + V	Modifier of Noun

Reduced adverbials

Reduced adverbials have the same properties as full adverbials. In particular, they begin with the subordinating conjunctions common to adverbial clauses, and they typically modify verbs. There are only two qualifications: (1) not all full adverbials may be reduced; (2) reduction occurs typically through the removal of a subject and a form of the verb *be*. Sentence [10a] illustrates a full finite adverbial and [10b] its reduction.

[10a]   *While she was living in Africa,* Sheila learned Swahili.
  [b]   *While living in Africa,* Sheila learned Swahili.

Gerunds

[11a]   *Giving grammar lectures* is always a challenge.
  [b]   *Bill's leaving town* confirmed his guilt.

Here again, we have almost complete sentences, but in forms that are different from an ordinary tensed sentence. The verb of these clauses has the morpheme-*ing* suffixed to it. (NB. This isn't the progressive -*ing*.) And when it has a subject, which is optional, the subject phrase may be in the genitive case, *Bill's* in [11b], although in many varieties (especially informal ones) it may be in the objective case:

[12]   I don't like *him being out late at night.*

Reduced relatives

Reduced relatives, also called **participles,** have the verb form ending in -*ing* (also -*en*). Most reduced relatives are simple, in that they contain no subject, as in [13a]:

[13a]   Anyone *hoping to get on the boat* should have a ticket.
   [b]   Anyone *who is hoping to get on the boat* should have a ticket.

Unlike the gerund, this *-ing* morpheme is that of the progressive; [13a] can be paraphrased as [13b]. (You might recall at this point our description of the *Whiz Test* in Chapter 7.) As we shall see, the reduced relative also contrasts in function with the gerund.

To-infinitives

[14]   We want *Bill to leave immediately.*
[15]   *To leave now* would cause a lot of trouble.

The italicized parts are *to*-infinitival clauses. The first one contains the subject *Bill* and is the object of the verb *want*. The second one has no overt subject; its subject is understood as something like *(for) us* or *(for) someone*. The subject of a nonfinite clause is generally optional. However, whenever an infinitival clause functions as the subject of its matrix, its subject, if it has one, must be preceded by *for*:

[16a]   *For us to leave now* would cause a lot of trouble.
   [b]   **Us to leave now* would cause a lot of trouble.

Some varieties of English require this *for* even when the infinitival clause functions as the object of the main clause, [17a], and even when the infinitival subject is omitted, [17b]. Standard English tends to omit it:

[17a]   We would like (for) you to have a wonderful time.
   [b]   We only came up here (for) to hear him preach.

Bare infinitives

The infinitival form of the verb can appear without *to*, both with and without an overt subject. This form of infinitival clause occurs frequently with verbs of perception, *see, hear, feel,* and others such as *do, let,* and *make.*

[18a]   *Leave immediately* is what he should do.
   [b]   I saw *John do it.*
   [c]   I heard *Mehta conduct Beethoven's Ninth.*
   [d]   I felt *it move under my hand.*
   [e]   We let *him come in.*
   [f]   We made *her leave.*

Auxiliary verbs in nonfinite constructions

Aside from modals, nonfinite VPs may have a full range of auxiliary verbs. A few of the possibilities are indicated below. (Note that the *first* auxiliary *never* carries a tense inflection.)

[19a]   It is exhilarating *to* **have jumped** *from a bungee cord.* (Infinitive without Subject)

[b]   It is wonderful *for Wanda to* **be jumping** *from a bungee cord.* (Infinitive with for-to + Subject)

[c]   Egbert regrets **having jumped** *from a bungee cord.* (Gerund without Subject)

[d]   *Waldo's* **being prevented** *from bungee jumping* relieved Wanda. (Passive Gerund with Subject)

[e]   **Having consulted** *the reputable sources,* I consulted my horoscope. (Simple Participle)

[f]   **Being advised,** I decided to face the bungee jump. (Passive Simple Participle)

[g]   *My guru* **having been consulted,** I decided to face the bungee jump. (Absolute Passive Participle with Subject)

10.5   FUNCTIONS OF SUBORDINATE CLAUSES

10.5.1   Clauses that function as modifiers of verbs (adverbial clauses)

Adverbial clauses are typically introduced by what have been traditionally called **subordinating conjunctions** and generally fulfill the same functions as AdvPs (see Chapter 7), indicating time, place, condition, cause, and purpose. They appear in the positions typical of AdvPs (initial, medial, and final). They're typically finite, but in some cases, they may be nonfinite. We provide examples of each of these types with their typical conjunctions. Note that nonfinite versions of adverbial clauses are elliptical versions of the fuller finite structures.

Time clauses

[20a]   *After you left the party,* things really began to swing.

[b]   *As soon as the mailman came,* Terry ran to the door.

[c]   *Before Reagan was elected,* there was more money for schools.

[d]   *Since the shuttle crashed,* NASA has been demoralized.

[21a]   *While he was swinging on the creeper,* Tarzan emitted a blood-curdling yell.

[b]   *While swinging on the creeper,* Tarzan emitted a blood-curdling yell. (Nonfinite)

[22a]   *When he was questioned by the police,* the suspect demanded to see his lawyers.

[b]   When questioned by the police, the suspect demanded to see his lawyers. (Nonfinite)

[23a]   *Before you get into trouble,* quit.

[b]   *Before getting into trouble,* quit. (Nonfinite)

Place clauses

[24a]   *Wherever you find cotton,* you will find the boll weevil.

[b]   Double quotes should be used only *where they are appropriate.*

[c]   Double quotes should be used only *where appropriate.* (Nonfinite)

Conditional clauses

[25a]　*If you understand this,* (then) you will be able to do the exercises.
　[b]　*Unless you understand this,* you will be unable to do the exercises.

Cause clauses

[26a]　*Because he hoped to elude his pursuers,* Fred continued his trek into the mountains.
　[b]　*Since/As funding is scarce,* research is hampered.
　[c]　*Being a clever fellow,* Fred was able to draw the correct conclusions. (Nonfinite)
　[d]　*Seated by the window,* the children could see everything that happened on the street. (Nonfinite)

Purpose clauses

[27]　We packed food for six meals *so (that) we could stay out in the forest overnight.*

Result clauses

[28a]　She was *so* stunned *that she couldn't speak.*
　[b]　The shooting star moved *so* quickly *that I almost missed it.*

EXERCISES　1. Make a list of the common subordinating conjunctions from the sentences above. Can you think of other subordinating conjunctions that aren't in the sentences, e.g., *until, once,* and *whenever?* Make up ten sentences that contain these conjunctions.

2. Provide some examples to demonstrate that adverbial clauses can, like AdvPs, appear in initial, medial, and final positions. Is one or more of these positions more common or natural? Does the status of the clause as finite or nonfinite affect its potential to occupy various positions?

10.5.2　Clauses that function in the nominal range

The subordinate clause in a complex sentence may function as its direct object, subject, or indirect object, as the object of a preposition, or as a complement.

10.5.2.1　Clauses that function as direct objects

[29a]　John claims *he has earned his first million already.*
　[b]　We believe *he exaggerates a great deal.*
　[c]　We prefer *(for) everyone to get along well.*
　[d]　We all enjoy *his visiting us.*

We can demonstrate that the embedded structures in [29] (sometimes called **complement clauses**) are the direct objects of the verbs *says, think, prefer,* and *enjoy* by using a number of tests. The first test is that NPs substitute for them:

[30a] John claims silly things.
  [b] We believe our suspicions.
  [c] We all prefer good relations.
  [d] We enjoy his visits.

We can also substitute demonstrative or other pronouns for them:

[31a] John claims this frequently.
  [b] We believe this now.
  [c] We prefer them.
  [d] We all enjoy them.

The embedded clauses bear the same grammatical relationship to the verbs of their sentences as the NPs that they replace. These are clearly direct object NPs, so the clauses they replace must also be direct objects.

We now introduce a slight complication of the pattern above. Sentences of [29a] and [29b] can be paraphrased as [32a] and [32b], respectively:

[32a] John claims that he has earned his first million already.
  [b] We believe that he exaggerates a great deal.

These sentences include the word *that* at the beginning of the embedded clause. Words which introduce clauses in this way have been given various names. Traditionally, as we saw in Chapter 6, they have been called **subordinating conjunctions,** a term we will reserve for the set of words that introduce adverbial clauses. We will most often call them **complementizers** because they introduce complement clauses.

The complementizer is part of the subordinate clause. We can show this by the fact that when we move the clause, the complementizer must also be moved:

[33a] It is *that he has earned a million* that John claims.
  [b] It is *that he exaggerates* that we believe.

Notice that if we try to leave the complementizer in its old position, the result is ungrammatical:

[34a] *It is he has earned a million that John claims *that*.
  [b] *It is he exaggerates that we believe *that*.

When we move elements, we move entire phrases, not just parts of them, so the complementizer is an integral part of an embedded sentence, although it has no other grammatical function within the clause.

The complementizer *that* isn't to be confused with the demonstrative pronoun *that.*

The two words just happen to be spelled identically, but within the system of English grammar they function rather differently. The demonstrative *that* contrasts with the demonstratives *this, these,* and *those,* with which it forms a subsystem within the grammar. The complementizer *that* doesn't contrast with the other demonstratives. There are no sentences of English in which an embedded clause is introduced by *this* or *those:*

[35]   *We believe this/these/those he is a great grammarian.

The complementizer *that* is optional when the embedded clause is a direct object, although not under other circumstances, e.g., when the clause is the subject:

[36a]   That he is a great grammarian isn't widely known.
   [b]   *He is a great grammarian isn't widely known.

EXERCISE   From newspapers collect twenty sentences containing finite subordinate clauses introduced by the complementizer *that* and twenty more without *that.* Is *that* truly optional or does its presence or absence convey some meaning?

Further support for our claim that these embedded clauses are direct objects comes from the fact that they can be passivized, just like most other object NPs:

[37a]   That he is a great grammarian is believed by many.
   [b]   (For everyone) to be home for Christmas is preferred by many.
   [c]   Visiting museums is enjoyed by many.

We will refer to the *for* which precedes the subject of infinitival clauses as a complementizer also.

EXERCISES   1. Find five more verbs that take direct object complement clauses.
   2. Make up five new complex sentences with subordinate clauses as their direct objects using the verbs you found for Exercise (1) and another five for verbs from the examples in the preceding section.
   3. Make a list of the tests for direct object clauses presented above. Using these tests, show that in each of the sentences you constructed in Exercise (2) your embedded clause is, in fact, the direct object.

Indirect question clauses are another type of direct object clause:

[38a]   I wonder *who the culprit is.*
   [b]   I know *what the thief took.*
   [c]   I asked him *whether he was ready to leave.*

[d] I told him *who to visit.*
[e] I don't know *who to ask.*

Indirect questions are embedded as the objects of verbs such as *wonder, know, tell,* and *ask.* They begin with a wh-word: *who, what, which, when, where,* and *why.* They may be either finite (e.g., [38a] to [38c]) or nonfinite (e.g., [38d] and [38e]). But they may not be gerunds:

[39]   *I asked him what visiting.

EXERCISE   Find another five verbs that take indirect question object clauses. Using tests such as those we used above, show that indirect questions are, in fact, direct objects.

There is a very interesting semantic distinction that can be drawn between types of (primarily) object clauses. The distinction is between **factive** and **nonfactive** interpretations. (Recall our brief discussion of these in Chapter 2.) Consider the following pair of sentences:

[40a] Greg believed that Alf left the keys at home.
[b] Greg remembered that Alf left the keys at home.

Sentence [40a] is consistent with either Alf's leaving or not leaving the keys at home; if it's true, then Alf may or may not have left the keys at home. Sentence [40b], on the other hand, is consistent only with Alf's leaving the keys at home, and if it's true, then Alf must have left the keys at home.
Notice too what happens when we negate these sentences:

[41a] Greg didn't believe that Alf left the keys at home.
[b] Greg didn't remember that Alf left the keys at home.

Sentence [41a] is again consistent with Alf leaving or not leaving the keys at home, and [41b] is again consistent only with Alf leaving the keys at home. Sentences like [40b] and [41b], in which the main clause contains a verb like *remember, forget,* or *realize,* are said to **presuppose** the truth of their complement clauses. That is, if the overall sentence is true (whether positive or negative), the object clause must also be true. Sentences that fulfill this requirement (and others) are called factive sentences. In this they contrast with sentences like [40a] and [41a], in which the main verb is like *believe* or *think.* These sentences don't presuppose the truth of the object clauses and are regarded as nonfactive sentences.

10.5.2.2   Clauses that function as subjects

Subordinate clauses can also appear as subjects of main clauses. They may be finite, [42a] to [42c], or nonfinite, like the infinitive of [42d] and the gerund of [42e]:

[42a] *That students enjoy grammar* proves my point.
[b] *That this may not work out* upsets us.

[c] *That he fled* will convince the jury of his guilt.
[d] *(For us) to leave now* would upset everyone.
[e] *(Our) leaving now* would upset everyone.

We can apply our usual types of tests to show that these embedded clauses are subjects. We can replace them with full NPs:

[43a] *This fact* proves my point.
[b] *The problem* upsets us.
[c] *His flight* will convince the jury of his guilt.
[d] *Our departure* would upset everyone.

The pronouns that appear in this position must be in the nominative case:

[44a] These/those are widely believed.
[b] *Them are widely believed.

Notice that when the subject is an embedded sentence, the verb is singular. That is, sentential subjects such as those above are regarded as singular.

EXERCISES
1. Find five more verbs that take complement clauses in subject position.
2. Make up ten new complex sentences with subordinate clauses as their subjects by using the verbs you found for Exercise (1) and the verbs of the sentences in the text.
3. For each of the sentences you constructed in Exercise (2), show that your embedded clause is, in fact, the subject. Use the tests above.

10.5.2.3 Clauses that function as indirect objects

Clauses can appear as indirect objects (IOs) also:

[45] We gave *whoever was there* a french pastry.

We can demonstrate that this indirect question is the IO of this sentence by applying the usual tests—Pro-sub and Passive:

[46a] We gave *him* a french pastry.
[b] Whoever was there was given a french pastry.

IO clauses are much more restricted in form than subject or direct object clauses. They seem to be restricted to clauses that refer to animate entities, which isn't altogether surprising when we consider the typical semantic roles of the IO phrase, namely those of recipient or beneficiary.

EXERCISES
1. Find five more verbs that take complement clauses in IO position.
2. Make up new complex sentences with subordinate clauses as their IOs by using the verbs you found for Exercise (1).
3. For each of the sentences you constructed in Exercise (2), show that the embedded clause is, in fact, the IO.

10.5.2.4 Clauses that function as objects of prepositions

Prepositions also may take sentential objects, most readily when they begin with *who(ever)* and similar words, [47a] to [47c]. Gerunds readily function as objects of prepositions (OPs), [47d]:

[47a] We gave the pastry to *whoever would eat it.*
  [b] We left the crumbs for *whichever birds came by.*
  [c] We slept in *what we had worn all day.*
  [d] We counted on *(his) getting back in time.*

We know that the clause is the object of the preposition that precedes it because if we substitute a pronoun for the clause, it must be in its object form:

[48] We gave the pastry to *her.*

We can also isolate the entire prepositional phrase:

[49a] It was *to whoever would eat them* that we gave the pastries.
  [b] It was *to her* that we gave the pastries.

We don't find *to-* or bare infinitival clauses as objects of prepositions, although it's possible to argue that there may be an understood or deleted preposition immediately before *for* in sentences such as:

[50] We are most eager — for Fred to return.

The arguments for this preposition are somewhat complicated, but worth noting here anyway. First, when the object of *eager* is a nonsentential NP, it must be governed by a preposition:

[51a] We are eager for his return.
  [b] *We are eager his return.

Second, in a construction called the **pseudocleft** (discussed below), both the preposition (P) and the complementizer (C) appear:

[52] What we are most eager *for* (P) is *for* (C) Fred to return.

[60a]   The man that/who sold us the boat skipped town.
  [b]   The boat that/which/Ø the man sold us broke down.
  [c]   The guy that/who/Ø we sold the boat to is very upset.
  [d]   The man whose boat we bought skipped town.
  [e]   The man that/who/Ø we bought the boat from skipped town.

EXERCISES   1. For each sentence below: (a) identify the relative clause; (b) determine whether a wh-word, *that,* or zero (Ø) introduces the clause; (c) give the headword modified by the clause; (d) locate the gap in the clause; (e) "normalize" the clause by expressing it as an independent sentence as in [58]; and (f) identify the function of the wh-word/*that*/Ø within the clause.
   a. The one that I choose will be very fortunate.
   b. Alice was the one who brought the whoopie cushion.
   c. Anyone you give it to will just throw it away.
   d. Zelda bought the pink flamingo that Scott liked so much.
   e. Wanda asked the man she considered the main suspect where he had been on the night of the robbery.
   f. They laugh best who laugh last.
   2. We have called *that* a complementizer when it introduces a noun clause or a relative clause. Using the four characteristics noted earlier, compare and contrast the behavior of *that* in the two types of clauses.

The restrictive relatives that we have been examining are interpreted as providing information necessary for identifying the referent of the entire NP. Another kind of relative clause, the **nonrestrictive** or **appositive,** only supplies extra information which isn't considered necessary to identify the referent of the NP:

[61a]   The claim, which is fully supported by the evidence, . . .
  [b]   The claim which is fully supported by the evidence . . .

The appositive or nonrestrictive relative, [61a], refers to some claim and then adds the supplementary information that the claim is fully supported. The reader/hearer is assumed to know which claim is being referred to without this extra information. The restrictive relative, [61b], refers to a claim which is assumed to be identifiable only by using the information in the relative clause to distinguish the intended claim from other claims.

One syntactic effect of this difference between appositive and restrictive relatives is that the head of an appositive, but not of a restrictive, may be a proper noun:

[62a]   Bill, who is well known to all of us, will sing his favorite tune "Home on the Range."
  [b]   *Bill who is well known to all of us will sing his favorite tune "Home on the Range."

The explanation for this is that the referents of proper nouns are assumed to be identifiable by hearers/readers without extra information. Restrictive relatives, whose information is assumed to be essential for the identification of the referent, are therefore redundant with proper nouns. Appositive relatives modifying proper nouns, whose information is assumed to be supplementary, aren't redundant. We do, however, find sentences such as the following, which might be used in a situation in which there are several individuals called Bill. In that case, the usual assumption associated with proper names may be suspended and the specific Bill being referred to can be identified by a restrictive clause:

[63] The Bill who has the rose between his teeth . . .

We turn now to the formal differences between restrictive and appositive relatives that we mentioned previously. Restrictive relative clauses may be introduced by either a wh-word, *that,* or zero. Nonrestrictive clauses may be introduced *only* by wh-words:

[64a] Mr. Horsefield, whom we have just met, . . .
  [b] *Mr. Horsefield, that we have just met, . . .
  [c] *Mr. Horsefield, we have just met, . . .

Moreover, restrictive relative clauses may be moved away from the nouns they modify, but appositives may not:

[65a] A man *who was from Iceland* came in.
  [b] A man came in *who was from Iceland.*
[66a] Bill, *who was from Iceland,* came in.
  [b] *Bill came in, *who was from Iceland.*

EXERCISES 1. The distinction between written restrictive and nonrestrictive relatives is indicated through punctuation. How is it indicated in speech?
2. In the following sentences, identify each relative clause and indicate whether it can be restrictive or nonrestrictive. (Punctuation has been omitted intentionally.) If a sentence can be either, discuss the difference of meaning.
   a. Everyone who viewed the exhibit was satisfied.
   b. The visitors who viewed the exhibit were satisfied.
   c. Wendy who comes from Wyoming knows a lot about ranching.
   d. I hit the brakes which caused the car to fishtail.

So far we have described only finite relative clauses. However, nonfinite clauses can also function as relatives:

[67a] The man *to see* is Fred Finkelheimer.
  [b] The man *standing near the entrance* is my father.

Sentence [67b] can be interpreted as a **reduced relative clause.** That is, it's an elliptical version of:

[68] The man *who is standing near the entrance* is my father.

Reduction of this sort is common when the implied material is a wh-word and one of the inflected forms of *be*. Note the similarity between reduced relatives and reduced adverbials: Both involve the deletion of a wh-word and a form of *be,* an ellipsis referred to by linguists as **whiz-deletion.**

Reduced relatives may also function as nonrestrictive modifiers:

[69]   Astrid, standing near the entrance, was almost trampled in the rush.

We should mention here too that other modifiers in NPs can be restrictive or nonrestrictive, such as PPs:

[70a]   The man in the iron mask . . .
   [b]   Bill, in the iron mask, . . .

One final matter pertaining to the forms of **participial** or **reduced relative clauses.** As these names suggest, the verb of the reduced relative clause is in participial form, either *-en* (past participial) or *-ing* (present participial) form, and elements of the clause are omitted. Consider:

[71a]   People sentenced to life in prison . . .
   [b]   Anyone walking on the grass . . .

And compare them with:

[72a]   People who were sentenced to life in prison . . .
   [b]   Anyone who is walking on the grass . . .

Clearly, the relative clauses in [71a] and [72a] are passives, and in [71a], the relative pronoun and the form of passive *be* are omitted. An analogous omission of *who is* occurs in [71b].

However, the terms past and present are a bit misleading, as they suggest that the relatives imply past or present time. The clauses aren't, in fact, restricted to these interpretations:

[73]   People sentenced to life in prison from now on will have to pay for their keep if the proposed new law goes into effect.
[74]   Anyone walking on the grass at that time was subject to a stiff fine.

In [73], the past participial relative actually refers to a future time, *from now on*. In [74], the present participial relative refers to a past time, *at that time.* In short, the actual time reference of the reduced relatives is governed by elements other than their verbs.

10.5.4   Miscellany

In this section, we describe grammatical operations that produce subordinate clauses that don't fit neatly in the preceding categories: **extraposition, NP-movement** (or **raising**), **tough-movement, cleft,** and **pseudocleft** constructions.

Extraposition

Clauses which are interpreted as subjects may occur not only in the main clause subject position but also at the right end of the main clause predicate. Compare the following pair:

[75a] *That Oscar writes poetry* upsets his parents.
 [b] It upsets his parents *that Oscar writes poetry.*

These two have essentially the same meanings. In both sentences, the italicized clause is interpreted as what upsets Oscar's parents. Note that in [75a] the clause appears as the subject of the main clause, whereas in [75b] that position is occupied by **dummy** or **expletive** *it* and the clause occurs at the end of the predicate. The rule which connects these two constructions is called **extraposition,** a name which suggest that the clause has been moved (-posed) outside (extra-) its normal position.

We have already exemplified another construction in which a clause is extraposed, but we repeat our example here for convenience:

[76a] A man who was from Iceland came in.
 [b] A man came in who was from Iceland.

Again, both sentences have identical meanings even though in [76b] the relative clause modifying *man* appears at the end of the predicate. The rule which links these two sentence types is called **extraposition from NP.**

One reason that English (and many other languages) allows extraposition and extraposition from an NP is that clauses tend to be relatively long, and so disrupt the subject-predicate structure of sentences. Sentences are generally easier to process (understand) when the clause has been extraposed. Another reason might be, as we mentioned earlier in this chapter, that while NPs require case marking, subordinate clauses don't, and so may be moved to positions which don't receive case.

NP-movement (raising) clauses

Consider now the following two sentences with almost identical meanings:

[77a] It seems that Oscar has upset his parents.
 [b] Oscar seems to have upset his parents.

In both sentences, *Oscar* is interpreted as the subject of *has/have upset his parents.* However, in [77a] it occurs as the subject of the subordinate clause, whereas in [77b] it occurs as the subject of the higher verb *seem.* Note that the clause in [77a] is finite, whereas the clause in [77b] is nonfinite. In fact, *Oscar* cannot occur as the subject of an infinitival clause after *seem, appear,* or *turn out:*

[78] *It seems Oscar to have upset his parents.

In general, these verbs require that the phrase understood as the subject of their infinitival complements be moved ("raised") to become the subject of the higher verb.

Tough-movement

A similar (though by no means identical) movement occurs in sentences in which adjectives, such as *easy* or *hard,* and NPs, such as *a pain* or *a treat,* function as the main predication. These are often cutely called **"tough-movement"** sentences. Tough-movement relates [79a] and [79b]:

[79a] It is tough to live with Hilda.
  [b] Hilda is tough to live with —.

Note that [79b] ends with a preposition whose object, *Hilda,* is missing, or more accurately, displaced. It appears as the subject of the main clause. Note too that the main clause subject of [79a] is the expletive *it.* This *it* doesn't refer to anything and occupies a position that receives no thematic role (which is why it's an expletive or dummy). *Hilda,* on the other hand, receives its thematic role from the subordinate verb and preposition. It's as if *Hilda* had been moved from the subordinate clause into the higher subject, hence the idea of movement.

A very reasonable question to ask at this point would be: Why does English maintain pairs of sentences such as [77a] and [77b] and [79a] and [79b] whose members have identical meanings? While we don't have a definitive answer, we believe that the reason has to do with the discourse functions of subjects. Typically, though by no means always, subjects function as the **topics** of their sentences (see Chapter 8). Topics refer to the entities that the sentences are about. So [77b] is about Oscar in a way that [77a] isn't; similarly, [79b] is about Hilda, whereas [79a] isn't. We would use the [77b] and [79b] sentences of these pairs in discourse contexts slightly different from the contexts in which we would use the [77a] and [79a] versions. (See Delahunty, 1991.)

We turn now to a pair of sentence types which have characteristics akin to finite relative clauses, the **cleft** and **pseudocleft** constructions.

Clefting

The following is a cleft sentence, and we will refer to the phrase in square brackets as its **focus** and to the italicized clause simply as its **clause:**

[80] It was [Henry Ford] *who invented the assembly line.*

Clefts consist of an expletive *it* higher subject, a form of *be,* a focus phrase (which may be any phrase type), and a clause which looks like (but actually isn't) a finite relative clause.

The clause is like a relative in that it may be introduced by a wh-word, *that* or (in some cases) nothing at all:

[81] It was Henry Ford (who/that) invented the assembly line.

It also contains a "gap," which is interpreted as if it were "filled" by the focus so that the clefts above mean essentially:

[82] Henry Ford invented the assembly line.

The fact that a cleft can be reduced in this way has led some grammarians to suggest that the focus was actually moved out of the clause into its position in the matrix.

Cleft foci are often interpreted as contrasting with some other phrase. For example, you might use a cleft such as the ones above if you thought that the hearer/reader believed that Roger Smith invented the assembly line:

[83]   It was Henry Ford, not Roger Smith, who invented the assembly line.

If the focus is a PP, then the sense of contrast may fade somewhat:

[84]   It was in 1789 that the French Revolution broke out.

The construction here suggests something like *specifically in 1789,* but it could also be used if a hearer believed that the French Revolution broke out in 1689 or 1799.

The clause of a cleft sentence is usually interpreted as "known" information, known either to the hearer or by people generally. It isn't, however, assumed to be currently in the hearer's consciousness (Delahunty, 1991; Prince, 1978).

Pseudoclefting

Like clefts, pseudoclefts "cleave" a sentence and contain a form of *be*:

[85]   *What irritates me* is [the amount of sports on TV].

Again, we will refer to the italicized as the pseudocleft clause, and to the bracketed phrase as its focus. The clause may begin only with the wh-word *what:*

[86a]   *Who plays golf is Fred.
  [b]   *Which ate the mouse was the cat.
  [c]   *When I arrived was lunchtime.

And again, the basic meaning may be represented by a sentence in which the focus phrase replaces *what:*

[87]   The amount of sports on TV irritates me.

But just as clefts don't mean exactly what their noncleft counterparts mean, neither do pseudoclefts and their counterparts. The clause of a pseudocleft represents information which the speaker assumes to be in the consciousness of the hearer at the time the sentence is uttered (Prince, 1978).

10.6   COORDINATION

Subordination occurs when one clause functions as a grammatical relation of another clause, but subordination isn't the only way in which clauses can be combined to compose a larger sentence. They can be combined without one being subordinated to another. Two clauses united into a single inclusive sentence without subordination are said to be **coordinate.** They're typically joined together by the **coordinating conjunctions** *and, or,* or *but:*

[88a] The king is in his counting house and the queen is in the parlor.
 [b] The police must charge you or they must release you.
 [c] You must remain here but your partner may go.

The sentences of [88] illustrate coordination of main (matrix) clauses. However, subordinate clauses, both finite and nonfinite, may be connected in this way:

[89a] We left [because we were tired] and [because the lecture was boring]. (Conjoined Adverbial Clauses)
 [b] Alex wanted [to sing] and [to play the piano]. (Conjoined Infinitives)
 [c] Anyone [who attends classes] and [who pays attention] should pass the course. (Conjoined Relative Clauses)
 [d] [Climbing Denali] and [winning the biathlon] were Meg's greatest accomplishments. (Conjoined Gerunds)

10.7 SUMMARY

In this chapter, we explored the major grammatical structures that enable English speakers to create sentences of infinite length and complexity. Despite the intricacy and variety they make possible, finite and nonfinite subordinate clauses are individually fairly simple. Each has a rather limited set of formal properties, and we have had to add very few functions to describe their workings. To see this more clearly, you might want to review Tables 10.1 to 10.3. But the process of embedding—of building structures within structures—multiplies the potential for variety exponentially. We have here only scratched the surface of that potential. But if you want to see some dramatic demonstrations, pick up a sonnet by Shakespeare, a poem by Dylan Thomas, or a piece of prose by Henry James, William Faulkner, or Virginia Woolf. Or pick up an essay that you have written recently. You will probably amaze yourself with the complexity of your own language.

REFERENCES AND RESOURCES

Delahunty, G. P. 1991. "The powerful pleonasm: a defense of expletive *It Is.*" *Written Communication,* 8:213–239.
Prince, E. 1978. "A Comparison of *Wh*-Clefts and *It*-Clefts in Discourse." *Language,* 54:883–906.

GLOSSARY

Absolute construction: a construction set apart grammatically from the rest of a sentence.

Adjective clause: see **relative clause.**

Adverbial clause: a subordinate clause introduced by a subordinating adverbial conjunction. See Chapter 6.

Appositive relative: see **nonrestrictive relative.**

Cause clause: an adverbial clause that begins with *because, since, as,* or an implied instance of one of these conjunctions denoting the cause of an event.

Clause: a grammatical construction that consists of a subject and a predicate; may be **finite** or **nonfinite.**

Cleft sentence: a sentence built on the pattern *It is/was X that . . . .*

Complement clause: a clause following verbs such as *say, think, prefer,* etc.

Complement of NP: a clause that follows a head noun such as *idea, fact,* etc. and denotes a specific instance of the class denoted by the head noun.

Complementizer: a word (e.g., *that*) which introduces a complement clause.

Complex sentence: a sentence that has at least one subordinate (embedded) clause.

Compound sentence: a sentence that has two or more main clauses, connected by a coordinating conjunction. See Chapter 6.

Conditional clause: an adverbial clause introduced by *if, unless,* etc.

Coordinating conjunction: a word that conjoins two or more grammatically equal elements, such as *and, but,* and *or.* See Chapter 6.

Coreference: see Chapter 6.

Dummy: see Chapter 7.

Embed: see Chapter 7.

Expletive: see Chapter 7.

Extraposition: a grammatical process in which a clause interpreted as a subject occurs at the end of its clause.

Factive: see Chapter 2.

Finite: a clause that has a present or past tense inflection or a modal auxiliary. See **nonfinite.**

Focus: a phrase in a cleft construction that follows *is/was.*

Gerund: a verb phrase that functions in the range of noun phrases (e.g., subject, object). See Chapter 5.

Independent clause: a finite clause that contains all of the required clausal elements; also a clause that is not subordinate to another clause. See **main clause, matrix clause.**

Indirect question clause: a clause beginning with a wh-word that functions in the range of a noun phrase.

Infinitive: see Chapter 5.

Main clause: the minimal finite clause of a sentence. See **subordinate clause.**

Matrix clause: a clause in which another clause is embedded.

Nonfactive: see Chapter 2.

Nonfinite: a clause that has no tense inflection or modal auxiliary. See **finite.**

Nonrestrictive relative (also called "**appositive relative**"): a relative clause that describes but doesn't limit the reference of a noun phrase.

Noun complement clause: a clause following nouns such as *fact* and *idea.*

NP-Movement: the movement of an NP from the subject of an infinitival subordinate clause into the subject position of a higher clause containing a verb such as *seem* and the movement of an object NP into the surface subject position in a passive sentence.

Object complement: see Chapter 5 and Chapter 8.

Participle: see Chapter 5 and Chapter 7.

Phrase: a grammatically unified structure that lacks a finite or nonfinite subject-verb relationship.

Place clause: an adverbial clause introduced by *where* or *wherever.*

Presuppose: see Chapter 2.

Pseudocleft: a sentence of the form *What X Vs is Y* ..., where X and Y are phrases.

Purpose clause: a subordinate adverbial clause that begins with *so* or *so that* and denotes the purpose of an event.

Raising: a process that moves a noun phrase from a lower clause into a higher clause.

Reduced adverbial: an adverbial clause, beginning with a subordinating adverbial conjunction, from which the subject and verb are omitted.

Reduced relative (also called "**participle clause**"): a relative clause that postmodifies a head noun with the forms *wh + be* implied. See **relative clause.**

Relative clause (also called "**adjective clause**"): a subordinate clause that postmodifies a head noun.

Restrictive relative clause: a relative clause that limits the reference of the head noun in a noun phrase. See **nonrestrictive relative.**

Result clause: a subordinate adverbial clause signaled by the construction *so . . . that* and denoting the result of an event.

Simple sentence: a sentence that contains only one clause.

Subject complement: see Chapter 5 and Chapter 8.

Subordinate clause: a clause connected to another clause by an actual or implied subordinating word.

Subordinating conjunction: a word that connects a subordinate clause to a higher clause.

Time clause: a subordinate adverbial clause connected to a higher clause by the words *after, as soon as, before, since,* etc. and denoting the time of an event.

Topic: a phrase that designates the entity that a sentence is about.

Tough-movement: a transformation that changes sentences such as *It is tough to live with Hilda* to *Hilda is tough to live with.* See **raising.**

Whiz-deletion: the deletion of expressions such as *which is* or *who was* for the purpose of reducing relative clauses.

11 GENERATIVE GRAMMAR

A theory of language
Aspects of the theory of syntax
Transition: Constraints and generalizations
Government-Binding theory

11.0   A THEORY OF LANGUAGE

We have several goals in this chapter. Foremost, we wish to present a brief outline of a current approach to language, known as **Government-Binding (GB)** theory, which was developed by Noam Chomsky and his coworkers during the 1980s. The GB approach currently commands the greatest interest in the field, and as teachers you are likely to encounter its influence during your career.

Our goal in presenting GB is to demonstrate how modern linguistic research is carried on. Specifically, we will demonstrate the construction of a theory and the ways in which it's justified. As we illustrated in Chapter 1, the awareness of theoretical concerns is an important counter to the assumptions about the nature of language that underlie the prescriptive grammars and handbooks that teachers are often required to use. These assumptions are generally simplistic and frequently wrong.

In describing GB, we will discuss what it assumes are the fundamental properties of human language. The most notable of these is the idea that language is **modular.** By this we mean that actual sentences are the result of interactions among various components of the grammar of a language. These **components** include a phonology, a morphology and lexicon, a syntax, a semantics, and a pragmatics. Each of these components is **autonomous,** in the sense that its characteristics are quite distinct from the characteristics of the other components and that each interacts in very limited ways with the other components. GB focuses almost exclusively on the syntax of natural language and proposes that the syntactic component is itself modular, comprising **modules** which we will describe in due course.

Because GB is the culmination of 35 years of linguistic research in the generative tradition, we approach it historically. We begin by examining the major ideas presented in Chomsky's *Aspects of the Theory of Syntax* (1965). We then describe some of the attempts to make the system more general. These will lead us into GB theory, the final focus of the chapter.

11.1   ASPECTS OF THE THEORY OF SYNTAX

In the following sections, we will discuss the major ideas proposed in *Aspects*. These include the goals Chomsky proposed for linguistic theory and, in particular, the ways in which linguistic theories are evaluated, the concept of **strict subcategorization,** and the need to differentiate different levels of syntactic representation, which he referred to as **deep structure** and **surface structure.**

11.1.1　Goals of generative grammar: Levels of adequacy

In *Aspects,* Chomsky argued that the goal of linguistics ought to be the understanding of the **competence** of an ideal native speaker of a language. As we noted in Chapter 1, competence is the knowledge that enables native speakers to produce, understand, and judge an indefinite number of sentences.

Chomsky distinguished linguistic competence from the production or comprehension of actual utterances in real situations, which he called **linguistic performance.** In actual language use, competence and performance are inextricably intertwined, so linguists must abstract away from performance factors such as differences between speaking and understanding, memory limitations, distractions, and the like when they want to describe and explain the grammatical competence of an ideal native speaker of a language.

He argued that many different descriptions could accurately represent the grammar of a given language so that in order to select the best description, linguists need a general theory of grammars, one which would apply to all languages. In other words, they need a theory of linguistic **universals.** A description that is consistent with the general theory is preferable to one that isn't. A description of a particular language that follows from a theory that lays out just which grammars and which grammatical devices (rules) are humanly possible can be viewed as derived from general principles. A grammar that follows logically from general principles, from linguistic universals, can be thought of as *explaining* the linguistic phenomena that it deals with. This concern with explanation and universals is an important difference between the generative approach to language and its predecessors.

Chomsky proposed that grammars must be judged against three *levels of adequacy*. A grammar meets the lowest level, that of **observational adequacy,** if it, like native speakers, correctly distinguishes expressions which are grammatically well-formed from those that are ill-formed. All that an observationally adequate grammar is required to do is to indicate for any expression whether it is or isn't grammatical. If you're unsure of the meanings of *grammatical* and *ungrammatical,* you should review Chapter 1.

A grammar is **descriptively adequate** if it's observationally adequate and assigns the same structures to sentences of the language as its speakers do. For example, it must be able to identify correctly the subject, direct object, and other grammatical categories in each sentence.

A grammar is **explanatorily adequate** if it's descriptively adequate and if the structures that it assigns to sentences are consistent with a set of **universal properties** of language, which in turn are those used by children acquiring their first language. For example, the rules must be structure dependent (see Chapter 1). That is, they must be expressed in terms of formal categories such as NP and VP rather than in terms of a numbered sequence of positions.

Many grammars are capable of being observationally adequate; fewer are descriptively adequate; and fewer still are explanatorily adequate. (See Figure 11.1.) Indeed, if the universals are properly formulated, then for any given language, ideally, only one explanatory grammar is possible. The generative linguist's job is to discover the set of universal

FIGURE 11.1.   Levels of Adequacy

Observationally adequate: GOOD
- Correctly distinguishes grammatical from ungrammatical sentences

Descriptively adequate: BETTER
- Correctly distinguishes grammatical from ungrammatical sentences
- Assigns correct analysis to sentences

Explanatorily adequate: BEST
- Correctly distinguishes grammatical from ungrammatical sentences
- Assigns correct analysis to sentences
- Analyses are expressed in universal categories

---

properties of language which when applied in the construction of the grammar of any language will yield the single grammar that speakers of that language actually construct as they learn it. The higher the level of adequacy, the richer the set of assumptions about the nature of language and of the human beings that learn and use it, and consequently the more constrained the grammar of any language.

11.1.2   Strict subcategorization

In the *Aspects* model, words are stored in a **lexicon,** a mental dictionary, and they're inserted into the **phrase structure trees** by special rules called **lexical insertion rules.** Let's briefly examine these parts of the grammar.

The lexicon of the grammar must contain every word known to an ideal native speaker/hearer. Each word must be associated with all of the idiosyncratic or unpredictable information particular to it, including its phonological form, any special morphophonological rules (such as exceptional plural or past tense marking), its meaning (or meanings), its part or parts of speech, and its strict subcategorization information.

Strict subcategorization information indicates, for example, whether a verb is intransitive, transitive, or otherwise. In general, the strict subcategorization information associated with a verb indicates what other elements must occur in the verb phrase into which the verb is inserted. This information is expressed as a **strict subcategorization frame.**

Put is a particularly useful example for our current purposes because it must be followed by NP and PP or AdvP, which we can represent as [$_{VP}$——— NP   PP/AdvP]. This expression indicates that *put* occurs in VPs (represented by the square brackets) in which it's followed by an NP and a PP or AdvP. Any sentence without either of these two phrases in its VP is ungrammatical:

[1a]   *We put.
 [b]   *We put the box.
 [c]   *We put under the table/away.
 [d]   We put the box under the table/away.

The lexical insertion rules insert words into tree structures that are compatible with their strict subcategorization frames. So they could insert *put* into:

[2] [$_{VP}$ —— [$_{NP}$ the hat] [$_{PP}$ on the cat]]

but not into:

[3] [$_{VP}$ —— [the printer]]

EXERCISE   What are the strict subcategorization frames for *kiss, observe, place,* and *laugh*. Remember that these frames include only the phrases and words that *must* accompany the verbs, if any.

11.1.3 Levels of syntactic representation: Deep structure, surface structure, and transformations

Consider the following sentences:

[4a] Bill looked up the number.
 [b] Bill looked the number up.

These two sentences differ only in the position of the particle *up*. In the first sentence, it occurs between the verb and the object; in the second sentence, to the right of the object. Both sentences contain the same words, and the phrases, particularly the NPs, perform the same grammatical functions in both. *Bill* is the subject; *the number* is the direct object. Moreover, the two sentences are synonymous. By this we mean specifically that the thematic roles (see Chapter 8) assigned to the NPs are the same in both sentences. *Bill* is the Agent and *the number* is the Theme. As native speakers we can assert these facts with certainty and expect universal agreement among English speakers. Because knowledge of the relationship between sentence pairs such as that above is part of every native English speaker's competence, it must be expressed in a generative grammar. At issue is how to do this.

We can assign the following analyses to sentences [4a] and [4b]:

[5a]

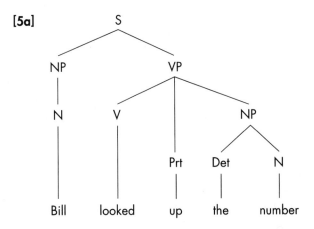

[b]

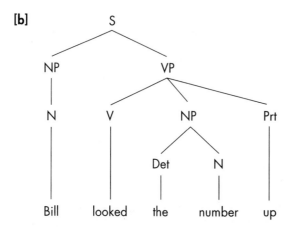

From the point of view of a generative linguist, these structures are generated by the phrase structure rules (PSRs):

[6] S → NP   VP
VP → V   Prt   NP (cf. tree [5a])
VP → V   NP   Prt (cf. tree [5b])

(Review Chapter 9 if you're unsure about formal diagrams and PSRs.) There are two VP expansion rules here, and since we wish to eliminate as much redundancy as possible, we can use the abbreviatory devices introduced in Chapter 9 to unify them:

[7] VP → V   (Prt)   NP   (Prt)

Prt is an abbreviation for *particle,* words that combine with verbs to create two-word verbal units, e.g., *look up, pick up, pick out.* As examples [4a] and [4b] show, a particle can occur between either the verb and its direct object or after the direct object.

However, [7] predicts that English sentences with two particles in their VPs ought to be grammatical, a false prediction, as [8] shows:

[8] *Bill looked up the number up.

The problem is that phrase structure rule [7] doesn't express the condition that if a sentence contains a particle in one position, it cannot also contain one in another position.

To express this condition, we need a **transformation,** i.e., a rule that changes one tree into another tree. These changes include moving elements of a tree from one position to another, deleting elements, and substituting one type of element for another (e.g., a pronoun for a full NP).

However, transformations presuppose a distinction between their inputs and outputs, i.e., between **deep structures** and **surface structures.**

Suppose that [5a] is the deep structure of both [4a] and [4b]. The surface structure of [4a] is identical in all relevant respects with its deep structure. The surface structure of [4b] is slightly different from its deep structure, specifically regarding the position of the particle. We account for this slight difference by positing a transformation, called **Particle Move-**

ment (**PM**), that moves a particle from its deep structure position beside its verb and places it to the right of the direct object. This yields the surface structure [5b].

The transformational approach has the advantage over the phrase structure approach of not making the false prediction that sentences such as [8] are grammatical, and of expressing, by the common deep structure, the knowledge of native speakers that pairs of sentences such as these are grammatically related. The grammar represents the two sentences as transformational variants of each other, analogous to the ways in which allophones and allomorphs are related to each other as variants of underlying abstract phonemes or morphemes. Assigning sentences a common deep structure also expresses the fact that the sentences are broadly synonymous with each other, specifically in that a given noun phrase will have the same thematic role in all of them.

EXERCISES
1. Create four pairs of sentences analogous to [4a] and [4b], using the particles *up, out, over,* and *on.*
2. Find five other verb + particle combinations.
3. What condition must be added to the particle movement transformation to account correctly for the following data?
   a. The witness picked Fred out.
   b. The witness picked out Fred.
   c. The witness picked him out.
   d. *The witness picked out him. [Emphasis on *out.*]

[That is, what condition must be added to ensure that the grammar does not predict that (d) is grammatical?]

11.1.3.1   A note on the discourse functions of Particle Movement

Particle Movement has no effect on the meaning of sentences to which it has been applied. The thematic roles of the NPs in the sentences affected by PM are exactly the same as those in sentences that are unaffected. Are both sentence types freely interchangeable in all contexts then?

The answer to this should be clear from the previous exercise. PM *must* apply if the object is a pronoun. It seems plausible to assume that at least one factor in determining where to place the particle is the informational status of the object NP. If the NP represents old, known, or given information (and pronouns are typically in this category), then the particle moves to the right. If the NP represents new information, the particle is placed between V and NP. This is an example of the interaction between the syntactic and pragmatic components of the grammar.

Another factor, and probably the more important one, is the length of the object NP. The longer the NP, the more likely the particle is to appear before, rather than after it, as the following sentences show:

[9a]   He looked it up.
 [b]   He looked the number up.
 [c]   He looked his boss's number up.
 [d]   ?He looked the number which he had written on the back of a match book up.

[e]   *He looked the number of the house where the cat that killed the rat that ate the malt lived up.

[f]   He looked up the number of the house where the cat that killed the rat that ate the malt lived.

These examples illustrate the effect that length (or *weight*) can have on where a phrase can occur in a sentence.

11.1.4   Topicalization and the assignment of thematic roles

Phrases are assigned **thematic** (or **theta**) roles by virtue of their grammatical relations within the sentence, specifically by virtue of their relation to a verb, preposition, or noun. Some, but by no means all, current theories make the **uniqueness assumption**—that an NP can be assigned *only one* thematic role in a particular sentence. In the interests of simplicity, we will adopt that assumption in this section.

We will assume also that *every* NP in a sentence must be assigned a thematic role. We will call this the **completeness assumption.**

It follows from these two assumptions that every NP in a sentence must be assigned one but no more than one thematic role.

Consider now the sentences:

[10a]   Bill carried Mary.
   [b]   Mary, Bill carried.

In both of these sentences, *Bill* is the Agent and *Mary* is the Theme. Note, however, that *Mary* occurs in two different positions in these sentences. In [10a] it occurs in the direct object position, whereas in [10b] it's in what is known as the **topic position.** Speakers of English know that both of these sentences assert that Bill carried Mary; in other words, *Mary* is the Theme. Let's assume that we have a rule whereby *carry* assigns Theme to its direct object in sentences like [10a]. Must we now assume that we need another rule to account for the assignment of Theme to *Mary* in the topic position? Conceivably so. Such a rule might say: Assign Theme to the NP directly to the left of the subject of the clause in which the assigning verb occurs. However, when we examine more data, we can see that this becomes impossible:

[11a]   Mary, Fred thinks that Bill carried.
   [b]   Mary, Susan believes that Fred thinks that Bill carried.
   [c]   Mary, I know that Susan believes that . . . that Bill carried.

EXERCISE   Insert one, two, and three further expressions of the form *NP Vs that* in the position occupied by the periods in [11c].

In each of the sentences of [11], *Mary* is understood as the Theme of *carried*. But we can insert as many *that*-clauses between *Mary* and *carried* as we wish. There is no principled limit to the number of such clauses. It follows that for an infinite number of sentences we would need an infinite number of rules to assign Theme to *Mary*. Clearly, such a set of rules couldn't exist in anyone's mind. We must therefore find an alternative way of assigning a thematic role to all of these different (but related) positions.

Rather than devise a complex set of rules that would directly assign Theme to *Mary* in all of these positions, transformational linguists have simplified the assignment process by assuming something like the following: A verb such as *carry* assigns Theme to its *deep structure* direct object, which may afterward be moved by transformations such as **Topicalization.** The moved phrase is thereafter always associated with its original position and so with its thematic role.

In support of this idea, note that we cannot put another NP into the object position and still interpret the resulting S as Mary is carried by Bill:

[12] Mary, Bill carried Susie.

We can only interpret *Mary* in [12] as an addressee and not as a direct object. *Susie* has taken over that role. Because *Mary* can no longer be associated with the direct object position, it cannot be interpreted as Theme. So the deep structure position with which a moved phrase is associated and from which it derives its thematic role must be empty.

Let's now ask about the position that the topicalized phrase occupies in surface structure. There are various possibilities. One is that Topicalization inserts the topicalized phrase directly under S. However, we will introduce a new node, **Comp** (for **Complementizer**), which requires a special phrase structure rule to generate it:

[13] S′ → Comp   S

[14]

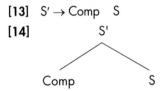

We will assume that Topicalization inserts the moved phrase into Comp. The surface structure of [10b] would therefore be represented as:

[15]

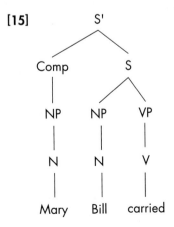

Comp is a position outside S that occurs in every S', pronounced *S-bar*. It's never assigned a thematic role directly. A phrase in Comp acquires its thematic role by virtue of its association with a deep structure position. This association is represented by the transformation that moves the phrase. As every NP must be assigned a thematic role, it follows that there can be no NP in Comp in deep structure. We will call positions to which no thematic role can be assigned directly **nonargument positions.** This is often abbreviated to **A′** (read *A-bar*) in the literature. **Argument positions** are those positions within S to which thematic roles *may* be assigned in deep structure. They include, as you no doubt guessed, subjects, objects, and objects of prepositions. We will discover later that while these positions may be assigned a thematic role, they occasionally aren't. So Topicalization moves a phrase from an A position to which a thematic role has been assigned to an A′ position.

Besides moving an NP, as in the examples above, Topicalization can move any phrase to Comp:

[16a] *Mary,* I like. (NP topic)
  [b] *Into the valley of death,* I will not go. (PP topic)
  [c] *Intelligent,* he isn't. (AP topic)
  [d] I said that Fred would go home, and *go home* he will. (VP topic)
  [e] *Quickly* she left. (AdvP topic)

EXERCISE   Draw the deep structure and surface structure trees for each sentence in [16].

11.1.4.1   Discourse functions of topicalization

Every native speaker of English knows that topicalized and untopicalized sentences express essentially the same message. The thematic roles of the various NPs in the sentences are unchanged by the movement. There is nonetheless a difference between the two forms. The untopicalized is a more general-purpose construction than the topicalized, which we would use only in special pragmatically distinct contexts.

The most typical reaction speakers of English have upon hearing sentences such as:

[17] The forks, you put on the left.

is that the entity or entities referred to by the topic NP have already been introduced (directly or indirectly) into the discourse. So [17] might occur as the answer to:

[18] Which side do I put the forks on?

A second and closely related use of topicalized sentences is to refer to an entity which is a member of a list of related entities which has already been introduced into the discourse. A typical other sentence to go along with [17] might be:

[19] and the knives you put on the right.

Knives and forks are members of the set of silverware items, and if you came upon a conversation in which [17] was the first sentence you heard, you could reasonably assume that the speakers had already mentioned silverware, and one speaker was now listing the individual members of the silverware set and telling, e.g., a child, where each one goes in a place setting. So the NP in topic position can refer to a member of a set of items which has already been introduced into the discourse.

To sum up our discussion of Topicalization: Topicalization moves any phrase from its position within S to the Comp position. The moved phrase retains the thematic role it was assigned at deep structure. The old position may not be filled with another phrase. No morphological changes occur to either the moved phrase or other elements of the sentence. Topicalization is used to refer to entitites that are members of sets or lists which have already been introduced into the discourse (Ward, 1988).

11.1.5 Subject-Auxiliary Inversion

As we noted in Chapter 8, the order of subject and first auxiliary verb is reversed in questions [20a] to [20e] and sentences that begin with negative adverbs such as *rarely* [21]:

[20a] Can I have another go?
  [b] Have you taken the trash out?
  [c] Are you leaving now?
  [d] Are you okay?
  [e] Have you any wool?
[21] Rarely have I seen such a magnificent sunset!

As you recall from Chapter 9, the immediate constituents of S are NP–Aux–VP. Using these as our base, we can relate a yes-no question to its declarative counterpart by assuming that both have the same deep structure (NP–Aux–VP), and that there is a transformation, called **Subject-Auxiliary Inversion (SAI)**, that moves Aux to the left of the subject in the question (Aux–NP–VP).

We will assume that Aux is **adjoined to S** rather than just inserted directly under it. Adjunction to S involves first creating a *second* S node above the original one and then inserting Aux (or more generally the adjoined phrase) under the newly created node. SAI applies to [22a] to give [22b]:

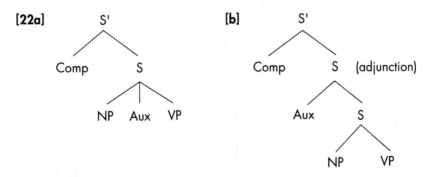

The technical reasons for adjunction need not detain us here.

EXERCISE   Draw the deep and surface structure trees for the sentences in [20] and [21].

In Chapter 8, we demonstrated that auxiliary verbs are optional and that they occur in the order:

[23]   (Modal)   (Perfective *have*)   (Progressive *be*)   (Passive *be*)

SAI affects only the first verb in the sequence regardless of which it is. In fact, we will assume that only the first auxiliary verb is actually in the Aux position when SAI applies. Later in this chapter, we will discuss the positions of the other verbs.

11.1.6   Wh-Movement

Wh-Movement is a transformation very similar to Topicalization in that it too moves a phrase to Comp. However, instead of operating on any phrase at all, Wh-Movement moves only those phrases that contain a wh-word. Wh-words include *who(m), what, when, where, why,* and *how.* Consider:

[24a]   You must give Bill what?
   [b]   What must you give Bill?

Here again, the grammatical and thematic relations are identical in the two sentences. Only the word order has changed. We explain these similarities by assuming that these sentences have identical deep structures and that they differ only in the transformations applied to them. In [24b], Wh-Movement has moved *what* to the front of the sentence (and SAI has moved *must*). In [24a], neither transformation has applied.

Other sentences in which Wh-Movement has applied include:

[25a]   What will you buy?
   [b]   Which book must you buy?
   [c]   Whose uncle have you met?
   [d]   Where have you been?
   [e]   Why weren't you home in time?
   [f]   How will you get there anyway?
   [g]   When must you leave?
   [h]   Who will you say gave you the furs?
   [i]   Who ate the cheese?

EXERCISE   Draw the deep and surface structure trees of the sentences in [25]. Did you put *who* in Comp in the surface structure of [25i] or did you leave it in the subject position? Why? Did you put *who* in Comp in the surface structure tree for sentence [25h]? Does this affect your analysis of [25i]? How?

11.1.6.1　Wh-Movement and Subject-Auxiliary Inversion

In several of the examples above, both Wh-Movement and SAI have occurred. In fact, it's typical of English direct wh-questions that they involve both transformations. We can represent the surface structure of such sentences as:

[26]

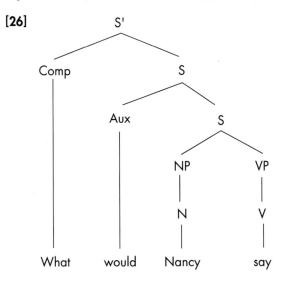

That is, Wh-Movement puts the wh-phrase into Comp and SAI adjoins Aux to S.

These two transformations can occur separately, and so the application of one isn't dependent on the application of the other. SAI occurs alone in yes-no interrogatives. Wh-Movement occurs alone in relative clauses:

[27a]　The cat which Bill must pet . . .
　[b]　*The cat which must Bill pet . . .

Wh-Movement may also occur in indirect questions without SAI:

[28]　We know what Nancy would say.

11.1.7　Imperative

Imperative sentences are generally without overt subjects, modals, or tense:

[29]　Get out!

There are reasons to believe, however, that imperative sentences do have deep structure subjects. First, English sentences in general have subjects, and it would be odd if one class of sentences lacked them. Second, and much more convincingly, imperatives interact with reflexive pronouns in ways that would be hard to explain if they had no subject. Consider:

[30a]　Bill shaved himself.
　[b]　You shaved yourself.

[c] I shaved myself.
[d] They shaved themselves.
[e] You shaved yourselves.
[f] We shaved ourselves.
[g] *You shaved myself/himself/herself/themselves/ourselves.

The reflexive pronoun in the direct object position must agree in person, number, and gender with the subject. That is, the form of the reflexive pronoun is dependent on the form of the subject. Clearly, for this to be the case, the reflexive pronoun must have a subject to depend on. Bearing this in mind consider:

[31] Shave yourself!
[32] *Shave myself/himself/herself/themselves/ourselves.

We can explain this pattern of data by assuming that underlying [31] is:

[33] You shave yourself.

Because the only reflexive that can co-occur with it is the second person reflexive (either singular or plural), the subject of a reflexive imperative must be *you*. But the subject *you* can be deleted, by a transformation called **Imperative Subject Deletion.**

The Aux of imperative sentences seems to be special. Nonimperative Aux phrases may contain a modal; an imperative Aux may not, even though an imperative sentence may contain other auxiliary verbs, as the following show:

[34a] Do close the door.
 [b] *Must close the door!
 [c] *Will eat your vegetables!
 [d] Have the dishes washed when I return!
 [e] Be studying when I return!
 [f] Be gone by daybreak!

If we assume that the Aux phrase can be occupied by either a modal or a marker which indicates that the sentence is an imperative, then Imperative Subject Deletion will correctly capture the facts. Consequently, the deep structure of *Close the door!* is:

[35]

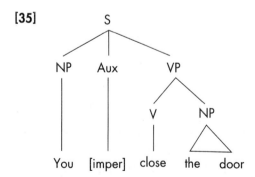

EXERCISE   Which applies first, imperative subject deletion or a rule which checks that a reflexive pronoun has an appropriate antecedent? Why?

11.1.7.1   A note on the pragmatics of imperatives

Imperatives are traditionally thought of as the form used for giving orders. Recent research suggests that there is more to be said about them than this, and that they raise interesting issues of language use. Fundamentally, a speaker using an imperative assumes that the addressee will do what the sentence expresses. However, studies of politeness suggest that speakers must concern themselves with their addressees' **face**, their public or personal self-image. They must be careful not to deny aspects of an addressee's self-image or unreasonably impose upon him or her. Imperatives can only be politely used when they don't violate aspects of an addressee's face.

Addressees can be assumed to be willing to cooperate with speakers without loss of face under a couple of types of circumstances: first, if the speaker has the authority to order the addressee to carry out the act expressed by the imperative; second, if the addressee can be assumed to want to carry out the act. For example, recipe directions are expressed in the imperative, at least partly because their readers may want to carry out the directions. Similarly, people who have asked for directions can be assumed to want to carry them out:

[36]   Take College Blvd. south for three blocks, then turn right on Mason, ...

Imperatives are polite also in (good) wishes:

[37a]   Have a wonderful time!
  [b]   Have a good day!

Or in offers:

[38a]   Let me take care of that.
  [b]   Have another piece of cake.
  [c]   Come on in.

Or in warnings:

[39]   Watch out!

EXERCISE   From the point of view of the preceding discussion, explain why the use of the imperative in the "wish" *Go to hell!* is impolite.

11.1.8 Verb Phrase Deletion

Another deletion rule deletes the VP of a sentence when it's identical to the VP of a preceding sentence, as in:

[40] Fred can go to the movies, and Mary can too.

We understand [40] as:

[41] Fred can go to the movies, and Mary can go to the movies too.

If we take [41] as representing the deep structure of [40] and posit a transformation that deletes the VP of the second clause when it's identical to the VP of an earlier clause, then we will have accounted for our understanding of these two sentences. In general, deletion can take place when it's possible to figure out easily from the context, linguistic or nonlinguistic, just what has been deleted. **Deletion under identity** as in [40] is a typical case in which the prior linguistic context allows the recovery of the deleted elements. Imperative Deletion is a case in which the deleted phrase is recoverable from the context.

VP Deletion is somewhat more complex than we have represented it here. When we examine it a bit more closely, we discover some interesting things about the structure of the VP. Consider the following set of sentences:

[42a] John must have been learning Spanish, and Fred must have been learning Spanish too.
[b] . . . and Fred must have been too.
[c] . . . and Fred must have too.
[d] . . . and Fred must too.

In sentences [42b] to [42d], respectively, we have deleted [V NP], [been V NP], [have been V NP]. In general, transformations operate on phrases rather than on arbitrary strings of words, and if we assume that this must be the case, then each of the sequences [V NP], [been V NP], and [have been V NP] must be a phrase. It follows that VP is composed of several levels of phrase structure, and that VP Deletion may apply to any of these levels:

[43]

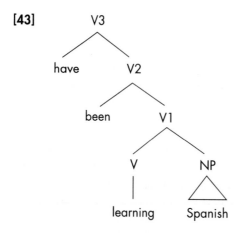

11.1.9   *There* Insertion

English contains pairs of sentences such as the following, which, like active and passive pairs, are essentially synonymous, but with some subtle differences:

[44a]   A unicorn is in the garden.
   [b]   There is a unicorn in the garden.

The second sentence differs from the first in that its subject contains *there* (which doesn't refer to a specific location) and the phrase that corresponds to the subject of the first sentence (*a unicorn*) occurs after the copula. How are we to represent the similarities and differences between such sentences?

   The generative grammarian's response has been to say that the sentences are transformationally related. They both have deep structures similar to [44a], but the derivation of [44b] involves a transformation which moves the subject phrase into the VP and inserts *there* into the vacated subject slot.

   Normally, English verbs agree with their surface structure subjects. In existential *there* sentences, however, the verb agrees with the NP that follows it in surface structure:

[45a]   There are unicorns in the garden.
   [b]   *There is unicorns in the garden.

Sentence [45b] is unacceptable in written or formal English, although its contracted form, [46], is acceptable in informal, colloquial varieties:

[46]   There's unicorns in the garden.

Many linguists would point to the fact that the verb of an existential *there* sentence agrees with the NP that follows it as evidence that this NP is the deep structure subject, moved by a transformation to the right of the verb. This transformation is known as *There* Insertion.

11.1.9.1   Some discourse functions of existential *there* sentences

No doubt you noticed that the deep structure subject of existential *there* sentences is typically an indefinite NP. Indefinite NPs typically represent information that is assumed to be new to the audience and typically is placed later in sentences. Old information is generally expressed early in a sentence, often in the subject. Topics are generally old information, and so are frequently expressed in the subject phrase. Obviously, discourse must have ways of introducing new topics, and *there* insertion sentences, by placing the new topic after the verb, are a natural way of accomplishing this. They're also used to assert the existence of entities and to summarize information (Huckin and Pesante, 1988).

11.1.10   Passive

Since we introduced the passive voice in Chapter 8, here we will merely describe the **Passive Transformation** as formulated in the *Aspects* model. Consider the following pair of sentences:

[47a] Bill wrote the book.
  [b] The book was written by Bill.

The thematic relations of *Bill* and *the book* are identical in these two sentences: *Bill* is the Agent, and *the book* is the Effected.

In an *Aspects* style analysis, the deep structures of synonymous active and passive sentences were taken to be identical, and the Passive Transformation (1) created the *by*-phrase, (2) moved the subject NP into it, (3) moved the direct object NP into the now vacant subject position, (4) inserted the verb *be,* and (5) changed the morphology of the verb to the passive participle form. The deep structure of [47a] and [47b] was:

[48a]

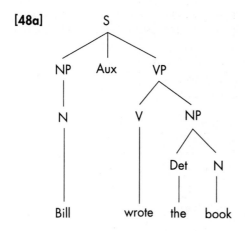

Sentence [47a] resulted when the Passive Transformation didn't apply to [48a]; sentence [47b] resulted when it did. The surface structure of [47b] was:

[48b]

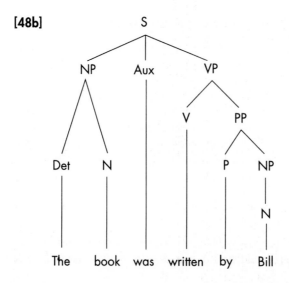

11.2 TRANSITION: CONSTRAINTS AND GENERALIZATIONS

During the 1970s, it became apparent that while the *Aspects* model was descriptively adequate, it was too powerful to be explanatorily adequate. There were so few **constraints** (i.e., restrictions) on transformations that almost any linguistic phenomenon could be described using them. As we have just seen, the passive transformation was a very powerful rule whose operations overlapped with those of several other components of the grammar, and consequently was quite redundant. One implication of the power of grammars of the *Aspects* type was that they represented languages that couldn't be learned in a finite amount of time. As a result, the focus of linguistic research shifted toward the task of limiting the descriptive power of the theory, a focus it has retained until now. The period we describe in this section is a transitional one between the *Aspects* (or "standard") theory and the current Government-Binding (GB) theory, which will be the subject of section 11.3. To give a sense of the thrust of this effort to limit the power of transformations, we begin by developing the concept of a **trace**.

11.2.1 Traces

English contains relative structures like the following:

[49] A cat such that Bill pets it

In this NP the pronoun *it* refers to the same thing as the phrase *a cat*. Such pronouns are called **resumptive pronouns.** They indicate the grammatical relationship that the head of the relative construction plays within the relative clause. In this case, the pronoun is the direct object of *pet*. However, [49] represents an unusual type of relative in English (although many other languages require resumptive pronouns in relative clauses). A more usual English relative would be:

[50] A cat which Bill pets

Here the object of *pet* is *which,* even though it's in the Comp position and not in the typical position for a direct object. That syntactic position was vacated by Wh-Movement and now appears to be empty. However, it's only apparently empty. We cannot, for example, insert another phrase into that position:

[51] *A cat which Bill pets the cat/dog/it

A similar restriction applies also in questions:

[52a] What did Bill pet?
  [b] *What did Bill pet the dog?

and in topicalized sentences:

[53a]   Pretzels he never eats.
  [b]   *Pretzels he never eats carrots.

So both Wh-Movement and Topicalization move a phrase into Comp and leave behind a position which cannot be refilled. We can explain why the evacuated position cannot be refilled if we assume that it's not really empty, that it's actually occupied by a resumptive pronoun that has grammatical and psychological reality but no pronunciation. We will refer to the silent element left in a position from which a phrase has been moved as a **trace**, which we will represent as [t] in our examples.

Both Wh-Movement and Topicalization represent a relationship between a deep structure position and a surface structure position that we can represent schematically as:

[54] $[_{Comp} XP]$ $\longleftrightarrow$ $[_{XP} t]$

The trace is of the same category as the moved phrase. In other words, the trace of a moved NP is an NP; of a moved PP is a PP; and so on for all categories. Moreover, traces have certain interesting effects. In many sentences, the sequence of words *want to* can be contracted to *wanna:*

[55]   I wanna go to bed.

However, there are instances when we cannot contract, specifically when a trace intervenes between *want* and *to:*

[56]   Who would you want [t] to sing the song?
[57]   *Who would you wanna sing the song?
[58]   You would want Bill to sing the song.

The trace left by the Wh-Movement of *who* in [56] and [57] is between *want* and *to* as *who* is understood as the subject of *sing,* just as *Bill* is in [58]. Just as we cannot contract *want* and *to* in [58] because *Bill* intervenes, neither can we contract them in [56] because the trace [t] intervenes. So traces are not nothing. They're categories which we can think of as akin to unpronounced resumptive pronouns.

Another way to look at traces left by moved constituents is to recall that verbs (particularly) are associated with strict subcategorization frames, whose violation results in ungrammatical sentences, as we saw earlier. However, look at the following sentences (recall that *put* requires NP and PP/AdvP):

[59a]   Where did we put the box?
  [b]   What did we put under the table?
  [c]   Under the table, what did we put?

We appear to be able to violate the subcategorization restrictions if Wh-Movement or Topicalization has taken place in the sentence.

If we view the subcategorization frame for *put* as indicating that this verb controls two positions in a VP, an NP, and a PP or AdvP, then the strict subcategorization requirements are fulfilled not only in deep structure but also in surface structure. We can represent the relevant aspects of the surface structure of [59a] as [59d]:

[59d] Where$_i$ did we put the box t$_i$?

Traces also explain why we cannot refill positions from which phrases have been moved: They are already filled. We leave it to you as an exercise to demonstrate that refilling the positions in [59a] to [59d] from which phrases have been moved results in ungrammaticality.

The movement of the constituents connects their new positions with their old positions, and so whatever thematic role the verb assigns to a trace is transmitted to the phrase in the new position. We can now think about movement as creating a connection between a phrase in one position with a trace in another, or between a deep structure position and a surface structure position.

It's by virtue of this connection that the moved phrase is assigned its thematic role. Clearly, the trace must be in a position to which a thematic role is assigned; otherwise the phrase with which it's connected will receive no role and the sentence will violate the completeness requirement. Clearly, too, the phrase must be moved to a position to which no thematic role has been assigned; otherwise it will receive two thematic roles, one by virtue of its position, the other by virtue of its connection with its trace. A sentence containing a phrase with more than one thematic role violates the uniqueness requirement.

We now have two ways of viewing the relationship between deep structure and surface structure. First, as in the earlier theory, a phrase is assigned its theta role in deep structure and may then be moved, still carrying its role. Second, in the more recent versions, a theta role is assigned to a deep structure (or **D-structure,** as it's now called) position. The phrase in that position may then be moved. The phrase receives its theta role by virtue of its connection with its D-structure position. This connection is indicated by assigning the trace and the moved phrase identical subscripts:

[60]   [XP]$_i$ ⟵⟶ [t]$_i$.

With the concept of trace under our belt, let's now revisit the passive. Recall that the Passive Transformation relates sentence pairs such as [47a] and [47b] repeated here:

[47a]   Bill wrote the book.
   [b]   The book was written by Bill.

It appeared to many linguists that creating structure (normally the job of PSRs), inserting words (normally done by lexical insertion rules in the deep structure), changing the morphology, as well as moving phrases about were far too much for a single transformation to accomplish.

More recent theories assume that the deep structures of the active and passive forms are similar but not identical, and the Passive Transformation is greatly simplified. All it does now is move an object NP into an empty subject position. In recent analyses, the deep structure of the active, [47a], remains [48a], while the deep structure of the passive, [47b], is [61]:

[61]

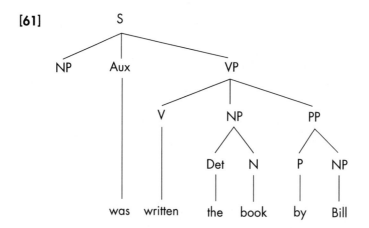

Notice that the deep structure subject NP is **empty:** That is, the position is there but it has no words or traces in it. The copula is already present in deep structure, as is the passive morphology on the main verb. The passive participle is assumed to be like an adjective and therefore to assign only one thematic role—to its direct object; the Agent role is assumed to be assigned by the preposition *by.* The subject is empty because no theta role is assigned to it. And because it's empty, it's available for the object NP to move into. The surface structure of [47b] in this theory is [62]:

[62]

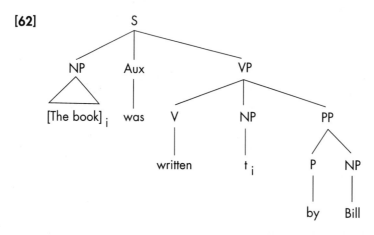

EXERCISE   Draw the deep structure and surface structure trees associated with the following sentences.
a. John was trailed by the FBI.
b. We were endangered by the accident.
c. This trail has been ruined by snowmobiles.

What are the active sentences that correspond to these? How does the deep structure of the passives represent what is common to both active and passive variants?

One very important implication of traces is that the information represented in deep structure is still represented in surface structure. What traces do is generalize deep structure throughout the entire derivation of a sentence. They preserve the deep structure even when transformations move elements of it far from their original positions. They also allow us, should we choose to do so, to view movement transformations as merely indicators of relationships between theta-marked positions and non-theta-marked positions, and thus avoid having to assume the existence of movement transformations. We will have more to say about this aspect of traces when we deal with the **projection principle** in section 11.3.

11.2.2 Noun Phrase Movement

Imagine the task of learning a grammar. If transformations could apply in a number of constructions, as Wh-Movement does in questions and in relative clauses, then the learner's task is simpler than if every construction had its own idiosyncratic transformational rules. The *Aspects* version of Passive was idiosyncratic to that construction. However, the more recent version, which merely moves an NP into subject position, besides being simpler, is also more general; it applies in other sentence types, most notably in what have been called **raising constructions** (see Chapter 10).

Complex sentences in which the main verb is one like *seem, appear,* or *happen* come in two surface versions. The first has an **expletive,** or **dummy** *it* in the main clause subject and a finite embedded clause:

[63] It seems that Oscar is here.

In the second version, the subject of the embedded clause replaces *it* and the embedded clause is an infinitival:

[64] Oscar seems to be here.

Clearly, these are almost completely synonymous. In particular, in both, *Oscar* is interpreted as the one who is here, even though it's the subject of the embedded clause only in the first type. How can we account for this interpretation of [64]?

Suppose we assume that the deep structure of [64] is:

[65] [$_{NP}$] seems Oscar to be here.

and that NP Movement moves the subject of the infinitival (*Oscar*) up into the empty subject of *seems* (shown in [65] as [$_{NP}$]). This movement is obligatory, as [66] shows:

[66] *It seems Oscar to be here.

Just why the movement is obligatory is an issue that the theory at this stage cannot explain, but later versions can.

It's important to notice at this point that *seem* and verbs like it assign no thematic role to their subjects. This is why we can have the dummy *it* in that position when the subordinate clause is finite but not an NP which must be assigned a theta role:

[67]   **Fred seems that Oscar is here.*

If *seem* were to assign a theta role to its subject, and we were to move the subject of the embedded clause into that position, it would then have two thematic roles and be in violation of the uniqueness condition.

The movement rule we have been discussing moves an NP into a position which has no thematic role. In fact, this is the only type of position into which a rule can move an NP. In both passive and raising constructions, the nonthematic position is the subject. This rule is referred to as **NP Movement.** Now from a learner's point of view all that needs to be learned is that passive and raising verbs don't assign theta roles to their subjects, thus allowing NP Movement to apply. We will see later just why NP Movement must apply in these cases. Immediately below we tackle the issue of why NP Movement, Wh-Movement, and Topicalization (in fact, movement rules in general) all move phrases upward. To do this, we must introduce the structural relationship called **c-command.**

11.2.3   C-command

Sentences in which the subject is a reflexive pronoun are ungrammatical:

[68]   **Himself shaved Bill.*

Generally, a reflexive *must* have an **antecedent.** This antecedent must (1) be close to the reflexive, usually in the same clause; (2) agree with it in number and gender; and (3) be higher up in the tree structure than the reflexive.

Personal pronouns also *may* have antecedents, although they can occur without them. Whenever a pronoun does have an antecedent, the antecedent must agree with the pronoun in number and gender, just like the reflexive, but must not be close to the pronoun—usually not in the same clause as it—and cannot be higher up in the tree than it. Thus we cannot say:

[69]   **He believes that Oscar is a genius.*

when we intend *he* and *Oscar* to refer to the same individual; i.e., when we intend *Oscar* to be the antecedent of *he*.

Exactly what we mean by "higher up" is what we explore in this section. To understand this discussion, you may need to refresh your memory of the relations between nodes that we described in Chapter 9, especially *domination* and *immediate domination*.

The notion that we have been expressing as "higher up" is actually a very specific structural relationship, called **c-command.**

A node X is said to c-command its sister nodes and all of the nodes dominated by them. That is, a node X c-commands any node Y, as long as neither X nor Y dominates the other, and the first *branching* node that dominates X also dominates Y. Thus both A and B c-command C, D, and E in:

[70]

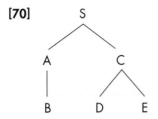

Because A and C are sister nodes, each c-commands the other and everything underneath it: A c-commands C, D, and E; C c-commands A and B. Neither D nor E c-commands A or B. This is because C, the first branching node to dominate D and E, doesn't dominate A. But B c-commands C, D, and E because the first branching node that dominates B is S, and S dominates C, D, and E.

Applying this notion to NP Movement and to reflexives and pronouns and their antecedents, we see that *NP Movement moves a phrase into a position which c-commands the position from which it came, i.e., it c-commands its trace.* The antecedent of a reflexive must c-command the reflexive. This requirement is violated in [68], which is why it's ungrammatical. A pronoun cannot c-command its antecedent, which is why [69] is ungrammatical.

EXERCISES

1. In tree [62] above, show that the moved NP c-commands its trace.
2. Draw the surface structure trees for sentences [68] and [69] and show that *himself* and *he* c-command their respective antecedents, *Bill* and *Oscar*.

The c-command relationship is very important. It crops up in many different situations, most notably in movement and in the relations between pronouns and reflexives and their antecedents. It represents a generalization about the structure in which items may be related to each other and is a good candidate for a linguistic universal. Clearly, no learner of a language, certainly not of a first language, is taught the structure, and it's difficult to see just how they could figure it out from the evidence available to them; so it's very likely part of our innate linguistic knowledge.

11.2.4   Generalizing phrase structure rules: X-bar theory

Each of the phrase structure rules we presented in Chapter 9 represented a single phrase. Thus we had one rule for NP and another for VP; we had a separate PSR for each phrase. We made no attempt to seek out similarities among the phrases. In this section, we do just that and describe the generalizations in **X′** (pronounced **X-bar**) **theory.**

First and foremost, notice that the head of each phrase gives its name to the phrase. Thus nouns head noun phrases, verbs head verb phrases, and prepositions head prepositional phrases. We don't find nouns heading adverbial phrases or adverbs heading the Aux. So if we use the variable X, then we can generalize this fact about phrase structures: Every XP (i.e., every phrase) contains a head, X. This is often referred to as the **endocentricity constraint.**

Second, let's separate the two aspects that early PSRs conflated, dominance and precedence, i.e., linear and hierarchical order. These two aspects can vary separately from one language to another. For example, in Japanese, the elements that correspond to English prepositions come after their objects rather than before. (Which is why they are called **postpositions.**) Ideally, a linguistic theory should be general enough to be able to represent the similarities and differences between languages with prepositions and those with postpositions. If we separate linear from hierarchical order, then we can do this. Hierarchically, English prepositional phrases and Japanese postpositional phrases are identical: They consist of a pre- or postposition head and its object. They differ in that the head precedes the object in English but follows it in Japanese:

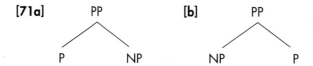

Similarly, English verbs precede their objects, but Japanese verbs follow theirs:

Generally, languages are fairly consistent in the order they assign to heads and objects. In English, a head generally precedes its objects; in Japanese, a head usually follows its objects. From the point of view of a learner, such a general pattern is much more easily learned than a language in which the order of head and object varies from phrase to phrase. We can represent this separation of linear and hierarchical organization in PSRs by separating elements on the right of the arrow by commas, indicating that they can occur in either order:

[73] PP → P, NP
[74] VP → V, NP

These rules now allow both the English and the Japanese orders, a development which expresses an important generalization.

But phrases are similar to each other in many other ways. Another major generalization is: All major class lexical items (i.e., Ns, Vs, As, and Ps) **project** phrasal categories which are at least three levels deep. That is, all phrases are of the following form:

[75]

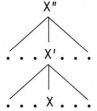

The highest, **X″** (pronounced X-double bar), is the **maximal projection** of the lexical item involved and corresponds to NP, VP, PP, and AP. The middle level, **X′** (pronounced X-bar), is a phrasal category which is less inclusive than X″. The lowest, **X,** level is the lexical (word) level.

   X-bar theory claims that phrases not only share the three-level organization set out above, but that the constituents of each level are consistent across phrases. X″ consists of an optional **specifier** (modifier) and X′:

[76] X″ → (Spec), X′

In P″ (i.e., PP), the specifier is an adverbial phrase:

[77] *Right* up his alley.

In N″ (i.e., NP), the specifier is an NP modifier, such as a genitive:

[78] *Bill's* book.

In V″ (i.e., VP), the specifier is an adverbial phrase:

[79] *Inadvertently* tripped.

In S, the specifier is the subject.

   X′ has two expansions: (1) X and its **complements** and (2) X′ and **adjuncts** (modifying phrases). Remember that complements are phrases that are strictly categorized by the words they complement and include direct and indirect objects and the objects of prepositions. Adjuncts are optional modifiers. (The asterisk after the category label indicates that more than one of the categories may occur.)

[80a] X′ → X, (XP*)
  [b] X′ → X′, (XP*)

   The complements of V and P are typically N″s (e.g., *win the game, in the pink*), whereas the complements of N and A are typically P″s (e.g., *students of linguistics, considerate of others*). Adjuncts are also typically P″s: e.g., *studied at MIT, at one with nature, student at MIT, aware in certain respects.* The following tree represents the general structure of phrases:

[81]

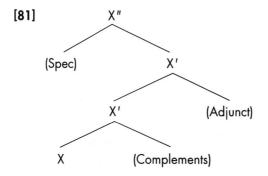

And the next tree provides an illustrative example:

[82]

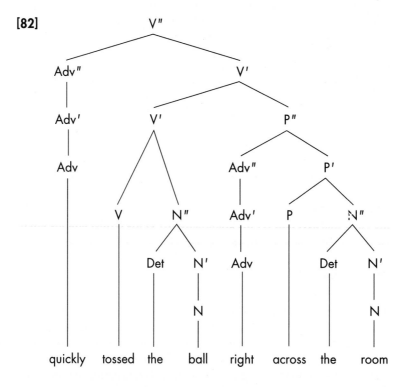

In the X′ theory of phrase structure, (1) the head of a phrase must belong to the lexical category which gives the phrase its name, (2) the linear and hierarchical structure must be separable so that we can represent the general ordering patterns that all phrases in a language exhibit, and so we can represent ordering differences between languages, and (3) the hierarchical structure of a phrase is fully determined by X-bar theory. Consequently, we no longer need PSRs like those we presented earlier. The information they represented can now be represented more simply and generally. We have simplified our grammatical theory by eliminating very specific rules and factoring out the information they represented and placing it in very general statements, which are good candidates for linguistic universals. The resulting grammars are consistent with these universals, are more easily learnable, and consequently are more explanatorily adequate. In the next section, we will explore a similar generalization of a set of restrictions on movement rules.

EXERCISE   In tree [82], put H next to the head of each phrase, A next to its adjunct, C next to its complement, and S next to its specifier.

11.2.5 Subjacency and cyclicity

Consider the following sentences:

[83a] Who$_i$ do you believe that Sally likes [t]$_i$?
  [b] Bill$_i$ I believe Sally likes [t]$_i$.
  [c] Who$_i$ do you think that Bill believes that Sally wants Fred to see [t]$_i$?

In [83a] to [83c], the phrases in Comp originate in embedded clauses. In [83c], the embedded clause is four sentences deep. It appears that Wh-Movement and Topicalization can move phrases to the topmost Comp from clauses that are indefinitely deeply embedded. However, there are restrictions, as [84] and [85] show:

[84]   *Who$_i$ do you believe the suggestion that Sally likes [t]$_i$?
[85]   *Bill$_i$, I believe the suggestion that Sally likes [t]$_i$.

It's the structural difference between [83a] and [83b] on the one hand and [84] and [85] on the other that accounts for the grammaticality of the former and the ungrammaticality of the latter. The structural difference is in the VP. The surface structure tree for [83a] and [83b] is:

[86]

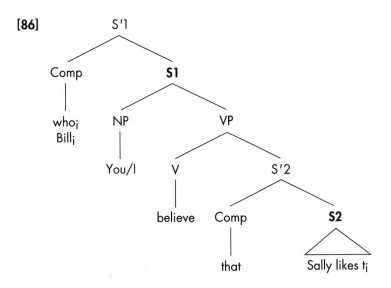

The surface structure tree for [84] and [85] is:

[87]

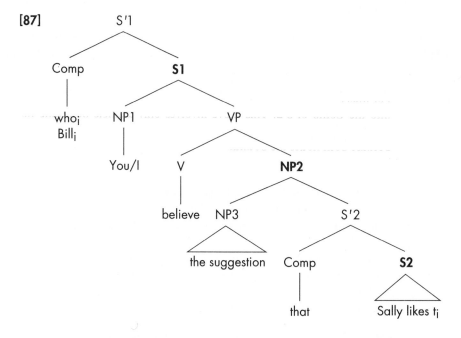

In [87] (= [84] and [85]), the embedded S'2 is directly dominated by NP2, whereas in [86] the embedded S'2 is directly dominated by VP. If we assume that Wh-Movement and Topicalization operate *cyclically* by moving a phrase from its deep structure position in a clause into the Comp of that clause, and from there into the next higher Comp, and the next, until the highest Comp is reached (a process called **Comp-to-Comp Movement**), then we have one part of the explanation for the ungrammaticality of [84] and [85].

Suppose we also assume that NP and S are special nodes, called **bounding nodes** (in bold characters in the diagrams), and that a movement transformation can only move a phrase across *one* bounding node at a time, a restriction called the **subjacency condition**. When we put this together with the Comp-to-Comp restriction, then we can see why [84] and [85] are ungrammatical. Who_i/$Bill_i$ would have to move first into the Comp of S'2 and then directly to the Comp of S'1. This second move crosses *both* NP2 and S1, two bounding nodes, thus violating the subjacency condition. Subjacency doesn't apply in [86] because only *one* bounding node, S1, intervenes between the lower Comp and the highest one. Thus, in general, phrases may move from Comp-to-Comp for indefinitely many Comps, as long as no two Comps are separated by more than a single bounding node.

If you have difficulty visualizing a phrase moving across other phrases, you might imagine the analysis tree as representing a set of nested boxes. Each phrase is a box, and each phrase is part of a larger phrase, and so each box is within a larger box up to the top S', the box that includes all the others. For a phrase to be moved, it must be extracted from whatever boxes it happens to be in. The bounding nodes represent special boxes; only one such box may be exited at a time. In the following diagram only the boxes representing the relevant nodes have been included.

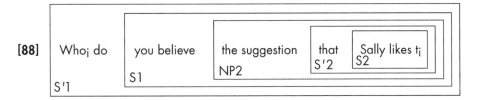

For *who*$_i$ to move from t_i to the leftmost or highest Comp, it must first be extracted from S2 into the Comp of S'2. This move involves only a single bounding node, so it poses no problem. To get to the highest Comp, *Who*$_i$ would have to be extracted from NP2 *and* S1. Because both nodes are bounding, this extraction results in ungrammaticality.

11.3 GOVERNMENT-BINDING THEORY

During the 1980s, generative theory underwent major revisions. Throughout the 1970s, Chomsky and his colleagues developed the notion of constraints on transformations and grammars. These efforts culminated in the early 1980s in what is now the primary generative theory of grammar, **Government-Binding (GB)** theory. GB has competitors, of course, including **Lexical Functional Grammar (LFG), Generalized Phrase Structure Grammar (GPSG),** and **Relational Grammar (RG).** These theories are described in several of the references listed at the end of this chapter (Sells, 1985; Newmeyer, 1986; van Riemsdijk and Williams, 1986; Horrocks, 1987; Borsley, 1991; Haegeman, 1991). We present GB here because it commands the greatest following among generative linguists. It has led to a great deal of research on English and a wide array of other languages, as well as to important research on first and second language acquisition. GB presents a number of substantive claims about both linguistic universals and language acquisition; it can, therefore, seriously claim a considerable degree of explanatory adequacy.

Successful theories, whether in linguistics or in some other field, have a way of eventually influencing what or how we teach in our schools. Ideas derived from generative linguistics have already been incorporated into developments such as the Whole Language movement. While we cannot predict just what influence GB theory will have, it has already led to much research in first and second language acquisition. Thus we expect that its influence will be felt initially in those areas—important areas when we consider the expected increase in enrollment of minority students, many of whom will be learning English in the schools.

In this section, we outline just what GB claims to be a theory of, namely, **core grammar,** and distinguish this from other, **peripheral,** aspects of grammar. A theory of core grammar is a theory of **linguistic universals** or of **universal grammar (UG).** We relate the concepts of core and periphery to ideas of **markedness.** We then introduce the **principles and parameters** approach adopted by GB. Core grammar consists of a number of principles which allow for some limited variation among languages. These are said to be **parameterized.** One such principle is the head parameter, which requires that each phrase contain a headword but which allows the head to appear before its complements, as in English, or after them, as in Japanese. The head parameter thus has two **settings,** head first or head last. GB is **modular.** That is, core grammar consists of a set of interacting components or sets of principles, called **modules.** We will describe the modules and their interactions. We will finish with an illustration of how the theory applies to a sentence.

11.3.1   Core and periphery

GB conceives of the grammar of a language as consisting of <u>a core set of principles and parameters shared by all languages and a set of peripheral phenomena</u>. Core grammar is held to be innate, i.e., to be part of the genetic endowment of human beings and without which human language is impossible. <u>Human beings are either born with or develop knowledge of the principles of core grammar as a part of their normal maturation</u>. It's only because we are endowed by nature with these principles that we are able to learn languages as we do. Other creatures don't have linguistic universals, and this is why they cannot acquire a human language. GB focuses almost exclusively on discovering the universal principles and parameters that constitute core grammar.

The following examples should clarify the distinction between core and peripheral phenomena. In English, attributive adjectives generally precede the nouns they modify (e.g., *new clothes*). In Italian (e.g., *uomo simpatico* lit. man nice, "nice man") and in Spanish (e.g., *escuela secondario* lit. school secondary, "secondary school"), attributive adjectives follow the nouns they modify. In each of these languages, however, there are a number of cases in which this pattern is violated. For example, in English, adjectives follow an indefinite noun or pronoun, *something new.* In Italian, the adjective *buono* generally precedes its noun. Compare *buona sera* "good evening" with *borsa nera* lit. purse black, "black purse." In English, sentences are required to have subjects and verbs, but we do find subjectless sentences, *Can't buy me love* and verbless sentences, *The bigger the better.* <u>Constructions that violate the general patterns of the language are deemed to be peripheral. Peripheral phenomena are learned later than core phenomena and perhaps require a different learning environment.</u>

As another illustration of the distinction between core and periphery, recall the discussion in Chapter 1 of preposition stranding. Within GB a number of explanations have been proposed for the fact that English allows preposition stranding but that most other languages, including French, Italian, and Spanish, don't. If we assume, as some GB theorists do, that in core grammar a movement rule cannot extract the object NP from a maximal phrasal projection, including PP, then English preposition stranding can be viewed as a marked, peripheral phenomenon, in contrast with the other languages which don't include this possibility.

The goal of GB is to discover the set of universal principles that constitute core grammar and to identify the parameter settings they allow. In this way, the theory will have a body of principles which are innate to human beings and which serve as the explanatory basis of linguistic similarities and differences.

11.3.2   Principles and parameters

Core grammar consists of a number of principles and the settings they allow. These principles limit the number of possible core grammars, and consequently facilitate the language learner's task by eliminating from consideration an indefinite number of logically conceivable grammars. One proposed universal is that all grammars are **structure dependent** (see Chapter 1). That is, every syntactic rule applies to a lexical or phrasal category by virtue of the structural relations it has to other parts of its sentence. No syntactic rule applies to an item just by virtue of its linear position in a string of words. For example, no language requires rules that simply reverse the order of the first and fourth words in a sentence. For another example, English Subject-Auxiliary Inversion applies to the auxiliary of the main clause (the highest S) of a question and not to the first (or second, or third, etc.) auxiliary in a sentence:

[89a]   Is the man who is riding the bike [t] Oscar?
  [b]   *Is the man who [t] riding the bike is Oscar?

Sentence [89b] is ungrammatical because it was generated by a movement rule which selected the first auxiliary rather than the Aux of the main clause. Such a rule wouldn't be structure dependent and so couldn't be a part of the core grammar of any language. No learner of a language would ever consider such a rule as part of the grammar of the language being learned. No learner of English would make the kind of mistake that [89b] represents. Structure dependence is a characteristic of the core grammar of all languages.

   Although children come to the task of acquiring a language already knowing a great deal about grammar, there are aspects of the target language that they must discover. After all, languages do differ from each other. A learner must identify the **parameter settings** for the target language. Parameters are statements that describe the universal characteristics of human language. These statements often allow for a very narrow range of differences among languages. For example, a child knows from UG that phrases have heads and complements. What she or he must discover is whether the head precedes or follows its complements in the target language. If that language is English, then it's enough for the child to be exposed to structures such as *To your room* or *Give grandma a kiss* to know that heads come first in that language. A few instances of this type of evidence are sufficient to allow children to set the head parameter to "head first." Analogous evidence in Japanese would indicate that the parameter must be set to "head final." (See Figure 11.2.)

11.3.3   Modularity

GB proposes that core grammar comprises several levels of representation, just like its predecessors. These levels include **D-structure,** which is similar to the deep structure of previous theories, **S-structure,** which is akin to surface structure, and one maximally simple and general movement transformation, **Move α (Move alpha),** which connects D-structure and S-structure. **Phonetic form** is derived from S-structure by the application of rules that spell out morphemes, delete elements, and conceivably move elements. New to GB is the level of **logical form.** This is derived from S-structure by rules, usually movement rules, which place elements such as quantifiers (e.g., *some, all*) in appropriate positions so that they can be correctly interpreted by rules of semantic interpretation. Logical form is the interface between language and other aspects of cognition. The following diagram illustrates the relationships among the levels of representation:

[90]

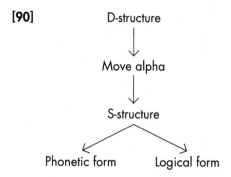

As in earlier models, D-structure is the level at which the lexicon and the phrase structure components meet and at which thematic roles are assigned to phrases. Move α can then move phrases about, leaving coindexed traces. S-structure is an abstraction from the actual sentence. It consists of lexical items, traces, and abstract morphemes such as *past,* which will be spelled out by the phonological rules.

The universal principles of core grammar proposed by GB are grouped into modules which interact with each other in restricted ways. We discuss each module in turn in the following sections. In Figure 11.3, we name and briefly describe what each module does.

FIGURE 11.2. Core Grammar

UNIVERSAL CORE GRAMMAR

Principles: e.g.,
  (a) All phrases have heads
  (b) Restrictions on movement transformations

Parameters: e.g., modifiers may precede or follow their head

ENGLISH CORE GRAMMAR

(a) Parameter set: Head first

ENGLISH PERIPHERAL GRAMMAR

(b) Preposition stranding

JAPANESE CORE GRAMMAR

(a) Parameter set: Head last
(b) No preposition stranding

JAPANESE PERIPHERAL GRAMMAR

11.3.3.1 Theta theory

Theta theory determines the assignment of thematic roles. Theta roles are assigned by lexical items, most particularly verbs and prepositions, but also by nouns, to NPs in D-structure. In the lexicon, each verb is associated with a number of thematic roles, each of

FIGURE 11.3 Government-Binding Model

Theta Theory
- Determines the assignment of thematic roles.
- Replaces earlier completeness and uniqueness conditions.
- Applies in D-structure.

Projection Principle
- Ensures that the strict subcategorization properties of the lexical items are transferred to all syntactic levels of representation.
- Motivates traces.
- Ensures that every sentence has a subject.

Bounding Theory
- Limits the range of movement.
- A generalization of the subjacency condition.

Government
- Structural relationship which lexical items bear to their complements and to a small set of other phrases.
- Affects distribution of anaphors and pronouns (binding).
- Affects assignment of case.

Binding Theory
- Constrains the relationships between anaphors (reflexive pronouns and reciprocals), pronouns, and full lexical NPs, and their antecedents.

Case Theory
- Determines where NPs can occur in a sentence.
- Assigns abstract case under government.

Control Theory
- Determines the interpretation of the understood subjects of infinitives.

which is correlated with the phrases that the verb strictly subcategorizes. These are referred to as the **internal theta roles.** Besides assigning theta roles to its complements, a verb may assign an **external theta role** to its subject NP, which isn't strictly subcategorized.

Positions to which theta roles can be assigned in D-structure are referred to as **argument (A) positions.** These include subjects, direct and indirect objects, and the objects of prepositions. Positions, such as Comp, to which theta roles cannot be assigned in D-structure are **nonargument (A-bar) positions.** Strictly subcategorized phrases are internal arguments; the subject is an external argument:

[91]

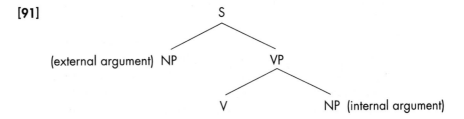

The **theta criterion** states that an NP can be assigned one and only one thematic role, and that every thematic role that the lexical items in a sentence can assign must be assigned. The theta criterion replaces our earlier uniqueness and completeness conditions. The theta criterion constrains the positions to which NPs can be moved. Specifically, an NP cannot be moved to a position which has already been assigned a thematic role. This is because it would thereby be assigned a second theta role. The positions that can be left without a theta role in D-structure are the subject position (of passive participles and of verbs like *seem*) and positions external to the clause structure, such as Comp. The theta criterion ensures that movement can only apply between a theta position and a nontheta position. Thus, in passives, Move α moves a phrase from an object position which has been assigned a theta role to a subject position which lacks a theta role. Move α also moves a wh-phrase from an argument position into Comp, a nonargument position.

The constraints imposed by the theta criterion on movement are important explanatory factors in the analysis of passive and raising constructions. In both constructions, the subject position isn't assigned a theta role in D-structure. This is because neither the passive participle nor verbs such as *seem, happen,* and *appear* assign an external theta role. Because the subject is assigned no theta role in D-structure, it's free to act as a **landing site** for a phrase moved from a position to which a theta role has been assigned.

The theta criterion also motivates traces. As we noted, a moved phrase is assumed to leave behind a trace in the position from which it moved. The trace is coindexed with the moved phrase. The pair, moved phrase and its coindexed trace(s), constitute a **chain:**

[92] $[XP]_i \longleftarrow \longrightarrow [t]_i$

Chains are explicit connections between moved phrases and the D-structure positions from which they derive their theta roles. In effect, the theta criterion requires that *every* chain be assigned a theta role and that *no* chain be assigned more than one theta role.

11.3.3.2   The projection principle

The **projection principle** expresses the idea that the syntactic structure of a sentence mirrors at every level the strict subcategorization characteristics of the lexical items in it. A sentence with a transitive verb must contain a direct object; a sentence with a bitransitive verb must contain two object NPs; a sentence containing an intransitive verb cannot contain an object NP. Thus syntactic structure is determined by the characteristics of the lexical items it contains.

Characteristics of the lexical items are assumed to determine the structure at every syntactic level; i.e., the projection principle holds at D-structure, S-structure, logical form, and phonetic form. We can state the projection principle as [93]:

[93]   Representations at each syntactic level are projected from the lexicon in that they observe properties of the lexical items.

Because the lexicon expresses only the strict subcategorization properties of lexical items, the projection principle as just stated would project only VP structure. The principle has been extended to include the stipulation that every S must contain a subject. Both principles together are referred to as the **extended projection principle.**

Along with the theta criterion, the projection principle also motivates traces. If instead of leaving a trace, movement were to entirely obliterate the position from which a phrase moved, then the resulting structure would violate the projection principle. Examples [94a] and [94b] represent alternative analyses of the surface structure of the relative clause *Which John caught*. In [94a], the object required by the transitive verb *caught* is still in its appropriate position; in [94b], on the other hand, *caught* is left without any object at all:

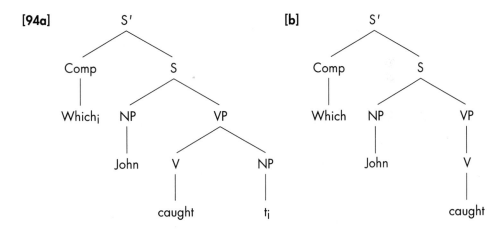

The extended projection principle requires that sentences in languages which don't require overt subjects, such as Spanish and Italian, must nonetheless have a syntactic subject position. For example, the Spanish sentence [95] has no overt subject:

[95] Tengo   sed.
      have-1st.sg. thirst
      (I) am thirsty

According to the projection principle, null subject sentences are not sentences without subjects; rather, they're sentences whose subject position hasn't had any lexical items inserted in it. Languages vary parametrically on whether or not they allow null subjects; i.e., they may have different settings of the **null subject parameter.**

In languages like English and French, which aren't null subject languages, the extended projection principle motivates the occurrence of expletive elements such as *it* and *there*, special elements which don't require theta roles.

We must note here that GB has a different conception of Aux from earlier theories. It replaces Aux with **Infl,** an abbreviation for **inflection.** Infl contains the features that determine subject-verb agreement. These are represented by a feature called **AGR.** Because subject-verb agreement occurs in some clauses but not in others, this is a binary feature, [±AGR]. Infl also indicates whether a clause is tensed, [±TENSE], and which tense is involved. Infl also may contain a modal verb. GB views S as a projection of Infl, so many recent publications represent S as *IP (Infl or I Phrase)*. When it's tensed, Infl can govern and assign case to the subject of its sentence. AGR in [96] stands for Agreement and represents the fact that in tensed English clauses the subject and the first verb agree with each other. A concrete example for the sentence *I might leave* appears as [97].

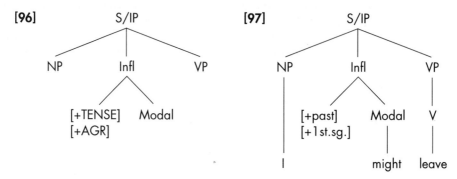

11.3.3.3 Bounding theory

Most, if not all, current theories assume that syntactic rules apply locally. For example, a verb assigns thematic roles to the complements in its own clause, not to phrases in lower or higher clauses. With respect to movement, local application means that Move α cannot move a phrase very far from its source position. In earlier theories, the idea of **locality** was expressed as **island constraints** or Ross's constraints after the linguist who initially developed them.

Ross noticed that it's possible to move a phrase out of an object (compare [98a] and [98b]), but not out of a subject. Compare [98c] with [98d]:

[98a]   He took [a photograph of Oscar].
 [b]   Who$_i$ did he take [a photograph of t$_i$].
 [c]   [A photograph of Oscar] was in the album.
 [d]   *Who$_i$ was [a photograph of t$_i$] in the album?

It's also impossible to move a phrase out of a clause which is the complement or modifier of a noun (a complex NP). Compare [99a] with [99b]:

[99a]   He considered [the fact that Oscar enjoys a good book].
 [b]   *What$_i$ did he consider [the fact that Oscar enjoys t$_i$].

It's also impossible to move a phrase out of a clause whose Comp already contains a wh-phrase (e.g., indirect questions). Compare [100a] with [100b]:

[100a]   I wonder [whether he bought a book].
 [b]   *What$_i$ do [$_S$ you wonder [whether [$_S$ he bought t$_i$]]].

Ross proposed separate constraints on movement for each of these (and other) cases. However, during the 1970s, all of these cases were subsumed under the subjacency condition. Remember that the subjacency condition prevents a phrase from being moved across more than one bounding node at a time. For *What*$_i$ to reach the highest Comp in [100b], it must cross the two S boundaries in one movement, thereby violating the subjacency condition. *What*$_i$ cannot land in the lowest Comp because that Comp is already occupied by *whether*.

In keeping with the thrust of modern linguistic theorizing, recent GB writings, following Chomsky (1986a), have replaced the list of bounding nodes with the very general hypothesis that all maximal projections (i.e., full phrases including S, NP, AP, PP, etc.) *except VP* are **barriers** to movement. So **bounding theory** (which replaces the subjacency condition) states that a phrase cannot cross more than one barrier in a single movement. Some languages adhere strictly to this restriction; others allow some marked (i.e., noncore, peripheral) movements. For example, English, as we noted, allows extraction of NPs from PPs:

[101]   Who$_i$ did you give the book to t$_i$

However, for the wh-phrase to get to its position in Comp from t_i in [102], the structure underlying **What$_i$ will the student of t$_i$ laugh?* would have to cross two barriers, NP1 and S1 (the maximal projection of Infl):

[102]

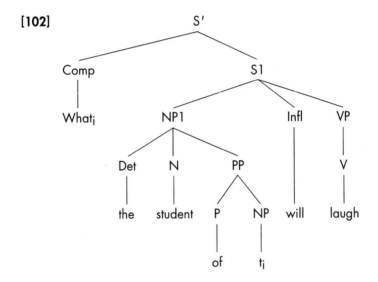

11.3.3.4   Government

In traditional grammar, verbs and prepositions are said to govern their objects and, by governing them, to determine their case. Verbs and prepositions assign case locally in languages like English and German. Bounding theory represents one aspect of locality; government represents another. **Government** is a structural relationship between a lexical head and its complements, as well as the subject of certain types of clauses. An element X

governs another element Y if X is the lexical head of a phrase of which Y is a constituent and no barrier to government separates X from Y. All maximal projections (including S', *but not S*) are barriers to government:

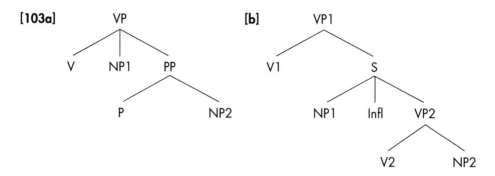

[103a] / [b]

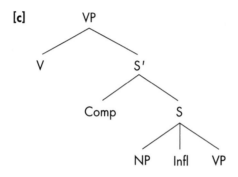

[c]

In [103a], V governs NP1 but not NP2 because the maximal projection PP intervenes; P governs NP2. In [103b], V1 governs NP1 even though S intervenes; it doesn't govern NP2 because VP2 intervenes. In [103c], V governs neither Comp nor NP because S' intervenes. In [103b] and [103c], if Infl were tensed, it would govern its subject NP.

Government is like c-command. In fact, a governor c-commands the nodes it governs. However, government is more restrictive than c-command. Any node can c-command any other node, as long as they are in the required structural configuration, but a governor must be a lexical category or Infl. A c-commanding node c-commands all its sister nodes and all of their daughters regardless of what nodes intervene. Government, however, can reach only a very limited distance downward; it's blocked by a maximal projection.

Government is a very restrictive structural relationship which is of crucial importance in defining both when case can be assigned and the distributions of anaphors and pronouns and their antecedents, as we will see in the next section.

11.3.3.5   Binding theory

Binding theory can be viewed as another locality constraint. It controls coreference relationships between (1) reflexive and reciprocal expressions (**anaphors**) and their antecedents,

(2) pronouns and their antecedents, and (3) **referring expressions,** i.e., nonpronominal, nonanaphoric NPs.

Let's examine these relationships one at a time. Reflexives and reciprocals (e.g., *each other*) must have antecedents that agree with them in person and number. The antecedent must (1) c-command the anaphor, (2) occur in an argument (A) position such as a subject or object, and (3) not be "too far away from" the anaphor. We will define what we mean by "not too far away from" in a moment. Consider:

[104]   John$_i$ shaved himself$_i$

In [104], *John$_i$* is the antecedent and *himself$_i$* is the anaphor. *John$_i$* is the subject of the clause and is therefore in an argument position. It also c-commands and agrees with the anaphor in number and person. They are both elements of the same clause and so aren't far from each other.

In [105] and [106], the antecedent, *John$_i$*, agrees with an anaphor, *himself$_i$* and c-commands it from an argument position. However, the two are too far away from each other: the antecedent is in the higher clause while the anaphor is in a finite subordinate clause:

[105]   *John$_i$ believes that Mary shaved himself$_i$
[106]   *John$_i$ believes that himself$_i$ shaved Mary

Sentences [107a] to [107c] are analogous to [104], [105], and [106], respectively. The only difference is that we have replaced the reflexive pronoun with the reciprocal *each other* and *John* with *John and Mary:*

[107a]   [John and Mary]$_i$ like [each other]$_i$.
  [b]   *[John and Mary]$_i$ believe that Oscar likes [each other]$_i$.
  [c]   *[John and Mary]$_i$ believe that [each other]$_i$ like Oscar.

Sentence [107a] is grammatical like [104]; sentences [107b] and [107c] are ungrammatical like [105] and [106].

In [108], the antecedent agrees with the anaphor, c-commands it from an A-position, but the two are in different clauses. Why then is [108] grammatical while [105] and [106], which also involve two clauses, aren't?

[108]   Lorenzo$_i$ believes himself$_i$ to be magnificent.

The answer lies in the differences between the two clauses. In [105], the anaphor *himself$_i$* is governed by *shaved.* In [106], *himself* is governed by the tensed Infl of the *that* clause. However, in [105] and [106], while the *that* clause contains both the anaphor and its governor, it doesn't contain the antecedent *John.* The following trees may make it easier to visualize these relationships:

[105a]

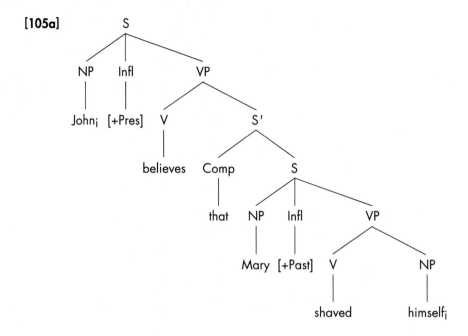

[106a]

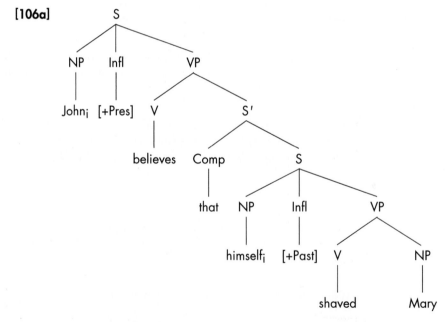

In [108], the lower Infl contains neither tense nor agreement. As a result, it cannot govern the subject of its clause. Because the complement of *believe* in [108] is an S rather than an S', the governor of the anaphor is the verb of the higher clause, *believes*. Consequently, the smallest S containing both the anaphor and its governor is the entire S (*Lorenzo$_i$ believes himself$_i$ to be magnificent*). This S does contain the antecedent of *himself*, namely, *Lorenzo*. Compare tree [108a] with trees [105a] and [106a].

[108a]

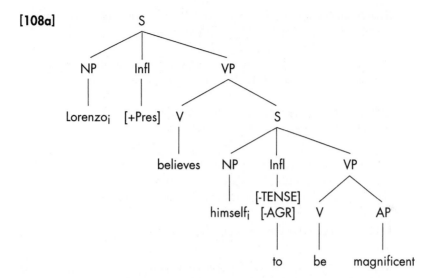

We call the smallest (i.e., the lowest) S that contains both an anaphor and its governor the **governing category** of the anaphor. Now we can formulate the general principle that relates anaphors and their antecedents. This is referred to as **Binding Principle A:**

[109]   An anaphor must be A-bound in its governing category.

That is, the antecedent must c-command the anaphor from an argument position within the lowest S that contains both the anaphor and its governor.

Consider now pronouns and their antecedents. Just as with anaphors, the antecedent of a pronoun must agree with it in number and person. However, the patterns of distribution of pronouns and anaphors are complementary. Consider the sentences:

[110a]   John$_i$ shaved him$_j$.
   [b]   *John$_i$ shaved him$_i$.
   [c]   John$_i$ believes that Mary shaved him$_i$.
   [d]   John$_i$ believes Mary to have shaved him$_i$.
   [e]   *John$_i$ believes him$_i$ to be magnificent.

In [110a] and [110b], the governing category for the pronoun is the entire sentence. This contains the antecedent, *John$_i$*. In [110a], *John$_i$* and *him* refer to different individuals; in [110b], they refer to the same individual. So a pronoun and its antecedent cannot be very close to each other. The governing category for the pronoun in [110c] and [110d] is the lower clause, which doesn't contain the antecedent; in both clauses, *him* is governed by *shaved*. In [110e], *believes* governs the pronoun so that the entire S is the governing category, and this contains the antecedent. When the governing category of the pronoun doesn't contain the antecedent, the sentence is grammatical; when the governing category of the pronoun does contain the antecedent, the sentence is ungrammatical. We can formulate this as **Binding Principle B:**

[111]   A pronominal must be A-free in its governing category.

That is, the antecedent of a pronoun cannot c-command that pronoun from an argument position within the pronoun's governing category.

Finally, let's consider the distribution of referring expressions **(R-expressions).** Referring expressions are referential NPs which are neither pronouns nor anaphors. Compare the following sentences with those above containing anaphors and pronouns:

[112a] *John$_i$ shaved John$_i$.
   [b] *John$_i$ thinks that Mary shaved John$_i$.

In [112a], the second R-expression, *John$_i$*, is A-bound in its governing category; in [112b], the second R-expression is A-bound though from outside its governing category. It appears that R-expressions cannot be A-bound. This is formulated in **Binding Principle C:**

[113] A referring expression must be A-free.

That is, a referring expression cannot be coreferential with any other expression which c-commands it from any argument position in the sentence.

11.3.3.6 **Case theory**

Case theory determines where NPs with overt lexical content can occur. Every NP with phonological content must be assigned a case but cannot be assigned more than one case. In this respect, case and thematic role assignment are alike. Any sentence which contains an NP which hasn't been assigned case is filtered out as ungrammatical by the **case filter:**

[114] A sentence is ungrammatical if it contains an NP which has phonetic content but no case.

Phrases other than NP don't need to be assigned case. The case filter checks NPs for case at S-structure.

Many languages, such as Latin and Finnish, have extensive inventories of overt, morphological cases. Latin nouns have multiple forms representing different cases, as the paradigm [115] illustrates:

[115] Nominative   puella ("girl")
           Accusative   puellam
           Genitive   puellae
           Dative   puellae
           Ablative   puellā

English nouns have minimal overt **case marking,** distinguishing only genitive from nongenitive. Still other languages, such as Chinese, have no overt case marking at all. Regardless of whether a language displays overt case marking, all languages involve **abstract case.** Abstract case is assigned by the following rules:

[116a] A tensed Infl assigns (abstract) nominative case to the subject of a sentence.
    [b] A verb assigns accusative case to its object.
    [c] A preposition assigns oblique case to its object.

[117]

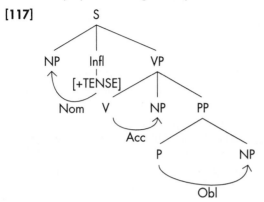

In each instance, the case assignor governs and is **adjacent** to the phrase to which it assigns case. Other cases are assigned in different ways. Genitive case is assigned to an NP modifier of an N. The second NP in a bitransitive VP is assigned case by virtue of its strict subcategorization.

Nouns and adjectives, however, even though they're lexical governors, don't assign case. This explains why their complements are PPs while the complements of V and P are NPs (cf. *Tape the movie; tape of the movie; Resent the intrusion; resentful of the intrusion*). Without the P the complement wouldn't be assigned case, so the sentence would be judged ungrammatical by the case filter. The case filter also explains why passive objects move: The passive participle, being a derived adjective, cannot assign case, so if the object NP remains in its D-structure position, the sentence will be filtered out by the case filter. Compare [118a] and [118b]:

[118a]   *It was written the book by Chomsky.
    [b]   The book was written by Chomsky.

Adjectives in raising constructions (e.g., *likely*) also don't assign case and raising is forced if the complement is an infinitival clause (e.g., *Bill is likely to be there*). Raising verbs are also assumed not to assign case, which accounts for the fact that they too force movement (e.g., *Bill seems to be here*).

The adjacency requirement on case assignment is subject to parametric variation. English doesn't allow anything to intervene between a V and its object (*He ate quickly the hotdog*); other languages such as Italian don't require adjacency between a case assignor and a case assignee (e.g., *Mangio velocemente il panino* "(He) ate quickly the sandwich").

11.3.3.7   Empty categories

Case theory determines the distribution of NPs with lexical content. However, besides such NPs, GB also recognizes a number of different types of **empty categories,** i.e., NPs without lexical content, represented by [e] in the sentences of [119].

[119a]   The book was written [e] by Chomsky.
   [b]   Which book did Chomsky write [e]?
   [c]   We persuaded Oscar [e] to be good.
   [d]   [e] ho fame.
       have-1st.sg. hunger.
      (I) am hungry.

The distribution of empty categories is largely determined by the binding principles. For each of the classes of overt expression whose distribution is determined by the binding principles, there is a corresponding empty category.

    Recall that every moved phrase leaves behind a trace at the position from which it was moved. Traces of NP Movement (from a theta position to an argument position in raising and passive constructions) are *anaphors* and are therefore subject to Binding Principle A. They must be A-bound in their governing categories. For example, [120a] is ungrammatical because t_i isn't A-bound in its governing category, S. (Note the different subscripts on *she_j* and t_i.)

[120a]   *Bill_i thinks that [$_S$ she_j will be hired t_i by IBM].

Compare this with a sentence in which the trace is properly bound:

[120b]   Bill_i thinks that [$_S$ she_i will be hired t_i by IBM].

    Traces of moved wh-phrases, on the other hand, are *R-expressions* and are subject to binding principle C. The R-expressions must be A-free but coindexed with a c-commanding wh-phrase in an A′ position such as Comp. Compare [121a] and [121b].

[121a]   *Who_i does he_i think t_i is ugly?
   [b]   *Does Bill_i think Bill_i is ugly?

In [121a], the trace is A-bound by *he_i*, so *who_i* and *he_i* are intended to refer to the same individual. Sentence [121b] is ungrammatical because the lower *Bill_i* is A-bound by the higher one. The lower *Bill_i* is therefore not A-free in its sentence, which is therefore ungrammatical. Compare it with [122a]:

[122a]   Who_j does he_i think t_j is ugly?
   [b]   Does Bill think Fred is ugly?

In [122a], *who_j* and *he_i* don't corefer (note the different subscripts), so the trace of *who* and *he* don't corefer. Consequently, the trace isn't A-bound in its governing category. In [122b], *Bill* and *Fred* refer to different individuals, so *Fred* is A-free in its sentence.

    Null subjects in Italian, Spanish, and other such languages are pronouns, and so subject to Binding Principle B. These must be A-free in their governing categories. They're represented by the notation **pro** (NB. lowercase). Underlying the sentence *Ho fame* "(I) am hungry" is:

[123]   pro ho fame.

The most interesting of the empty categories occurs as the empty subject of infinitival clauses in English and similar languages. This is represented as **PRO** (NB. uppercase). Remember that the extended projection principle requires that all clauses have subjects. Underlying [119c] is [124]:

[124] We persuaded Oscar PRO to be good.

PRO is simultaneously subject to Binding Principles A and B, which means that it must be simultaneously A-bound and A-free in its governing category. This contradiction is resolved by assuming that PRO cannot be governed. From the assumption that PRO cannot be governed it follows that PRO cannot receive case. From this it follows that the position PRO occupies cannot be occupied by a lexically filled NP because this would violate the case filter. Compare [124] with [125]:

[125] *We persuaded Oscar Lady Marshmallow to be good.

We deal with the interpretation of PRO in the next section.

11.3.3.8 Control theory

Control theory determines the interpretation of PRO, the subject of English infinitival clauses. Recall that PRO cannot be governed and therefore cannot be case marked, and so it must be empty. It has no overt analogue, as [125] demonstrates.

PRO does occur in subject position and therefore may receive a theta role from the VP of its clause. However, its reference is determined from outside that clause. It may be coreferential with a phrase in a higher clause of its sentence. This coreferential phrase is referred to as the **controller of PRO**. Sometimes the controller is the subject of the higher clause, as in [126a], which means approximately [126b]:

[126a] Oscar promised PRO to leave.
   [b] Oscar$_i$ promised that he$_i$ would leave.

Sometimes the controller is an object in the higher clause, as in [127a], which means approximately [127b]:

[127a] Oscar told Sylvia PRO to leave.
   [b] Oscar told Sylvia$_i$ that she$_i$ should leave.

According to Sag and Pollard (1991), there are three major classes of verbs that take infinitival complements whose subjects are controlled. Class 1 contains verbs like *promise* and includes *agree, vow, try,* and *intend.* These verbs denote a commitment, and the NP representing the entity making the commitment (i.e., the Agent) is the controller:

[128] I$_i$ promised/tried/agreed/intended PRO$_i$ to leave.

Class 2 contains verbs like *want,* such as *wish, expect,* and *hope.* These denote a mental state, and the NP representing the Experiencer of the state is the controller:

[129] I$_i$ wanted/wished/expected/hoped PRO$_i$ to leave.

Class 3 verbs include verbs like *tell,* such as *force, persuade, order,* and *command.* These denote situations in which one entity influences another. The NP representing the influenced entity (i.e., the Patient) is the controller:

[130] I$_i$ told/forced/persuaded/ordered Oscar$_j$ PRO$_j$ to leave.

11.3.3.9 A general example

A sentence is grammatical if its structure and derivation are consistent with all of the principles of GB theory. We illustrate how they apply to the structure in Figure 11.4 which underlies the sentence:

[131]   Who does he think Oscar persuaded to shave himself?

In Figure 11.4, the extended projection principle is satisfied because each of the Ss has a subject and the phrases subcategorized by the verbs are represented in the structure; *persuade* subcategorizes an NP and an S, *think* subcategorizes an S'. All NPs are assigned theta roles and all theta roles that are available have been assigned, so the theta criterion is satisfied. *Think* assigns Experiencer (Exp) to its subject; *persuaded* assigns Agent (Ag) to its subject and Patient (Pat) to its object; *shave* assigns Agent to its subject and Patient to its object.

The case filter is satisfied: The subjects of S1 and S2 are governed by tensed Infls, and so they're assigned nominative case; the objects of *persuade* and *behave* are governed by their respective verbs, and so are assigned accusative case; PRO is in an ungoverned position, and so correctly cannot be assigned case; the sentential complements don't require case.

Control theory is satisfied because PRO is coindexed with the trace, t_i, of the object NP in S2.

Binding theory is satisfied because the anaphor *himself* is A-bound in its governing category, S3, by PRO; t_i in S2 is trace of *who$_i$* and therefore a referring expression; it's A-free. *Oscar* is also A-free. *He$_j$* is A-free in its governing category, S1.

Move α has moved *who$_i$* from t_i in S2, first into the Comp of S'2, then into Comp of S'1, leaving coindexed traces at each stop, as required.

The trace in S2 is coindexed with and c-commanded by the trace in S'2 and by *who$_i$* in S'1.

Bounding theory is satisfied because the two traces are separated from each other by only a single barrier (S2), and the trace in Comp of S'2 is separated from *who$_i$* in Comp of S'1 by only a single barrier (S1).

Sentences are ungrammatical if they violate any of the principles. For example, if *Oscar* and *he* referred to the same individual, the sentence would be ungrammatical because it would violate Principle C of the binding theory. If the subject of S3 were lexically filled, the sentence would violate the case filter. If *persuade* had no direct object NP, its subcategorization frame would not have been projected onto the syntactic structure and the projection principle would have been violated. Also, the theta criterion would have been violated because the patient role assigned by *persuade* to its object couldn't have been assigned.

Conclusion

In this section, we outlined GB claims about **core grammar,** which we distinguished from **peripheral** aspects of grammar. A theory of core grammar is a theory of <u>universal</u>

FIGURE 11.4   Structure underlying sentence [131]

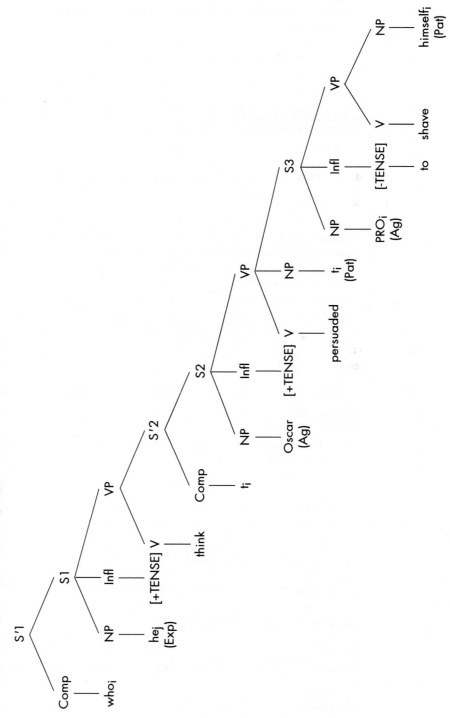

grammar. We then introduced the **principles and parameters** approach adopted by GB. Core grammar consists of a number of principles which allow for some limited variation, or **parameterization,** among languages. One such principle is the head parameter, which has two **settings,** head first or head last. GB is **modular.** That is, core grammar consists of a set of interacting sets of principles. We described the modules and their interactions and ended with an illustration of how the theory applies to a sentence.

REFERENCES AND RESOURCES

Borsley, R. D. 1991. *Syntactic Theory: A Unified Approach.* London: Edward Arnold.
Chomsky, N. 1957. *Syntactic Structures.* The Hague: Mouton.
———. 1965. *Aspects of the Theory of Syntax.* Cambridge, MA: MIT Press.
———. 1981. *Lectures on Government and Binding.* Dordrecht: Foris.
———. 1986a. *Barriers.* Cambridge, MA: MIT Press.
———. 1986b. *Knowledge of Language.* New York: Praeger.
Haegeman, L. 1991. *Introduction to Government and Binding Theory.* Oxford: Blackwell.
Horrocks, G. 1987. *Generative Grammar.* London: Longman.
Huckin, T., and L. Pesante. 1988. "Existential *there.*" *Written Communication,* 5(3):368–391.
Newmeyer, F. 1986. *Linguistic Theory in America.* Orlando, FL: Academic Press.
Sag, I., and C. Pollard. 1991. "An Integrated Theory of Complement Control." *Language,* 67 (1):63–113.
Sells, P. 1985. *Lectures on Contemporary Syntactic Theory.* Stanford, CA: CSLI.
van Riemsdijk, H., and E. Williams. 1986. *Introduction to the Theory of Grammar.* Cambridge, MA: MIT Press.
Ward, G. 1988. *The Semantics and Pragmatics of Preposing.* New York: Garland.

GLOSSARY

Abstract case: nominative, accusative, or oblique case assigned to an overt noun phrase of a sentence based on its underlying structure.

Adjacency: the position of nodes in a tree diagram where one node is right beside another node.

Adjoin: to change a tree diagram by creating a node grammatically equal to some other node and attaching a moved node and the original node as daughters of the new node.

Adjunct: in X′ theory, a constituent of a phrase that isn't strictly subcategorized by the headword of the phrase. See **complement, specifier.**

AGR: the abbreviation for agreement; features of inflectional agreement between the subject and the predicate.

Anaphors: reflexive and reciprocal pronouns.

Antecedent: a full noun phrase that denotes the same entity as a pronoun.

Argument (A) positions: those positions within S to which thematic roles *may* be assigned in deep structure.

Autonomous: the term applied to grammatical components that have distinct characteristics and specific restricted interactions with other components.

Barrier: a maximal projection (S, NP, AP, PP, but *not* VP) that limits the movement of a phrase by transformations; a phrase cannot cross more than one barrier in a single movement.

Binding: the relationships of anaphors, pronouns, and full lexical NPs to their antecedents.

Binding principle: a restriction on the relation between an expression and its antecedent.

Binding Principle A: an anaphor must be A-bound in its governing category.

Binding Principle B: a pronominal must be A-free in its governing category.

Binding Principle C: a referring expression must be A-free.

Bounding: restrictions on the movement of a phrase by transformations. See **barrier, island constraint, subjacency.**

C-command: a relation between two nodes, X and Y, where node X c-commands node Y, as long as neither X nor Y dominates the other, and the first *branching* node that dominates X also dominates Y.

Case filter: a restriction that marks a sentence as ungrammatical if it contains an NP which has phonetic content but no abstract case.

Case marking: a marking (nominative, accusative, oblique, etc.) assigned by rules to a noun phrase; may be realized by concrete case inflections. See **abstract case.**

Chain: a set composed of a moved phrase and at least one trace, all with the same index.

Comp: the abbreviation for complementizer; a node dominated by S′ that may serve as a landing site for wh-words or topics; a nonargument position.

Comp-to-Comp Movement: the path of transformations (Wh-Movement and Topicalization) that move a phrase from its deep structure position in a clause into the Comp of that clause, and from there into the next higher Comp, and the next, until the highest Comp is reached.

Competence: see Chapter 1.

Complement: in X′ theory, a constituent of a phrase that is strictly subcategorized by the headword of a phrase; e.g., direct and indirect objects and the objects of prepositions. See **adjunct, specifier.**

Completeness assumption: the assumption that every semantic role associated with verbs, prepositions, etc. is assigned to an NP in an S. See **uniqueness assumption.**

Component: a well-defined aspect of language structure, e.g., phonology, morphology, syntax, semantics.

Constraint: a restriction on linguistic rules.

Control theory: the theory that determines the interpretation of the understood subjects of infinitives.

Controller of PRO: a noun phrase that is coreferential with PRO. See **PRO** and **Pro.**

Core grammar: universal features of language, as realized in the grammar of a particular language. See **markedness, peripheral grammar, universal grammar.**

Deep structure (also called "**D-structure**"): the structure created by phrase structure rules and lexical insertion.

Deletion: the removal of part of a tree structure by a transformation.

Deletion under identity: the deletion of the second of two identical phrases. See **deletion.**

Descriptive adequacy: the level of adequacy of a grammar that is observationally adequate and assigns the same structures to sentences of the language as its speakers do. See **explanatory adequacy, observational adequacy.**

Dummy: see Chapter 7.

Empty category: a phrase without lexical content.

Endocentricity constraint: the principle that the head of each phrase gives its name to the phrase; e.g., nouns head noun phrases, verbs head verb phrases, and prepositions head prepositional phrases.

Explanatory adequacy: a level of adequacy of a grammar that is descriptively adequate and that assigns structures to sentences consistent with the set of **universal properties** of language used by children acquiring their first language.

Expletive: see Chapter 7.

Extended projection principle: the principle that the syntactic structure of a sentence mirrors at every level the strict subcategorization characteristics of the lexical items in it, as well as the syntactic characteristics of the subject.

External theta role: the theta role assigned by a verb to its subject. See **internal theta role.**

Face: a pragmatic concept indicating the public and/or personal image of speaker or addressee.

GB: the abbreviation of Government-Binding theory.

Generalized phrase structure grammar: a generative theory of language; an alternative to **Government-Binding** theory.

Governing category: the smallest (lowest) S that contains both an expression and its governor.

Government-Binding: a theory of generative grammar developed by Noam Chomsky.

Government: the structural relationship which lexical items bear to their complements and to a small set of other phrases.

Imperative Subject Deletion: a transformation that deletes the subject *you* of an imperative sentence.

Infl: the abbreviation of inflection; the category node of a tree diagram that contains the features that determine subject-verb agreement. See **AGR.**

Internal theta role: the theta role assigned by a verb to its complements. See **external theta role.**

Island constraint: a local restriction on movement transformations. See **bounding.**

Landing site: a node (e.g., Comp) to which a phrase is moved by a transformation.

Lexical functional grammar: a generative theory of language; an alternative to **Government-Binding theory.**

Lexical insertion rule: a rule that inserts a word into a tree structure according to its strict subcategorization restrictions.

Lexicon: a model of a native speaker's representation of the meaning and grammatical status of the words in a language.

Locality: a restriction of grammatical rules to limited portions of a tree structure.

Logical form: a level of semantic representation, derived from S-structure, that provides an interface between language and other aspects of cognition.

Marked: a specification of a form not in accord with the principles of **universal grammar.**

Maximal projection: the largest bar-projection of a phrase, represented as X″.

Module: a self-contained component of language; e.g., phonology, syntax. See **component.**

Move alpha (α): a principle that allows any element to be moved to any position in a tree.

Nonargument position: a node in a tree diagram to which no thematic role can be assigned in deep structure; abbreviated **A'** (A-bar).

NP Movement: a transformation that moves the subject of an infinitival up into the empty subject position of a verb such as *seems* and which moves the D-structure object into the subject position in passive sentences.

Null subject parameter: a parameter of language acquisition that defines whether a sentence must have a subject position with any lexical items inserted in it.

Observational adequacy: the quality of a grammar that correctly distinguishes expressions which are grammatically well-formed from those that are ill-formed. See **descriptive adequacy, explanatory adequacy.**

Parameter: a set of linguistic possibilities, often one or two choices, that defines a specific aspect of language. See **settings.**

Parameterization/Parameterized: the property of allowing a choice of linguistic structures. See **parameter, parameter settings,** and **settings.**

Parameter settings: the choices of structures allowed within a parameter. See **parameter** and **settings.**

Particle Movement: a transformation that moves a particle to the right of its object.

Passive Transformation: a transformation that changes an underlying tree structure into a derived structure whose underlying object appears as the surface subject.

Performance: see Chapter 1.

Peripheral grammar: aspects of language that don't correspond to universal patterns of language. See **core grammar, marked.**

Phonetic form: the grammatical level which represents the phonological form of sentences.

Phrase structure rule: see Chapter 9.

Postposition: in Japanese, elements that correspond to English prepositions but come after their objects rather than before them.

Principle: general statements in universal grammar that specify the nature of structures possible in the core grammar of a language; e.g., **structure dependent.**

Principles and parameters: a model of possible human language structures and of language acquisition in GB theory.

Pro: an abbreviation for **pronoun;** also the empty category that appears in null subject positions in languages such as Italian and Spanish.

PRO: the empty category that occurs as the subject of infinitival clauses in English and similar languages; subject to control by a coreferential phrase in a higher clause.

Projection principle: the principle that the syntactic structure of a sentence mirrors at every level the strict subcategorization characteristics of the lexical items in it.

Raising: a transformation which moves an element from a lower clause into a higher clause.

Raising constructions: sentence types in which a phrase has been raised. See **raising.**

Referring expression (R-expressions): see Chapter 2.

Relational grammar: a generative theory of language; an alternative to **Government-Binding** theory.

Resumptive pronoun: a pronoun that indicates the grammatical function that the head of a relative construction plays within the relative clause.

Settings: the choices of structure allowed within a parameter.

Specifier: in X′ theory, an optional modifier within a phrase. See **adjunct, complement.**

Strict subcategorization: a lexical restriction on what other elements must occur in a phrase into which a word is inserted.

Strict subcategorization frame: a formula that indicates what categories and expressions are strictly subcategorized by a word.

Structure dependent: the principle that every syntactic rule applies to a lexical or phrasal category by virtue of the structural relations it has to other parts of its sentence.

Subjacency: the restriction that a movement transformation can only move a phrase across one **bounding node** at a time.

Subject-Auxiliary Inversion (SAI): a transformation that moves an Aux to the left of the subject in a question.

Surface structure (also called "**S-Structure**"): the tree diagram that results after the application of all transformations.

Thematic role (also called "**theta role**"): see Chapter 8.

***There* Insertion:** a transformation that moves a deep structure subject to the right of the verb and inserts the dummy element *there* into the vacated subject position.

Theta criterion: the stipulation that an NP can be assigned one and only one thematic role, and that every thematic role that the lexical items in a sentence can assign must be assigned.

Theta role: see **thematic role.** See also Chapter 8.

Theta theory: the module of the GB model that determines the assignment of thematic roles.

Topicalization: a transformation which moves a non-wh-phrase into Comp.

Topic position: a position at the front of an English sentence where topicalized information is placed.

Trace: the abstract marker [t] left in a position from which a phrase has been moved.

Transformation: a rule that changes one tree into another.

Uniqueness assumption: the assumption that an NP can be assigned *only* one thematic role in a particular sentence. See **completeness assumption.**

Universal: a specific characteristic of all human languages.

Universal grammar: characteristics common to all human languages, including design principles of language.

VP Deletion: a transformation that deletes a VP under identity with another VP.

Wh-Movement: a transformation that moves a wh-phrase into Comp.

X-bar theory: a model used to describe phrase structure rules in their most general formulations.

PART THREE

Some Applications of Language Study

Until now we have treated English as if it were a uniform system, i.e., as if all of us spoke it identically in all circumstances. This useful idealization makes our initial forays into the study of language a bit easier. But the time has come for us to recognize that language isn't uniform. It varies with speakers and with the circumstances in which it's used. People from different areas, social classes, and ethnic groups, and from different times use different versions of the language. The circumstances in which we use language affect the forms we choose and the ways in which we deploy them. When writing, we generally have time to plan what we wish to express and ordinarily take the time to edit what we have written. When speaking, we typically do so spontaneously, generally without having the time to plan far ahead or the opportunity to consider carefully just how we might express our intentions. So our written language differs from our spoken language. In a language as varied and as widely used as English, it's only to be expected that some forms of the language but not others are deemed appropriate in writing. The rules of usage, of course, dictate which forms are and which aren't acceptable.

In the three chapters that follow, we investigate this variation in language, the circumstances in which it arises, and the rules that have grown around it. In Chapter 12, we discuss the differences between spoken and written language. These differences include differences in the forms of the language and in its organization. We relate these linguistic differences to differences in the situations in which written and spoken language are produced and interpreted and to the different expectations we have of the two modes.

In Chapter 13, we turn our attention to the variation in languages and correlate it with various social factors. We begin with the most familiar variants, those associated with different regions of the English-speaking world. We then extend our discussion to ethnic varieties, focusing on three U.S. ethnic groups: Blacks, Chicanos, and Native Americans. We have chosen Black English because it's the variety of a very important group in American society and one which most if not all teachers come in contact with. It's also the best researched of all U.S. varieties. We describe some features of Chicano English because Chicanos are a large and growing population in school systems throughout the country, again one that most teachers will need to be familiar with. While Blacks and Chicanos are well represented in schools around the country, Native Americans are rather less visible, even though they too are to be found in all states. Because their languages and cultures vary greatly, and because so little research has been done on their English varieties, we focus on some varieties spoken in the southwest. We could have described the English of Japanese, Chinese, Korean, Vietnamese, Portuguese, German, or Jewish Americans, to mention but a few. However, members of these groups don't appear to have as much difficulty getting through the school systems as do Blacks, Chicanos, and Native Americans. We hope that a sympathetic, respectful, and informed approach on the part of teachers to their varieties—and indeed to all varieties—will make schools less alien, more encouraging, and more enabling to speakers of these varieties.

We continue in Chapter 13 with a discussion of a currently controversial linguistic issue—language and sex (or gender). We discuss some issues that are pertinent to the question of whether English is "sexist" and to linguistic differences between males and females. These differences develop very early in people's lives and a range of explanations have been offered for them. Chapter 13 includes discussion of the standardization of English with particular focus on the two main codification tools—dictionaries and grammars. We complete the chapter by examining issues that arise in educational settings from the variation in English, focusing especially on achievement tests. We argue that teachers should familiarize themselves with the assumptions about language that the tests used in their schools reflect and that they should be prepared to ignore or adapt tests that are based on unrealistic assumptions about the nature of language.

In Chapter 14, we consider the issue of usage, i.e., codified expectations regarding linguistic form. Usage statements are often presented as "grammar" but, in fact, represent an aspect of the standardization of the language. Their goal is uniformity in the service of broader communication. They attempt to achieve this goal by claiming that one, and only one, of the available ways of expressing a particular meaning is acceptable. However, as we demonstrate, many usage statements are expressed in terms that stigmatize the alternative expressions and thereby also stigmatize their speakers. Moreover, the standard forms aren't a politically and socially neutral choice. Because they represent the variety spoken natively by white middle- and upper-class people, the standard forms give those groups a significant social and educational advantage over people who must learn both school subjects and a new linguistic variety in which to express them.

12 SPOKEN AND WRITTEN LANGUAGE

KEY CONCEPTS

Speaking and writing
Differences between speech and writing
Spoken and written language from the producer's perspective
Spoken and written language from the receiver's perspective
Linguistic characteristics of oral and written texts
The flow of information

12.0   SPEAKING AND WRITING

With few exceptions (e.g., Palmer and Blandford, 1969), grammars of English have emphasized the written language almost exclusively. Sometimes spoken language has been rejected out-of-hand as sloppy and imperfect; sometimes it has simply been ignored as a source of information about English. This exclusiveness extends further to a concentration on the grammar of literary works and formal essays with little attention paid to the English written for business, the sciences, personal communication, and the many other purposes which the language serves.

Linguists, in contrast, argue that the primary manifestation of language is speech. They offer several reasons. First, children initially acquire the spoken tongue. Second, the self-conscious learning of the inner workings of language (i.e., grammar) and of specialized skills (such as writing) develops after—and perhaps on the basis of—oral language. Such skills, moreover, are often imperfectly learned and exhibit considerable variation among speakers. Third, spoken language historically preceded writing. Western writing systems date back only to about 3000 B.C., while speech goes back at least 30,000 years. Finally, societies continue to exist and function to the present day with no written language. For instance, the Jemez Indians of New Mexico staunchly refuse to allow so much as a tape recording, much less a written record, of their speech.

Recently, teachers of English have begun to acknowledge the importance of oral language. As a purely practical matter, elementary school teachers must instruct students with only oral knowledge of English; teachers of older children occasionally encounter fully or functionally illiterate individuals (either native or nonnative speakers). But there are also significant theoretical reasons to recognize the importance of the spoken word, particularly for writing. On the negative side, weak writers often rely too heavily on the spoken idiom (Shaughnessy, 1977). Thus teachers must become familiar

335

with oral influences on students' prose. More positively, the understanding of spoken language may provide a key to establishing a transition for all students between the spoken and written modes. Finally, oral influences frequently appear in literary works. Modern poetry, in particular, explores the rich communicative potential of the spoken language.

EXERCISES

1. Examine the following (constructed) sample. Which features represent an oral influence?

   I am taking a non-art majors course which is a very fun course. First of all, we learned about line where we had to work with unity, line, and repetition. After that we started with curved and diagonal lines. Then we went into value and this is the lightness and darkness of a color. And what we did was we took up a picture and blew it up to a larger size and used black, white, and gray. To give shape to our art work but not actually reproducing the original art work. Then we began working with perspective and we worked with one-point and two-point perspective and we drew boxes and then we used color and value to color these boxes to show depth and position where they are at. And now we are working with perspective again but we are also, besides working with lines and boxes, we are working with circles and ovals. And one thing we learned the other day was that when you draw a glass you don't just draw a straight line at the bottom, just like the top of the glass is round where you drink out of it. It is a very fun course and I hope to gain a lot of information out of it. I think that every person should be required to take this course because it gives you a better idea of how you are to draw things and when you see something whether it is a dish or house or tree or whatever, you will have a better idea of how lines and curves make up this object.

2. Analyze the use of oral features in the following poem by Katharyn Howd Machan.

   Hazel Tells LaVerne

   last night
   im cleanin out my
   howard johnsons ladies room
   when all of a sudden
   up pops this frog
   musta come from the sewer
   swimmin aroun an tryin ta
   climb up the sida the bowl
   so i goes ta flushm down
   but sohelpmegod he starts talkin
   bout a golden ball

an how i can be a princess
me a princess
well my mouth drops
all the way to the floor
an he says
kiss me just kiss me
once on the nose
well i screams
ya little green pervert
an i hitsm with my mop
an has ta flush
the toilet down three times
me
a princess

(Printed with permission © 1976.)

12.1 DIFFERENCES BETWEEN SPEECH AND WRITING

In this section, we will consider such variations from three perspectives, that of the speaker/writer (section 12.2), that of the hearer/reader (section 12.3), and that of the text produced (section 12.4). Some of the differences may initially appear self-evident. However, their consequences for understanding communication—and for teaching it—are considerable. Only recently have teachers of English become aware of the extent of these differences and of their impact on pedagogy.

Both speech and writing come in many varieties. In this section, we will concentrate on formal essay writing such as is taught in traditional composition courses. Sometimes we will note characteristics of professional prose or literature, but these forms will not be our main concern. The treatment of speech will focus on casual conversation between individuals acquainted with each other and discussion of nontechnical topics known to all participants. Occasionally, we will refer to other varieties such as classroom lectures and formal public speaking.

Also, we will use the word **text** in a slightly unfamiliar way, but one that is common in the study of language units larger than sentences, a study called **discourse analysis** (see Chapter 2). A **text** is any unified and complete body of language selected for analysis. Depending on the object of our study, a text may thus be a novel, poem, piece of nonfiction, advertisement, as well as any unified part of these forms—e.g., chapters, paragraphs, stanzas, acts, etc. The notion of text also applies to speech and includes whole conversations, speeches, lectures, as well as their unified parts—e.g., introductions, digressions, and perorations. The nature of any text considered in this chapter will be clear from context. (When we intend to refer to an academic textbook, we will use the word "textbook" rather than "text.")

12.2   SPOKEN AND WRITTEN LANGUAGE FROM THE PRODUCER'S PERSPECTIVE

In this section, we examine differences between speech and writing from the perspective of the speaker or writer.

12.2.1   Writing is a solitary act

In contrast to the immediate feedback available to speakers, writers rarely have direct access to the response of an audience during the process of composing. Imagine yourself, for instance, in a computerized classroom, where your teacher could, from time to time, respond immediately as you typed a draft of an essay. Aside from obvious discomfort, would your essay turn out better or worse? Many writing teachers argue that the result would be better since in receiving information about our audience's positive or negative responses, writers can elaborate on positive points and avoid or repair problematic concerns.

Skilled writers ordinarily make many adjustments to accommodate an absent audience, including a projection of their authorial "voice" and revision of individual features of their text, such as we will note later in this chapter (Halpern, 1984). Failure to make such adjustments can result in an essay that presents only the egocentric position of the writer (Collins and Williamson, 1984).

EXERCISE

1. Conversation provides ways to "repair" problems in understanding as they arise. Examine the following conversation. Identify the communicative problem that arises. How do the speakers resolve that problem? Can you think of any analogous problem that may occur in writing? How would you go about solving that problem?

   > *Holly* (1): I'm looking for a copy of the *I Ching*.
   > *Clerk* (2): What's that?
   > *Holly* (3): Oh, it's a book on Chinese philosophy.
   > *Clerk* (4): I'm sorry, we don't carry anything like that.

2. Compare the response of Holly (3) to the dust jacket description of the *I Ching*:

   > The *I Ching*, or *Book of Changes*, is one of the first efforts of the human mind to place itself within the universe. It has exerted a living influence in China for three thousand years, and interest in it has been spreading in the West. First set down in the dawn of history as a book of oracles, the *Book of Changes* deepened in meaning when ethical values were attached to the oracular pronouncements; it became a book of wisdom, eventually one of the Five Classics of Confucianism, and provided the common source for both Confucianist and Taoist philosophy. (Wilhelm, 1977)

How would the clerk have reacted had Holly addressed the paragraph to him? Under what circumstances would one speak a paragraph like this? What sort of "voice" does this passage have?

12.2.2 Writing is more extended in time than speech

The solitude of the composing process has at least one advantage: it allows writers to conceal the often extreme effort and time required to create a text. Few of us need any reminder of the laborious nature of writing. The temporal extension of the process is less easily estimated, however. For well over a decade, writing specialists have studied the activities of writers during the composing process. They have examined writers' experiences of discovery (Perl and Egendorf, 1986), abstraction (Berthoff, 1986), and linear thinking (Harris and Wachs, 1986).

Teachers of composition usually urge students to proceed in three stages, **prewriting, drafting,** and **revision.** Let's consider these stages in more detail.

Prewriting is mainly a planning stage. Now all communication has a certain element of goal-setting and planning to reach that goal. You may, for instance, want to borrow some class notes from a friend (your goal). Consciously or not, you might plan to achieve that goal by phoning your friend, engaging her in a bit of friendly warm-up conversation, and then popping your request. Along the way, certain subgoals might emerge in the course of the conversation—e.g., consoling your friend on the results of a grammar test, sharing insights about a novel read in a nineteenth-century literature class, etc. Planning in writing is analogous, although more extensive. Typically, one plans not only general (global) goals and strategies but also (local) subgoals and strategies. The difference between speech and writing in this regard is most pronounced in formal essay composition. A note to your friend asking for the class notes might require about the same preparation time as the telephone conversation.

The time spent in **drafting** even an informal letter, however, is significantly longer in writing than in speech. Relatively little is known about the precise process that people use in creating sentences, although the discipline of psycholinguistics has begun to study this matter in recent years (Matsuhashi, 1981). Whatever the mechanism of sentence production, however, writing clearly takes more time, if for no other reason than that the tongue is faster than the hand. Physical speed, though, is relatively trivial in comparison to the psychological consequences of diminished speed, an increased awareness of the act of composing and transcribing. We shall say more on this point in the following section on self-consciousness.

The final stage of writing, **revision,** has no clear analogue with speech. Of course, we do correct ourselves in the middle of sentences, repronouncing words, reframing grammatical constructions, etc. But rarely do we recast the language of an entire sentence. Conversational turns such as "Let me rephrase that . . ." usually appear in formal spoken circumstances, i.e., those situations most resembling the formality of writing. Needless to say, conversationalists never move paragraphs around, add topic sentences, transition words, etc.

12.2.3   Writing is more self-conscious than speech

Self-consciousness, also called **monitoring,** is the psychological consequence of time extension. In writing, we are hyperaware of our *act* of communication—in addition to our consciousness of the message we intend to convey. The mechanism of self-consciousness, as James Moffett (1982, 1985) has argued, is our **inner speech.** Inner speech is the individual's internal monologue, perhaps a remnant of infantile babbling. Inner speech is used for several important cognitive processes—experimentation, problem solving, evaluating, and self-analysis. Moffett proposes that inner speech, useful though it may be, has its negative side:

> . . . left to itself, without guidance of conscious will, our inner speech tends to repeat itself in the direction of obsession. We have habits and limits. We recycle the same ideas and images, ride on the same trains of thoughts, and reach familiar conclusions. By means of redundant inner speech we maintain a whole world view of reality, a sort of sustained hallucination, usually shared to some degree by family, friends, and compatriots. (Moffett, 1985: p. 305)

For Moffett, composition (like meditation) requires "will and conscious direction" (p. 306) to control and build upon the materials of inner speech. Moffett's hypothesis thus suggests a reason for the essential role of self-consciousness in writing.

Since our words are such an intimate part of our selves, the extensive degree of self-consciousness necessarily involves an acute awareness of our language as we write. Particularly in the drafting and revision stages, vocabulary and grammatical structure become the object of intense critical awareness. For this reason, it's not surprising that the self-conscious study of English grammar has historically been so closely allied to the analysis of written language. Nevertheless, very little research exists to show that extensive conscious awareness of the details of grammar contributes to the actual process of composition, except perhaps in the revision activities that address specific prescriptive dictates.

12.2.4   Written language relies less heavily on context than spoken language

The word "context" has a range of senses. This book will use the term in three distinct ways:

1. **Verbal context:** The language preceding and following a given piece of text (sentence, paragraph, etc.)
2. **Situational context:** The factors in the immediate circumstances of a text that bear on its interpretation; e.g., time and place of utterance, identity, age, sex, relative social status of speaker and hearer, objects in the immediate surroundings, purpose of the interaction, etc.
3. **Cultural context:** The body of information and customs shared by participants in communication

The verbal context of the sentence *Written language relies less heavily on context than spoken language* is thus all of the words that precede and follow it in this book. Notice, though, that not all of the verbal context is relevant to the sentence. One might suppose that the nearer one sentence is to another, the more contextually relevant it is. While this supposition holds generally, it's far too simplistic. For example, a cross-reference in an earlier or later chapter of this book might evoke this section as a context. Likewise, one might return a conversation to a previous topic by saying [1]:

[1]   What were we talking about before the phone rang?

Verbal context may be indicated in writing, though less frequently in speech, in various ways. One is the use of **discourse markers** such as *above, below, on the previous page,* and *in the last chapter.* Other discourse markers serve as signs that the speaker has planned the topics that she or he is going to address:

[2a]   I have three questions to ask you.
 [b]   The Roman Empire fell because of several interrelated factors.

English, and perhaps all languages, also has a set of devices that indicate local contextual relationships between sentences. These devices are called **cohesion markers** (Halliday and Hasan, 1976). Five types of phenomena contribute to cohesive ties. (Underlined forms indicate cohesive markers; those in boldface denote the item that they tie back to.)

1. Reference
   My cat's name is Hoboken. <u>He</u> enjoys birds for breakfast.
2. Substitution
   Hoboken enjoys chasing **birds.** He caught <u>one</u> yesterday.
3. Ellipsis
   Hoboken **moved fast.** The bird didn't _____.
4. Conjunction
   The bird tried to escape. <u>However</u>, Hoboken was too fast.
5. Lexical relationships.
   Hoboken is a skillful hunter. Most <u>felines</u> are.

Although both spoken and written language contain cohesive elements, there is more pressure on writers to employ them since writing cannot depend on extralinguistic context in any reliable way.

EXERCISE   Select any paragraph from this chapter and identify any discourse markers and cohesive devices it contains. Identify each type, using Halliday and Hasan's framework.

Situational context is limited in writing because writer and reader are unavailable to each other. Consider a sign on a bulletin board with only the words *English Literature Club*

Meets Here Today. One might reasonably assume that *here* refers to the room where the sign appears. However, if the sign appeared in a corridor, a more likely interpretation would view *here* as designating the entire building. Finally, if the words appeared not as a sign but as a school newspaper headline, the interpretation would broaden to mean "somewhere on campus." *Today* causes even more problems since you have no guarantee that you're reading the sign on the day of the meeting. You might assume that the meeting isn't tomorrow, unless you think that someone is trying to trick you. But you might have some suspicion that the meeting might have taken place yesterday or sometime recently, knowing that people who post signs often don't remove them once they go out of date. Of course, in speech no such problems of interpretation would arise. You would immediately recognize *today* as the day on which the sentence was uttered, and you could resolve any uncertainty about where *here* is by asking your interlocutor. (For more on this topic, see Chapter 2.)

How could the sign be worded to avoid vagueness? Perhaps something like this would do: *English Literature Club Meeting, July 3, 1994, 116 Snooze Hall*. Unlike *here* and *there*, which often single out some aspect of situational context, the specific date and room number identify an absolute rather than a relative time and place.

EXERCISE   We haven't discussed in detail how other situational factors can be relevant to the interpretation of an utterance. Can you devise examples of where other situational factors listed in (2) on p. 340 may apply? To what extent can such factors be expressed in writing? How? Can you think of situational factors that are (actually or potentially) *not* relevant to the interpretation of an utterance?

Finally, cultural context plays a role in both speech and writing. Consider two ministories in [3a] and [3b]. Which one makes more "sense"?

[3a] John went to a restaurant. He asked the waitress for coq au vin. He paid the check and left.

[b]   John went to the park. He asked the midget for the mouse. He picked up the box and left. (Schank and Childers, 1984: pp. 114, 116)

Even if you don't know any French or haute cuisine, chances are that [3a] is more "natural" than [3b], which contains no potentially obscure vocabulary. The property of natural relatedness of parts of a text is what most English teachers refer to as **coherence**, an essential property of both writing and speech. The means by which individuals establish coherence have only recently been studied, primarily by researchers in artificial intelligence. It turns out that machines are unable to supply information from cultural context unless it's specifically programmed into their memories. This deficiency has spurred researchers in artificial intelligence to explore what exactly speakers do in responding culturally. One suggestion put forth by Roger Schank is that speakers possess a body of **scripts** (also called **schemata** or **frames**), which are "prepackaged sets of expectations, inferences, and knowledge that are applied in common situations, like a blueprint for action without the details filled in" (p. 114). Passage [3a] above is coherent, suggests Schank, because we possess a "restaurant script"; [3b] is incoherent because we don't have a "mouse-buying script" (though we do have a "purchasing script," which accounts for the partial normality of [3b]).

Although coherence is a property of all normal (e.g., nonschizophrenic) discourse, there is some reason to believe that writing differs somewhat from speech. One factor is the role of **semantic abbreviation** (Collins and Williamson, 1984). Through this process, communicators omit or leave inexplicit certain information, on the assumption that the audience will supply it through script-based knowledge. Thus in [3a] above, we assume that John ate the coq au vin even though that detail isn't overtly stated. Such semantic abbreviation would likely occur in both writing and speech.

However, it has been suggested that writing, at least of the highest quality, reflects a considerable degree of variation in the way in which semantic abbreviation is practiced in various rhetorical contexts (Collins and Williamson, 1984). One might also hypothesize that writing tends to activate a larger number of scripts than speech, thus creating a sense of greater complexity or depth. Unfortunately, no research on this possibility has been carried out. Finally, one might hypothesize that much literature makes extensive use of multiple and heterogenous scripts. Consider, for example, these lines from Wallace Stevens's "The Emperor of Ice Cream."

> Call the roller of big cigars,
> The muscular one, and bid him whip
> In kitchen cups concupiscent curds.

(From *Collected Poems of Wallace Stevens*. Copyright 1923 and renewed 1951 by Wallace Stevens. Reprinted by permission of Alfred A. Knopf, Inc.)

EXERCISE   Identify the scripts evoked in the passage by Stevens's poem. In what ways might a reader react to such apparent incoherence? Now consider William Carlos Williams's "The Red Wheelbarrow." This poem seems to rely only on a single script. What is it? How do you account for the poetic quality of this poem? (Many beginning students, incidentally, refuse to recognize it as poetry.)

> so much depends
> upon
>
> a red wheel
> barrow
>
> glazed with rain
> water
>
> beside the white
> chickens.

(William Carlos Williams: *The Collected Poems of William Carlos Williams, 1909-1939, Vol. I.* Copyright 1938 by New Directions Publishing Corp. Reprinted by permission of New Directions Publishing Corp.)

12.2.5 By and large, written language is learned, while spoken language is acquired

The distinction between learning and acquisition is important to an understanding of language skills. **Learning** implies conscious, relatively structured activity. It's based on general abilities such as attention, patience, tolerance for ambiguity, analytic and organizational skills, etc. Such abilities are variable from person to person. **Acquisition,** in contrast, is the unconscious development of knowledge through experience and through (usually unconscious) experimentation. It depends on innate capacities common to all members of a species, and hence is largely invariable. Such capacities aren't general but, rather, are specific to a particular domain, such as language.

To understand this distinction more concretely, consider a nonlinguistic example, learning to walk. Human children, even those born with physical complications, have the genetic capacity to walk, although they don't walk at birth. By the end of their first year, children have consistently initiated crawling and have tried to stand upright by themselves. Parental encouragement and physical support plays a negligible role in the process. Shortly after this point, children succeed in standing upright, taking their first steps, running, and getting into endless trouble as they use their locomotion to explore the world. To this point, all has been a matter of acquisition.

Learning arises when children use their acquired abilities for specific purposes. For instance, a child may take up soccer and develop skills at dribbling and kicking a ball while running. Another may learn ballet, where specialized steps are learned such as walking *en pointe* (on tiptoe) and *entrechat* (jumping and crossing one's legs simultaneously). Learned skills normally require instruction from a teacher, although exceptional individuals might learn the soccer or ballet moves through reading books or by watching skilled players or performers. Learning normally requires extended practice, although again gifted individuals may pick up certain skills with no obvious effort. The overall result in any case will be a considerable diversity within the human species in specialized learned skills in locomotion.

Acquisition and its genetic underpinnings help to explain differences among species. A bear, for instance, is genetically programmed to walk on all four legs practically at birth. It's not programmed to walk on two legs, although it's capable of standing upright for specific purposes such as picking berries or raiding beehives. In captivity, a bear can learn to walk upright, although it will not do so regularly given its druthers.

Language is like walking in that it's initially acquired, not learned. The acquisition process accounts for the early development in children of their linguistic competence, their unconscious sense of the rules of their language. Through a combination of genetic factors, exposure to language, and the process of experimenting with utterances, preschool children gradually change their talk so that it more and more closely resembles that of adults. Of course, some trivial amount of learning does take place, as parents occasionally attempt to teach their offspring such details as irregular verb morphology (e.g., to say *brought* rather than *bringed*). However, parents don't teach children any significant amount of language. Indeed, evidence suggests that even the small amount of conscious instruction administered by some parents has no significant effect even on those details of their children's language singled out for comment. The major role of parents appears to be that of providing an environment with reasonable verbal stimulation. On that basis, the acquisition process works almost automatically.

Learned linguistic skills build upon the foundation of acquired competence. In the spoken arena, these skills include public speaking (giving speeches, debating), television and radio broadcasting, interviewing, and performing in plays. Writing, in its many forms, is largely a learned skill. Parents spend small fortunes on preschool materials designed to make their children aware of the formation of letters. Grade schools build on basic orthographic skills by developing students' ability to spell correctly and to write in a cursive script. At this point, conscious instruction in composition begins, instruction that may last beyond the university years. Sometimes a considerable portion of writing instruction is devoted to the formal study of grammar, on the supposition that grammatical self-consciousness will contribute to a writer's development.

As in the case of walking, the learning and the acquisition of writing skills are intertwined. Most advanced writing skills probably derive from experience and experimentation, two factors common to learning and acquisition. Thus some writing teachers claim that extensive reading will improve one's writing. Also, writing teachers sometimes require students to keep journals or to imitate the styles of prose models presented in texts. Finally, many students learn to write in their academic disciplines largely through exposure to the literature that they read in professional journals and texts. A major issue in current composition studies is the relative effectiveness of formal teaching and conscious learning.

12.3 SPOKEN AND WRITTEN LANGUAGE FROM THE RECEIVER'S PERSPECTIVE

12.3.1 Parallels between readers and listeners

Many of the characteristics that pertain to writers and speakers also apply to readers and listeners. Reading, for instance, is generally a solitary act, except in such cases as parents reading to their children and authors reading their works aloud to an audience. While the writer must estimate the reader's background knowledge of a subject, the reader lacks the opportunity to ask for clarification of an obscure point.

Second, reading is also extended in time, although not nearly as much as writing. Two issues arise in regard to temporality—readability and speed of reading. **Readability** is a formulaic measure of readers' ease in comprehending sentences. Sentences identified as having a low readability level (often expressed as an academic grade level) presumably can be read faster than those with a high readability level. Thus a sentence with a fourth-grade readability would be more easily and speedily comprehended than one with a twelfth-grade index. There are at least two dozen formulas for calculating readability. Table 12.1 represents the readability scores of sentences [4a] to [4d] below, which have roughly the same meaning: the four readability scores result from four slightly different formulas for measuring readability:

[4a]   The sick old man went to his doctor, but the doctor wasn't able to see him until the next day.

[b]   The ailing octogenarian visited his osteopath, but the physician was unable to consult with the ancient gentleman until the following day.

[c] Though the sick old man went to his doctor, it wasn't until the next day that the doctor could see him.

[d] The sick old man went to his doctor, who was unable to see him until the next day.

TABLE 12.1 Readability Scores

Sentence	Kincaid	Auto	Coleman-Liau	Flesch
[4a]	4.3	5.4	3.2	4.0
[4b]	14.9	15.1	15.3	17.0
[4c]	4.5	6.9	4.5	4.0
[4d]	3.7	4.3	3.5	4.0

Readability in each of the four systems in Table 12.1 is based on various factors, the most common being word length, word familiarity, and sentence length. (The internal grammatical complexity of sentences is rarely calculated because of the limited capacity of computer parsing programs when these systems were designed.) Using a mathematical formula, the system assigns a grade level to a sentence. For instance, the Kincaid formula puts sentence [4a] at early fourth grade and sentence [4b] near the end of grade 14—i.e., second semester college sophomore level.

As you can observe, the scores differ somewhat in the grade level indexing. Sentence [4a] is indexed two grade levels apart by Auto and Coleman-Liau. Sentence [4c] diverges by almost three levels between Auto and Coleman-Liau. Apparently, Auto tends to estimate higher levels—at least for simpler sentences, largely because of the way in which various factors are weighted. Second, the Flesch formula assigns the same score (4.0) to sentences [4a], [4c], and [4d], while the other systems differentiate them. Since the three sentences differ mainly in grammatical structure rather than in vocabulary, one might doubt the sensitivity of the Flesch formula to syntactic variation. As we have noted, however, none of the four formulas takes into account the impact on readability of syntax (e.g., the adverbial clause in [4c] and the relative clause in [4d]). In fact, three indexes assign sentence [4d] a lower score than the simply coordinated sentence [4a]. About the only consensus of the measures emerges on the scoring of the overwritten sentence [4b], and even there the range of grade levels is two.

In spite of some serious doubts that emerge about current readability formulas, the basic notion seems both intuitively sound and practically important for teaching reading, writing, and literary stylistics. Since readability depends on grammatical structure as well as on sentence length and the frequency and length of vocabulary, reliable scoring will depend on the development of new systems that are more sensitive to syntax. In addition, grammatical analysis must develop beyond the intuitive bases of many traditional studies and must move toward a degree of exactness that can serve usefully in mathematical processes such as the calculation of reading ease.

Speed-reading is a highly commercialized technique designed to promote retention in reading. Regardless of marketing claims for speed-reading, any gain in speed is achieved by specific techniques of eye fixation and movement which, at least in the early stages, require a considerable amount of effort to learn. Moreover, the actual speed of reading remains a complex interplay of the readability of a passage and the reader's strategies. It appears unlikely that even the fastest readers interpret written messages anywhere near as rapidly and effortlessly as they interpret speech.

A third parallel between reading and listening is that reading is normally less self-conscious than writing, although more so than listening. One obvious self-conscious activity is taking notes on a text, although this activity may properly be considered an act of writing superimposed on the reading process. More important is the *depth of processing* that reading allows. Our consciousness appears to have various levels, ranging from the superficial to the deep. Our experiences may register to us on any level, a fact supported by psychological studies of memory (Clark and Clark, 1977). If someone introduces another person to us, we may only superficially process the new name and hence find ourselves embarrassed not to recall it just a few minutes later. Many self-help memory programs provide tips on remembering information by increasing our depth of processing. Thus if we are introduced to Jane Hunter, we are urged to create a mental image—e.g., Tarzan's companion stalking a lion. A similar level of self-conscious effort required to increase memory is expected in reading. With academic prose, for instance, one looks for organization, technical terms, definitions, etc. In prose fiction, one reads for theme, characterization, plot, and other literary components. Even the reading of newspaper reports calls for specific attention to the who, what, when, where, how, and why of an event.

Fourth, the same contextual restrictions that affect writers also impinge on readers. While the writer can only project the degree of context relevant to the understanding of a work, readers face the task of determining which works fit their personal needs and backgrounds. Thus a person with a basic interest in cactus plants would more appropriately select an elementary handbook on succulent houseplants than the *Cactus and Succulent Journal,* a professional publication filled with learned botanical studies. The training required to comprehend the contents of the journal form a part of its context.

Finally, reading—unlike listening—is a learned skill, developed almost simultaneously with writing. Again, there are complexities. One can take seminars in listening skills, where emphasis is placed on attention and on the inferences that one can draw about speakers. Moreover, people acquire certain reading skills not only through conscious learning but also through experience and experiment. Probably the most obvious acquired skill is the ability to read poetry, particularly "complex" poetry such as that taught in most literature courses.

Besides these parallels with the writing situation, we will explore two further characteristics of reading that are relevant to the classroom. The first is the extent of tolerance for error. The second is the dynamic nature of the reading process.

12.3.2.   Tolerance for errors

Many teachers and students believe that the study of grammar has as its main goal the elimination of error from one's written prose. As we argued in the Introduction to Part One, grammatical study has other and more important justifications. Nevertheless, few would deny that readers' tolerance for error in writing is far lower than in speech. We might attribute this fact to the rigidity imposed by a supposed need for consistency in published works, itself a product of lack of feedback. Some linguists have referred to the consciously articulated norms as defining a variety of language called Edited American English (EAE), a dialect native to no one. EAE serves as the norm imposed by teachers, publishers, and handbooks to assure the uniformity of publishable prose. Needless to say, EAE is an artificial ideal, and one met rarely even by "educated" adults.

As we observe in Chapter 14, the status of a standard dialect derives from economic and political rather than from linguistic factors. Any dialect—standard or not—is capable of expressing infinitely subtle gradations of meanings and of producing the most exquisite works of literature. The existence of a dialect such as EAE is a fact of life, and perhaps a practical necessity. But EAE has no inherent linguistic superiority over any other dialect of English.

It's also a fact of life that readers make judgments about errors in what they read. Until recently, it was assumed that errors reflected the laziness and stupidity of individuals. More recently, however, English teachers have begun to view at least some mistakes as signs of creative processes such as experimentation which provide evidence about learners' assumptions about EAE in the intermediate stages of its development. The first evidence to favor this view arose from **error analysis** studies of students learning English as a foreign language. For instance, a foreign learner might utter the sentence *Does John can speak?* Although ungrammatical according to rules of competence, this sentence tells us that the speaker has acquired the general principle that English questions require a verb to be placed in front of the subject, i.e. subject-auxiliary inversion. The nonnative has also recognized that, in many cases, a form of the verb *do* serves as the inverted verb. The major refinement needed for the speaker is to sort out the variations on inversion when the sentence contains an auxiliary such as a modal, *have,* or *be.* In short, errors often indicate general assumptions made by speakers; the job of the teacher is to point out where the general assumptions fail to apply because of the structural complexities of English.

Teachers of English to native speakers have come to realize that their students follow some of the same processes as nonnative speakers—although the actual errors made by the two groups differ. A pioneer work in this field is Mina Shaughnessy's *Errors and Expectations* (Shaughnessy, 1977). This study surveys errors of grammar, vocabulary, and spelling, viewing them as signs that a writer is progressing through stages of growth, from basic to intermediate to advanced. Significantly, no stage escapes errors; rather, the nature of the "imperfections" becomes increasingly more subtle in accord with growing sophistication. However, unlike foreign speakers who approach English with a well-defined linguistic background, basic monolingual writing "bears traces of the different pressures and codes and confusions that have gone to make up 'English' as the student sees it" (1977: p. 100). As a result:

> At times variant and standard forms mix, as if students had half-learned two inflectional systems; hypercorrections that belong to no system jut out in unexpected places; idiosyncratic schemes of punctuation and spelling substitute for systems that were never learned and possibly never taught; evasive circumlocutions, syntactical derailments, timid script, and near-guesses fog the meaning. (p. 100)

EXERCISE   Below are some sentences produced by native and nonnative learners of written English. Identify which ones you think are from native speakers and which come from nonnatives. In each case, try to identify what general principle might account for the error.

a. The dog was chasing its' tail.
b. The dog chasing its tail.
c. The bus that I took it was late.
d. To successfully accomplish the ban, smokers should first become aware of how advertisers use the media to sell the cigarette.
e. The publicized opinions of these questions are biased.
f. If us youngsters are incapable of handling the situation, we shouldn't be punished when we fail to do it.

A related issue is that of the seriousness of errors—i.e., **error gravity**. Although readers notice errors, not all errors are created equal; some have serious consequences for the communicative process while others are relatively cosmetic. Once again, gravity studies originated with errors of nonnative speakers learning English. The general conclusions indicate that errors differ in their impact on intelligibility. Paradoxically perhaps, cosmetic errors such as misspellings are often noticeable to any reader while potentially more serious ones may be perceptible only to trained editors or to English teachers.

Consider, for example, the following sentence:

[5]   Since the harvest was good, was rain a lot last year.

This sentence contains two kinds of errors, **global** and **local** (Burt and Kiparsky, 1972: pp. 6–7). Local errors affect single clauses. For instance, omission of *it* and the wrong form of the past tense are local errors in the clause, which presumably should read . . . *it rained a lot last year*. In contrast, global errors affect the relationships among clauses, sentences, or larger parts of texts. In the example above, the faulty placement of *since* is global because it reverses the cause-and-effect relationship between the two clauses. You can determine for yourself whether you perceived the local error more easily than the global one. Most people fasten upon the local slips, even though they're far less likely to cause communicative confusion than global problems. Error gravity studies suggest that teachers should concentrate initially on those problems that interfere with communication. Less critical weaknesses may well be delayed to later stages in a writer's development.

Besides nonnative speakers, teachers often encounter students who speak other varieties of English (see Chapter 13). Sentences such as those in [6] are grammatical for many people:

[6a]   He lost.
 [b]   I done finish my work.
 [c]   That house needs painted.
 [d]   He run into a tree.
 [e]   Nobody don't like Henry.

Teachers should realize the legitimacy of these forms in students' spoken variety and should recognize that "correction" of a student's variety in the direction of EAE will probably sound arbitrary and even strange to the student. As in the case of parental commentary on early childhood "errors," simple correction will very likely have no effect. Successful instruction calls for conscious recognition by both teachers and students of the validity of the student's native variant and of the artificiality of EAE.

12.3.3 Language processing

Communication involves at least three cognitive processes: **memory, attention,** and **expectation.** (These three poles correspond to orientations to past, present, and future, respectively.) **Memory** stores past information, on either a short or long term basis, and allows it to be "reactivated" on demand. **Attention** focuses the recipient on the message as it's delivered. **Expectation** directs the recipient toward future possibilities in the message's transmission. Both spoken and written communication rely on all of these processes. There is, however, some reason to believe that they receive unequal emphases in the two modes. In particular, spoken language appears to emphasize attention over memory and expectation, whereas writing brings memory and expectation to a standing more equal to that of attention.

Attention in conversation to another person's words is a matter not just of courtesy but also of self-interest. Listeners carefully monitor the stream of another's discourse in a continuous effort to locate places where they may insert their own contributions to the conversation. As research into conversational behavior has shown, we cannot begin our conversational turn at any place; we seek out certain sensitive spots in another's speech which allow us to inject our comments. In reading, however, we have by definition granted the floor to the writer for an extended time; and since the writer is absent, we have no direct way of interrupting.

However, at least two pressures exert themselves to prevent our continuous processing of the written message. First, our inner speech urges us to respond to the text immediately rather than withholding our reactions until later. Second, potential distractions from the situational context (a blaring stereo or a chatty roommate) may threaten to divert us from the task of reading. Attention thus results from the need to suppress forces that might sidetrack our central purpose. One might wonder whether speech or writing calls for greater attention than the other. This question may be unanswerable. Since speech calls for aural and writing for visual attention, a quantitative comparison of the two modes may be less important than a qualitative one.

The different role of memory in speech and writing appears most clearly in **back references**—allusions to information assumed to exist from previous interaction between communicators. In writing, such interaction is mainly limited to information created through prior linguistic context, including familiarity with other texts. However, given the possibility of very long texts, a back reference might require a reader to recall a context in an earlier volume, which may have been read years previously. More commonly, a chapter of a book may contain a back reference of several hundred pages. Two influences on memory must be distinguished. One is textual proximity, measured in words, sentences, paragraphs, chapters, volumes, etc. The other is temporal proximity, measured in the (largely uncontrollable) time between the reader's recognition of the back reference and the time when the reader actually encountered the material referred to. In speech, the situation is somewhat different. Generally, one refers back to information that occurs only in previous stages of the current conversation—usually a short time from a back-referring expression. In addition, the information subject to back-reference is more varied than in writing since it can include knowledge derived from situational context. Thus, in departing from a dinner party, you may compliment your hosts on their preparation of the coq au vin, even though the name of the entrée never arose during the course of the evening.

Another memory difference involves the permanence of written prose as opposed to the ephemeral quality of speech. Try an experiment. Make up a moderately long sentence and say it to someone. Then ask your hearer to write down the sentence verbatim. Unless warned in advance of the nature of the task, virtually no one will succeed in recording the sentence perfectly. The reason is that in oral language, listeners factor out the essence or **gist** of a sentence to store in their memories. They discard the grammatical form of the sentence and store it in a simplified version based on its meaning. In writing, the exact grammatical form of a sentence is permanently on record. A written sentence is also subject to repeated rereading, immediate or eventual. While this fact seems to relieve one's memory from excessive storage, it may actually have the contrary effect. Since grammatical form may contribute to subtle differences of meaning, readers cannot rely on the simplifying task of representing a gist, but instead, must represent more subtle dimensions of the text.

Take a simple example. Suppose that you're studying for a history test and encounter in your textbook the following statement:

[7] Demonstrations during the Vietnam War tended to make the government take a hard line on military buildup.

Had you heard this sentence orally in a discussion with a classmate, you probably would have simplified the utterance to a simple cause-effect relationship between demonstrations and the government's hard line on military buildup. In reading this sentence for a test, however, you would have to give closer attention to and then later recall the words *tended to,* which represent a qualification on an otherwise absolute statement. In this way, heightened attention to, and detailed memory of, the form of sentences is important in writing, whereas in speech memory for their rough content usually suffices.

Finally, expectations play a different role in speech and in writing. Probably the clearest indication of anticipation in speech is the common practice of a hearer completing the utterance of a speaker. Such activities indicate the listener's sensitivity to the speaker. However, such anticipations are extremely limited in scope, usually to a single sentence. On occasion, we can easily determine in advance the overall goals of another; however, we can rarely foresee the exact form of discussion that person will adopt to achieve this goal. Written texts also allow readers to anticipate the ends of sentences. Moreover, they contain formal devices to allow readers to anticipate both goals and strategies in significant detail. For instance, an introductory paragraph of an essay or chapter of a book will often indicate topics covered, perspectives on the topic, whether the text will be informative or argumentative, and what structure the discussion will take. Also, topic sentences of paragraphs regularly tell readers what to expect in ensuing sentences. In this way, expectation plays a more extensive role in writing than in speech.

As psycholinguists have long pointed out, participants in communication are very active. But their activity is highly structured—by their knowledge of the world, by their linguistic competence, and by specific features of texts. We thus proceed in the next section to examine the textual dimension of speech and writing.

12.4   LINGUISTIC CHARACTERISTICS OF ORAL AND WRITTEN TEXTS

One way of distinguishing writing and speech is to count the sorts of linguistic items that appear in each. A major source of information on this issue is the large number of statistical analyses of English. Many of these have been made for educational purposes, chiefly the determination of reading levels for school textbooks. Unfortunately, most of these studies deal only with written sources. Because of their pedagogical importance, however, and because they serve as potential backgrounds for further analysis of oral English, we will briefly describe some of the major studies.

The first attempt at extensive statistical analysis of English is the Thorndike and Lorge Word Count (Thorndike and Lorge, 1944). From the 1920s to the 1940s, education professors Edward L. Thorndike and Irving Lorge conducted a series of counts. Their most comprehensive work is *The Teacher's Wordbook of 30,000 Words*. (See Table 12.2.) The study was based on a **corpus** (i.e., a set of texts) of around 4.5 million words, distributed among five classes:

1. A general (G) category, summarizing four different counts
2. One (T) emphasizing "frequency in readers, textbooks, the Bible, and the English classics"
3. One (L) including recent (around 1939–1944) and popular magazines
4. One (J) including books recommended for grades 3 to 8
5. One (S) from books directed to juveniles and adults.

The number in any column represents the number of times per million words that a given word occurs; thus the word *abbreviate* occurs once per million overall, eight times in the textbook, biblical, and literary sample, and not at all in the grade school sample. Items marked AA are roughly the first 1000 most frequent words in the samples; such words are listed separately in the book. Items identified with an A are in the second 1000 most frequent words. The letter M identifies the 1000 most frequent items in the subsamples.

Thorndike and Lorge suggest that such counts can supply textbook writers and reading teachers with information that is useful in vocabulary teaching and in selecting texts for different grade levels of students. Here, for instance, is their recommendation for grade 4 of words whose meanings should be known:

> If it is an AA or A word or a word marked 49, 48, etc., down to 20 (except for a few words of interest only to adults or too hard to understand—such as *administration*—or if it is marked 100 or higher in the J column. (p. xi)

(Words between 49 and 20 are among the 4000 most common words in the sample.)

The Thorndike-Lorge Word Count remained a benchmark, even though its corpus was out-of-date, until 1971, when *The American Heritage Word Frequency Book* appeared

TABLE 12.2 Thorndike-Lorge Word Count

a to above

	G	T	L	J	S		G	T	L	J	S
a	AA	M	M	M	M	abeyance	1	10	3	0	11
Aaron	2	28	6	5	14	abhor	7	115	8	8	12
aback	2	10	15	11	12	abhorrence	1	14	1	2	7
abandon	38	119	150	130	285	abhorrent	1	11	6	3	0
abandoned (adj.)	3	11	14	12	27	abide	22	125	43	93	150
abandonment	3	10	16	3	39	ability	49	130	312	108	340
abase	1	14	2	0	5	abject	4	57	0	7	15
abash	3	16	14	24	13	abjure	1	11	2	2	9
abate	7	57	20	20	33	ablaze	2	7	15	16	5
abatement	1	10	5	2	4	able	AA	700	930	857	940
abbé	3	7	18	0	44	able-bodied	1	2	10	9	6
abbess	1	14	3	9	1	ablution	1	10	3	1	4
abbey	11	57	19	51	83	ably	1	14	9	3	5
abbot	10	38	20	86	41	abnormal	5	28	43	1	18
Abbott	3	19	11	2	22	aboard	21	115	121	80	68
abbreviate	1	8	8	0	5	abode	16	130	20	81	63
abbreviation	1	12	1	4	7	abolish	18	90	50	16	135
abdicate	1	16	4	1	6	abolition	7	50	17	12	49
abdication	1	10	3	5	9	abolitionist	1	11	1	2	5
abdomen	7	28	49	39	18	abominable	6	57	20	19	14
abdominal	2	28	16	0	5	abomination	2	28	2	2	9
Abe	8	12	119	5	14	aboriginal	2	11	6	5	21
abed	1	16	6	8	6	about	AA	M	M	M	M
Aberdeen	1	16	5	0	6	above	AA	M	941	M	?
abet	1	7	6	1	6						

(Carroll, Davies, and Richman, 1971). This statistical analysis was undertaken by the American Heritage Publishing Company to serve as a basis for the production of *The American Heritage School Dictionary.* Its corpus includes over 5 million words, distributed among written texts by grade level (3 to 9) and by seventeen subject areas. See Table 12.3.

This study is far more sophisticated statistically than the Thorndike-Lorge, and consequently, a bit more difficult for the nonspecialist to understand. In Table 12.3, column F gives the overall number of a word's appearance in the sample. The D column measures the spread of the word across the subject-matter categories—the higher the D-number (between 0.0000 and 0.9999), the more likely the word will occur in a variety of subject areas. The U-figure indicates a word's frequency per million words, adjusted so that a word spread among subject matters receives a higher score than words clustered in a single subject. The Standard Frequency Index (SFI), however, is perhaps the most revealing statistic. The SFI ranges from 0 to 90; the higher the number, the more likely the word is to occur; thus the article *the* has an SFI of 88.6, *disprove* has 40.1, and *elocution* has 24.6. A word-type with an SFI of 90 could be expected to occur once every 10 words; one with an SFI of 80

TABLE 12.3   Selected Word Frequencies

Word	F	D	U	SFI
a	124,959	0.9948	24441	83.9
abdomen	42	0.4052	3.7563	45.7
abolitionist	2	0.2408	0.1204	30.8
above	2,298	0.9659	437.70	66.4
absorb	52	0.6624	7.0693	48.5
acacia	4	0.4845	0.4027	36.0

Source: Carroll et al. 1971. *The American Heritage Word Frequency Book.* Boston, MA: Houghton Mifflin Co.

would be expected to occur once every 100 words; words with an SFI of 40 would be expected every million words; and an index of 10 suggests a word's appearance one time in a billion. Notice from Table 12.3 that minor class words occur much more frequently and in a greater range of text types than the major class ones.

Unfortunately, neither Thorndike-Lorge nor *The American Heritage Word Frequency Book* provides any direct information on grammatical characteristics of texts. Pioneer work in this field has recently advanced through statistical analysis of the Brown University Corpus. This corpus contains around 1 million words (500 samples of 2000 words each), distributed through fifteen types of texts (**genres**), including journalistic (reportage, editorials, reviews), popular lore, skills and hobbies, belles lettres (biography, etc.), scientific, humor, and fiction (general, mystery, science, adventure and western, romance). The published statistical analyses (Kučera and Francis, 1967; Francis and Kučera 1982) include a vocabulary ranking for adult texts comparable to the American Heritage's analysis of texts for a younger audience. More important, information appears on sentence length and structure (noun phrases, pronouns, verb phrases, adverbials, and connectives). For example, one can learn that informative prose contains about 85% active sentences to 15% passive (Francis and Kučera, 1982: p. 554). Such information is potentially useful to teachers. First, it demonstrates that "writing" isn't a monolithic category but allows for significant variety, with several different genres. Second, it suggests possible norms for composition teachers. Rather than telling students to avoid the passive voice altogether, instructors might make the more realistic suggestion that use of voice varies with a writer's purpose and recognize that a recommendation simply to limit the number of passives is misleading.

Statistical studies of written English shed no direct light on oral usage, although recently analyses of oral material have been made (Svartik and Quirk, 1980; Johansson, 1982). Direct comparisons between the two modes are more valuable. Most such studies have been carried out by researchers in speech departments. Generally, they examine only deliberate, prepared speeches, primarily by public figures who have produced written texts on the same topics. Analyses of these texts have produced a general consensus on a few characteristics that distinguish speech and writing:

1. Speech has a higher proportion of personal words such as *father, doctor, human, who.*
2. Speech contains more first and second person pronouns.

3. Spoken thought units are shorter. (A "thought unit" is "a sequence of words that could grammatically comprise a separate sentence without leaving a sentence fragment." *John and Mary ran and played* is one thought unit. *John ran; Mary played* is two.)
4. Oral language has more repetition. This feature is measured as the number of different words in a text.
5. Speech contains more monosyllabic words.
6. Speech uses more familiar words—that is, more words from the first 1000 on the Thorndike-Lorge list. (Einhorn, 1978)

Even though such studies deal with oratorical speech (which may have been written out in advance), they support what one might intuitively suspect as differences between speech and writing.

As linguists have become more aware of the need for a clearer understanding of speech, they have begun to collect and analyze samples of oral language, sometimes comparing them with samples of writing. These studies, for the most part, are descriptive. They don't make the assumption that spoken English is a uniform variety of language, but rather, that the language consists of an indefinitely large number of genres, which are categories of texts grouped together according to common "subject-matter, purpose, and style in addition to situational parameters such as the relation between the communicative participants, the relation of the participants to the external context, and the relation of the participants to the text itself" (Biber, 1988: p. 70).

To this point, our discussion has mainly focused on face-to-face conversation and academic prose. When we consider a broader range of genres, the picture becomes much more complex. Researchers such as Douglas Biber (1985, 1986, 1988) have demonstrated that there is a continuum between speech and writing (Ede, 1987). Moreover, genres such as formal speech may overlap with certain features of written language. Biber draws on both the Brown University Corpus and the London-Lund Corpus of Spoken English (Svartik and Quirk, 1980). The latter includes speech genres of face-to-face conversation; telephone conversation; public conversation, debates, and interviews; spontaneous speeches; and planned speeches. Biber's analysis identifies over forty linguistic features and employs a computer to count and compare their occurrence in texts of each genre. These features include such markers as verb tense (present versus past), personal pronouns (first and second versus third), place and time adverbs, questions, nominalizations, passives, relative clauses, infinitives, subordinators, prepositional phrases, and others. The descriptive features can also be organized into functional categories. For instance, past tense and third person pronouns are typical of a narrative, reportorial style. Present tense, first and second person pronouns, and questions express contextualization to the immediate situation and participants. The statistical technique of **factor analysis** can then represent each text as a cluster of related features. In this way, similarities and differences among texts can be determined, eventually producing a linguistic and quantitative portrayal of genres and subgenres. Thus it's possible to distinguish between press writing and other genres, as well as among the subgenres of reportorial writing, editorials, and film reviews.

Let's consider some concrete examples. Genres and subgenres can be compared through six categories derived from the factor analysis:

1. Involved versus Informational
2. Narrative versus Nonnarrative
3. Explicit versus Situation-Dependent
4. Overt Expression of Persuasion
5. Abstract versus Nonabstract Information
6. On-line Informational Elaboration.

Telephone conversations show a high degree of personal involvement, whereas academic texts (humanities and science) show very little involvement. Political press reportage shows a moderate amount of narrative; financial press reportage shows a tendency to avoid narrative. References in technology and engineering prose are relatively explicit in their pronoun use. Sports broadcasts, not surprisingly, use a considerable number of situational references. Letters to the editor are higher on the scale of persuasion than personal editorials. Natural science academic prose is considerably more abstract than its counterparts in the humanities, while society press reportage shows little evidence of abstraction. The prize for the greatest elaboration of information goes to mathematics academic prose; personal telephone conversation shows relatively little.

Genre analysis of this sort often supports our intuitive sense of differences, although occasionally there are surprises and enigmas. (Spontaneous speeches, for instance, average considerably fewer nouns than prepared speeches—157.7 versus 189.1.) The values of genre analysis are its explicitness and the possibilities it offers of showing interrelationships among types of texts and their language. As computer parsing of English becomes more sophisticated and capable of analyzing larger structures, such technology could become a significant educational tool. Early versions of such programs are already available in the classroom in the form of text editors that provide advice based on numerical information about a text. Statistics, however, don't interpret themselves. And as data accumulate, interpretation becomes increasingly complex. Further, teachers shouldn't accept as fact the interpretation of a software designer; quite often these individuals merely transmit without question the prescriptive and social biases enshrined in manuals and handbooks.

12.5   THE FLOW OF INFORMATION

The study of details of texts tells us little about larger questions of textual structure, i.e., the way in which sentences relate to each other. In this section, we consider an important structuring principle of spoken and written texts—that of topicality. Topics govern the organization of texts beyond individual sentences.

The notion of **topic** is familiar to students of writing, who are regularly informed that every paragraph should contain a topic sentence. And although professional writers don't use clearly defined topic sentences in every single paragraph (Braddock, 1974), their inclusion is well accepted as a standard in Edited American English. In spoken language, topic likewise plays an important, if less clearly defined, role. Topic helps to create the **coherence** of a text by providing a conceptual center in the form of a script around which individual sentences revolve. In writing, such perceptual centers result from preplanning; in conversation, they develop "on-line" to fit the goals of the participants. Let's illustrate this notion. Consider the following dialogue. (Letters identify the two speakers; numbers indicate their utterances.)

[8] *E1:* I went to Yosemite National Park.

  F1: did you

  E2: yeah—it's beautiful there right throughout the year

  F2: I have relatives in California and that's their favorite park because they enjoy camping a lot

  E3: oh yeah

  F3: they go round camping

  E4: I must admit I hate camping

  (Brown and Yule, 1983; slightly emended)

This example contains shifts from E's trip to Yosemite to F's relatives to E's dislike of camping—three topics in a very short space. Most likely, E didn't foresee the turn that the conversation would take. Nevertheless, the interchange has a topical logic, a logic built on the principle that cooperative conversation adheres to the maxim of Relevance (see Chapter 2). A second principle is that each sentence in a discourse normally contains two types of information. **Given information** is familiar to both participants from either preceding utterances or shared schematic background. **New information** represents the contribution of each succeeding sentence to the accumulating stockpile of context. These two principles result in a constant interplay among the utterances. To demonstrate, let's examine the conversation more closely.

Table 12.4 lists the pairs of utterances that show topical connections. It further identifies material devoted to topical connection (Given) and material that adds new information to the interchange. (The latter material occurs in the first of the two sentences identified in each row.)

Several important points emerge from this analysis. First, much of the passage is devoted to the maintenance of balance between speakers, both of whom have a desire to contribute. (Indeed, it's this desire that prompts topic-shifting.) Balancing appears in F-1 and E-3, where each speaker agrees to maintain the topic of the previous utterance. Second, a goodly portion of the conversation is devoted to maintaining topical orientation, although from one turn to the next. The transmission of new information represents only a partial dimension of speech. In fact, some utterances (F-1, E-3, and the redundant F-3) appear to convey no new information. This isn't to deny the importance of those three utterances but

TABLE 12.4 Given and New Information in Conversation

	Given Information	New Information
E-1	I	went to Yosemite National Park
F-1	go/went (elided)	(none)
E-2	yeah (response to question) there/Yosemite N. P.	beautiful throughout the year
F-2	that's, Park/Yosemite N. P.	relatives, California favorite, camping
E-3	(none)	(none)
F-3	they, camping	(none)
E-4	camping	I hate

rather to demonstrate their functional utility. The dialogue without those three comments would resemble robot talk.

Third, the language furnishes a variety of devices to allow **cohesion** between conversational turns. The dialogue illustrates just a few: exact verbal repetition (e.g., *camping*), pronouns *(they, that's)*, adverbs *(there)*, and ellipsis (in F-1). Fourth, conversation isn't strictly linear; i.e., one utterance doesn't necessarily tie in with only the previous one but may **skip-connect** to a remark that occurred previously in the discourse. In the passage above, both E-2 and F-3 skip-connect over the previous speaker's utterance.

Written language, as we have suggested, makes use of topical organization, but in a much different way. First, the content, number, and order of topics are typically preplanned by writers. Second, discourse and local topics tend to be explicitly identified through introductions and initial or final sentences of paragraphs. Third, topics typically receive extended discussion, usually through several sentences in a paragraph. Finally, because less time is devoted to social interaction than in speech, proportionately more goes to the conveyance of new information, although the overlap of given and new is still maintained. Perhaps this last characteristic accounts for the tendency to elevate writing over speech. If one prefers cognitive over social processes, writing has a clear advantage.

EXERCISE   In the text below, identify the topics and the devices that signal topical organization and coherence; also note given and new information.

> *E-1:* Hi, Art, how ya doin'?
>
> *F-2:* Pretty good. How's your knee?
>
> *E-3:* Good. Much better.
>
> *F-4:* Still doing OT?
>
> *E-5:* Not really. Go to the pool about twice a week, just do laps and stuff.
>
> *F-6:* Well, that's pretty good exercise.
>
> *E-7:* Yeah, I need it. Been putting on weight lately.
>
> *F-8:* You and me both. Look at this set of love handles. I've been putting in so much overtime, I haven't been getting to the gym very much.
>
> *F-9:* Really? How come you've been so busy at the office?
>
> *F-10:* Well, we put out this ad in *Consumer Today* and people have been writing us and calling us like crazy. It's good news and bad news. The good news is we got business to beat the band; the bad news is I don't get a summer vacation.

REFERENCES AND RESOURCES

Berthoff, Ann E. 1986. "Abstraction as a Speculative Instrument." In Donald McQuade, ed., *The Territory of Language*. Carbondale, IL: Southern Illinois University Press, 227–237.

Biber, Douglas. 1985. "Investigating Macroscopic Textual Variation through Multifeature/Multidimensional Analyses." *Linguistics*, 23:337–360.

———. 1986. "Spoken and Written Textual Dimensions in English." *Language*, 62(2):384–414.

————. 1988. *Variation across Speech and Writing*. Cambridge: Cambridge University Press.

Braddock, R. 1974. "The Frequency and Placement of Topic Sentences in Expository Prose." *Research in the Teaching of English,* 8:287–302.

Brown, Gillian, and George Yule. 1983. *Discourse Analysis*. Cambridge: Cambridge University Press.

Burt, Marina K., and Carol Kiparsky. 1972. *The Gooficon*. Rowley, MA: Newbury House Publishers, Inc.

Carroll, John B., Peter Davies, and Barry Richman. 1971. *The American Heritage Word Frequency Book*. Boston, MA: Houghton Mifflin Company.

Clark, Herbert H., and Eve V. Clark. 1977. *The Psychology of Language*. New York: Harcourt Brace Jovanovich.

Collins, James L., and Michael M. Williamson. 1984. "Assigned Rhetorical Context and Semantic Abbreviation in Writing." In Richard Beach and Lillian S. Bridwell, eds., *New Directions in Composition Research*. New York: Guilford Press, 285–295.

Ede, Lisa. 1987. "New Perspectives on the Speaking-Writing Relationship: Implications for Teachers of Basic Writing." In Theresa Enos, ed., *A Sourcebook for Basic Writing Teachers*. New York: Random House, 318–327.

Einhorn, Lois. 1978. "Oral and Written Style: An Examination of Differences." *The Southern Speech Communication Journal,* 43:302–311.

Francis, W. Nelson, and Henry Kučera. 1982. *Frequency Analysis of English Usage: Lexicon and Grammar*. Boston, MA: Houghton-Mifflin.

Halliday, M. A. K., and Ruqaiya Hasan. 1976. *Cohesion in English*. London: Longman.

Halpern, Jeanne W. 1984. "Differences between Speaking and Writing and Their Implications for Teaching." *College Composition and Communication,* 35:345–357.

Harris, Muriel, and Mary Wachs. 1986. "Simultaneous and Successive Cognitive Processing and Writing Skills." *Written Communication* 3:449–470.

Johansson, Stig, ed. 1982. *Computer Corpora in English Language Research*. Bergen: Norwegian Computing Centre for the Humanities.

Kučera, Henry, and W. Nelson Francis. 1967. *Computational Analysis of Present-Day American English*. Providence, RI: Brown University Press.

Matsuhashi, Ann. 1981. "Pausing and Planning: The Tempo of Written Discourse Production." *Research in the Teaching of English,* 15(2):113–134.

Moffett, James. 1982. "Writing, Inner Speech, and Meditation." *College English,* 44(3):231–246.

————. 1985. "Liberating Inner Speech." *College Composition and Communication,* 33(3):304–308.

Palmer, Harold E., and F. G. Blandford. 1969. *A Grammar of Spoken English,* 3d ed. Cambridge: Heffer.

Perl, Sondra, and Arthur Egendorf. 1986. "The Process of Creative Discovery: Theory, Research, and Implications for Teaching." In Donald McQuade, ed., *The Territory of Language*. Carbondale, IL: Southern Illinois University Press, 251–268.

Schank, Roger, with Peter G. Childers. 1984. *The Cognitive Computer*. Reading, MA: Addison-Wesley Publishing Co.

Shaughnessy, Mina P. 1977. *Errors and Expectations*. New York: Oxford University Press.

Svartik, Jan, and Randolph Quirk, eds. 1980. *A Corpus of English Conversation*. Lund: CWK Gleerup.

Thorndike, E. L., and Irving Lorge. 1944. *The Teacher's Wordbook of 30,000 Words*. New York: Teachers College, Columbia University.

Wilhelm, Richard. 1977. *The I Ching,* 3d ed. Translated by Cary F. Baynes. Princeton, NJ: Princeton University Press.

GLOSSARY

Acquisition: a development of abilities resulting from genetic factors, often accompanied by experience and unconscious experimentation. See **learning.**

Back reference: an explicit mention of information from previous interaction between communicators, either within the same text or to another text.

Coherence: the property of a text by which its various parts create a natural sense of connectedness around a central topic.

Cohesion: specific linguistic expressions (cohesion markers) in a text that contribute to coherence. Such devices may be conjunctions, ellipses, lexical relationships, reference, and substitution.

Corpus: a collection of texts coded to allow for computer analysis of their linguistic or literary characteristics.

Discourse analysis: the study of structural properties of language units larger than sentences; includes coherence and cohesion, topicality, conversational rules, etc.

Discourse marker: a specific expression that refers to some property of a text beyond the structure of a single sentence; includes cohesive devices and phrases like *as follows.*

Error analysis: the study of linguistic errors in speech or writing that attempts to classify them, determine their severity (gravity), and explore their causes; often not based narrowly on prescriptive rules.

Error gravity: degree of seriousness of errors. See **global error, local error.**

Factor analysis: a statistical technique that attempts to identify common elements underlying a set of measurements or to identify an underlying pattern of relationships.

Frame: see **schema.**

Genre: any distinguishable type of spoken or written text; e.g., newspaper editorial, comic book, story, business letter, joke, etc.

Gist: the simplified semantic content of a sentence, normally the only aspect of a sentence remembered after it's processed.

Given information: information assumed to be relevant to an utterance because it has been previously mentioned or is assumed as common background knowledge. See **new information.**

Global error: any error that affects two or more clauses. See **local error.**

Inner speech: the nonvocalized language production that is accessible to our consciousness.

Learning: the development of specialized skills through conscious, relatively structured, activity. See **acquisition.**

Local error: any error that affects a single clause. See **global error.**

Monitoring: consciously directing one's attention to the act of producing an utterance or a piece of written language.

New information: information not assumed to be available to communicators from either previous text or background knowledge. See **given information.**

Readability: a formulaic measure of readers' ease in comprehending texts.

Schema: a body of information or experience organized in the mind as a network of related concepts.

Script: see **schema.**

Semantic abbreviation: the omission in communication of material assumed to be known to the receiver of the message. See **given information.**

Skip-connect: a linguistic tie between an utterance and some other utterance not immediately preceding it.

Standard frequency index (SFI): a mathematical measure of the probability of a word's occurrence in a text.

Text: any unified body of language, whether spoken or written.

Topic: a central notion upon which a text or a part of a text is focused.

13 LINGUISTIC VARIATION

13.0 REGIONAL, SOCIAL, AND TEMPORAL VARIATION

While it's impossible to be unaware of the fact that people from different parts of the English-speaking world speak more or less different forms of the language, many people don't realize that linguistic variation is functional and efficient. For example, if we come across a text in which *lift* is used to refer to an elevator, we have evidence that the text might have been written by someone from England (or one of the other English-speaking areas influenced by British English). Similarly, if we hear someone say *y'all* we can generally assume that the person is from the southern area of the United States. In general, it's possible to glean a great deal of information about (among other things) where speakers are from, what social class or ethnic group they belong to, and how formal they consider the speech situation. This information is communicated indirectly by the speaker's pronunciation, choice of lexical items, morphology, and syntax. It doesn't need to be expressed directly, and this indirectness constitutes the efficiency and functionality of linguistic variation. By using particular variants, speakers can provide considerable information about themselves.

EXERCISE   What other differences can you think of between British and American English?

Language variation, besides being functional, is also inevitable. No two speakers speak identically. The differences among individuals can come to represent differences between groups, and to the extent that individuals and groups wish to differentiate themselves, these linguistic differences will be maintained. In fact, all languages comprise a great deal of variation, even languages spoken by relatively few people. Moreover, the speech of single individuals varies also, and no group of speakers, however internally homogeneous, is limited to only a single, invariant way of speaking.

EXERCISE   Identify three expressions that you would use with your closest friends but not with your parents, teachers, or bosses.

    The fact that language is variable implies that languages inevitably change over time. The English spoken from the eighth through the eleventh centuries (called Old English) had many more inflections than modern English. Old English nouns had as many as six different forms, e.g., *scip,* (ship), *scipes, scipe, scipu, scipa, scipum.* These inflections indicated different cases and numbers. In the sixteenth century, Shakespeare's characters could use *-st* and *-th* as the second and third person singular endings on present tense verbs, such as *Hast thou?* and *She doth.* We no longer use these endings. The changes that affect a language are generally indications of neither progress nor decay (Aitchison, 1991). If the language loses something, such as inflectional endings, it finds other ways, such as prepositions and word order, to express what the inflections used to express.

    As you're well aware at this point, languages consist of a number of interacting components, including a sound system; a morphology and word system; a syntax; a semantics; a pragmatics; and a discourse component. Each of these may vary and varieties of a language may differ from each other in any or all of these components.

    We are perhaps most familiar with varieties that differ from each other in pronunciation. Two varieties that differ only in pronunciation are said to differ in **accent.** A major variation in both British and American pronunciation concerns the ways in which speakers treat the sound represented by the letter *r.* When *r* occurs after a vowel and at the end of a word, as in *car,* or before a consonant, as in *card,* then many speakers, especially in southern England and in eastern New England, don't pronounce the *r.*

EXERCISE   What other differences in pronunciation can you think of between British and American English?

    Varieties differ too in their morphologies. For example, southern varieties of American English add *all* to *you* to create a plural form, *y'all.*

    Varieties differ in the words they use. In American English, we find different words used for the same referent, *submarine/hoagie/torpedo sandwich, bucket/pail, earthworm/night-crawler, quilt/comforter.*

    Varieties differ in their syntax as well. Some southern dialects allow two modals in the same clause, *I might could get there in time.* Many varieties allow double negatives, *I don't have no money.*

    Varieties also differ in their discourse patterns. Speakers of southern varieties are more likely to use *Sir* and *Ma'am* than northern variety speakers. In some areas, working-class parents are more likely to give their children direct commands than their middle- and upper-class neighbors. Heath (1983) discovered that Black and white speakers in one southern area differ in their willingness to tell stories. Many speakers of Black English vernacular are proficient in routines such as "sounding," "the dozens," and rap.

English speakers, like speakers of all languages, have beliefs and attitudes about language varieties and their speakers. Some people believe that there is only one correct form of the language and that all variation is unnecessary deviation. Others go so far as to view some variants as indications of individual moral laxity and even of societal decay. Our position—that of the vast majority of linguists and sociolinguists—is that it's impossible to make valid inferences about people's moral character, intelligence, educability, or affability on the basis of their speech alone. Moreover, beliefs of that sort may stand in the way of students' educational success.

EXERCISE   What do you think about sentences with "double negatives," or *come, seen,* or *dove* as past tenses? What about the people who use these forms?

By the time we are 5 or 6 years old we are aware that differences in language indicate differences in speakers' regional, social, and ethnic backgrounds. We may be aware also that we don't speak to our parents and our friends in the same way, and that we use specialized expressions for particular tasks. All of the types of linguistic variation described above (phonological, morphological, etc.) may correlate with these social and geographic factors.

13.1 REGIONAL VARIATION

Regional variation is perhaps most familiar to us. We are very much aware that people from other English-speaking countries have their own accents and their own lexical items. Many Irish-English speakers pronounce *t* at the ends of words like *hit* almost as an *s*. They also use expressions such as *I'm after eating my lunch* to indicate events that occurred very shortly before the time they're reported. One major difference between American and other varieties of English is that in the United States, *t* and *d* between a stressed and an unstressed vowel are pronounced identically; both sound very much like *d* (phonetically a voiced, alveolar flap, [D]); in other varieties, they're pronounced differently. For many U.S. speakers, *writer* and *rider* are pronounced identically; for other English speakers, they're almost always differentiated.

Within the United States, linguists distinguish a number of major regional varieties, or **dialects** (see Figure 13.1), including Upper North (which encompasses the area between New England and the eastern edge of the Dakotas), Northwest, Lower North, and Upper and Lower South. Eastern New England and many of the southern dialects frequently omit *r* when it occurs after a vowel, in words like *far, farm*. Speakers in the Lower North area tend to pronounce *don* and *dawn* identically. Southern speakers tend to reduce diphthongs to single vowels, pronouncing *time* somewhat like *tam*. In the midwest and west many speakers pronounce *merry, Mary, marry,* and even *Murray* alike, all with [ɛ]. Vernacular speakers in the Appalachian region prefix progressive verbs with *a-, We're going a-shooting*.

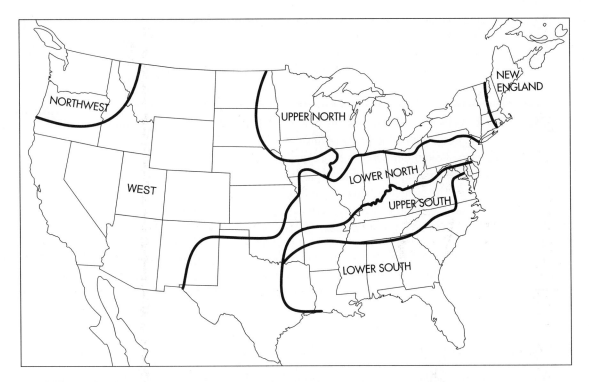

FIGURE 13.1   Major U.S. dialect areas. (Adapted from Carver 1989:248)

Southern speakers and many Upper South speakers use *y'all*. Southern speakers are also likely to say *quarter till* in contrast to *quarter to* and *quarter of*. In the north central states *dip* is used to refer to "the sweet liquid poured over pudding," whereas in the southwest and other areas, it refers to a spicy sauce eaten with chips (Cassidy, 1982).

EXERCISE   From Figure 13.1, identify the dialect area that you live in. What expressions, other than the ones mentioned above, are characteristic of your area?

13.2   SOCIAL VARIATION

Some linguistic variants are associated with social classes or ethnic groups. In New York City, *r* is dropped after vowels primarily by working- and lower-class speakers. In almost every area where English is spoken, the sounds ordinarily written as *th*, are pronounced in at least two ways—as either the interdental fricatives /θ/ and /ð/ or [t] and [d]. The former pronunciations are more prestigious than the stereotyped *dese* and *dose*.

Morphology also varies with social group. In many areas of the country, working- and lower-class speakers use distinct forms of verbs, including *come* and *seen* as past tense forms and *went* as a past participle. There is also frequent use of *them* as the plural of *that*, e.g., *them books; hisself, theirselves* for *himself, themselves.*

Syntactic variants associated with vernacular speakers include double modals, multiple negatives, and subject-auxiliary inversion in indirect questions.

EXERCISES
1. Which of the expressions below have social associations? Can you identify the group with which they're linked?
   a. I axed him what is his name?
   b. Mary brung me them flowers.
   c. The swimmers dove right in.
   d. dog (with nasalized vowel)
   e. We ett [ɛt] our lunches.

2. What items of pronunciation, morphology, or syntax distinguish the different social classes in your area?

13.3   ETHNIC VARIATION

Demographic studies indicate that the proportion of ethnic "minority" students enrolled in public schools in the United States will increase considerably over the next decade. In many parts of the country, "minority" students already constitute more than half the enrollment. In this section, we will briefly describe some of the linguistic characteristics of Black English (BE), Chicano English (CE), and some Native American English (NAE) varieties. We have chosen these varieties for a number of reasons. First, Blacks and Chicanos are the two largest minority groups in the country and both are growing. Second, the varieties represent two different reasons for variation. BE developed over the almost 400 years since the first Blacks were brought as slaves to the Americas. It may have been a pidgin at first, which later became a creole. It's now a much studied variety of English, which shares many of its features with other varieties of the language, although it may retain some features that derive from its pidgin and creole past. Chicano English and Native American varieties are "contact" varieties. They developed from the contact between English and other languages. In the case of CE, the contact is between English and Spanish, particularly in the areas along the United States/Mexican border. Third, all three varieties tend to be stigmatized, often even by their own speakers, who are at greater risk of educational failure than speakers of other varieties of English.

While we use the ethnic adjectives Black, Chicano, and Native American to refer to these varieties, it's very important to remember, first, that not all Blacks speak BE, nor all Chicanos CE, nor all Native Americans NAE, and second, that the varieties are spoken by people who are closely associated with the speakers of these varieties but who wouldn't otherwise be regarded as Black, Hispanic, or Native American. It's also important to remember that none of the varieties is without internal variation. Not all speakers of BE or CE speak them in exactly the same way, so it's better to regard them as sets of very similar varieties. NAE refers to varieties of English spoken by Native Americans from many different native language backgrounds and from many different tribes and cultures, so it doesn't refer to a single uniform variety either. Finally, many Blacks, Chicanos, and Native Americans speak other varieties of English, most notably standard American English.

EXERCISE   What other ethnic varieties do you think exist in the United States? Which of these do you think are contact varieties, and which languages are involved?

13.3.1   Black English

Of all the American dialects, BE is closest to the southern variety. Both are nonrhotic, i.e., both omit *r* after a vowel in words like *car, card, floor,* and *fourth.* BE speakers may also omit *l* in similar situations, pronouncing *help* as *hep,* and *toll* as *toe.* BE speakers may pronounce pairs of words such as *poor* and *poe, sure* and *show,* and *your* and *you* identically. Other dialect speakers distinguish these words by modifying the vowel of the ones from which *r* has been dropped. BE speakers may also omit *r* between vowels, an omission not available in other varieties; *Carol* and *Cal, Paris* and *pass* may be pronounced similarly.

Speakers of standard English (SE) frequently omit the last consonant in words such as *find, cold, fact,* and *rest* when the next word begins with a consonant; *old car* may be pronounced as *ol car.* This omission is often called **final consonant cluster simplification (FCCS).** BE speakers can apply FCCS in contexts where it would be unlikely for speakers of SE, notably when the next word begins with a vowel; they may pronounce *cold out* as *col out.*

Many words and expressions that are familiar to and used by SE speakers derive from BE. Perhaps the best-known current word is *rap.* Others that were borrowed earlier from BE include *cool* indicating approval, *dig* meaning to understand, *man* as a term of address, *fox* denoting a beautiful woman, *nitty-gritty, up-tight,* and *right on.*

BE morphology differs from SE and in certain respects from other vernacular varieties. All varieties of English allow contraction of various forms of *be.* SE speakers can say *I'm/you're/he's* for *I am/you are/he is.* BE (like white southern English) takes the contraction process a step further and allows the complete omission of *are: You fired* for *You are fired.* BE goes the next step and allows the omission of *is: He fired.* We can represent the possibilities and the varieties that make use of them in Table 13.1. The lower section of Table 13.1

TABLE 13.1

	Full Forms	**Contracted**	**Are Deletion**	**Is Deletion**
	He is here	He's here	—	He here
	We are here	We're here	We here	—
Standard English	Yes	Yes	No	No
White Southern NSE	Yes	Yes	Yes	No
Black English	Yes	Yes	Yes	Yes

illustrates an important characteristic of the relations among dialects. Dialects of a language share a great many features (e.g., full and contracted forms of *be*) and where they differ, they do so incrementally. With respect to contraction and deletion of *be*, SE and BE are two steps apart, with white southern English between them.

Besides the omission of *is*, BE has several other unique verbal characteristics:

1. Invariant habitual *be*, as in *He be there every day*. This form of the verb doesn't change as the subject of its clause changes, *They be there every day*. It denotes a typical or habitual state, or a recurrent action.
2. *Been* to indicate an event that occurred in the past but which continues to be relevant at the time of utterance, *You been paid your dues* for approximately *You have already paid your dues*.
3. Deletion of the second consonant of a cluster before a vowel, *lif' up* for *lift up*.
4. Devoicing of final stops in stressed syllables, *bit* for *bid*, *back* for *bag*.
5. Omission of the *-s/-es* suffix that indicates (a) third person singular present tense *(he talk* for *he talks)*, (b) plural *(four horse* for *four horses)*, and (c) genitive *(Bill hat* for *Bill's hat)*. (Wolfram, 1991: p. 108)

While dialects and varieties differ from each other in their grammatical patterns, they also differ statistically rather than categorically. For instance, BE speakers may omit the plural marker in 10 to 20% of the positions in which it could occur. This means, of course, that they include the plural marker in the other 80 to 90%. So the difference between SE and BE in this respect isn't a simple, categorical presence versus absence of the plural marker, but rather, categorical versus variable presence.

BE and some white southern varieties use *done* to indicate that an event has been completed, *I done forgot what you wanted* (Wolfram, 1991: p. 287), meaning I have forgotten what you wanted.

BE syntax shares some features with other varieties, most notably, multiple negation and double modals. It also allows the substitution of *it* for *there* in existential *there* sentences. Where SE requires *There was a bad crash on Main*, BE (and other, particularly southern, varieties) allows *It was a bad crash on Main*.

BE speakers' discourse patterns differ in a number of ways from those of SE speakers. The "man of words" is very highly regarded in Black culture. We are all familiar with such excellent Black orators as Martin Luther King, Jr., and with the skills of Black ministers. We are also familiar with the pattern of responses from the congregation to Black ministers' words. In recent years, we have become familiar with rap forms of poetry. Less familiar are verbal competitions among African-American boys and young men called "the dozens" or "sounding." These involve ritual insults, typically to the participants' families, especially to their mothers. Each participant is required to produce a ritual insult that tops the one that immediately precedes it. The winner is the person who produces the final, untoppable riposte. The insults are ritualistic because each participant must be careful not to say something that may describe another's family too accurately. Failure to maintain this distance can result in serious, nonritual conflict. Labov collected the following sound in New York City. We quote it and Labov's comments:

C1: Your momma's a peanut man!
C2: Your momma's a ice-man!
C3: Your momma's a fire man!
C4: Your momma's a truck driver!
C5: Your father sell crackerjacks!
C6: Your momma *look* like a crackerjack!

"The last sound in this series cannot be topped, and the sounding goes off in a completely different direction" (Labov, 1972b: pp. 346–347).

The oratory exhibited by Black ministers, preachers, and politicians, and the verbal agility required of successful rappers and sounders clearly imply great skill in the use of language. Unfortunately, the skills most admired by young Blacks are often rejected by school systems and teachers. Not surprisingly, therefore, it's often the young people who are most skillful in Black cultural uses of language who reject the values of the school.

EXERCISE   Listen to a Black orator, such as a political or religious leader. What linguistic features characterize his or her speech? If you can, tape the speaker addressing a Black audience and a white (or multiracial) audience. Does the language differ in the two cases? If so, in what ways?

13.3.2 Chicano English

Chicano English is one of several Hispanic varieties of English. Other Hispanic varieties include those spoken by Cuban-Americans in Florida, those spoken by Puerto Ricans in New York City, and those spoken by Hispanic populations who have been in the southwestern United States for centuries and who look to Spain for linguistic and cultural models. CE is, as we mentioned, a contact variety. By this we mean that it's used in communities in which Spanish is also used. It's not that every CE speaker also speaks Spanish, but many certainly do. CE is a set of relatively stable varieties of English used by Americans of Mexican descent in communities around the country, particularly the major urban ones, but also in southwestern rural communities. It's the variety of choice for people who wish to demonstrate their loyalty to those communities, and it distinguishes them from those who identify with Mexican or Anglo-American values.

The features that distinguish CE from other English varieties are of three main kinds. First, there are a few features that can be traced to the influence of Spanish; second, there are those features that are unique to CE but which cannot be uncontroversially traced to Spanish; and third, there are those features that CE shares with other vernacular varieties of English.

One phenomenon closely associated with CE is **code switching**, which involves the use of two languages within a single interaction, and even within a single utterance. This use of two languages is very common among bilinguals and in bilingual communities everywhere. In the following example, transcribed from a real conversation, the Spanish is italicized:

Code Switching	English Translation
Fui ayer con el doctor. Boy, they certainly make money. *Me cobro* twenty dollars. *Fijese* a two minute visit *y con trece pacientes en el* office. Thirteen times twenty—*son* $260. *Ademas de lo que pagan en los hospitales. Hijole! Porque no me hice* doctor instead of accountant.	Yesterday I went to the doctor. Boy, they certainly make money. He charged me twenty dollars. Imagine a two minute visit and with 13 patients in the office. Thirteen times twenty—it's $260. Besides what they pay him in the hospitals. My goodness. Why didn't I become a doctor instead of an accountant.

(Penfield and Ornstein-Galicia, 1985: p. 15)

Clearly, in order to be able to code-switch, one must be skilled in both languages. However, not all CE speakers can speak Spanish. The native language of many Chicanos is English, so CE must not be mistaken for a variety of learner English. Nor may its features, even the few that are uncontroversially traceable to Spanish origins, be viewed as errors made by people who have only a poor command of English. Its patterns are internally consistent and have been stable for decades. It must be remarked, however, that both CE and learner varieties of English are spoken in Mexican-American communities. CE is spoken by people for whom English is a native language (even if not their only language); the learner varieties are spoken by children learning English and recent immigrants. Our interest here is primarily in CE.

One stereotype of Hispanic English that isn't a regular feature of CE, although it does occur in the variety, is the insertion of a vowel, often [ɛ] at the beginning of words that begin with s followed by a stop consonant, such as *school, stop, scared.* These are pronounced as *eschool, estop, escared* by many native Spanish speakers learning English because Spanish regularly inserts a vowel at the beginning of such words. Perhaps because this pattern is so highly stigmatized, it's not a regular feature of CE.

Linguists who have studied CE agree that CE speakers' substitution of the voiceless velar fricative [x] for [h] is due to the influence of Mexican Spanish, e.g., [x]*ave* for *have.* The fact that many frequently occurring English words begin with h (e.g., *he*) makes this substitution a salient indicator of CE, even though it's very unlikely to cause any miscommunication in interactions between CE speakers and speakers of other varieties.

CE speakers tend to alternate [č] and [š], sometimes pronouncing *check* as *check* and sometimes as *sheck;* sometimes pronouncing *show* as *chow* and sometimes as *show.* Because Spanish has [č] but not [š], we should expect CE speakers to substitute [č] wherever English has [š] but never to substitute [š] for [č]. Clearly, nothing as simple as direct influence from Spanish can explain these substitutions.

CE speakers may pronounce [v] as [f] in word and root final positions (e.g., *give* as *gif*), as [β] (a voiced, bilabial fricative), [b], or [v] between vowels: e.g., *le[β]el* (level), *li[b]ing* (living).

A phonological characteristic of CE that affects the pronunciation of English inflectional morphemes is devoicing of [z] to [s], particularly at the ends of words, e.g., *Al's* as *Al*[s], *cars* as *car*[s], *goes* as *goe*[s]. These pronunciations affect the English plural, genitive, and third person singular present tense.

CE speakers may systematically substitute lax vowels for English tense [i], [e], and [u], pronouncing them as [I], [ɛ], and [U], respectively. They may say *nid* for *need, spik* for *speak, fill* for *feel,* and *mel* for *mail.* They may also substitute *y* for *j* in words such as *just.*

Features that CE has in common with BE and other vernacular varieties are the substitution of *d* for *th* in words such as *this* and *that* and the simplification of word and root final consonant clusters, e.g., pronouncing *second* as *secon* and *friends* as *frens.* As in spoken American standard English, CE speakers pronounce pairs such as *which* and *witch, where* and *wear* identically.

CE shares the grammatical feature of multiple negation with other vernacular varieties and uses *more* to mean *more often, More I use English* (Penfield and Ornstein-Galicia, 1985: p. 52). In embedded wh-questions, CE speakers may invert the subject and the auxiliary, as in . . . *they asked them where did they live* (Wald, 1984: p. 25). They also tend to drop the past tense marker *-ed,* pronouncing *kissed* as *kiss.*

Lexically, CE speakers may use *borrow* for both borrow and lend and *out from* to mean away from.

EXERCISE   Make a brief list of stereotypical CE features. Then try to discover whether Chicanos actually use those features, and if they do, how frequently.

13.3.3   Native American varieties of English (NAE)

Many Native Americans speak their ancestral languages and one or more varieties of English. Many speak standard English as well as a variety that shares characteristics with other nonstandard varieties of English and which is influenced by the ancestral language. Some Native Americans speak their ancestral languages and a nonstandard variety of English, others speak only their ancestral languages, and still others speak only a nonstandard variety of English. Because there are several hundred Native American languages, there are numerous Native American varieties of English in the United States, perhaps as many as 200. Obviously, we can deal with only a tiny fraction of their characteristics here. Our discussion is based on papers in Leap (1977).

A number of southwestern NAE varieties, including Hopi, Isletan, Mojave, and Navajo, simplify consonant clusters, e.g., pronouncing *student* as *studen.* In this respect, the NAE varieties are similar to BE, although all of these varieties differ according to which consonant clusters are simplified and how they're simplified.

NAE speakers also use multiple negation and uninflected *be,* although once again, they differ in detail from other varieties of English.

Other characteristics of NAE may be due to the influence of the ancestral community languages. For instance, the Cheyenne, Hopi, Isletan Tiwa, Mojave, and Navajo languages tend to devoice final consonants, and so do the local varieties of English, giving *jop* for *job.*

Hopi, Mojave, and Navajo speakers fairly consistently drop the *-ed* marker of the past tense, e.g., using *worship* for *worshipped,* perhaps because these languages don't have a past/present tense system analogous to English.

In Isletan English, speakers use what is known as the **cognate object construction.** This involves using a verb and a direct object where other varieties would use just a verb, e.g., *People take participation in the mass* (cf. People participate in the mass), and *They have vision of the edge of the plaza* (cf. They see the edge of the plaza).

SE and Isletan English differ also in their patterns of subject-verb agreement. In SE, in the third person present tense, if the subject is singular, and therefore unsuffixed, the verb is suffixed with *-s* (*The* **boy goes** *there every morning*); if the subject is plural and therefore suffixed with *-s*, the verb is unsuffixed (*The* **boys go** *there every morning*). In Isletan English, the agreement pattern requires that if either the verb or the subject is suffixed, then the other must be suffixed too; e.g., *There are some parties that* **goes** *on over there* (the subject has plural reference), *It have to be somebody in the corn groups* (the subject has singular reference).

EXERCISE   What reactions do you have when you hear people speaking a nonstandard ethnic variety?

13.4 LANGUAGE, SEX, AND GENDER

The relationship of language, sex, and gender has been an area of intense research in the last 15 years or so. Several issues have emerged. Perhaps the one most familiar to nonspecialists is that of sexism in language—the issue of whether English systematically discriminates against women in its lexicon and in its patterns of use. A second issue is whether men and women, or more generally, males and females, speak different varieties. The research suggests that they may. The third issue is how to explain why males and females differ linguistically. The fourth issue is whether males and females view the world differently, are viewed differently, and are socialized differently because of their linguistic differences.

13.4.1 Sexism in language

English contains a number of expressions that many people, both men and women, find objectionable. After indefinite pronouns like *everyone* and *anyone* the pronoun required by prescriptive grammarians is *he* and its related forms, even though *everyone/anyone* refer to both men and women and *he* is the masculine pronoun. For example, *Everyone is required to remove his shoes upon entering.* Similarly, expressions such as *mankind* refer to both men and women, and *chairmen, policemen,* and *mailmen* may be women. The language seems to suggest that the typical human being is a man.

Until recently, there was no title abbreviation for women that didn't indicate their marital status. Women were either *Miss* or *Mrs.* The corresponding male title *Mr.* gives no indication of whether a man is married. This asymmetry prompted people to begin using

Ms. for women when their marital status wasn't relevant. There are still no titles that distinguish married from unmarried men, so the asymmetry persists.

Because of these asymmetries, many organizations, including the National Council of Teachers of English (NCTE) and the Linguistic Society of America (LSA), have passed resolutions requiring participants at their conferences and authors of their publications to use "gender-neutral" or nonsexist language. That is, they should use expressions that include reference to both genders where appropriate and to use gendered pronouns such as *he* only when males alone are intended. The following LSA guidelines are quite typical:

1. Avoid so-called masculine generics such as the pronoun *he* (*his,* etc.) with sex-indefinite antecedents or *man* and its compounds (except in unambiguous reference to males).

   Although such forms have long been endorsed by prescriptive grammarians, in current usage they are not interpreted as unproblematically including both sexes equally, and tend to suggest that the default human being is male.
2. Avoid using genuine generics as if they referred only to males (e.g., "Speakers use language for many purposes—to argue with their wives. . . ." or "Americans use lots of obscenities but not around women.").
3. Avoid adding modifiers or suffixes to nouns to mark sex of referents unnecessarily. Such usage promotes sexual stereotyping in one of two ways.
   a. By highlighting referent sex, modification can signal a general presupposition that referents will be of the other sex *(lady professor, male secretary)* and thus that these referents are aberrant.
   b. Conventionalized gender-marking "naturalizes" the presumptive or unmarked sex of the noun's referents *(stewardess, cleaning lady).*
4. Use parallel forms of reference for women and men, e.g., do not cite a male scholar by surname only and a female scholar by first name plus surname or construct examples with a cast of characters like executive "Mr. Smith" and his secretary "Mary." (*LSA Bulletin* 135, March 1992: p. 8)

EXERCISE   Make a list of sexist expressions, including the ones mentioned above. For each one, find a gender-neutral expression that could replace it.

13.4.2 *"Generic" he*

"Generic" *he* may be viewed from two perspectives. The first, gender bias, we discussed earlier. The second is the level of style or formality.

In formal standard English, the variety used in highly edited written or spoken genres, the prescriptive tradition requires that we use *he* when the antecedent is an indefinite pronoun. The basis is that the formal varieties treat the indefinites as singulars, even though their reference may be plural. The verb in the following sentence is singular and agrees with its subject: *Everyone is required to remove his shoes.*

In informal spoken English, including spoken standard English, many if not most speakers use forms of the pronoun *they,* the third person plural, which isn't marked for gender. Informally, most of us are likely to say *Everyone has to take their shoes off.* Prescriptive grammarians object to structures such as this on the basis that a singular antecedent should be matched to a singular pronoun, and if the indefinites are singular, as the subject-verb agreement pattern suggests, then the pronouns should be singular too.

Various ways of avoiding the pitfalls of sexism and grammatical agreement have been suggested, such as the use of *he or she* and their various inflected forms: *Everyone is required to remove his or her shoes,* or the use of a plural antecedent and *they: All are required to remove their shoes.* Unfortunately, none of the proposed solutions are as stylistically felicitous as one would like. Ironically, the use of *they* after indefinite antecedents was fully acceptable until the nineteenth century when prescriptive grammarians banished it.

Another pattern of pronoun use (rather than grammar) is the choice of masculine pronouns after expressions such as *doctor* and feminine pronouns after *nurse,* e.g., *A doctor should be willing to care for his patients at any hour of the day.* This isn't a matter of grammar; if the doctor is a woman, then we are required by the grammar of English to use the feminine pronoun. Analogously, if the nurse is a man, we must use the masculine. However, when the sex of the doctor is unknown, we tend to use *he;* when the sex of the nurse is unknown, we tend to use *she,* even though there are female doctors and male nurses. The usage appears to reflect two aspects of our society. First, doctors have higher status than nurses, and second, the higher status professions have been and still are dominated by men and the lower status ones are occupied primarily by women.

As a final example of the imbalance in the way the language and its use refers to males and females, consider the four words *man, woman, boy, girl.* From a purely semantic point of view, the difference between *boy* and *girl* should be identical to the difference between *man* and *woman,* and the difference between *man* and *boy* should be identical to the difference between *woman* and *girl.* We can represent the semantics as follows:

	MALE	**FEMALE**
ADULT	man	woman
NONADULT	boy	girl

However, *boy* is used to refer to males until they're about 18 years old, whereas *girl* is used to refer to females much older than that.

13.4.3 Male and female varieties

Do men and women speak different varieties of English? If they do, when do these differences develop? Generally, men and women do speak differently from each other and the differences develop very early in life.

There is considerable research that suggests that girls are slightly more linguistically precocious than boys. Girls babble earlier than boys, produce their first words earlier, and have more words by 18 months. Girls' phonology, morphology, vocabulary, syntax, semantics, comprehension, and reading are more advanced than boys' throughout childhood. How these maturational differences relate to the differences we find in the forms used by women and men is a matter of speculation. It's with these latter differences that we are concerned in this section. [For very readable surveys, see Baron (1986) and Coates (1986).]

Most English speakers alternate to some degree between pronouncing the suffix *-ing* "with and without the g" (i.e., between [Iŋ] and [In]). For most English-speaking communities, the pronunciation with [Iŋ] is more prestigious than the one without. The [Iŋ] pronunciation tends to occur more frequently in more formal contexts; [In] occurs more frequently in less formal interactions. Fischer (1958) studied two groups of boys and girls in New England. The groups were of 3 to 6 year olds and 7 to 10 year olds. For both groups, the girls used the prestigious [Iŋ] forms significantly more often than the boys. Similar studies have examined other variables in Edinburgh, Scotland (Romaine, 1978); Glasgow, Scotland (Macauley, 1978); and Reading, England (Cheshire, 1982b), as well as in Montreal and Tehran. In all of these studies, women and girls tend to use the standard, prestige forms more often than men and boys.

Girls also seem to be more polite than boys. For example, they tend to mitigate disagreements by adding *I think* (Perkins, 1983). Girls tend to laugh more in interactions with boys than in all-girl interactions. While both boys and girls accommodate their styles to children of the other sex, girls accommodate more than boys.

Women continue the patterns they acquired as girls and for the most part continue to use more prestige forms than men and to use politeness markers more frequently; they say *Please* and *Thank you* more frequently. Women and girls use fewer direct commands and fewer taboo items than boys and men. In conversations, men take longer turns and are more likely to interrupt other speakers than women. Women do more conversational **backchanneling** to keep the conversation going; i.e., they say *uhhuh* and *Is that so?* more frequently than men. Men and women tend to talk about different topics when they're in same-sex groups. In one study, male university students tended to talk about sports, competition, aggression, and "doing things." College women, on the other hand, talked about themselves, their feelings, their relationships, their homes, and their families. When they got together, the men talked less about aggression and women talked less about home and family (Aries, 1976).

EXERCISE   Are these descriptions consistent with your experience? Check your intuitions by systematically observing actual same- and mixed-sex interactions.

13.4.4   Why do these differences exist?

Various attempts have been made to explain why women are more likely to use more prestige forms, to be more polite, and to work more at maintaining conversations than men. We summarize some of these explanations here:

1. Women assume greater responsibility for transmitting the culture, and are therefore more sensitive to the norms of acceptable behavior.

2. Women are less secure than men, and linguistic insecurity is manifested in the tendency to use a greater number of prestige forms.

3. Women and men have traditionally had (and continue to have, in spite of recent improvements) different occupations and to belong to different social networks. Women are still more likely than men to remain at home and are therefore less subject to peer pressure than men. Because they often don't know the people they interact with very well, women's interactions are somewhat more formal.

4. Linguistic differences between men and women reflect differences in power and prestige. Men's tendency to interrupt and take longer conversational turns can be understood as reflecting different degrees of power. Moreover, studies suggest that the characteristics of women's language and language use aren't the sole property of women; men in situations in which they have little power tend to use similar interactional strategies. Social psychologists have demonstrated that women with prestigious accents are perceived as more competent, independent, adventurous, and feminine, as well as less weak than women with less prestigious varieties.

5. Men and women differ in their assumptions about their relationships to others. Men tend to be more individualistic and to arrange themselves in competitive hierarchies. Women tend to be more egalitarian and to be more other-oriented. They tend to maintain relationships and to be more cooperative and more caring about others. The differences in preferred topics, backchanneling, conversation maintenance, politeness, turn length, and interruption would follow from the differences in socialization and assumptions.

6. Men tend to be rewarded for being tough; women for being feminine and polite. Men are therefore rewarded for language that reflects toughness; women are rewarded for language that is polite and correct. Sociolinguistic research has demonstrated that women, particularly younger, working-class women, are becoming more like men in their use of less prestigious variants. This suggests that the same peer pressures and values that determine men's (linguistic) behavior can also apply to women.

EXERCISES   1. What, if any, changes have you noticed in women's speech in recent years?
2. For each of the explanations above, select the data given in the text (and any other data you care to add) that are consistent with each explanation.

13.4.5 Do these differences matter?

These linguistic differences are important in several ways. They reflect the different identities and values of their users and are important in differentially socializing men and women. They may also be a factor in the educational and occupational differences between males and females.

The different expectations that men and women bring to interactions may be a factor in miscommunication between the sexes (Tannen, 1990). Men are less likely than women to disclose information about themselves, and their reactions to women's disclosures about themselves are frequently quite the opposite of what women expect or desire. Self-disclosure for women is an opportunity to discuss problems, to alleviate frustrations, and to share experiences. Women often describe the events of their days when they come home from work; men are less likely to do so. For women, this talk is usually intended to elicit understanding and solidarity, to maintain or develop a relationship. Men, on the other hand, often react to women's descriptions of their experiences by acting as if they had been asked to solve problems. They tend to lecture and give advice.

Boys and girls are socialized differently. Boys are expected to be more verbally aggressive; girls more passive and quiet. In classrooms, this can have the effect of drawing teachers' attention to boys far more than to girls. Boys get this attention by either misbehaving or aggressively answering teachers' questions. In either case, the boys are rewarded with attention. In fact, teachers have been shown to pay up to twice as much attention to boys as to girls, often without having any awareness of the difference (Spender, 1982). This has the fairly predictable effect of enhancing boys' self-esteem and reducing girls'.

EXERCISE   Observe a class. Do males still talk more in class than females? Do they get more attention from the teacher?

Even though girls do better than boys in early school years, this success is typically in languages and humanities rather than in mathematical and scientific subjects. This differentiation in skills tracks girls into relatively less prestigious careers and boys into the fields that offer greater income, status, and power.

As a final note to this topic, it's important to recognize that although the styles we have portrayed as typically male and typically female differ quantitatively as well as qualitatively, neither style is exclusively male or female. As Tannen (1986) illustrates, the same kinds of misunderstandings can arise among men and among women. More importantly perhaps, neither style is better in any absolute sense than the other. It's their differences in mixed interactions that cause confusion and distress. In mixed interactions, it's typically the male style that dominates; it imposes interpretations regardless of whether they were the ones intended. We don't believe that the problems can be solved by either side adopting the style of the other. Each style can be effective in specific situations. Some situations require assertion; others require the ability to listen and empathize. In keeping with the point of view we espouse throughout this book, we believe that solutions are more likely to emerge when we add rather than subtract skills. Education should improve knowledge and skills, and thereby enhance people's self-esteem and opportunities.

EXERCISE   Think of ways to find out whether you as a teacher respond differently to males and females. Would you change? How? Why?

13.5   REGISTERS

While everyone is familiar with linguistic differences among speakers from different sexes, ethnic groups, social classes, and regions, we aren't quite as aware of variation in the speech of individuals. Nonetheless, none of us speaks in the same way to our friends as we do to our bosses. **Stylistic variation** refers to variation in the speech and writing of individuals and the conditions that determine it. As Halliday (1978: p. 33) expresses it, **registers** are linguistic varieties that correspond to different uses of language. Halliday proposes that registers represent **tenor, field,** and **mode. Tenor** refers to the relationships between the participants and includes what other researchers have referred to as levels of formality or style. **Field** includes the topic and the purposes of the interaction. **Mode** refers to the medium—whether the language is written or spoken.

EXERCISE   What other contextual factors do you think affect the vocabulary, morphology, syntax, phonology, semantics, and pragmatics we use? You might consider the roles, relative ranks, and relationships among participants; the time and place where the interaction takes place; whether we are being serious or playful; and the genre. Make up or, better yet, find real examples of language which reflects contextual factors.

13.5.1   Tenor

We begin by examining the effects of formality on speakers' choices of variants. In New York City, William Labov (1972a) designed sociolinguistic interviewing techniques to study the effects of contextual changes on speech. He defined five separate contexts or levels of formality: **casual speech,** in which participants pay attention to what they're saying rather than to how they're saying it; **careful speech,** in which interviewees answer the interviewer's questions; **reading style,** in which they read a paragraph of text; **word lists,** in which they read a series of single words; **minimal pairs,** in which they read sets of word pairs that differ from each other only on a single sound—in some pairs, the sound is the one hypothesized to vary with context, e.g., *dock* versus *dark*. These contexts range from those in which minimal attention is paid to speech to those in which maximum attention is paid.

Labov used these different contexts to study the pronunciations of **sociolinguistic variables,** a set of alternative ways of pronouncing a phoneme which are ranked according to their prestige. Thus the sociolinguistic variable (r) has two values in New York City (NYC), zero and [r], i.e., the omission of *r* entirely and its pronunciation.

It's important to emphasize here that from a linguistic point of view, it's entirely arbitrary whether people choose the zero or the [r] variant. Neither pronunciation is linguistically better or worse than the other. Whatever prestige is associated with one value of a variant is determined by who uses it and the circumstances in which it occurs, and the prestige may indeed be quite fleeting. Until the 1960s, omission of *r* was the more prestigious NYC pronunciation, as it still is in England; currently in New York, it's more prestigious to pronounce your *r*s.

Labov discovered that the great majority of NYC speakers consistently replaced stigmatized (zero) variants with prestige variants as the speech situation became more formal. For example, he discovered that speakers pronounced *r* less than 20 percent of the time in casual speech, up to 36 percent in careful speech and reading style, up to 60 percent in word lists, and up to 80 percent in minimal pairs. Clearly, the more attention people pay to speech, the more often they will pronounce r and, more generally, the greater will be their use of prestige values of variants.

Linguists have studied the behavior of English speakers in several countries with respect to many sociolinguistic variables, including the ways in which *-ing, th* in words such as *thin* and *then,* and the vowels of words such as *jazz, cap,* and *off, lost* are pronounced. In each of the studies, patterns similar to those discovered by Labov were found. That is, in each case as the context became more formal, less prestigious pronunciations became less frequent and more prestigious ones became more frequent: [In] was replaced by [Iŋ], [t] and [d] were replaced by [θ] and [ð], respectively.

As we have seen, Labov's basic idea was that the formality continuum correlates directly with the degree of attention paid by speakers to how they're speaking. Other researchers have focused on the nature of the relationships among participants. Roger Brown and Albert Gilman (1960) proposed that the dimensions of power and solidarity underlie differential patterns of speech, particularly address in American English and the choice of second person pronoun in languages such as Spanish, Italian, and French, which distinguish between familiar and formal pronouns (e.g., Fr. *tu, vous*). By **power,** Brown and Gilman mean the amount of influence and control (or prestige and status) that participants wield. When two participants in an interaction differ significantly in power, e.g., a managing director and a doorman, then in American English, the more powerful is very likely to address the less powerful by his or her first name *(Good morning, George),* whereas the less powerful will very likely address the more powerful by his or her title and last name *(Good morning, Miss Smith).* The difference in power is reflected in the asymmetry in address terms. (See also Brown and Ford, 1961.)

In **solidarity,** Brown and Gilman include similarities of various sorts among participants, such as liking each other, being about the same age, having gone to the same school, belonging to the same profession, or having the same status. People who are strongly solidary interact frequently and know each other well. The greater the solidarity between participants, the greater the likelihood that they will address each other symmetrically. Two students of the same age, taking the same class, are very likely to address each other by their first names. Two faculty members at the same institution are also very likely to address each other by their first names. Adults who have little in common and who don't know each other very well, i.e., have low solidarity, are likely to address each other by their titles and last names. As they get to know each other and to discover that they have things in common, they're likely to shift to first names. Thus linguistic patterns reflect social relationships and change as relationships change.

EXERCISE   How do you think that two people who address each other asymmetrically might change to using the same forms? What would happen if you were to decide unilaterally to address your parents, teachers, or bosses by their first names?

13.5.2 Field

Field, as we noted, includes the purposes and topics of discussion. Of the two aspects, purpose is perhaps the more important, as it can determine both the topic and how it will be expressed. If our goal is to buy a car, then we will talk about the car, its history, its condition. If we talk about the weather or some other neutral subject, it will only be to establish a relationship within which to facilitate the deal. Telephone solicitors usually begin their pitch with "How are you today?" presumably to establish a friendly relationship, but this actually just warns us that a salespitch is coming. In a casual conversation, we might talk about several topics; indeed, typical conversations range smoothly over many.

By **topic** we mean the subject matter of the discourse, or part of a discourse, such as English grammar, math, our health, our most recent game of basketball, the visit to Paris last summer, politics, or religion. Topic affects primarily the vocabulary we use, but it does so in conjunction with the factors of formality and **technicality.** By **technicality** we mean the degree to which we use words derived from specific disciplines, professions, or crafts in precisely the ways in which practitioners use them most carefully. For example, a cabinet-maker may casually and nontechnically refer to changing the *blade* on a saw; in a more technical context, she might say that she is going to put on a ¾-*inch dado blade.* In a nontechnical discussion, a linguist might use the word *sound* to refer to what he would call a *phoneme* in a more technical context.

Topic, formality, and technicality affect our word choices in at least two ways. First, they can determine the words we use; some items can be referred to only with specific words. In a technical discussion of trigonometry, we would use the word *cosine* to refer to cosines. Any other expression is likely to be imprecise and misleading. We can often determine the subject matter and the level of technicality from the terms used: *macrophage* and *lipoprotein* suggest a technical discussion of organic chemistry; *quark* suggests particle physics; *byte* suggests computers.

Second, these three factors can determine the meaning of expressions. The word *morphology* means word forms in the context of a linguistics discussion, but the form and structure of animals and plants in biology. *Rip* means to cut along the grain of a piece of wood in the context of woodworking, but to tear a piece of cloth or similar material otherwise.

Each profession, craft, discipline, and field has its own special terms and meanings. To practitioners these are technical terms with specific meanings; to outsiders they may seem like obfuscatory jargon. For insiders they are not only essential for accurate communication, but they also indicate proficiency in the field.

EXERCISE   For a list of technical terms in linguistics, see our glossaries. Make a short list of technical terms from some sport or hobby that you're knowledgeable about. What is the technical meaning of each term? Do the terms have other meanings outside the context of the sport or hobby?

13.5.3 Mode

Mode refers primarily to spoken and written language. However, these two are ends of a continuum rather than simple opposites. People write out papers they will ultimately read aloud and dictate to a secretary or into a recorder what is intended to be written. It's even more accurate to view these modes as but two of a number of interacting factors, including whether the participants are face-to-face, as opposed to communicating by such **channels** as radio, television, telephone, answering machines, FAX, or E-mail, as well as by more traditional forms of written communication such as letters, journals, and books.

More important than the differences that result from the media of speech and writing are the differences due to the different situations in which speech and writing are ordinarily used. Speech occurs typically in face-to-face interaction; writing doesn't. In face-to-face communication, the parties can use space, time, and person deictics freely. In non-face-to-face interactions, they must make these aspects of context explicit by substituting nondeictic expressions. (See Chapter 2 for a discussion of deictics.) Stubbs (1980) has compiled a list of the formal devices available to either speech or writing but not to both:

Spoken and written language aren't simple translations of each other. Indeed, we haven't yet developed a writing system which can represent all of the characteristics of spoken language. For instance, the English alphabet consists of 26 letters, and so only very inadequately represents the more than forty phonemes of the language. More importantly, the intonation patterns that communicate whether an utterance is a statement, question, or command, or whether it's said jokingly or seriously, cannot be indicated, nor can the tempo of speech. (For a more detailed discussion of the relations between spoken and written language, see Chapter 12.)

> *Speech* (conversation): intonation, pitch, stress, rhythm, speed of utterance, pausing, silences, variation in loudness; other paralinguistic features, including aspiration, laughter, voice quality; timing, including simultaneous speech; co-occurrence with proxemic and kinesic signals; availability of physical context.
>
> *Writing* (printed material): spacing between words; punctuation, including parentheses; typography, including style of typeface, italicization, underlining, upper and lower case; capitalization to indicate sentence beginnings and proper nouns; inverted commas, for instance, to indicate that a term is being used critically (*Chimpanzees' 'language' is . . .*); graphics, including lines, shapes, borders, diagrams, tables; abbreviations; logograms, for example, &; layout, including paragraphing, spacing, margination, pagination, footnotes, headings and sub-headings; permanence and therefore availability of co-text. (Stubbs, 1980: p. 117, quoted in Milroy and Milroy, 1985: p. 142).

Another difference between speech and writing that comes from their typical contexts of use is their difference in formality. Writing is typically more formal than speech. This seems to be a reflection of both the necessity and opportunity of paying attention to the expression. Typically, one doesn't have a chance to formulate what one wishes to say, revise it, and then deliver it. Speech is produced "on-line"; it's unplanned. Writing, on the other hand, typically does allow for revision of the language and content before being sent. As a result, our traditions expect us to make use of that time by paying attention to how we express ourselves; we are expected to make use of the opportunity to edit. This attention to form results in more formal language; we use the more prestigious forms, e.g., we spell *-ing* as *-ing* even though we might say [In], and we write *whom* where we would probably say *who*. Our writing traditions restrict us considerably; in many instances, we are expected to follow the codified norms of written English. We will discuss the notion of language codification in our section on standardization below.

13.5.4   Genre

We have discussed the concepts of tenor, field, and mode as if they occurred separately. This is an analytic illusion. The three come together in the notion of **genre**. A **genre** is a text type, such as a Shakespearean sonnet, a university lecture, an essay in the *New Yorker,* a newspaper article, a Harlequin romance, or a telephone conversation. Each of these types of texts has characteristics that represent tenor, field, and mode. For example, a Shakespearean sonnet is very restricted in its form; it must have fourteen lines and a particular rhyme scheme and metrical pattern. The publishers of Harlequin romances provide very specific guidelines for their writers: the hero and heroine must have certain characteristics, the plot must meet certain specifications, the settings must be somewhat exotic, and the degree of explicit sexual content must be carefully controlled.

Other genres aren't so constrained. Casual conversations are spoken in face-to-face interactions; they may be about any topic, and can be between participants with any degree of solidarity and with any status relationship. They represent specific values of these factors. Because different values are reflected in a legal document, we find different expressions in the two. For example, in a rental agreement, the parties to the lease are referred to as *Tenant* and *Landlord* rather than by their names or by pronouns; we find expressions such as *pursuant to, hereinafter, covenants, hereby,* and *estoppel,* expressions we typically don't use in casual conversation.

EXERCISE   Check your lease or other legal document and make a list of other expressions and meanings specific to the legal genre.

For a description of a very systematic approach to the differences among genres, see our discussion of Biber's research in Chapter 12.

13.5.5   Speech communities

Although we have approached the topic of variation by distinguishing between variation correlated with users from variation correlated with uses of the language, Labov discovered, and others have confirmed, that the two types of variation are, in fact, tightly connected. Labov found that in a **speech community** the different classes of speakers all evaluated values of variants in the same way and all followed the same general patterns. To take an example, all classes of speakers in NYC pronounced *r* more frequently as the speech context became more formal; speakers from different classes differed from each other only in the frequency with which they pronounced *r*s. Figure 13.2 displays the pattern (adapted from Labov, 1968: p. 244).

In general, the most prestigious and powerful social groups use the most prestigious variants most frequently and the least prestigious social groups use the less prestigious variants most frequently. But all social groups agree about the relative prestige of variants, and all increase the frequency with which they use the more prestigious variants as the situation becomes more formal. This agreement about the variants and the rules for their use was taken by Labov as a defining characteristic of a speech community.

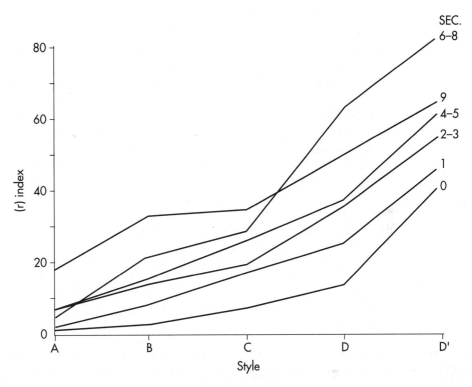

FIGURE 13.2   Frequency of use of *r* by class and formality in New York City (Adapted from Labov, 1968: p. 114)

13.6   A BRIEF HISTORY OF THE STANDARDIZATION OF ENGLISH

Written English, especially its spelling, morphology, and syntax are highly standardized. By **standardization** we mean the attempt to promote uniformity of form and meaning by eliminating variation. Standardization involves several processes. First, of course, people must *perceive a need* to intervene in the language. As societies become more complex and centralized, individuals and governments require a uniform linguistic variety that will be used and understood consistently by a majority of the people, and which will act as a unifying force. Second, they (overtly or covertly) *select* a variety and promote it as the common one. Third, this variety must be *accepted* by the relevant people, particularly those with power. Fourth, if it's accepted, then the variety can be *developed* so as to be able to perform as required in the government, administrative, legal, educational, intellectual, and religious domains. Fifth, a means must be created of defining and disseminating this variety; it must be *codified*. Dictionaries, grammars, and manuals of style are produced. Sixth, ways of *maintaining* the standard must evolve. Education, publishing, and the "complaint" tradition all contribute to the maintenance of standard English.

For about 300 years after the Norman conquest in 1066 A.D., French and Latin were the two primary languages of administration, law, scholarship, and religion in England, and consequently, there was little call for a standardized English. However, the fourteenth century saw the beginning of the restoration of English as a language of administration, literature, and religion. By 1476, when he set up England's first printing press, Caxton was dismayed by the range of variation in the language. He perceived that the linguistic variation that existed in England at the time made speakers from one region incomprehensible to speakers from another region. So he chose to print the variety of the Southeast Midlands. He justified his choice by claiming that "the men of Mercia, who are from the middle of England and as it were partners with the ends, understand the northern and southern languages better than the northerners and southerners understand each other."

Caxton wasn't the first to perceive the need for a common variety of English. English commerce had grown and prospered greatly over the previous century. England had become a unified state subject to a monarch who resided in Westminster, just outside London. It had also begun to compete with powerful centralized European kingdoms such as France (with which it was involved at this period in the Hundred Years War). These developments had already fostered the use of specific dialects as modes of wider communication, most particularly, the dialect of the Southeast Midlands and London. Caxton probably was encouraged in his choice of this dialect because it was the variety native to the wealthy London merchants, many of whom had migrated from the midlands. This was the variety in which they had been carrying out their business correspondence for about a century before Caxton. It had also become the English variety used in official government documents. Nationalistic, commercial, and administrative forces all pointed toward the need for a standard English and toward the choice of the Southeast Midlands variety to fulfill that need.

One of the effects of the introduction of printing was to reduce the amount of variation in spelling. However, this initial fixing of English spelling occurred before a major change, called the **Great Vowel Shift,** affected the majority of English long vowels. As a result, once the spelling was fixed, pronunciation and spelling began to drift apart so that the pronunciations associated with English vowel letters are currently quite varied and quite different from the pronunciations accorded them in either earlier forms of English or other European languages.

By the end of the sixteenth century English was the main language of almost all public domains of English life. It was used in religion, education, administration, and scholarship. The English Renaissance brought English scholars into contact with classical texts and languages, from which they borrowed enormous numbers of words. As a result, English became sufficiently developed to be able to function effectively in all these domains.

In spite of its obvious effectiveness in these domains, many people felt that the language required regulation. Some felt that the massive infusions of classical borrowings were inappropriate and recommended a return to a native English vocabulary. Others felt that they couldn't rely on their own judgment in choosing appropriate English words and constructions. They had nothing analogous to the grammars and rhetorics of the classical languages to guide them. Many felt that English was subject to such rapid change that their writings would be as inaccessible to subsequent generations as Old English was to them and as Chaucer was becoming. These feelings led in the early eighteenth century to a call for an academy modeled on that of France, which would "ascertain" the language, i.e., settle doubtful usage. This proposal was discussed at length and eventually rejected on various grounds, including that it violated the spirit of English freedom and individuality. (A similar debate occurred in the United States after the American revolution with identical results.) The task of fixing the language subsequently fell to private individuals.

Various movements during these centuries contributed to the codification of English. In the eighteenth and nineteenth centuries, the orthoepist movement attempted to correct pronunciation, and lexicographers, rhetoricians, and grammarians attempted to fix its spelling, words, morphology, syntax, and usage. To complete this section, we will briefly examine the development of the English dictionary and of school grammar (a topic we return to in Chapter 14).

13.6.1 Dictionaries

When we consult a modern dictionary, especially a comprehensive or unabridged one such as the *Oxford English Dictionary (OED)* or Webster's *New Twentieth Century,* we do so with a number of expectations. From an organizational point of view, we expect the dictionary to list its entries alphabetically. We expect it to contain any word we inquire about and to include the names of mythological characters; historical personages; names of the capitals of states and countries; specialized lists of words, such as biblical terms; and also such supplementary information as lists of universities and colleges. For each entry, we expect the dictionary to tell us authoritatively its part of speech, its etymology, how to spell and pronounce it, what meanings to associate with it, and how to use it appropriately. In many dictionaries, its history, meanings, and uses will be illustrated by carefully chosen quotations from respected texts.

While we might think that it's only a matter of common sense that dictionaries should have these characteristics, there is, in fact, nothing natural or inevitable about them. The modern dictionary is the product of a history that dates only from the late eighteenth century. Before that, the individual characteristics that we consider a package developed independently of each other. Even something as apparently sensible as alphabetical ordering wasn't fully used (although it was known) until 1604. Dictionaries fulfill a desire created by particular historical and cultural circumstances. Before the eighteenth century, there was little need for dictionaries with modern characteristics. The modern dictionary fulfills a desire for authoritative information based on the usages of prestigious users of the language.

All of the elements of the modern dictionary are present in Dr. Samuel Johnson's *A Dictionary of the English Language* (1755), published in two large folio volumes containing 40,000 entries. Johnson's contributions to lexicography were three: (1) he recognized that words may have multiple senses, which for the most part he clearly and carefully (if occasionally idiosyncratically) defined; (2) he richly illustrated the meanings and use of each entry with quotations from literary and scholarly works, and (3) he labeled words that he believed his readers should avoid with such terms as "cant," "low," "ludicrous."

EXERCISES   1. Discuss Johnson's comment on *lesser:* "A barbarous corruption of *less,* formed by the vulgar from the habit of terminating comparatives in *-er;* afterwards adopted by poets, and then by writers of prose." What inferences do you think might be drawn by Johnson or his readers about someone who uses the form *lesser?*

   2. Johnson defined *lexicographer* as follows: "A writer of dictionaries; a harmless drudge that busies himself in tracing the original and detailing the significance of words." Are lexicographers really harmless?

According to the introduction to his dictionary, Johnson at first intended to stabilize (or **fix**) the language for all time. As he labored, he realized the inevitability of language change and decided that the best he could do was to "give longevity to that which its own nature forbids to be immortal." In particular, he abandoned the hope of fixing English pronunciation. Nonetheless, even though he did occasionally recognize more than one spelling for a word, his dictionary was instrumental in fixing English spelling, in large measure because of Johnson's own prestige and authority, bolstered considerably by the fact that he based his decisions primarily on upper-class usage.

In the new United States, debate raged regarding the language such a newly independent country should have. In the late eighteenth and early nineteenth centuries, Noah Webster produced a grammar, a reader, a speller, and a number of dictionaries. Besides being anxious to improve the deficiencies he saw in Johnson's work, Webster was caught up in the movement to Americanize English and was successful in distinguishing some American spellings from their British counterparts (e.g., *ax* for *axe*, *tire* for *tyre*), although not nearly as many as he originally intended. The major systematic changes he introduced are:

BRITISH	UNITED STATES	EXAMPLES
-our	-or	neighbour/neighbor
-re	-er	theatre/theater
-dge-	-dg-	judgement/judgment
-que	-ck	cheque/check
-ce	-se	defence/defense
-exion	-ection	inflexion/inflection
-ise	-ize	realise/realize
-CC-	-C-	waggon/wagon
		travelled/traveled

(-CC- represents double consonants.)

In 1857, a project began that proved a monument to nineteenth-century historical scholarship—the *Oxford English Dictionary* project. The authors aimed at including every word that appeared in English since 1150, with accurate etymologies, and their various forms and meanings. The OED was published in twelve volumes between 1884 and 1928. Its first supplement appeared in 1933 and later supplements appeared in the 1970s and 1980s. It was made available in a two-volume microprint edition in 1971, and as a result, has become widely known. It has recently been published in a second updated edition and in computer readable form.

The expectation dies hard that a dictionary will warn its readers about words, especially those to which objection might be taken because they're informal, obscene, or slang. However, in 1961, the Merriam-Webster Company published Webster's *Third New International Dictionary,* which abandoned the prescriptive practices of previous editions and confined itself to describing the language. The outcry was such that many institutions refused to accept the *Third* as their guide and continued with the second edition of 1934. The American Heritage Publishing Company was so concerned with Merriam-Webster's dereliction of its duty that American Heritage offered to buy the rights to the dictionary and to recall all copies of the "defective" edition. When American Heritage was refused, it decided to publish a dictionary of its own. American Heritage assembled a 100-member panel which included writers, journalists, and a single linguist. The editors consulted this panel about controversial usages and included their responses in the entries. However, this procedure failed in its goal to provide consistent guidance. The panel members were as divided about those usages as the rest of us, which, of course, is why the usages are controversial in the first place. [For a revealing and entertaining discussion of usage panels, see Baron (1982).]

13.6.2 Grammars

Should we use *It is me* or *It is I, Who did you see?* or *Whom did you see?, Who did you speak to?* or *To whom did you speak?* Do multiple ("double") negatives intensify the negation or "destroy each other"? The fact that we continue to be concerned with shibboleths like these is a testament to the power of the late eighteenth-century grammarians who set out to codify the grammar of English.

In the late eighteenth century, people placed great faith in the orderliness and rationality of the universe. If Newton could demonstrate the laws of gravity and Linnaeus could create a system for classifying plants and animals, then surely rational order could be imposed on language. Added to the assumption of orderliness were the results of centuries of scholarship in the classical languages and even considerable knowledge of earlier forms of English, as well as a strong sense of the disorderly energy of English. The temper of the times was ideally suited to the task of regulating the language.

According to Archbishop Lowth, a clergyman with a knowledge of Latin, Greek, Hebrew, various modern languages, and Old English, "Grammar is very much neglected." He set out to remedy this deficiency by writing *A Short Introduction to English Grammar,* which appeared in 1762 and went through twenty-two editions in the eighteenth century. Lowth's grammar was imitated by many other authors of English grammars. Indeed, many used Lowth's technique of stating a rule, giving examples of its use, and then giving examples of its violation, often culled from well-respected writers. In fact, Lowth's own wording of particular rules crops up in numerous grammars written during the nineteenth and even twentieth centuries, most notoriously, his claim that "Two negatives in English destroy each other, or are equivalent to an affirmative" (Lowth, 1762/1979: p. 95).

The concept of grammar that we have inherited from the eighteenth century is quite different from the one we have presented throughout this book. According to the American Lindley Murray, one of Lowth's more successful imitators and author of *An English Grammar,* first published in 1795 and frequently reissued throughout the nineteenth century, "English grammar is the art of speaking and writing the English language with propriety." This definition focuses on language use rather than on the language system itself, a confusion that remains to this day.

Eighteenth-century grammarians were agreed that the language needed regulation. When they disagreed, it was primarily over the criteria to be used in justifying the regulations. There were two main positions. The first, represented by Joseph Priestley in his *Rudiments of English Grammar* (1761), held that current use among certain groups of people was the only guide. The idea that certain groups of people spoke the best English has a long history. Just who spoke that variety changed from one century to another. Caxton, as we saw, preferred the Mercian dialect because it could be understood by northerners and southerners as well as by the men of "myddle englond." By the early sixteenth century, the preferred variety was that used in the royal court. By the seventeenth century, the favored variety had shifted to that of the learned and cultivated. By the eighteenth century, this had narrowed to the speech of the universities. Common use was a criterion preferred by only a minority of the grammarians who codified English.

The second, and ultimately dominant point of view, appealed to a range of criteria, including logic, linguistic history, clarity, and personal taste. Lowth's claim that "Two negatives . . . are equivalent to an affirmative" is derived from logic and mathematics. However, English (like many other languages) has used double, and indeed, multiple, negation throughout its history to indicate the force of a speaker's denial. Chaucer and Shakespeare used it, as did most writers until the eighteenth century, and as speakers of nonstandard varieties do to this day.

Linguistic history was also called into service. For example, because Latin used a preposition which could be translated as *from* rather than one meaning *to* with the Latin original for *averse,* English speakers should use *averse from* rather than *averse to.*

Notions of clarity were also used to support a choice. Murray held it to be a "capital rule" that the words which are most closely related to each other semantically "should be placed in the sentence as near to each other as possible." From this it follows that *He only eats cake* is unacceptably vague or ambiguous and that if we mean that the only thing he eats is cake, then we should say *He eats only cake.*

Sometimes authors relied on their own taste. Murray asserts that the practice of separating "the preposition from its noun in order to connect different prepositions with the same noun: as, 'To suppose the zodiac and planets to be efficient of, and antecedent to, themselves.' . . . is always inelegant." He also claimed that placing a preposition before a relative pronoun is more "graceful" than stranding the preposition. However, the amount of justification for a particular choice varied greatly from one writer to another. Some were content merely to assert their preferences as rules.

What appears to have occurred in the late eighteenth century is that the preferred and dispreferred expressions were in competition among speakers generally, including among the wealthy and educated. Grammarians standardizing the language felt that they had to eliminate all but one variant. Occasionally, they felt the need to justify their choices, and so searched for criteria.

The choice of criteria allowed certain inferences about the speaker or writer who used a dispreferred form. Because multiple negatives were banned on logical grounds, one who used them could be assumed to be illogical. If a construction was inelegant, then its users lacked taste. As a result, the choices and criteria used by the eighteenth-century grammarians licensed the negative inferences that are still made about people who use the dispreferred forms. There is, of course, no linguistic reason to prefer one of these disputed forms over another, so judgments based on them are really social evaluations of their users regardless of whether or not they're expressed as linguistic judgments. If grammar is the art of writing and speaking with propriety, then by definition those who fail to adhere to the canons laid down by the grammarians speak and write improperly.

A further motivation for the appearance and popularity of grammars such as Lowth's and Murray's was that the late eighteenth century was a time of considerable upward social mobility. It's well known from modern sociolinguistic studies that upwardly mobile people tend to be "linguistically insecure"; i.e., they tend to assume that their speech may not be correct, and that there is a correct form of speech which they can learn and which will allow them to pass without comment within the class to which they aspire. Prescriptive grammars fulfilled a need among these upwardly mobile speakers. People who learned the rules that the grammars laid down and who avoided the objectionable expressions could expect to be accepted in their new class.

Although eighteenth-century standardizers set out to regulate and fix the entire language (i.e., to prevent it from changing further), they had only mixed success. They succeeded primarily in eliminating some variation from formal written English. They managed to fix English spelling; we tolerate very little spelling variation and a number of attempted reforms since that time have failed. These standardizers also managed to ban a number of constructions from written English (some quite useful, such as multiple negation). And they succeeded in convincing English speakers to retain certain morphological contrasts which would probably have disappeared by now (*whom* versus *who*). Although there is still the widespread belief that some pronunciations are better than others, standard English is pronounced in many accents, so they failed to standardize English pronunciation. They also failed to eliminate morphological and syntactic variation from the spoken language. In particular, the standardizers failed to eliminate variation that is important for speakers' personal and social identities. Unfortunately, they succeeded in setting up a logic that allows nonstandard speakers to be judged illogical, uneducated, even ineducable, on the basis of their speech.

13.7   LANGUAGE BELIEFS AND ATTITUDES

We all have beliefs and attitudes about languages and their varieties. Some of these are harmless, such as the belief that French is the most appropriate language for love. Others reflect their holders' chauvinism, such as Voltaire's notion that French mirrored thought better than other languages. Others are aesthetic judgments, and so can be admittedly subjective, such as an enjoyment of southern accents or the sound of Japanese. Others, as we will see, aren't at all benign and can affect people's reputations and economic well-being.

Probably there are no speech communities in which people don't have language attitudes. Nonetheless, people don't always report their beliefs accurately when asked directly about them. As a result, linguists and psychologists have devised methods of eliciting these beliefs indirectly. Perhaps the most effective (certainly the best-known and most widely used) technique is the **matched guise test.** This involves finding speakers who are fluent in two languages or language varieties and having them tape-record the same message in their two varieties. When a number of these bilingual or bidialectal tapes have been made, they're played to subjects who are then asked to evaluate them in various ways. We illustrate this graphically in Figure 13.3.

Luhman (1990) used the matched guise technique in a study of the language attitudes of university graduates in Kentucky. Fifty university graduates from various parts of Kentucky were asked to rate tapes of speakers who were fluent in SE and Appalachian English according to various characteristics, including education, intelligence, economic status, and success. The SE guises were rated consistently and significantly higher than the Appalachian ones. Matched guise studies have compared the beliefs about SE and a large number of other English dialects (as well as many pairs of languages). The results have been consistent with

Real Speaker
(For example, Mary Smith)

Mary Smith speaking SE   Mary Smith speaking NSE
  (= Speaker guise A)   (= Speaker guise B)

Evaluators

"Guise A is taller, better-educated, more intelligent, wealthy, successful, and attractive than guise B."

FIGURE 13.3   The Matched Guise Technique

those of the Kentucky study: SE speakers are rated higher than NSE speakers on factors such as intelligence, competence, education, and success.

Where do such beliefs come from? Perhaps their single most important source is the ideology of standardization (Leith, 1983; Milroy and Milroy, 1985). Recall that standardization aims at linguistic uniformity in the service of functional efficiency. In theory, if everyone were to use the same forms with the same meanings, then miscommunication would be less likely. Unfortunately, the process of standardizing English included stereotyping and stigmatizing varieties that didn't conform to the prescribed norms. Milroy and Milroy (1985: p. 40) characterize the assumptions underlying this aspect of standardization as:

1. There is one and only one correct way of speaking and/or writing English.
2. Deviations from this norm are illiteracies, or barbarisms, and non-standard forms are irregular and perversely deviant.
3. People ought to use the standard language and it is quite right to discriminate against non-standard users, as such usage is a sign of stupidity, ignorance, perversity, moral degeneracy, etc.

Attitudes toward linguistic varieties also reflect attitudes toward, and beliefs about, their speakers. We tend to attribute our beliefs about the speakers to their varieties. Generally though, linguists and sociolinguists take the position that language attitudes are fundamentally attitudes about speakers.

Until very recently, children speaking NSE varieties were frequently assumed to suffer from cognitive or cultural deficits and were often placed in classes for the retarded. While few academics would now support the *deficit theory* of NSE, some teachers and student teachers may still subscribe to a version of it. Cecil (1988) reports that teachers had significantly higher expectations for the SE guises when they rated tapes of Black children speaking BE and SE on a matched guise test. For better or worse, students tend to fulfill their teachers' expectations.

But it's not only teachers who have these beliefs. Students do too, and at a very early age. U.S. children as young as 3 years old can already distinguish between SE and BE, and already believe that SE is better. Middle- and upper-class children very accurately reflect the general societal beliefs about varieties. Black children do not reflect these beliefs as accurately, but nonetheless, they generally agree with the evaluation of SE speech.

The matched guise studies show that SE is associated with the positive characteristics of the power dimension—greater prestige, intelligence, competence, success, and status. NSE varieties are negatively associated with these aspects of power—lower status, less intelligence, success, and prestige. SE and SE speakers are accorded overt **prestige,** i.e., positive values espoused by powerful elements of society. Speakers are generally aware of which elements are overtly prestigious and which are stigmatized.

EXERCISE   Imagine that you are answering a "grammar hotline" and a caller who identifies herself as a "middle-aged educated lady" asks for advice on correcting the grammar of her fiancé, "a man who is a fine person, but has only a high school education."
1. How would you respond to this caller?
2. What grammatical errors do you think this man might make?
3. Why would the "lady" want to correct her fiancé's grammar?
4. Do you think that the fiancé would appreciate her efforts?
5. Could there be any significance to the fact that the caller characterizes herself as a "lady" (rather than a woman) and her fiancé as a "man" (rather than a gentleman)?

13.7.1 Why do stigmatized varieties persist?

We mentioned earlier that people's speech provides evidence about where they're from, their social class, and their ethnic group. From the speaker's point of view, her choice of variants is an act of identity. It communicates her position in a multidimensional social and cultural space, most especially, membership in kin, friendship, residence, and workplace groups. People for whom these identities are extremely important will refuse to give up the linguistic characteristics that communicate them, even though they know that retaining their identities can be disadvantageous. For these people, the solidarity advantages of retaining NSE varieties outweigh the potential power associated with more prestigious speech.

Matched guise tests have shown that there are very positive values associated with NS varieties. For example, arguments presented in SE are rated as intelligent and logical, whereas arguments presented in the raters' own NSE variety are reported to be more persuasive. Speakers of SE are rated as successful but distant and not very reliable; NSE speakers are rated as less successful but more friendly and attractive. NSE variants are also widely regarded as indicating toughness, and because many men value toughness, they tend to adopt NS variants.

Members of the lowest social classes generally speak the most stigmatized NSE varieties. They often belong to **dense** and **multiplex** networks of friends and family. In a dense network, everybody knows everybody else. In a multiplex network, members are connected to each other by many types of ties. Members may be each other's workmates, cousins, friends, as well as neighbors. Although such close-knit groups provide a great deal of support and security for their members, a network can effectively constrain its members' behavior by threatening to cut them off from this support. As language is often an indicator of allegiance to a group, a member who begins to use more prestigious variants risks sacrificing the solidarity of the network for uncertain social status. Few choose status.

EXERCISE   To get a sense of the difficulties facing NSE speakers who attempt to use SE at home, try speaking very carefully, correctly, and formally to your family and close friends (without telling them why, of course). What reactions did they have? What did they say to you? Will you continue to speak to them in this way?

NSE variants persist because they're powerful symbols of group membership. Because people generally view the groups they belong to more favorably than other groups, and because their own self-esteem is partly derived from the esteem in which they hold their groups, they cannot easily relinquish the linguistic characteristics that symbolize their group membership. In general, while standard forms are associated with looser networks, stigmatized forms are maintained by close-knit networks, whose power would be hard to overestimate. Such networks mediate between individuals and the larger society and transmit the knowledge and values associated with languages, language varieties, and language functions. If a network values the forms and functions of language favored by the educational system, then its members may have the motivation to enhance their skills in those functions and thereby gain an educational advantage. On the other hand, if the network doesn't value these functions, members may lack the motivation to develop their skills in the formal, planned, relatively context-free discourses of the school.

We have used the expression **overt prestige** to characterize the evaluation accorded a variety by society as a whole. Overt prestige is associated with power and social status. However, NSE varieties are accorded **covert prestige** (group membership, solidarity, and toughness) by their speakers (and by many who don't typically speak them). These two forces pull in opposite directions. In his studies of Black teenage peer groups, Labov (1972b) has shown a positive correlation between the degree of membership in the group and the use of BE forms. The core members used BE forms most frequently, peripheral members used them less, and boys who didn't belong to the groups at all, used them the least. Because of the importance of its covert prestige, students may be very unwilling or even unable to give up a NS variety just because teachers and others tell them that doing so is important for their social advancement. Given the uncertainty of this advancement, their choice isn't entirely unrealistic.

13.7.2   Linguistic accommodation

What happens when speakers of different dialects must communicate with each other? There are several possibilities. One or both could speak in a way that is more similar to the other's dialect. That is, they could **converge** toward the other's variety by reducing the linguistic differences between them. Alternatively, they could **diverge**, i.e., increase the differences between their varieties. Or they could neither converge nor diverge. What reasons could speakers have for choosing one or the other of these possibilities? **Accommodation theory,** developed by the social psychologist Howard Giles and his associates, attempts to answer these questions (Giles and Powesland, 1975; Giles and St. Clair, 1979, 1985).

EXERCISE   Make a list of the changes you make to your speech as you speak to someone who isn't fully fluent in English, such as a young child or a foreigner. What are those changes designed to do?

By converging, speakers reduce the differences between them. In doing so, they can increase comprehensibility and may be viewed more favorably by their audiences. When speakers of prestigious forms of a language converge toward the less prestigious variety of their audience, they may be perceived as kinder and more trustworthy. Convergence is often interpreted as a desire for the other's social approval. Students who converge toward their teachers' varieties are more likely to be perceived as better, more intelligent, and more cooperative. They're likely also to become more comprehensible because speakers of SE are generally not very familiar with NSE varieties. Teachers may view nonconvergence as indicating that the student has no interest in their approval or in education.

However, there are complicating factors. Audiences will generally view convergence on a speaker's part favorably unless they believe that the speaker is converging because either he has to or he is being manipulative. When members of groups which are suspicious of each other attempt to communicate, they may view convergence as due to pressure or deviousness. When speakers don't converge, audiences may assume that this is because they don't want to do so rather than because they cannot. That is, the members of such groups may attribute negative or hostile motives to speakers whether or not they converge.

As we noted earlier, NSE varieties persist because they can indicate their speakers' social identities. When speakers from different groups speak to each other, they may wish to accentuate rather than minimize their differences—because either the groups are hostile to each other or one group feels that its legitimacy is under attack or one (or both) feels that the other's attitudes, habits, or appearances are undesirable. In such situations, speakers may diverge by increasing their linguistic differences.

Ethnic group members, such as Blacks, Chicanos, and Native Americans who value their ethnic identities and wish to maintain them and thereby maintain their distinctiveness from the majority culture, signal their intentions by using their native English varieties with both members of their own groups and outsiders. Speech divergence in interactions with outsiders, particularly representatives of the majority culture, can make ethnic members feel favorably distinct.

EXERCISE   Review your analysis of your tape of a Black orator. Did she or he accommodate to the non-Black audience? How did you react to this? How do you think the audience was affected?

13.8   EDUCATIONAL ISSUES

No normal student, whether a speaker of SE or NSE, comes to school with only a single linguistic variety. Each student comes with a **linguistic repertoire** of varieties to choose from. This repertoire and the knowledge of when to use each variety constitute the student's **communicative competence.** The goal of English language education is to provide students with the opportunity to add to their linguistic repertoire and to enhance their communicative competence. Specifically, because students' repertoires may initially be limited to informal varieties suitable for face-to-face interaction, the goals are (1) to add to students' knowledge of SE forms and their meanings and (2) to add to their ability to use SE in the formal contexts in which they must be able to function in later education and in the workplace.

Because many of those formal contexts employ written SE, students need to add to their reading and writing skills in such genres as the formal term paper and various types of essay. Teachers need to be thoroughly familiar with the conventions of these genres, especially their linguistic and organizational characteristics. Unfortunately, they cannot always depend on the accuracy of textbooks, writing handbooks, and style manuals, especially with regard to the appropriate linguistic forms. These books derive primarily from the eighteenth-century prescriptive grammars and rhetorics rather than from current research into the actual practices of professional writers. As an exercise, students and teachers might compare the textbook recommendations with the forms used by professional writers of the genres being studied. [See Delahunty (1991) on expletive *It is;* Garvey and Lindstrom (1989) on passive; Huckin and Pesante (1988) on existential *There.*]

Even though SE is required for public, formal uses, and is associated with the dimension of power, it's important to remember that students' NSE varieties are extremely important to their identities and are appropriate in contexts in which SE might not be, e.g., at home or among friends. Fortunately, learning standard English doesn't require unlearning or abandoning native NSE varieties or other languages. Many people are skilled users of both a native NSE variety and SE. The teacher's role is to provide the opportunity, the encouragement, and the models for students to add SE to their repertoire of linguistic skills. Because teachers' expectations of students can be based on students' linguistic varieties and can effectively determine students' school performance, it's very important that teachers be aware of their own language attitudes and their effects.

As Cheshire (1982a) has demonstrated, students who speak NSE varieties become confused when teachers don't distinguish clearly among native dialect forms, target SE forms, and forms that occur in neither. For this reason, teachers should become very familiar with the details of their students' dialects. This requires that they put aside any feelings that nonstandard forms indicate laziness or stupidity, and carefully observe what forms are used and in what circumstances. Teachers must also avoid assuming that because a group of people uses a particular form, its members use *only* that form. Remember that even the lowest classes studied by Labov in NYC used some *r* and even the highest classes occasionally omitted it. The use of a form is typically variable and its frequency increases or decreases as the context shifts. Studying data of this sort requires tape-recording the speech of native speakers under a variety of circumstances, transcribing the tapes accurately, counting the occurrences of each value of the variable, and comparing the percentages of occurrence of each value across contexts. This is a time-consuming task, but it's one which students find fascinating. The results include not only increased understanding of the local dialect but also increased awareness and respect for it among students and teachers. [For an amusing and very readable discussion of these and related issues, see Andersson and Trudgill (1990).]

EXERCISE   Make a list of all the nonstandard expressions in a batch of your students' essays. For each expression, determine whether it derives from the students' native variety, from their imperfect grasp of SE forms, or from informal spoken English. You might consult Wolfram (1991) for this exercise.

13.8.1   Speech and language testing

At many points in their school careers, U.S. children are subjected to standardized tests of their knowledge and achievement. Most of these tests depend on language and many attempt to assess children's linguistic skills. It's notorious that children from poorer sections of society, especially minority and NSE-speaking children, do much more poorly on these tests than children of white, educated, middle-class parents. Through the early 1970s, educators routinely interpreted this fact as indicating that these children were linguistically deficient, due to either their genetic or their cultural inheritance. Since that time, sociolinguistic research has helped to discredit this interpretation and to focus attention instead on the linguistic and sociolinguistic differences among these groups and on the linguistic and sociolinguistic deficiencies of the tests themselves.

As we have emphasized in a number of places in this book, from a linguistic point of view, all languages and all varieties of languages are equal in their complexity and all normal adult speakers control equally complex grammars. No varieties are underdeveloped versions of other varieties and no normal adults, regardless of their varieties, are linguistically deficient. (This isn't to deny the important social differences among varieties.) It follows that tests that take the variety of one group as their norm will inevitably be unreliable guides to the abilities of other groups. The fact that many standardized tests take standard English as their norm, and especially a very formal, written version of the standard, means that speakers who don't control SE will do less well on the tests than speakers who do control it. Such tests are often interpreted as indicators of children's linguistic ability in its entirety. However, the best that can be assumed is that the tests assess their subjects' control of SE, and even this interpretation may be too optimistic. The discussion that follows is based on Wolfram 1991, but see also Wolfram and Christian 1989.

EXERCISE   Standardized tests are "normed" on particular populations. That is, they take the responses of a particular group as the basis for evaluating the responses of everyone to whom the test is administered. On which groups are the tests administered in your school district normed? How representative are those groups of the students in your district? What implications does this have for the validity and fairness of the test results?

As we mentioned, some tests are rigidly normed on SE and responses that aren't expressed in SE are judged to be incorrect regardless of how appropriate their meaning and form might otherwise be. For example, the California Achievement Test (CAT), includes questions like the following, which asks lower-level elementary schoolchildren to choose from the italicized forms the one that they think is correct:

Beth *came/come* home and cried.

A child who chose *come* would be scored lower in linguistic ability than one who chose *came,* even though *come* is widely used by NSE speakers throughout the English-speaking world as the past tense of *come.*

Not only does the CAT expect SE, it expects a very formal version of it. The correct choice in *When can/may I come again?* is *may,* in spite of the fact that even SE speakers use *can* in all but the most formal occasions.

Some dialects substitute sounds that are acquired earlier for those that are acquired later, just as children do. In a number of English and U.S. varieties, particularly BE, adults use [f] and [v] for [θ] and [ð], pronouncing pairs such as *with* and *whiff* alike. Children who speak these varieties natively are likely to be assessed as having underdeveloped auditory perception skills by tests such as the Wepman Auditory Discrimination Test, even though adult speakers of their varieties use exactly the same forms.

Many tests focus on grammatical morphemes as an easily quantified indicator of syntactic ability. The Illinois Test of Psycholinguistic Abilities (ITPA) includes the following routine: the testor shows the child two pictures, one with one bed the other with two beds, and says "Here is one bed and here are two ———" and the child is expected to supply the missing form. Only *beds,* the SE form, may be scored as correct. Because some NSE varieties allow the omission of plural markers, especially after numerals, their speakers may be judged to have defective morphology and syntax, and perhaps even to have no understanding of number.

EXERCISE   Do the standardized tests used in your school district accept only SE? If not, how do they accommodate dialect variation?

It might be argued that these linguistic problems can be rectified simply by allowing genuine NSE forms as well as SE forms to count as correct (and some tests exist which do make allowances for grammatical and lexical differences among varieties). However, the sociolinguistic problems associated with many standardized tests are much more serious.

Recall that social groups may differ in how they use language. They can differ in the kinds of linguistic routines they employ and in the rules governing how much one person may say to another. Some tests (and probably all classrooms) include a three part routine called the **test cycle**: the teacher elicits information, the student responds with the information, and the teacher provides feedback. The following example is from Milroy and Milroy (1985: pp. 147–148):

T: Those letters have special names.
Do you know what it is?
What is the name we give to those letters?

S: Vowels.

T: They're vowels aren't they?

In routines like this, the teacher or testor is assumed to know the answer, and the children are expected to display their knowledge. Educated middle-class parents encourage display of this sort even in very young children, who become quite familiar with the routine. Whether teachers developed the routine and middle-class people simply adopted it or vice versa, white middle-class children typically enter school prepared for this type of interaction with their teachers.

Children of other social classes may not be familiar with the routine, as their parents may not use it. In fact, many may find that telling someone what they already obviously know violates their own social norms. Others may feel that whatever they say is likely to be used against them, and so they say little or nothing in response to teachers' and testors' attempts at elicitation. This reticence can be compounded if the children have learned (as many working-class children have) that they should be seen but not heard by adults. Many Black children who are extremely voluble among their peers have been judged nonverbal because they responded with silence to unfamiliar white adult testors. In general, if tests and the testing situation mean different things to different groups of subjects, then they cannot in principle measure the same skills in all children.

Finally, some tests such as the Peabody Picture Vocabulary Test (PPVT) are based on wrong assumptions about the nature of language. PPVT purports to assess "word knowledge." It does so by asking subjects to select from a set of pictures of things or activities the one that can be labeled by the word given by the testor. Besides the fact that some of the words are dialectally restricted and some of the items and activities are culture specific, this assumes that "word knowledge" is merely the ability to pair a word and its referent. As we saw in earlier chapters, lexical knowledge includes knowledge about how a word is pronounced; what other words it's morphologically related to; which syntactic categories it may belong to; what inflections it can take; how to use it in sentences; what other words and concepts it's related to; what levels of style it occurs in, and what it entails, presupposes, and implicates (Wolfram, 1991: p. 236).

EXERCISE   How do the tests used in your school district assess word knowledge?

13.8.2   What's to be done?

If tests are to be used to evaluate children's overall language development, then they should be designed to take dialect variation into account. Some such tests are available, such as the Bankson Language Screening Test; others can be appropriately adapted, such as Developmental Sentence Scoring and Content Form and Use Analysis. Because teachers and testors may have to assume responsibility for adapting tests to accommodate linguistic variation, they will have to become familiar with the native varieties of the students they evaluate.

Because some children retreat to silence in the formal testing situation and because a sampling of morphological knowledge is an inadequate indicator of a child's syntactic knowledge, it's important to get a sample of the child's spontaneous speech, preferably with peers. Even a 10-minute sample can give a great deal of information about a child's grammatical knowledge.

If standardized tests which are normed on SE and accept only SE responses as correct must be used, then they should be interpreted cautiously. At best, they may give an indication of the student's knowledge of formal SE. (See Milroy and Milroy, 1985; Wolfram, 1991.)

EXERCISE   Get together a small group of students (preferably friends) who have done poorly on some standardized test of their linguistic abilities.
1. Reduce the sociolinguistic difference between the students and the testor by having an adult member of their own social group administer the test.
2. Accept local NSE forms as well as SE forms in response to test items.
3. Tape the students as they perform a school task together without an adult present.

What picture of the students' linguistic abilities emerges under these circumstances. How does it compare with their initial test scores?

13.9   CONCLUSION

A realistic understanding of linguistic variation, its social correlates, and its implications for education, especially for language testing, is vitally important for today's English teacher. We have tried to give as broad an account of variation as space allows; however, we have barely scratched the surface. We hope that you will read the books and articles in our sources and further reading list.

Besides presenting teachers with challenging issues, linguistic variation can also be a valuable educational resource. In itself it's of great interest to students, who are always eager to learn more about how people speak. And it can provide readily available raw material for data gathering, analysis, and hypothesis testing, the steps in critical thinking and scientific inquiry. Students can study the forms used in their own communities, the sociolinguistic rules governing their use, the attitudes of different community members toward them and their users, and how they're used in literature. They can evaluate the prescriptions of handbooks and textbooks by comparing them with data they collect from books and magazines. Open, informed discussion of language can not only help reduce the prejudices of students and teachers, but it can also alleviate the difficulties faced by many minority and dialect-speaking children in the schools, and thereby alleviate some of their teachers' difficulties. [See Wolfram and Christian (1989).]

REFERENCES AND RESOURCES

Aitchison, J. 1991. *Language Change: Progress or Decay?* 2d ed. Cambridge: Cambridge University Press.

Andersson, L., and P. Trudgill. 1990. *Bad Language.* Oxford: Blackwell.

Aries, E. 1976. "Interaction Patterns and Themes of Male, Female, and Mixed Groups." *Small Group Behavior,* 7:7–18.

Bailey, R. W., and M. Görlach, eds. 1982. *English as a World Language.* Ann Arbor, MI: University of Michigan Press.

Baron, D. E. 1982. *Grammar and Good Taste.* New Haven, CT: Yale University Press.

———. 1986. *Grammar and Gender.* New Haven, CT: Yale University Press.

Brown, R. and A. Gilman. 1960. "The Pronouns of Power and Solidarity." In T.A. Sebeok, ed., *Style in Language.* Cambridge, MA: The MIT Press, 253–276.

———, and M. Ford. 1961. "Address in American English." *Journal of Abnormal Psychology,* 62:375–385.

Burling, R. 1973. *English in Black and White.* New York: Holt, Rinehart and Winston.

Carver, C. M. 1989. *American Regional Dialects.* Ann Arbor, MI: University of Michigan Press.

Cassidy, F. G. 1982. "Geographical Variation of English in the United States." In R. W. Bailey and M. Görlach, eds., *English as a World Language.* Ann Arbor, MI: University of Michigan Press.

Cecil, N. L. 1988. "Black Dialect and Academic Success: A Study of Teacher Expectations." *Reading Improvement,* 25:34–38.

Chambers, J. K., and P. Trudgill. 1980. *Dialectology.* Cambridge: Cambridge University Press.

Cheshire, J. 1982a. "Dialect Features and Linguistic Conflict." *Educational Review,* 34(1):53–67.

———. 1982b. *Variation in an English Dialect.* Cambridge: Cambridge University Press.

Coates, J. 1986. *Women, Men and Language.* London: Longman.

Delahunty, G. 1991. "The Powerful Pleonasm." *Written Communication,* 8(2):213–239.

Fischer, J. L. 1958. "Social Influences on the Choice of a Linguistic Variant." *Word,* 14:47–56.

Garvey, J., and D. Lindstrom. 1989. "Pros' Prose Meets Writer's Workbench." *Computers and Composition,* 6(2):81–109.

Giles, H., and P. F. Powesland. 1975. *Speech Style and Social Evaluation.* London: Academic Press.

Giles, H., and R. N. St. Clair, eds. 1979. *Language and Social Psychology.* Baltimore, MD: University Park Press.

———. 1985. *Recent Advances in Language, Communication, and Social Psychology.* London: Lawrence Erlbaum Associates.

Halliday, M. A. K. 1978. *Language as Social Semiotic.* Baltimore, MD: University Park Press.

Heath, S. B. 1983. *Ways with Words.* Cambridge: Cambridge University Press.

Huckin, T., and L. Pesante. 1988. "Existential *there.*" *Written Communication,* 5(3):368–391.

Labov, W. 1968. "The Reflection of Social Processes in Linguistic Structure." In J. Fishman, ed., *Readings in the Sociology of Language.* The Hague: Mouton, 240–251.

———. 1972a. *Sociolinguistic Patterns.* Philadelphia, PA: University of Pennsylvania Press.

———. 1972b. *Language in the Inner City: Studies in the Black English Vernacular.* Philadelphia, PA: University of Pennsylvania Press.

Leap, W. 1977. *Papers in Southwestern English II: Studies in Southwestern Indian English.* San Antonio, TX: Trinity University.

Leith, D. 1983. *A Social History of English.* London: Routledge & Kegan Paul.

Lowth, R. 1762/1979. *A Short Introduction to English Grammar.* Scholars' Facsimile Editions. New York: Delmar.

Luhman, R. 1990. "Appalachian English Stereotypes: Language Attitudes in Kentucky." *Language in Society,* 19:331–348.

Macauley, R. 1978. "Variation and Consistency in Glaswegian English." In P. Trudgill, ed., *Sociolinguistic Patterns in British English.* London: Edward Arnold.

McCrum, R., W. Cran, and R. McNeil. 1986. *The Story of English*. New York: Viking.

Milroy, J., and L. Milroy. 1985. *Authority in Language: Investigating Language Prescription and Standardization*. London: Routledge & Kegan Paul.

Murray, L. 1795/1819. *An English Grammar*. New York: Collins.

Ornstein-Galicia, J., ed. 1984. *Form and Function in Chicano English*. Rowley, MA: Newbury House.

Penfield, J., and J. Ornstein-Galicia. 1985. *Chicano English: An Ethnic Dialect*. Amsterdam: John Benjamins.

Perkins, M. 1983. *Modal Expressions in English*. London: Frances Pinter.

Priestley, J. 1761. *Rudiments of English Grammar*. London: Griffiths.

Romaine, S. 1978. "Post vocalic /r/ in Scottish English: Sound Change in Progress?" In P. Trudgill, ed., *Sociolinguistic Patterns in British English*. London: Edward Arnold.

Ryan, E. Bouchard. 1979. "Why Do Low-Prestige Language Varieties Persist?" In H. Giles and R. N. St. Clair, eds., *Language and Social Psychology*. Baltimore, MD: University Park Press.

Spender, D. 1982. *Invisible Women—The Schooling Scandal*. London: Writers' and Readers' Publishing Cooperative.

Stubbs, M. 1980. *Language and Literacy: The Sociolinguistics of Reading and Writing*. London: Routledge & Kegan Paul.

Tannen, D. 1986. *That's Not What I Meant!* New York: Ballantine.

———. 1990. *You Just Don't Understand: Women and Men in Conversation*. New York: Ballantine.

Toon, T. E. 1982. "Variation in Contemporary American English." In R. W. Bailey and M. Görlach, eds., *English as a World Language*. Ann Arbor, MI: University of Michigan Press.

Trudgill, P., ed., 1978. *Sociolinguistic Patterns in British English*. London: Edward Arnold.

———. 1986. *Dialects in Contact*. Oxford: Blackwell.

Wald, B. 1984. "The Status of Chicano English as a Dialect of American English." In J. Ornstein-Galicia, ed., *Form and Function in Chicano English*. Rowley, MA: Newbury House.

Wolfram, W. 1991. *Dialects and American English*. Englewood Cliffs, NJ: Prentice-Hall, Inc.

———, and D. Christian. 1989. *Dialects and Education: Issues and Answers*. Englewood Cliffs, NJ: Prentice-Hall, Inc.

GLOSSARY

Accent: the pronunciation of a particular variety of a language; e.g., British, southern United States, Chicano English, female speech.

Accommodation theory: a theory drawn from social psychology that attempts to account for how differing groups or individuals adjust to each other. See **convergence**, **divergence**.

Backchanneling: a conversational behavior in which an addressee makes sounds such as *uh-huh* to indicate attention to the speaker.

Careful speech: the language used by a person answering an interviewer's questions; more formal than **casual speech.**

Casual speech: the everyday spoken language used in informal situations, without attention to one's language.

Channel: the physical device for carrying the language signal; e.g., radio, television, telephone, answering machines, FAX, or E-mail, as well as more traditional forms of written communication such as letters, journals, books, and face-to-face talk.

Code switching: the use of two languages within a single communicative interaction, or within a single utterance.

Codification: the process by which a language variety is defined and disseminated through dictionaries, grammars, and manuals of style.

Cognate object construction: the grammatical construction in which a verb and a direct object are equivalent to a single verb, often with the verb and object having the same root; e.g., *dream a dream* (= to dream); *take a bath* (= to bathe).

Communicative competence: the unconscious knowledge that speakers have of the rules governing when to use the varieties of language within their **linguistic repertoires.**

Convergence: a process in communication when speakers of different varieties attempt to speak more like each other. See **accommodation theory, divergence.**

Dense network: a network with many connections among its members. See **multiplex network.**

Dialect: (a) in nonlinguistic usage, often a language variety viewed as a departure from an assumed standard norm. (b) In linguistics, an older term for the word "variety." (c) In linguistics, a language variety defined in terms of characteristics of its users. See **register.**

Divergence: a process in communication when speakers of two different varieties increase the differences between them. See **accommodation theory, convergence.**

Field: the topic and purpose of a communicative act. See **tenor** and **mode.**

Final consonant cluster simplification: the reduction of two or more consonants at the end of a word to fewer consonants; e.g., pronouncing *last night* as *las' night.*

Fix (eighteenth-century use): to prevent a language from changing.

Genre: see Chapter 12.

Great Vowel Shift: a change in the pronunciation of English long vowels that occurred approximately 1400–1500 A.D. For instance, the pronunciation of goose changed from [go:s] to [gu:s].

Linguistic repertoire: the set of language varieties available to an individual or speech community.

Matched guise test: a technique for determining the relative prestige of varieties: a single speaker produces utterances in two varieties, each of which is independently evaluated by subjects unaware that the utterances are from the same speaker.

Minimal pair style: the level of pronunciation at which speakers are at their highest level of awareness of pronunciation, even more so than when reading **word lists.**

Mode: the medium of communication—speech, writing. See **field** and **tenor.**

Multiplex network: a network with many different types of connections among members. See **dense network.**

Network: a structure made up of points (e.g., members of a group) and connections among them (e.g., friendship, kinship, shared values, language varieties, occupations, etc.).

Power: the relationship between people where one can control the behavior of another; based on strength, age, wealth, social structure, etc. See **solidarity.**

Prestige, overt and covert: a positive valuation of a member by a group; overt prestige is based on power and social standing; covert prestige derives from one's possession of the group's values.

Reading style: the type of articulation used in reading, usually showing greater attention to pronunciation than **careful speech.**

Register: a linguistic variety that corresponds to different uses of language; e.g., scientific, literary, religious. See **dialect**.

Sociolinguistic variable: a linguistic feature (phonological, morphological, syntactic, lexical, discourse) correlated with both level of formality and social standing.

Solidarity: the relationship between people based on shared values and experiences. See **power**.

Speech community: a group of people who share norms for the use of languages and language varieties in discourse.

Standardization: the attempt to promote uniformity of form and meaning in a language by eliminating variation.

Stylistic variation: a broad term indicating any variation in the speech or writing of individuals, along with the conditions that determine the variation. See **register** and **dialect (c)**.

Technicality: the degree to which a text contains precisely defined words from specific disciplines, professions, crafts, or other domains.

Tenor: the relationships between participants in communication, including social status, degree of familiarity, formality, etc. See **register**.

Test cycle: a routine used in teaching where (a) the teacher elicits information, (b) the student responds, and (c) the teacher provides feedback.

Topic: the subject matter of a discourse or of any part of a discourse.

Word list style: the level of speech in which speakers are highly attentive to pronunciation, even more so than in **reading style**.

14 USAGE

14.0   THE NATURE OF USAGE

It's a familiar scene. You have just informed a new acquaintance that you're an English major or an English teacher. The response is perfectly predictable: "Well, I guess I'll have to watch my grammar." No one says "Well, I guess I'll have to sprinkle my conversation with allusions to Shakespeare." or "Can you recommend some good writers?" The general public stereotypes students and teachers of English mainly as custodians of correctness in grammar.

In such circumstances as the above, the authors typically respond by reassuring our squirming acquaintance: "Don't worry, I'm off duty." By adopting the police idiom, we consciously point out the stereotype—that we have been charged with the duty of protecting the language by nabbing unwary violators of linguistic laws, the laws of usage.

For many people, their awareness of rules of usage causes severe insecurity and recalls unpleasant experiences early in their education, experiences reinforced throughout their adult life through the media and other agencies. Awareness of the rules, of course, doesn't entail adherence to them. Indeed, part of many people's linguistic consciousness is the belief that they don't observe the rules.

In general, statements of usage concern questions of what is correct and incorrect, right and wrong, in language. But usage statements have a variety of emphases. Some govern grammatical structure—e.g., subjects must agree in number with their verbs. Others address matters of clarity—e.g., a pronoun should have a specific, identifiable referent. Usage statements also address broader ethical issues—e.g., passives should be avoided because they allow writers to conceal the identity of persons who perform certain actions. Finally, some usage statements address sensitive social and political issues—e.g., suggestions to replace the so-called generic "he" with a pronoun that isn't gender distinct.

Usage statements are the province of prescriptive grammar. We distinguished earlier (in Chapter 1) between descriptive and prescriptive views of language. Descriptive approaches seek to identify what native speakers unconsciously sense as natural in their native language and to discover the underlying principles that explain why certain structures are natural and others aren't. Prescriptive grammar, on the other hand, specifies what forms of language speakers should or shouldn't use in speaking or in writing.

Teachers routinely make prescriptions, often in the form of corrections on compositions. Teachers also provide more detailed or more practical explanations of rules that students encounter in writing handbooks. Logically, effective prescription depends on accurate description of both the language itself and the way speakers and writers typically use it. Unfortunately, many of the corrections that teachers make are founded mainly on handbooks, and many handbook rules are based on assumed (i.e., unquestioned) general practice, as well as on personal preference and questionable assumptions about language.

There is one further element pertinent to the classroom. That is the fact that errors have attached to them various negative judgments: "lazy," "stupid," "illiterate," "substan-dard," "crude," "insensitive," "sexist." Those who possess—or think they do—a highly developed metalinguistic self-consciousness (teachers, trained speakers, writers, and other well-educated individuals) take pride in their verbal ability and frequently look down upon those who don't possess it—their students, the general public, the less educated. While such linguistic pride is justifiable in moderation, it's often overweening to the point of hubris. One wouldn't expect a physician to scorn her patients because they're ill or a plumber to laugh at a customer whose drains are clogged. Yet, in fact, such attitudes do at times lurk in the minds and behavior of the linguistically privileged.

The value placed in American society on correctness suggests the inevitability of usage strictures. Usage rules reflect the influence of the educationally, socially, and economically dominant segment of society. But they also powerfully color the attitudes of all speakers toward their personal knowledge of the language. To acknowledge the role of usage in this way should lead us toward a careful study of usage—particularly of those facets that raise issues of power and of personal sensitivity.

In this chapter, we begin by surveying the various sources of prescriptions. The bulk of the chapter examines different kinds of prescriptions and illustrates ways in which teachers can evaluate their merits. Finally, we develop a philosophy of usage that respects the language of students while providing them access to standard English.

EXERCISE   Consider the following, based on Hofstadter (1981):

Their is four errors in this sentence. Can you find them?

What are the four errors? Which could occur only in writing? In speech? Are there other sorts of errors in the sentence? Try to reconstruct the mental processes you used to find the errors. Are these the same processes that you use in normal listening and reading?

Most formally trained writers appear to have a form of a heightened conscious-ness of language—or what is called *metalinguistic awareness*. (Hartwell, 1985). Metalinguistic awareness appears as the consciousness of language *as language*. To what extent did you use your metalinguistic awareness in doing this exercise?

14.1 SOURCES OF USAGE STATEMENTS

Rules of usage aren't universal in language. Some languages, like French, have formal academies that attempt—sometimes with temporary success—to create uniformity. Others, such as German and Spanish, are casually regulated by the influence of political centers prominent because of their power or prestige. Still others have no centralizing or standardizing forces at all. English stands between French and Spanish/German in the degree of overt regulation. In this section, we will examine the sources of control over English.

The controls that influence the language today haven't always existed. Middle English, spoken from about 1100 to 1450 A.D., reflected the prominence of London and its speech. In the Renaissance, the speech of the royal court, one variant of London English, provided the norm of polite speech. Renaissance written style was influenced by both the ornate Latinate prose of Cicero and the plain style of the new scientists of the age (Gordon, 1966; Chapters 7 and 8). It wasn't until the eighteenth century that self-professed grammarians sought to regulate the language and to render it immune to any change. Writers such as Robert Lowth (a bishop), Joseph Priestley (a scientist), and George Campbell (a rhetorician) attempted to adjudicate among disputed uses and to provide the degree of certainty that the rising middle class demanded. Their decisions were often defended through complex arguments, using a variety of criteria: the practice of the aristocracy, writings of the most-respected authors, euphony (pleasing sound), simplicity, logical analogy, and prevailing practice. At the same time, dictionaries of English appeared in large numbers, including Samuel Johnson's *A Dictionary of the English Language,* which remained the British standard until the beginning of the twentieth century (Baugh and Cable, 1978).

In nineteenth-century America, the "melting-pot" mentality lent another motivation for linguistic uniformity and certainty. The educator Lindley Murray obliged the nation by borrowing the usage rules from the eighteenth-century logical grammarians, simplifying their work by stating only their conclusions, while leaving their arguments to languish in scholarly libraries. America's answer to Johnson appeared at the midcentury in the persons of Noah Webster and Joseph Worcester, whose dictionaries declared the linguistic independence of the colonies from England.

The history of usage shows some surprises. Campbell, for instance, pondered the merits of *backward* versus *backwards* as adverbs, preferring *backwards* on the grounds that *backward* already served as an adjective. Most modern dictionaries still regard the two forms as interchangeable as adverbs. Campbell also argued against the verb *unloose,* which by analogy with *untie* ought to mean "tie." This idiomatic oddity has been ignored in modern times, although many more have arisen to take its place. The eighteenth century, however, has made its mark on modern usage. For instance, the so-called "generic" use of the masculine pronoun to refer to words such as *anyone* or *someone* stems from that period.

EXERCISE   The sonnet below was written by Sir Philip Sidney. What grammar rule does Sidney appeal to? What is his conception of "grammar" and its position in society? How do you think that Stella would respond to the speaker's importunity?

> O grammar-rules, O now your virtues show;
> So children still read you with awful eyes,
> As my young dove may, in your precepts wise,
> Her grant to me by her own virtue show;
> For late, with heart most high, with eyes most low,
> I craved the thing which ever she denies;

She, lightning Love displaying Venus' skies,
   Lest once should not be heard, twice said, No, No!
Sing then, my muse, now Io Paean sing;
   Heav'ns envy not at my high triumphing,
   But grammar's force with sweet success confirm;
For grammar says,—oh this, dear Stella, weigh,—
   For grammar says,—to grammar who says nay?—
   That in one speech two negatives affirm!

Sonnet 63 from "Astrophel and Stella," (Hebel and Hudson, 1929)

Meanwhile, new usage questions arise daily. Should we, for instance, unabashedly coin verbs from nouns, as in *to parent* or *to impact?* Are those who season their speech with *you know, like,* and *I mean* to be censured? Teachers can expect to face many such questions throughout their careers. The options for answering the questions boil down to two: accepting the conclusions of someone else and developing one's own judgments. While we will argue later in favor of the latter, a knowledge of the sources of usage statements can be helpful in providing a larger set of data and a wider diversity of opinion than might ordinarily be available to a teacher.

The influences on matters of usage include individual English teachers, professional English organizations, writing handbooks, dictionaries, and the popular press.

14.1.1   English teachers and usage

High school and college teachers often act as transmitters rather than as arbiters of usage. In either formal grammar courses or composition units, most teachers simply accept the positions presented by their textbooks and pass them on to their students. To some extent, one can justify this practice. First, it's dangerous to undermine the authority of one's textbook when one disagrees with a few details. Second, most of the usage rules in textbooks are so well-established that they reflect an overwhelming consensus about conventions of writing. Unfortunately, the really interesting and controversial questions of usage, e.g., those related to clarity of meaning (e.g., ambiguity, obscurity), sexism, or dishonesty are often either ignored or shifted over to discussions of style.

Uncritical acceptance of textbook pronouncements is neither inevitable nor desirable. Teachers have the obligation to develop critical thinking skills in regard to language as well as in literary matters. Later in this chapter, we will illustrate the critical analysis of selected usage items. We encourage teachers and textbook committees to examine texts carefully for out-of-date, inaccurate, arbitrary, or trivial rules. Without the informed criticism of teachers, publishers will have no incentive to provide advice that meets the needs of students and of society.

Let's take an initial example of critical awareness of rules. What form of the verb *try* would you use in sentence [1]?

[1]   If Claire (would have tried/had tried) harder, she might have succeeded.

The textbook from which this example is drawn (*Scope English, Grammar and Composition, Level Five*, p. 307) accepts only *had tried,* calling *would have tried* "a common error in spoken English." The justification for *had tried* is:

> The . . . verbs . . . refer to unreal conditions in the past. They are in the past-subjunctive form. As you can see, the past-subjunctive form is the same as the past-perfect indicative form.

What's wrong with this treatment of unreal conditions? First, the comments occur within a discussion of the subjunctive, a form rarely used in English. Granted that the subjunctive is occasionally needed, on what grounds is *would have finished* incorrect? Apparently, the only reason is that the text says so. (One might at least point out that *had tried* is briefer than *would have tried.* However, *would have tried* (but not *had tried*) indicates unreality in sentence [2]; why doesn't it indicate unreality in [1]?

[2] Harold would have tried harder. (But he didn't.)

The textbook statement is also vague. By calling *would have tried* "a common error in spoken English," does it mean to suggest that it's not an error, common or uncommon, in writing? Sentence [2], moreover, isn't restricted to speech. Also, how much self-consciousness do students need to apply this rule? Is it reasonable to expect students to recall such a minor point? Does the teacher actually use the so-called "correct" form in his or her own speech? Finally, notice that the example associates failure with a female name. Do other examples show males failing an equal number of times?

You might object that such questions are quibbles, but they aren't. They illustrate the application of close analysis applied to textbooks. Unfortunately, teachers sometimes reserve their critical skills for works of literature. But there is no reason—or excuse—for a competent teacher not to turn a sharp eye to the books that will influence the linguistic consciousness of students.

14.1.2 Professional English organizations

Of the many professional organizations in English, the major one for teachers is the National Council of Teachers of English (NCTE). NCTE publishes several journals, books, and other documents on language policy and usage.

NCTE puts out three journals devoted to different levels of instruction. *College Composition and Communication* (CCC), as the title implies, addresses the most advanced level of instruction, although many of the articles and reviews are of general interest. The *English Journal* publishes articles designed for high school teachers, while *Elementary English* focuses on the primary grades. Each journal provides plentiful information in many areas pertaining to the discipline. In addition, NCTE publishes numerous books and pamphlets on language and literature, some of which reflect the policy-making arm of the council and hence concern matters of usage (see Finegan, 1980: pp. 88–91). Information on these publications can be obtained by writing to the NCTE at 1111 Kenyon Road, Urbana, IL 61801.

14.1.3   Writing handbooks

While professional organizations provide a wealth of resources for the teacher, they don't have as great an impact as they should. There are two reasons for this situation. First, not many teachers of English participate extensively in professional societies, particularly at the national level. Second, teachers rely on handbooks of usage put out by major publishers. Such works serve as useful catalogs of standard prescriptive rules, although they tend to omit open questions of current relevance. Table 14.1 lists some of the major usage handbooks.

TABLE 14.1.   Selected Handbooks of English

Barnet & Stubbs's Practical Guide to Writing (Little, Brown)
The Brief English Handbook (Little, Brown)
Brief Handbook for Writers (Prentice-Hall)
The Confident Writer (W. W. Norton)
The Essential English Handbook and Rhetoric (Bobbs-Merrill)
Handbook for Writers (Simon & Schuster)
Harbrace College Handbook (Harcourt Brace Jovanovich)
New English Handbook (Wadsworth Publishing Company)
The Portable English Handbook (Holt, Rinehart and Winston)
Rules for Writers (St. Martin's Press)
A Writer's Reference (St. Martin's Press)

In terms of topics covered, all of these works are nearly interchangeable. They differ mainly in their length and detail. Most provide examples and exercises. They're written for the college-level student and often serve as secondary texts in composition courses. (Some composition textbooks also include relatively brief handbooks.)

These works are also largely interchangeable in presenting usage as simply an extensive body of codified linguistic laws that one must obey. There is little or no effort to suggest how the rules can be acquired in ways that will transfer to the writing process since exercises are overwhelmingly in drill-and-practice format. Occasionally, the more thorough works will mention variation in usage. *The Confident Writer,* for example, notes that "conventions of grammar and punctuation are often debatable and change frequently" (p. 11). This point appears in the introduction to the work, which users rarely consult. It does affect certain entries, such as that for not splitting an infinitive, which is described as "not descriptive of modern English" (p. 293). Likewise, the manual devotes over four pages to the avoidance of sexually discriminatory language (pp. 332–336).

EXERCISE   Select three handbooks of usage and compare their treatment of any of the following:

split infinitives
ending a sentence with a preposition
case of pronouns
generic pronouns (use of "he" to refer to males or females)

Note the publication dates of the handbooks. Can you see differences in the works in their (1) degree of authoritarianism, (2) awareness of the variation between speech and writing, and (3) recognition of changing usage.

14.1.4   Dictionaries

Dictionaries probably have the greatest impact on the vocabulary usage of the general public because they're widely owned and easily consulted. Surprisingly, dictionaries differ considerably in the amount and nature of their usage information. The differences arise from both the beliefs of lexicographers about usage and the need of dictionary publishers to sell their works.

The major dictionaries of contemporary American English are listed in Table 14.2. The first two are unabridged; the remainder are college/adult-level desk references. Although these works have slightly different policies on usage and methods for expressing usage judgments, their editors all claim that their dictionary doesn't adopt an authoritarian position, but rather aims to inform and guide the reader. The statements below by dictionary editors are typical:

> A number of entries for words posing special problems of confused or disputed usage include . . . brief articles that provide the dictionary user with suitable guidance on the usage in question. The guidance offered is never based merely on received opinion, though opinions are often noted, but typically on both a review of the historical background and a careful evaluation of what citations reveal about actual contemporary practice. (*Webster's New Collegiate Dictionary*, 9th ed., p. 6)

> It is our hope that readers will find this Dictionary a reliable and friendly guide to our language's treasury of words—the tools of communication and understanding. (*American Heritage Dictionary*, p. 8)

There are also several notable dictionaries of usage which often provide more thorough—and occasionally more entertaining—discussion of problem areas. Some of the most popular ones appear in Table 14.3.

Examples of disputed lexical items abound: *irregardless; disinterested* versus *uninter-*

TABLE 14.2   Major Dictionaries of American English

Random House Dictionary of the English Language (RHD). 2d ed. Random House, 1987.
Webster's Third New International Dictionary (WNID3). Merriam-Webster Inc., 1961.
American Heritage Dictionary of the English Language (AHD). 2d College ed. Houghton Mifflin, 1982.
The Random House College Dictionary (RHCD). Random House, 1988.
Webster's New Collegiate Dictionary (WNCD9). 9th ed. Merriam-Webster, Inc., 1987.
Webster's New World Dictionary of American English (WNWD). 2d College ed., 1988.

TABLE 14.3   Dictionaries of Usage

Bernstein, Theodore M., *The Careful Writer*. New York: Atheneum, 1965.
Copperud, R., *American Usage and Style: The Consensus*. Van Nostrand Reinhold, 1980.
Evans, B. and Evans, C., *A Dictionary of Contemporary American Usage*. Random House, 1957.
Fowler, H. W., *A Dictionary of Modern English Usage*. Clarendon Press, 1965.
Maggio, Rosalie, *The Nonsexist Word Finder*. Oryx Press, 1987.
Morris, W. and Morris, M., *Harper Dictionary of Contemporary Usage*. Harper & Row, 1985.
Shaw, H., *Dictionary of Problem Words and Expressions*. McGraw-Hill, Inc., 1975.
Urdang, Laurence, *The Dictionary of Confusable Words*. Facts on File, 1988.

---

ested; gift (verb); *bad/ly* (feel _____); *aggravate* (_____ a person); *most* (_____ everyone); *hopefully*. Some of these items are uncommon, but most occur fairly often, particularly in spoken English. Here are some sample entries for *hopefully*:

[3a]   . . . 2. It is hoped; if all goes well: *Hopefully, we'll win.* (*The Random House College Dictionary*)

[b]   . . . 2. It is to be hoped (that) [to leave early, *hopefully* by six]: regarded by some as a loose usage, but widely current. (*Webster's New World Dictionary of American English*)

[c]   . . . 2. It is hoped; if all goes well: *Hopefully, we will get to the show on time.* [1630–40; HOPEFUL + LY]
   —Usage. Although some strongly object to its use as a sentence modifier, HOPEFULLY meaning "it is to be hoped (that)" has been in use since the 1930s and is fully standard in all varieties of speech and writing: *Hopefully, tensions between the two nations will ease.* This use of HOPEFULLY is parallel to that of *certainly, curiously, frankly, regrettably,* and other sentence modifiers. (*Random House Dictionary of the English Language*)

[d]   The adverb *hopefully* is often heard in the sense of "we hope" in such sentences as "*Hopefully,* the war will soon be ended." Would you [professional writers] accept such a formulation?
   In speech Yes: 42%, No: 58%
   In writing Yes: 24%, No: 76% (Morris and Morris, *Harper Dictionary of Contemporary Usage,* 1985)

[e]   Since [1960] . . . it has been more and more widely used in the sense *it is hoped,* as in "A new session will meet late in the spring to vote new credits, hopefully at a reduced figure." . . . This misuse is protested by five critics and American Heritage. Considering how widespread it has become, however, the protests are probably in vain. *The Standard College Dictionary,* Random House, and *Webster's New World* have already admitted it as standard, in function like an adverbial clause modifying a whole sentence: "Hopefully, I'll finish next week." (Copperud, *American Usage and Style: The Consensus,* 1980)

EXERCISES   1. Using the passages above, answer the following:
   a. Which two passages contain an apparent historical contradiction?

b. Which of the statements support use of *hopefully* as a sentence adverbial in standard English? How do they do so?
c. What specific guidance do passages (d) and (e) provide the user?
d. Describe the tone of each passage. (Is it reasonable? emotional? sarcastic, etc.?)
e. Which of the passages provides the most convincing support for its conclusion?
2. Select one of the controversial usages noted in this section, or identify one of your own. Consult three conventional dictionaries and three dictionaries of usage. Write a paragraph or two summarizing the conclusions and evaluating them.

14.1.5 The popular press

In a lively and provocative anatomy of usage as a symptom of the supposed decline of English, Geoffrey Nunberg (1983) observes:

> If we are bent on finding a decline in standards, the place to look is not in the language itself but in the way it is talked about. In the profusion of new books and articles on the state of the language, and in most new usage books, the moral note, if it is sounded at all, is either wavering or shrill. What is largely missing is the idea that there is any pleasure or instruction to be derived from considering what makes good usage good. (p. 32)

The targets of Nunberg's remarks include not only the academic establishment but also the popular press, particularly the cadre of journalists who have set themselves up as arbiters of usage. There is a small but influential group of these individuals; Table 14.4 identifies the main commentators and some of their works on language.

TABLE 14.4   Popular Books on Usage

James Kilpatrick, *The Ear Is Human: A Handbook of Homophones and Other Confusions.* Andrews and McMeel, 1985.
  The Writer's Art, Andrews and McMeel, 1985.
Richard Mitchell, *Less Than Words Can Say.* Little, Brown, 1981.
Edwin Newman, *I Must Say.* Warner Books, 1989.
  A Civil Tongue. Warner Books, 1983.
  Strictly Speaking: Will America Be the Death of English?. Indianapolis: Bobbs-Merrill, 1974.
William Safire, *Words of Wisdom.* Simon & Schuster, 1990.
  You Could Look It Up. Henry Holt & Co., 1989.
  Take My Word for It. Times Books, 1986.
  What's the Good Word?. Times Books, 1982.
John Simon, *Paradigms Lost: Reflections on Literacy and Its Decline.* Penguin, 1981.

The influence of the press arises because of its immediate, sometimes even daily or weekly, appearance before the general reading public. Syndicated articles are often recycled as books that enjoy wide circulation, particularly among those members of the general public who care about linguistic propriety. Most of these writers express themselves wittily and effectively. They regularly provide an entertaining, informative collection of supposed linguistic oddities, and thus supply useful data for debate.

In a sense these authors also provide "pleasure and instruction," the first of which at least is lacking in most other reference sources. But the pleasure comes in the police action—in nabbing an unsuspecting bureaucrat, politician, author, or—best of all—a fellow grammarian in some verbal solecism. Most of the books above and the articles on which they're based are largely formulaic, consisting in the public display and ridicule of the erring usage and of its perpetrator. The instruction usually falls under the heading of "X should have known better" or "The language is going to hell." Occasionally, a brief attempt is made to frame a logical defense of the author's preference, as was done in the eighteenth century; but as often as not the reader is invited to accept the preference because it represents the opinion of a published writer.

An extreme, but graphic, illustration of the tenor of the popular journalists' comments is John Simon's commentary on the "generic *he*" [as quoted in Nunberg (1983: p. 34)]:

> The fact that some people are too thickheaded to grasp, for example, that *anyone* is singular, as the *one* in it plainly denotes, does not obligate those who know better to tolerate *anyone can do as they please*. The correct form is, of course, *anyone may do as he pleases,* but in America, in informal usage, *can* has pretty much replaced *may* in this sense, and there is nothing more to be done about it; but we cannot and must not let *one* become plural. That way madness lies.

> And don't let fanatical feminists convince you that it must be *as he or she pleases,* which is clumsy and usually serves no other purpose than that of placating the kind of extremist who does not deserve to be placated. The impersonal *he* covers both sexes; . . .

While Simon's name-calling and cheap shots at feminists are obvious, they serve to disguise a fallacious linguistic argument. Simon assumes that the fact that *anyone* contains the word *one* makes it singular. However, the word has another part to it, namely, *any.* Now consider the following:

[4] Do you have any apples?
  [a] Yes, I have one.
  [b] Yes, I have several.

That *any* can occur with either a singular or a plural response suggests that it cover *both* singular and plural. Likewise, if you entered a room and asked *Does anyone have an apple?* you would hardly be linguistically offended if more than one person offered you the fruit. Moreover, sentence [4] would sound rather odd if *apples* weren't plural. So the presence of *one* in *anyone* doesn't render the word singular, any more than the presence of the word *horse* in *sawhorse* would allow you to ride away on one. In addition, changes of number are historically documented. The clearest case is the pronoun *you*, which originally referred only to the plural; it gradually shifted to its current reference to both singular and plural during the Renaissance. No massive rise in insanity is documented in the period. Moreover, psycholinguistic research has demonstrated that while *he* (and *man*) "covers both sexes" it certainly does not do so equitably (see, for example, MacKay, 1983; Schneider and Hacker, 1973).

The word *hopefully* offers a useful comparison between general reference works and the pronouncements of writers. One book that falls into both categories is William and Mary Morris's *Harper Dictionary of Contemporary Usage.* This collection draws on the opinions of a panel of writers who served as the usage panel for the *American Heritage Dictionary.* The generalized statistical conclusions are presented in [3d] above. But along with these synopses, the Morrises include quoted opinions from panel members. The following are typical reactions to *hopefully:*

[5a] "No. Slack-jawed, common, sleazy." (Shana Alexander)

[b] "It is barbaric, illiterate, offensive, damnable, and inexcusable." (Hal Borland)

[c] "I can't see any reason why not." (Ben Lucien Burman)

[d] "Yes. It depersonalizes the expression and that is good. . . . No one cares if *I* hope the war is over and *we* has to be defined—the adverb makes a kind of general unspecific yearning that suits many occasions." (Robert Crichton)

[e] "Mea culpa—I can see myself writing it—but it's wrong." (Thomas Fleming)

[f] "Sloppy but useful." (Elizabeth Janeway)

[g] "Chalk sqeaking on a blackboard is to be preferred to this usage. I don't accept it, but I fear we are all stuck with it." (Charles Kuralt)

[h] "You ask if I would accept it and I say No but I have to. It is awful." (Francis Robinson)

[i] "How do you not accept it? By squirming more obviously? I'm thinking of *all* my students and some of my colleagues." (Mark Schorer)

[j] "Hopefully has become a shorthand for 'I hope,' and it eliminates the pronoun in third-person writing." (Earl Ubell)

[k] "The most horrible usage of our time." (T. Harry Williams)

EXERCISE   Considering the opinions on *hopefully* expressed above, discuss the following:

a. What differences of opinion do you see among these writers?

b. Describe how the tone of these statements differs from that of the standard reference works.

c. Besides the authority of each author, what support for or against the usage is provided?

d. The German language has a word, *hoffentlich,* that is parallel to *hopefully* as a sentence adverb, except that its usage is completely uncontroversial. Adopting the position of many of the writers above, what conclusions would you draw about the quality of the German language?

14.2 SOME EXAMPLES OF USAGE STATEMENTS

Usage statements apply to a range of topics, including pronunciation, punctuation, vocabulary, syntax, and style. To examine these areas and to observe the style in which strictures are expressed, we will consider a representative sample of rules. In each case, we will have two aims: (1) to illustrate the types of prescriptions made and (2) to suggest how a teacher might evaluate the rule as an account of actual practice and as a statement that might help one's students.

You should be aware at the start of some of the common phraseology of prescriptivism. Some telltale expressions are: "good," "bad," "correct," "incorrect," "awkward," "misleading," "should (not)," "ought," and "do (not)." These expressions will help you to distinguish between prescriptive and descriptive claims about the language. Doing so is important because many prescriptions covertly rest upon descriptive assumptions that may or may not be valid.

14.2.1 Pronunciation

[6] You say ee-ther and I say eye-ther,
You say nee-ther, and I say ny-ther
Ee-ther, eye-ther, nee-ther, ny-ther
Let's call the whole thing off!

You like po-ta-to and I like po-tah-to,
You like to-ma-to and I like to-mah-to
Po-ta-to, po-tah-to, to-ma-to, to-mah-to!
Let's call the whole thing off!
(from George and Ira Gershwin, "Let's Call the Whole Thing Off," 1937)

[7] tomato (təma′to, mā′to)
(*American Heritage Dictionary*, 1st ed.)

[8] medieval: ". . . should be pronounced in four syllables" (p. 97)
erudite: ". . . traditionally, E-roo-dyt. Now usually AIR-yoo-dyt" (p. 52)
banal: "BAY-nal. Also buh-NAL" (p. 16)
plantain: "PLAN-tin. Do not say PLAN-tain" (p. 118)
February: "FEB-roo-er-ee. Do not say FEB-yoo-er-ee" (p. 55)
(Richard Harrington Elster, *There Is No Zoo in Zoology*, 1988)

Fortunately for humanity, couples rarely break off a relationship, as Gershwin's frivolous pair consider doing, over differences in pronunciation. (Other divisive issues for them are *laugh-ter* versus *lawf-ter, va-nill-a* versus *va-nell-a, pa-ja-mas* versus *pa-jah-mas, oy-sters* versus *er-sters*.) Indeed, we rarely correct—or even comment upon—another's pronunciation. Perhaps you can recall one of those discomforting incidents where you were forced into correcting someone else, perhaps because a particular word was unavoidable and you, knowing the normal pronunciation, didn't want to use a version that you believed incorrect. Perhaps the exchange went something like this:

[9] A: What a delicious gateau (= [gætu])
     B: Thank you, that's the first time I've ever made a gateau (= [gæto])
     A: How do you say it?
     B: [gæto]—or at least that's the way I've always heard it. But I could be wrong.
     A: Oh, no you're probably right. I never was any good at French.

This interchange, like many that concern metalinguistic issues, is loaded with hedges and apologies. Note that A, the "offender," raises the issue; she or he could simply have let it pass, perhaps feeling quietly embarrassed. With the issue in the open, B cannot back down completely, but hedges twice—once by stating that she is only basing her speech on personal experience rather than on some higher authority and again by noting the possibility of her own error. A courteously accedes to B's qualifications and offers an apology to balance her hedges. Aside from the correction of very young children, we rarely feel comfortable admonishing another person, even a foreigner, for mispronunciation and will do so only for serious reasons. For instance, as a 9 year old, one of the authors was in a grocery store with his mother. Approaching the baking equipment, the author mispronounced (intentionally) the word *baster* as [bæstər]. He was corrected in no uncertain terms.

A more common case where we look for the "correct" pronunciation of a word arises when we are truly uncertain of how to say it. Such words may be technical (e.g., *monanthous, synecdoche*), foreign (e.g., *creche, ersatz, bushido*), rare (e.g., *trepan, quipu, quenon*), or new to the language (e.g., *kvetch, cyborg*).

EXERCISE   How would you pronounce each of the controversial words in [6] to [9]? Look each word up in a current unabridged dictionary. (For new words, you may have to consult a specialized work such as Merriam-Webster's *12,000 Words*.)

A common source of "correct" pronunciation is a desk or unabridged dictionary. As example [7] shows, dictionaries sometimes provide more than one pronunciation, usually with the assumption that the one given first is more common. The reason for including multiple pronunciations is that dictionaries self-consciously adopt a descriptive rather than a prescriptive stance. In many cases—e.g., that of Gershwin's lovers—the reference work will support both usages, and hence fail to resolve anything. In cases where one finds a single pronunciation, readers will feel either satisfied, if they have their usage confirmed, or embarrassed, if they discover that they have consistently "mispronounced" the word.

Actual direct prescriptions of pronunciation are infrequent outside speech classes. The emphasis on pure pronunciation (*orthoepy*) goes back to the late eighteenth century, when professional speaking courses developed. Highly monitored pronunciation is valuable to many who must speak in public: e.g., politicians, clergy, lawyers, actors, broadcasters, and teachers. There is thus at least a practical motivation for a uniform "correct" speech.

On the popular front, the desire for improvement of one's speech has prompted two recent books that purport to establish the platinum pronunciation of many vexing words in English: Charles Harrington Elster's *There Is No Zoo in Zoology* (Macmillan, 1988) and *Is There a Cow in Moscow?* (Macmillan, 1990). The tenor of Elster's approach is indicated by the first book's subtitle *and Other Beastly Mispronunciations: An Opinionated Guide for the Well-Spoken*. Many of Elster's preferences are based on his consultation of dictionaries, both past and present. Thus he notes both the traditional as well as recent version of *erudite;* likewise, an older pronunciation of *banal* as BAN-ul (rhyming with *channel*) is given. For the most part, the dictionary serves as Elster's authority. His rationale for not saying PLAN-tain, for instance, is its failure to appear in dictionaries. However, another principle appears to operate, at least covertly: a preference for a pronunciation that most closely corresponds with the spelling. This seems to underlie Elster's preference for the four-syllable articulation of *medieval* and for the stilted enunciation of *February*. The latter word, in fact, forces him to forsake his reliance on dictionaries, most of which list the stigmatized and vastly more frequent pronunciation as the first.

The issue of frequency and usage is controversial. Elster clearly assumes that the usage of the "careful" minority is to be preferred over that of the (presumably careless) majority. Nevertheless, the dictum of careful spelling pronunciation isn't followed consistently in the book; Elster returns to the "majority rules" principle in preferring the word *balm* without the /l/ and *often* without the /t/.

14.2.2 Punctuation

[10] As a rule, do not write sentence fragments. The term fragment refers to a nonsentence beginning with a capital letter and ending with a period. Although written as if it were a sentence, a fragment is only a part of a sentence—such as a phrase or subordinate clause:

FRAGMENTS	SENTENCES
My father always planting a spring garden.	My father always plants a spring garden.
Because he likes to eat vegetables.	He likes to eat vegetables.
Which help the body to combat infection.	He likes to eat vegetables which help the
For example, yellow and green ones.	body to combat infection—for example,
(*Harbrace College Handbook,* 10th ed., p. 26)	yellow and green ones.

[11] Do not punctuate phrases, dependent clauses, and other fragments as sentences. Most fragments in student writing are phrases, clauses, and occasionally other constructions that depend for their meaning on independent clauses immediately preceding them.
(*Prentice-Hall Handbook for Writers,* 9th ed., pp. 54–55)

[12] Comma splice
Do not connect two main clauses with only a comma. Placing a comma between two main clauses without a coordinating conjunction (*and, but, for, or, nor, so, yet*) results in the comma fault or comma splice.

COMMA SPLICE   I avoided desserts, I was trying to lose weight.
(*Prentice-Hall Handbook for Writers,* 9th ed., pp. 60–61)

[13]   Run-together or fused sentences
Do not omit punctuation between main clauses. Such omission results in run-together or fused sentences—that is, two grammatically complete thoughts with no separate punctuation.
(*Prentice-Hall Handbook for Writers,* 9th ed., p. 62)

The rules of punctuation are legion. We have selected three rules that are clearly related to one another, in that they call upon the much touted ability called "sentence sense." That is, teachers assume that those who regularly write fragments, comma splices, and run-ons don't know what a sentence is.

Recent handbooks, of which the Harbrace and the Prentice-Hall are representative, share a consensus on these issues. Most of them recognize that fragments are acceptable—indeed, common—in speech. They agree that, used occasionally and consciously for special effects in writing, fragments are acceptable. Handbooks also offer plentiful examples of incorrect sentences, together with a variety of possible revisions. Most of them provide helpful exercises.

In spite of the apparent high quality of the handbooks—and similar sections in composition texts—some students persist in making these basic errors. What is the explanation? First, as we argued in Chapter 1, no native speaker of any language lacks an intuition of what is a grammatical sentence in their language. It follows that the diagnosis of "deficient sentence sense" may distract teachers from a more realistic analysis of the problem. Second, the explanation of the errors is couched in technical grammatical terms such as phrase, subordinate clause, dependent clause, and coordinating conjunction. Now students who commit the errors in question are the least likely to know the technical terminology and the most likely to be frustrated with English studies. And they will most certainly not follow such advice as the *Harbrace Handbook* gives to help writers to spot problems:

[14]   Before handing in a composition, proofread each word group written as a sentence. First, be sure that it has at least one subject and one predicate. . . . Next, be sure that the word group is not a dependent clause beginning with a subordinating conjunction or a relative pronoun. . . . (p. 27)

Commendable advice—but it's unrealistic to believe that even conscientious students who choose to apply it will be able to exercise the degree of metalinguistic control over their language that the advice calls for. How, for example, can students "be sure"? The answer, of course, is that students can only be sure if they rely on their intuitions. And that takes us back to the claim that students naturally know what is and what isn't a sentence.

What must students really know in order to master the rules of sentence punctuation? Of first importance, they must have a distinct sense of the differences between speech and writing (see Chapter 12). Handbooks routinely point out the frequency of fragments in spoken language (although almost never with real-life examples). However, they never point out that comma splices and run-ons don't occur in speech; they're possible errors only in writing. Writers of fragments, comma splices, and run-ons don't need to be drilled on "sentence sense"; they need to confront the speech-writing dichotomy. This lesson, of course, isn't limited to the "basic" writers in one's class. The translation of speech into writing concerns even the most professional prose artist because punctuation provides only an imperfect record of suprasegmental features of speech—pitch patterns, stresses, and pauses.

14.2.3 Lexical usage

EXERCISE Circle the appropriate word in the sentences below. (Preferred usages appear at the end of this section.)
a. I cannot cope/deal with any more pressure.
b. I cannot cope/deal.
c. I inferred/implied from your comments that you don't approve of heavy metal music.
d. Your comments infer/imply that you don't approve of heavy metal music.
e. I can't infer/imply whether you approve of heavy metal music.
f. Warren inferred/implied that I approve of heavy metal music.

In dictionaries and handbooks, lexical usage often focuses on commonly confused lexical pairs, such as those in the exercise above. Commentary often attempts to distinguish each word by either drawing sharp conceptual boundaries (as in [15]) or relegating one of the words to a "lower" situational status (as in [16]):

[15] *Infer* and *imply,* in their most frequently used senses, are carefully distinguished in modern usage. To *imply* is to state indirectly, hint, or intimate: *The report implies that we were to blame.* To *infer* is to draw a conclusion or make a decision based on facts or indications: *Reading the report led him to infer that we were to blame.* In these senses the words are not interchangeable. Although *infer* sometimes appears in examples such as the first, it is not acceptable there, according to 92 per cent of the Usage Panel. (*American Heritage Dictionary*)

[16] cope (kop) intr.v. **coped, coping, copes.** 1. To contend or strive, especially on even terms or with success. Used with *with.* 2. *Informal.* to contend with difficulties and act to overcome them. See Usage note. . . .
Usage: *cope,* employed without *with* and its specific object, is still most appropriate to informal usage: *A successful applicant must be able to cope.* The example is acceptable in formal writing to only 43 per cent of the Usage Panel. (*American Heritage Dictionary,* 1st ed.)

These entries illustrate one strategy peculiar to the *American Heritage Dictionary.* AHD relies on a usage panel composed of "experts" on language—in fact, mostly professional writers. Their opinion is expressed not as categorical, as in other dictionaries, but as a percentage of agreement. In cases such as *cope,* this procedure can be unnerving to a reader since percentages close to 50 amount to the toss of a coin rather than to the firm guidance that the public expects.

The common strategy of AHD for *infer* and *imply* is to sort out the supposedly clear central senses of each word and then to dispatch the allegedly inappropriate uses. This rhetorically effective technique runs into one small problem, immediately apparent if we examine a similar usage note in a different dictionary:

[17]   Sir Thomas More is the first writer known to have used both *infer* and *imply* in their approved senses (1529). He is also the first to have used *infer* in a sense close to the meaning of *imply* (about 1530). Both of these uses of *infer* coexisted without comment until some time around the end of World War I. Since then, senses 3 [= indicate] and 4 [= suggest, hint] have been frequently condemned as an undesirable blurring of a useful distinction. Their use, esp. with a personal subject, will still incur the wrath of some in spite of the usage of four centuries and the fact that in a given instance the meaning will be clear from the context. (*Webster's New Collegiate Dictionary,* 9th ed.)

The historical approach typical of Merriam-Webster dictionaries calls into question the claim that the two senses of *infer* and *imply* are actually distinct in modern usage—a fact that would comfort a secure reader but might deeply trouble the insecure. The rhetorical strategy here, one common to many dictionaries, is the implicit "if . . . then" statement: IF you use the word *infer* in certain senses, THEN you can expect to incur the wrath of some.

The AHD treatment of *cope* in [16] illustrates the attempt to distinguish *cope* from *contend* not on the basis of meaning differences but through appeal to levels of style. The meanings of terms such as *informal, colloquial,* and *nonstandard* are *not* obvious to ordinary users of dictionaries. Students must be made aware of these technical terms by consulting the introduction to the dictionary. In the AHD comment, the usage panel has ruled on the word's use only in formal writing; no information can be directly gleaned about the word's appropriateness in informal writing or informal speech. Those who want to pursue the matter in more detail should consult a book that summarizes the opinions of the usage panel, William and Mary Morris's *Harper Dictionary of Contemporary Usage.* Incidentally, WNCD9 provides no usage entry for *cope,* and the most recent edition of AHD omits the note in the 2d College ed. (1985).

Usage questions often concern items in the language that are undergoing historical change. The case of *infer* indicates a reopening of a historical case long after common practice had merged certain senses of *infer* and *imply.* Perhaps post-World War I prescriptivists sensed an apparent injustice in one word encroaching on the semantic territory of another. But such invasions continue. *Cope* intrudes upon the territory of *contend,* which can appear as an intransitive verb. But language operates far more like a natural system such as genetic coding than like the human system of politics and warfare. Like genes, language can be manipulated, but only according to its own principles. Powerful as they appear, human attempts to regulate any language and its history are feeble.

ANSWER TO   (a) either, (b) neither, (c) inferred, (d) imply, (e) either, (f) either.
EXERCISE

14.2.4   Syntax

Before you read further, complete the exercise in [18]:

[18]   Choose the form of the verb in parentheses that sounds the most natural to you.

SET A
   [a]   The reasons for the delay (was/were) never revealed.
   [b]   Merle and his brother (is/are) singing the national anthem.
   [c]   Neither Wanda nor her playing partners (has/have) arrived.
   [d]   There (is/are) five good reasons to eat broccoli.
   [e]   They are the ones that (has/have) to be painted.
   [f]   Some (has/have) chosen to stay.

SET B
   [g]   Microeconomics (is/are) extremely difficult.
   [h]   The stars and stripes (warm/warms) the heart of most Americans.
   [i]   Good and bad taste (is/are) acquired through experience.
   [j]   Either the fans or the umpire (is/are) wrong.
   [k]   Larry is one of those people who (is/are) always late.
   [l]   Larry is one who (is/are) always late.
   [m]   No one, not even the players, (want/wants) to postpone the game.
   [n]   No one (want/wants) to postpone the game.
   [o]   Sarah, as well as her cousin, (has/have) joined the team.

EXERCISE   Find a friend (not an English major) and ask him or her to do the exercise above. Be sure to stress that they make the most *natural* choice.

Syntactic rules of usage cover a wide range of topics, including parts of speech, verb tenses, pronoun reference, coordination and subordination, placement of modifiers, and sentence problems. Most of the rules cover not only grammar but also areas where grammar interacts with meaning. A treatment of pronoun reference, for example, might highlight a sentence such as [19]:

[19]   Was it Mary or Zelda that volunteered her/their time?

The common handbook doctrine is that nouns coordinated by *or* or *nor* (e.g., *Mary or Zelda*) are considered as singular because *or* has a distributive meaning—i.e., one or the other but not both. In fact, the "both" interpretation is logically possible, although the person who asks the question in [19] clearly assumes the distributive interpretation.

Even such a simple case quickly runs into problems, as [20] suggests:

[20] Was it Harry or Zelda that volunteered her/his/their/his or her time?

The only choice here consistent with the prescriptive rule is *his or her,* although handbooks regularly warn against overuse of the combination in favor of *their.* The facts of English spoken usage suggest that *their* is far more naturally used in this context; moreover, *their* offers a true gender-neutral pronoun. Regardless of the logic of this argument, not even the most "liberated" of the the handbook authors has accepted it.

Rather than following out this particular issue, however, let's consider a set of syntactic rules that we have already noted—subject-verb agreement (SVAG). In this matter, handbooks are in nearly complete agreement on their prescriptions. The formulations below are generic:

[21] **[a]** Words that intervene between a (simple) subject and a verb don't affect agreement.
e.g., The call of the loons always sooth*es* me.

[b] Coordinated subjects are plural unless (i) they refer to the same entity or (ii) are premodified by *every* or *each.*
e.g., Zubin and Zelda make an ideal couple.
i. The president and CEO is Wanda.
ii. Each boy and girl has a desk.

[c] When subjects are coordinated by *either/or* or *neither/nor,* the verb agrees with the closest one.
e.g., Either Esther or Edgar has your key.
Either the natives or the tourists have to adapt.
Either the natives or the consul has to adapt.
Either the consul or the natives have to adapt.

[d] After *there is/are,* the subject follows the verb and agrees with it.

[e] Verbs in relative clauses agree with the antecedent of a subject relative pronoun (*who, which, that,* etc.).
e.g., Those are changes that *have* to be made.

[f] When used alone as subjects, the words *either, neither, one, everybody,* and *anyone* are normally singular. Depending on the context, the words *all, any, half, most, none,* and *some* may be either singular or plural.
e.g., Everybody is going.
Some of the water has evaporated.
None of the members are going.

These rules take the form of an extensive list, with the implication that students should memorize the list. The subparts of the rule cover a wide range of syntactic structures: prepositional phrases [21a], coordinations [21b] and [21c], inversions [21d], subordinate clauses [21e], and indefinite pronouns and quantifiers [21f]. Moreover, the rules rely heavily on grammatical terminology, occasionally leaving important terms undefined, particularly the term *context*. Also, the emphasis is overwhelmingly on particularized cases rather than on general principles of either subject-verb agreement or agreement in general. Finally, usage surveys show that, for sentences such as *None of the members is/are going,* English speakers are evenly divided in their choice of *is* and *are* (Celce-Murcia and Larsen-Freeman 1983: 39). Clearly, SVAG is one of the most complex points of English grammar.

Even though SVAG rules are among the most difficult in the language, teachers often expect their students to have no trouble in conforming to the rules. Unfortunately, such expectations rarely are met. Students seem, almost perversely at times, to ignore the rules or to apply them arbitrarily in their own writing and speech. While we may view such errors as the result of laziness or dullness, we shouldn't do so before considering some flaws in the rules themselves.

No one would deny that agreement of a subject and its verb is a grammatical fact of English, a fact of competence. A subject in the third person singular with a present-tense verb calls for the ending -s or -es (phonemically, /s/, /z/, or /ɪz/ on the main verb or the first auxiliary verb, excluding modals:

[22a] The horse runs.
  [b] The horse is running.
  [c] The horse has run.
  [d] The horse will run.

The verb *be* exceptionally requires a wider range of agreement in all persons and in the past as well as in the present tense; e.g.:

[23a] I am running.
  [b] You were running.
  [c] She was running.
  [d] They were running.

SVAG reflects a historical relic from Old English, where all verbs were inflected as variously as *be*. Over the past thousand years, virtually all of the verb inflections have disappeared—except for the third person singular present tense. Why this form should be so persistent is open to speculation; note that we do quite well without agreement in the past tense of verbs other than *be*. And if one were to hold a contest to nominate the greatest improvement in English, eliminating SVAG would receive many votes from teachers and students.

Historical circumstances aside, English provides many instances where speakers regularly vary in the way in which they apply this rule of competence. In such instances, prescriptivists step in to add a morass of subrules which have nothing to do with competence at all. The prescriptivist principle seems to be that if any variation exists in language, then one must be right and all others wrong.

Exercise [18] at the beginning of this section illustrates several factors that influence the way in which speakers apply the competence rule (not the prescriptive one!) of SVAG. SET A presents examples that reflect the rules of competence straightforwardly; presumably no student would need to learn any explicit rules to produce them. SET B introduces problem cases, only some of which are directly addressed by prescriptions.

The first factor that complicates SVAG is reference. The prescriptive rules take reference into account occasionally, as in [18h], which accounts for a choice of *warms* as a verb agreeing with *stars* and *stripes,* although some speakers will choose *warm.* But do *stars* and *stripes* denote the same entity? Not unless one cannot distinguish a star from a stripe. Unlike the example (i) in rule [21b], *stars* and *stripes* don't *individually* denote the same entity, i.e., the flag. This is perhaps semantic hairsplitting, but it does indicate a loophole in the rule. Example [18i] provides a reversed case, where a singular subject is modified by two coordinated adjectives which *are* interpreted distributively. Another loophole appears in [18g], where a plural noun denotes a referentially singular item (note also *aerobics, scissors,* and sometimes *sports*). So reference is a slippery notion in the rules.

The second factor that affects competence is the material that intervenes between the subject and the verb. In simple cases, proximity isn't a factor in agreement (rule [21a]). Sometimes a word rivals the true subject for agreement—e.g., the object of a preposition (*delay* in [18a]). However, other parts of the rule contradict this precept. Example [21c] runs blatantly afoul of it by selecting the nearest of two coordinated nouns for agreement. Less obvious is rule [21f]. Compare *Some of the crowd have left* with *Some of the water has evaporated.* These examples suggest that the context relevant to agreement is precisely the material that occurs between the simple subject and the verb.

Actually, proximity may disguise further indeterminacies. For instance, appositives as in [18m] sometimes contribute to the plurality of the subject. Similarly, "as well as" in [18o] means nearly the same as "and," and thus throws a sentence into the scope of rule [21b] for coordinated subjects.

One might argue that SVAG simply has myriad exceptions that students must learn to master. But the exceptions don't prove the rule, they annihilate it. They suggest that the actual **competence** rule of agreement isn't a matter of grammar at all but of semantics. That is, the rule has a form something like the following: if the subject has a singular meaning, it's singular; if it has a plural meaning, it's plural. The exceptions of the traditional prescriptive rule are, in fact, closer to the real rule that speakers employ—even though individuals don't necessarily employ it in the same way. The reason that students have so much trouble with SVAG prescriptions is that those prescriptions *contradict* the rules that are in their heads as a part of their competence. Those writers who do master the prescriptive principles have learned to suspend—temporarily—their normal competence to fit the handbook rules. But it's futile to expect any but a minority of students to develop such metalinguistic abilities.

14.2.5 Style

Stylistic rules include recommendations, usually found in composition textbooks, handbooks, or computerized text editors about the relative merits of certain syntactic, or sometimes lexical, possibilities. Stylistic rules differ from syntactic rules in that they concern sentences that are correctly formed (in both prescriptive and descriptive senses) and that have no gross problems of meaning such as being ambiguous or incomprehensible.

One example of a stylistic rule affects the use of the passive. This construction is usually described in both syntactic and semantic terms, as in [24] and [25]:

[24] The passive construction (or passive voice) reverses the usual active who-does-what? model of the English sentence. The passive highlights the

recipient, target, or product of the action by pulling it out in front of the verb. The verb changes from *wrote* to *was written,* from *will pay* to *will be paid.* The doer or agent appears after *by* (or may be omitted altogether).
Active: The working poor, not the idle rich, **pay** most of our taxes.
Passive: Most of our taxes are **paid** by the working poor, not the idle rich. (*New English Handbook,* 3d ed., p. 739)

[25]   Passive voice: The form of the verb which shows that its subject does not act but is the object or receiver of the action: "The ham was sliced by Emily." (*Harbrace College Handbook,* 10th ed., p. 520)

In these examples, semantic description includes expressions such as "who-does-what?" "recipient, target, or product of the action," "doer or agent," "does not act," and "the object or receiver of the action." Syntactic expressions include "verb," "subject," and "after *by.*"

Handbooks and other manuals not only describe the structure of the passive; they also prescribe ways in which it should be used, particularly in writing. An example appears in [26]:

[26]   For good reason, good writers prefer the active voice most of the time. It is clearer and more direct, and it packs more punch. Also it immediately identifies the responsible actor. . . . Passive voice tends to be unemphatic and wordy. . . . It is sometimes evasive. . . . The passive voice is not always bad, however. You should not tie yourself into a pretzel to avoid it. Sometimes it is awkward to state the subject of a sentence. . . . When used with finesse and restraint, the passive voice can even add variety to prose. . . . The problem is misuse. Pseudoscientific and pseudoofficial prose is everywhere, tempting writers into the passive voice. Resist. Write in the active voice whenever you can. (*Writing Worth Reading,* 2d ed., pp. 284–285)

A critical examination of this example reveals some significant weaknesses of both description and prescription.

Descriptively, the portrayal of the passive is highly oversimplified. For instance, not all active sentences have agents as subjects:

[27a] Prisoners in many countries endure horrendous torture.
  [b] Yesterday saw a change in the weather.

Sentence [27a] also shows that active voice sentences can omit mention of the agent entirely. In addition, handbooks regularly ignore "statal" passives, as in [28]:

[28] The door was closed.

Sentence (28) is actually ambiguous between the statal interpretation (= is in the condition of "closedness") and the dynamic (= some agent closed the door). Statal passives, however, cannot be expressed actively without awkwardness. This is a crucial omission, given that the advice usually offered by manuals is to substitute an active for a passive voice. Incidentally, computerized style analyzers are currently incapable of distinguishing dynamic from statal passives.

The major flaw in descriptions of the passive, however, is the limitation to syntax and semantics. Traditional handbooks pay almost no attention to the discourse functions of the passive. Most examples of passive usage provide only single sentences completely devoid of context, as in [24] and [25]. (In defense of the handbooks, even linguists haven't until recently turned their attention to these functions.) We will indicate below how an awareness of the role of passive in discourse might enlighten the issue.

The prescriptive side of the passive shows a strong consensus that it has basically a negative influence, except in a few select cases. The first assumption is that the passive is a minority usage. That assumption is correct, except that it fails to recognize how large a minority it is. A study by Garvey and Lindstrom (1989) examined professionally written essays used in freshman composition readers as models for students' writing. Authors included such names as Jonathan Swift, Isaac Asimov, George Orwell, Mark Twain, E. B. White, Russell Baker, H. L. Mencken, Bruce Catton, Jessica Mitford, and James Thurber. In 1000-word samples, professionals used passive voice nearly 10% of the time, more frequently, in fact, than a similar sample of freshman composition students. Another study showed that the agent was omitted in the passive around 85% of the time (Celce-Murcia and Larsen-Freeman, 1983: p. 225).

The hostility toward passive goes beyond the issue of frequency. Indeed, many other minority usages (e.g., concessive clauses) are never singled out for censure. The disapproval of passive is basically moral or ethical, as [26] clearly indicates. The passive allows—perhaps even tempts—writers to commit the literary equivalent of sin: evasiveness, wordiness, self-importance, dullness. The passive is associated with bureaucrats and (pseudo)scientists. Handbooks do occasionally acknowledge that just as it's tolerable to tell a "white lie" to protect someone's feelings, one is allowed to commit a passive if no other alternative exists. And just as one might use a profanity with "finesse and restraint" to add punch to one's writing, one might deliberately employ the passive to add variety. In general, though, passive control is the literary equivalent of self-control.

In defense of the passive, we must note its basically positive role in language. While it allows the omission of an agent, that omission isn't always evasive. The agent may be unknown as in [29], irrelevant as in [30], or obvious as in [31]:

[29]   Alan's father was killed in Vietnam.
[30]   Order was restored to the courtroom.
[31]   The Cubs played the Mets last night. Once more, the Cubs were defeated.

The passive also plays a variety of roles in discourse. First, it sometimes conveys certain presuppositions:

[32a]   The dissolution of the government was not caused by the scandal.
  [b]   The scandal did not cause the dissolution of the government.

While [32a] strongly suggests that the government was dissolved, [32b] doesn't. Thus the active and passive versions of a sentence aren't entirely synonymous.

Second, passives allow continuity of topic. Sentence [33], for instance, can most naturally be followed by only one of the sentences in [34]:

[33]   Beaver dams are true works of architecture.

[34a] For instance, they are constructed on principles related to the geodesic dome.
  [b] For instance, beavers construct them on principles related to the geodesic dome.

Example [34b], moreover, suggests that beavers actually know the principles of the geodesic dome.

A third discourse function of the passive is to allow the agent to be expressed as new information, particularly by being placed in a *by*-phrase at the end of the sentence:

[35a] I like your new lithograph.
  [b] Thanks, it was done by Bev Doolittle.

These examples indicate the need to present the passive in realistic discourse contexts. Those contexts may be linguistic (one or more preceding sentences) or extralinguistic (scientific writing, journalism, conversation).

We believe that the passive voice should be taught as one among many options for expressing similar ideas. Teachers, handbooks, and composition texts should encourage students to explore options for their own writing and to discover the differences that choices make in their communication.

14.3   USAGE AND EDUCATION

The school system is the major social institution responsible for educating students in the intricacies of standard English usage, a task for which English teachers are assigned primary responsibility. In this, the final section of the book, we return briefly to the investigation of language varieties, particularly standard English. We examine the roles of linguistic variation in education, especially with regard to students' rights and needs and teachers' responses. We discussed aspects of these topics in Chapter 13 and briefly reiterate and develop that discussion here because it represents the basis of our approach to teaching usage.

14.3.1   The varieties of English

Truly a world language, modern English has approximately 400 million native speakers throughout the world: in Britain, Ireland, the United States, Canada, Australia, New Zealand, the Caribbean, India, and Africa. Millions more speak the language as a second language in Africa and India; and throughout the world, many more speak it as a foreign language. Estimates of the numbers of English users around the globe range from about 700 million to between 1 and 2 billion people. Only Chinese has more speakers (although they use a number of mutually unintelligible dialects and Chinese lacks the range of international functions that English has).

English is one of only six official languages of the United Nations. It is the official or national language in several countries, including Britain, Ireland, Canada, the United States, Australia, New Zealand, India (and several Indian states), Kenya, and Singapore. It's used for international maritime and air traffic communication. About 80% of all computer information is stored in English; 75% of the world's mail, telex, and cable traffic is in English; more than 50% of the world's technical and scientific publications are printed in English (McCrum, Cran, and McNeil, 1986: pp. 19–20).

English is used as both a spoken language and a written one, from the most intimate communication to the most formal. It's used in very restricted contexts where accurate communication on a narrow range of topics is essential, as in maritime and air traffic communication; it has developed specialized terminology and constructions for these uses. French aircraft with French crews landing in Cameroun speak English with the traffic controllers in the control tower; Philippino officers on Greek-owned, Panamanian-registered oil tankers docking in Kuwait communicate with the port authorities in English. Scholars at international conferences on scientific topics speak to each other and read papers in English. It's used by monolingual native speakers for all their linguistic exchanges, from the bedroom to the boardroom.

English has by a sizable margin the largest vocabulary of the major languages. The *Oxford English Dictionary* lists approximately 500,000 words, in comparison with estimates of 185,000 for German and 100,000 for French.

Clearly, a language with such diverse speakers and uses must be expected to be varied, and English is indeed very varied. It includes "native" varieties, such as the dialects of Britain. It also includes varieties which show greater or lesser degrees of influence from the languages with which English came in contact through exploration, conquest, and colonization: Welsh, Scottish, Irish, Canadian, American, and South African English, as well as the new Englishes of the Caribbean, India, and East Africa. Each of these areas has characteristic varieties of their own English, many with distinctive literatures.

The many varieties of English can be conceptualized, as in Chapter 13, according to whether they correlate with language users or uses (or both). **Dialects** are varieties associated with users. English dialects include a number of national and numerous regional, socioeconomic and ethnic varieties. **Registers** are varieties associated with uses. English registers include the range of variation associated with different levels of formality, different modes of communication such as reading and writing, various spoken and written genres, the specialized varieties associated with particular occupations and topics. (See Figure 14.1.) Writing handbooks and textbooks often stigmatize the vocabularies of these specialized varieties with the pejorative term "jargon," but few occupations lack specialized terms. (The study of English literature and language is no exception.)

FIGURE 14.1 Varieties of English

VARIETIES	
DIALECTS	**REGISTERS**
Regional	Formality
Socioeconomic	Mode of communication
Ethnic	Genre
Gender	Occupation
	Topic

English has two dominant national standard varieties—British and American. National standards may vary on any or all of the components of language: sound system, morphology, word stock, syntax, semantics, and pragmatics. The British and American standards, as we have seen, differ from each other primarily in a small number of spelling conventions (e.g., *-our* for *-or* in words such as *honor; -re* for *-er* in *theater; -ise* for *-ize* in *recognize*), in a small number of lexical items (e.g., *elevator* for *lift*); and in intonation patterns. Each of the two standard varieties is readily interpretable to a speaker of the other and to many speakers of nonstandard (NS) varieties.

In the United States, there is considerable regional variation and even more social variation, with a number of important ethnic varieties, including Black and Hispanic English. From a purely linguistic perspective, all languages and varieties are created equal. They come from the same basic mold and can express whatever their speakers need them to express. Some may express certain meanings more economically than others, having perhaps individual words where others must resort to circumlocution. All allow for the expansion of their vocabularies; all allow the generation of an infinite number of sentences; all can be developed to express the range of meanings required to function in the modern world. There are no primitive languages, nor are there any languages or varieties with such restricted vocabularies that their speakers must eke out their meanings with gestures.

From a social point of view, however, some varieties (most notably the standard ones) are more prestigious than others. Speakers evaluate linguistic variants—and their users—on the basis of language beliefs and attitudes, many of which have no basis in linguistic fact. A variety's prestige is derived from that of its users and of the situations in which it's used, not from any strictly linguistic characteristics—a fact often missed in discussions of linguistic variation. Clearly, standard written English and the varieties closest to it are accorded the greatest prestige.

14.3.2   Usage and standard English

A standard variety of a language typically serves in a range of socially important domains, such as the law, education, scholarship, technology, science, and government. These are formal, public domains characterized by the use of written, planned, message-oriented language. Standard varieties have written forms that are extensively codified through dictionaries, grammars, and handbooks of style.

From a sociolinguistic point of view, standard English (SE) combines features of both dialect and register. It approximates the native variety of certain social groups, particularly the educated middle and upper classes. It's required in certain contexts of use, typically the more formal and prestigious ones, and most particularly, in written communication. SE has such great prestige that many people believe that it's the only legitimate form of the language and view all other varieties as deviations or degenerations from it. They view **nonstandard** varieties as **substandard**.

SE has been subject to considerable codification through various sources. The effect, and often the conscious goal, of codification is to eliminate certain kinds of variants, primarily optional variants (e.g., *which* as a restrictive relative pronoun). Codification also has a more covert effect: the elimination of forms used by less prestigious groups in the community and by most speakers in less formal circumstances (e.g., *who* as relative or interrogative pronoun when serving as the object of a verb or preposition). In American English, pronunciation is much less codified than the other components, and indeed, people speak SE in a range of accents. In contrast, the syntax, morphology, vocabulary, and semantics of spoken SE are highly influenced by its written forms, particularly in the most formal spoken genres. Writing, of course, reflects the greatest degree of codification.

14.3.3   Usage in the classroom: Students' needs and rights

Teachers' and students' attitudes toward variety in English reflect those prevalent in the society. They range from general tolerance to a rigid rejection of variation as indicating social and linguistic decay. Some who have learned too well the editorial proprieties of formal written English find it very difficult to relinquish these authoritarian attitudes.

One of the greatest and most empowering goals of English teachers should be to educate students about language varieties, their speakers, and their expected contexts of use. Students often entertain serious misconceptions about language variation, and often view NS speakers as uneducated and even stupid. Instruction should lead them to confront the fact that all languages vary at all times, and that language variation and language change—its close relative—are natural and inevitable. Language awareness education promotes an understanding that social values associate particular variants with particular contextual circumstances, that certain varieties are expected under certain circumstances, and that all variants and their speakers deserve respect.

In addition, students must confront the social impact of SE. SE isn't simply a variety that one must acquire to appear in public print. It's not merely a piece of equipment necessary for success. It's not just another register expected under certain circumstances and not under others. Rather, it's native—or at least easily accessible—to certain groups, notably the middle and upper classes. The fact that it's required for the more lucrative and prestigious positions in the society privileges these classes but marginalizes those for whom it's not native. When we teach the narrow handbook usage strictures in an uncritical fashion, simply as a part of developing writing skills, we covertly teach the values of the classes to which the usage comes most easily.

EXERCISE   In a short essay on usage, William F. Buckley, Jr. suggests that decisions on acceptability in language be based on the usage of those who are "expertly trained and congenitally gifted." (*American Heritage Dictionary*, 2d College ed. p. 32.) What attitudes does this suggestion indicate toward (1) the relative status of various speakers of the language and (2) the relation of language variation to genetics?

The learning of usage should thus find its place not only in the composition classroom but also in the broader curriculum of language study. That curriculum should provide students with (1) as broad a knowledge as possible of the sociolinguistic characteristics of English, (2) a good working knowledge of its standard grammar, (3) an understanding of the various approaches to grammar, (4) the relations between spoken and written language, and (5) the relations among language, personal and social identity, and education. Students need an understanding of language structure, variation, and use which is sufficiently sophisticated for them to recognize and combat their own linguistic assumptions and prejudices and those of others. Tolerance of diversity in language goes hand in hand with tolerance of diversity in race, ethnicity, religion, and gender. Much contemporary research indicates that such awareness and tolerance will help students to develop advanced skills in English literature and composition as well as to learn other languages.

Because of the intimate relationships among language variety, social identity, and group membership, the English education of all speakers should be aimed at expanding their linguistic repertoires (Halliday, 1978; Edwards, 1985), adding to the range of circumstances in which they can produce the appropriate linguistic forms. Students have a right to an opportunity to acquire productive control of SE, without having to abandon their native variety (Stubbs, 1986).

14.3.4   Usage in the classroom: The role of the teacher

Those who believe that their job as English teachers will be to eradicate NS forms from their students' linguistic repertoires risk alienating students from education and from the social and economic advantages it makes possible. Alternatively, they risk alienating students from their families and friends, from the sociocultural background from which they entered the school and to which they return every afternoon. Because dialects indicate individual and social identity and membership in particular social groups, pressing students to abandon their native varieties forces them to choose between the values of the larger society, which we referred to in Chapter 13 as *power,* and the values of their home communities, which we referred to as *solidarity.* A change in language variety may signal that speakers are distancing themselves from their interlocutors, reducing their solidarity, and opting for status. The choice of linguistic variety may trigger ideological interpretations, as happened in Chicago among Black honors students, who, as they became more proficient in SE and dropped their Black speech, were taunted as "white" by their peers.

The teaching of SE should be sociolinguistically informed and linguistically accurate. The way in which language and language varieties are discussed in classrooms and textbooks is of crucial importance. Teachers must be able to identify in students' writing those forms (e.g., sentence fragments) that are characteristic of spoken language, which tends to be informal, unplanned, and listener-oriented. They must also be able to distinguish between forms which regularly occur in their students' native dialect (e.g., *lay* for SE *lie*), and forms which they produce in writing but which don't occur in either SE or the students' native variety (Cheshire, 1982). Only the latter are real errors, and even these may be due to the students' incomplete learning of SE forms, a sort of interdialect, indicative of their assumptions about the grammar of SE.

Few, if any, textbooks used in local school districts make these distinctions. They characterize all forms outside the standard norms as "incorrect" or "ungrammatical." These terms can only suggest to students that there is something wrong with their own language, or (ridiculously) that they don't speak English. By the time children are 5 or 6 years of age, and regardless of their ethnic or socioeconomic background, they're capable of varying their speech to match their audiences. They speak differently to their parents, their younger siblings, and to their peers. Teachers can build upon this knowledge of variation by presenting SE as another set of variants used in specific circumstances, most particularly, in writing. Also, more accurate, less stigmatizing terms, such as "typical" or "usual," should indicate the teacher's respect and tolerance for linguistic and social diversity and allow students to retain their linguistic self-respect.

If teachers do use terms such as "incorrect" or even "inappropriate," they should make clear to their students just who decides which expressions are correct/appropriate and incorrect/inappropriate, and who benefits from the decision.

Sociolinguistic and educational linguistic research suggests that many students, particularly those from poorer and especially from minority backgrounds, may, in fact, be quite skilled users of spoken varieties (Labov, 1972). However, they have generally had less opportunity to learn the more formal, planned, message-oriented, context-independent varieties closest to written language and most favored by the schools and society. Middle- and upper-class children, whose values and culture are reflected in the schools, and whose parents know the kinds of discourse expected in this and other formal contexts, have had more exposure to and, consequently, greater skills in the expected kinds of language use. Their considerable advantage shows up in higher grades and lower drop-out rates.

Students' language skills provide a valuable resource that teachers can examine and make use of. Classroom activities such as storytelling and role-playing can sensitize students to each other's verbal abilities. They can also provide enlightenment about the importance of personal and social identities reflected in language varieties. A sociolinguistic approach to SE and language variation helps students to understand the society in which they live and to build on skills they already possess. This applies particularly to nonnative speakers of English, who often speak a nonstandard variety of their first language. Like NSE students, these students should be encouraged to expand their skills into the more formal varieties of their native languages.

Because of the richness of the linguistic resources that students bring to the school, teachers can encourage students to discuss language as much as possible, and under a variety of topics—social, literary, political, moral, and ethical—rather than just in the context of teaching composition, which is where the topic usually is addressed. Moreover, since language crosses so many disciplinary boundaries, teachers outside the English faculty can add to the richness of language instruction through social studies, geography, and history, to name but a few.

Because the varieties used by their students may not be described already, teachers need to be able to recognize and describe the patterns in those varieties, and to use their descriptions as the basis for comparison with SE and as a topic of discussion in class.

Teachers need to develop students' ability to spot fallacies in claims about language made by their peers, the public, and even linguists. Units on logic and critical thinking can invite students to test grammatical and usage claims presented in textbooks and writing handbooks. Consider, for example, the common claim that the following sentence is ungrammatical because it uses *good,* allegedly an adjective, as an adverb.

[36]   He's doing very good.

Sentences such as [36] are very common and grammatical in NSE and, indeed, occur in the informal speech of people who are perfectly capable of expressing themselves in consistent

SE. In those varieties, *good* does, of course, modify the verb, and if adverbs are defined as words that modify verbs, then in those varieties *good* is an adverb. All that needs to be said is that in more formal varieties the usual form of the adverb is *well,* not *good.*

Traditional definitions of parts of speech provide other useful candidates for such activities. In this way, teachers can lead students to discover for themselves the analytic criteria, such as those in Chapters 5 and 6, that successfully classify words. Other possibilities are definitions of grammatical functions such as subjects and stylistic preferences such as the use of expletive *it.* In this framework, claims about language appear as hypotheses. Students identify the kind of data to which the claim applies and the types of texts in which that data occur, then collect the data and evaluate the hypotheses. Luckily, the data for linguistic analysis are cheap, probably the cheapest that any scholar could hope for. The data are also unlimited, consisting of the utterances of individual speakers and judgments of their well-formedness and appropriateness to their contexts. They can be collected from a range of contexts, formal or informal, spoken or written, from native or nonnative speakers, and analyzed accordingly.

Clearly, high school textbooks and handbooks are designed for students rather than for their teachers, so it's reasonable to expect teachers to know more than is in the texts and to be able to evaluate what is in them. Their evaluations ought to be based on the accuracy of the statements made in the texts and on the suitability of the assumptions that underlie the approach to language and grammar presented in the books.

Teachers should be particularly aware of the terminology in which much of the usage advice is couched. Such apparently neutral terms as "clear" and "concise" represent ideological commitments and reflect social class and group values. Other cultures, other socioeconomic groups, and other ethnic groups may prefer very different rhetorical effects, e.g., allusion and circumlocution, to reflect very different values such as respect for the addressee. Surely, there is a place here for politeness, which may clash with saying exactly what you mean.

Words such as "clear" and "concise" beg lots of questions. For example, clear to whom? Clarity can only be gauged relative to a specific audience and depends on the assumptions or knowledge shared by audience and writer. Conciseness and the way in which it's reflected in textbooks and writing handbooks as word counting suggests that writing is to be judged by the same standards that we use to judge commercial enterprises. It's almost as if the underlying assumption were that words are coins to be hoarded, as textbooks total up the number of words saved by replacing a passive or an expletive construction.

Another value-laden pair of terms is "strong" and "weak," as applied to certain words and constructions. The rhetorical advice is consistent: we should eliminate the weak. Does this apply to all domains of life? Isn't that what happened to the American Indians, to small savers with accounts in savings and loan associations? The rhetoric of strength is the rhetoric of dominating one's audience. It's reasonable to ask what we lose by adopting such a position and to consider whether most modern communication takes the form of debate.

We could argue about the implications of these terms and about whether the values they reflect are good or bad. You may, as we do, very well prefer to read clear, concise, vigorous prose. What is objectionable is the use of terms as if they were objective and neutral, transparent to all rather than opaque terms, freighted with social values, which favor some and discriminate against others. They're presented as "unmarked" or "natural" terms, which don't have to be examined. As recent feminist discussions of the "generic" pronoun *he* reveal, and as much modern literary criticism attempts to teach us, one person's unmarked term is another's call to battle. Examination of this marking structure reveals social, political, and economic interests, which otherwise remain hidden. It reminds us that "language is used for social control" (Stubbs, 1986: p. 60). Teachers, whose duty it is to teach SE, must recognize and acknowledge that we are agents of social control.

But as Stubbs continues, "the mechanisms of such control are describable and understandable and some escape is possible" (p. 60). Teachers have the duty to make SE available to students, to free themselves from assumptions that make SE seem natural and inevitable, to convey to students the motivations behind approved and disapproved linguistic choices and to acknowledge that these choices become mechanisms for the maintenance of power. What would we think of physics teachers who introduced students to atomic physics but failed to discuss the dangers of radiation? Of chemistry teachers who failed to mention the ecological dangers of chemicals? Of social studies teachers who never mentioned the social, economic, and cultural effects of government policies? Of history teachers who taught about colonialism without mentioning its destruction of conquered peoples and their cultures? Shouldn't it seem strange then that English teachers, who routinely discuss the social, political, and ideological characteristics of literary texts and their authors, ignore those very same features of the language variety that they ask their students to learn and use?

The choice of a language variety or of a particular usage is not value free; it's not merely a matter of clear communication, of convenience, or of a lingua franca. The choice privileges some people and marginalizes others; it's a political statement of values, of power, of hegemony, of stewardship, of gatekeeping. Those who fail to see this aren't neutral; they uncritically support the status quo.

The argument that language instruction—particularly grammar—should be taught only in the context of teaching composition is, by virtue of what it denies students (knowledge of other linguistic varieties, their sociolinguistic characteristics, and social values), a profoundly disturbing political decision. The language in which variants are evaluated ("incorrect/ungrammatical") misrepresents the linguistic and sociolinguistic facts and betrays the underlying sociopolitical dimension. Moreover, the values which students bring to school and which are signaled by their choice of language forms may be quite distinct from those enshrined in SE and SE teaching. For example, one prominent English series of high school English texts presents SE as the language of the business world. The choice is revealing. Surely education ought to be more than a mere thrall of business.

More generally, the range of contexts in which commentary on language and languages, their forms, functions, histories, and patterns of use are relevant and pertinent in junior high and high school is very broad and includes at least English language arts, foreign languages, social studies, history, geography, and psychology.

To the extent that all education involves teaching and learning new terminology and new ways of writing, then all classes, including chemistry, physics, auto repair, and basket weaving, provide opportunities to comment on the registers of English. In other words, all teachers, regardless of their specialities, would benefit from an understanding of the nature of language and particularly of language variation. A critical literacy regarding language ought to be a significant part of every teacher's training. As British educators express it, we need to distribute language study, not just composition, "across the curriculum" (Hawkins, 1984).

14.3.5 Conclusion

Some of the positions on usage expressed above may seem "radical." However, most of them derive from or repeat notions published in a policy statement put out in 1974 by the National Council of Teachers of English. Entitled *Students' Rights to Their Own Language,* this document has largely been ignored by teachers, trainers of teachers, and textbooks.

We may assume that English is—or ought to be—a unified, melting-pot language. In fact, the language has never been more varied in its history. As it develops as a world language, that variation is likely to increase rather than decrease. The ability to negotiate the variety of the language is thus not only a humanizing activity but will become even more of a practical necessity for students of the future.

Students have the right to the opportunity to learn standard English. They also have the right to respect for their identities and for their social milieu. Teachers should attempt to provide their students with a critical understanding of the nature of language and its relations to the world. Teachers need to develop skills in communicating with the three audiences that they will have to address professionally: their students, their colleagues and peers, and the public (usually in the form of students' parents). In each case, the critical factor is expertise in the subject matter. We encourage teachers to make the pursuit of language study an activity as lifelong as reading literature.

REFERENCES AND RESOURCES

Baron, Dennis. 1982. *Grammar and Good Taste.* New Haven, CT: Yale University Press.

Baugh, Albert, and Thomas Cable. 1978. *A History of the English Language.* Englewood Cliffs, NJ: Prentice-Hall, Inc.

Celce-Murcia, Marianne, and Diane Larsen-Freeman. 1983. *The Grammar Book.* Rowley, MA: Newbury House Publishers, Inc.

Cheshire, Jenny. 1982. "Dialect Features and Linguistic Conflict in Schools." *Educational Review,* 34(1):53–67.

Crowley, Tony. 1989. *Standard English and the Politics of Language.* Urbana, IL: University of Illinois Press.

Delahunty, Gerald P., and Margaret F. Sweany. Unpublished ms. "Passive Structures, Meanings and Uses: A Critique of Usage Handbooks and Computerized Style Analyzers."

Edwards, J. 1985. *Language, Society and Identity.* Oxford: Blackwell.

Elster, C.H. 1988. *There is no Zoo in Zoology.* London: Macmillan.

———. 1990. *Is There a Cow in Moscow?* London: Macmillan.

Finegan, Edward. 1980. *Attitudes Toward English Usage.* New York: Teachers College Press, Columbia University.

Garvey, James J., and David H. Lindstrom. 1989. "Pros' Prose Meets Writer's Workbench: Analysis of Typical Models for First-Year Writing Courses." *Computers and Composition,* 6(2):81–109.

Gordon, Ian. A. 1966. *The Movement of English Prose.* Bloomington, IN: Indiana University Press.

Halliday, M. A. K. 1970. "Language Structure and Language Function." In J. Lyons, ed., *New Horizons in Linguistics.* Harmondsworth: Penguin, 140–165.

Halliday, M. A. K. 1978. *Language as Social Semiotic.* Baltimore, MD: University Park Press.

Hartwell, P. 1985. "Grammar, Grammars, and the Teaching of Grammar." *College English,* 47(2):105–127.

Hawkins, E. 1984. *Awareness of Language: An Introduction.* Cambridge: Cambridge University Press.

Hebel, J.W., and H.H. Hudson. 1929. *Poetry of the English Renaissance 1509–1660.* New York: Appleton-Century-Crofts, Inc.

Hofstadter, Douglas R. 1981. "Metamagical Themas." *Scientific American,* 244(1):22–32.

Kramarae, Cheris, Muriel Schwartz, and William M. O'Barr, eds., 1984. *Language and Power.* Beverly Hills, CA: Sage Publications.

Labov, W. 1972. "The Logic of Nonstandard English." In *Language in the Inner City.* Philadelphia, PA: University of Pennsylvania Press, 201–240.

MacKay, D. 1983. "Prescriptive Grammar and the Pronoun Problem." In B. Thorne, N. Henley, and C. Kramarae, eds., *Language, Gender and Society.* Rowley, MA: Newbury House, pp. 38–53.

Marckwardt, Albert. 1982. "The New Webster Dictionary: A Critical Appraisal." In Harold B. Allen and Michael D. Linn, eds., *Readings in Applied English Linguistics.* New York: Alfred A. Knopf, 476–483.

McCrum, R., W. Cran, and R. McNeil. 1986. *The Story of English.* New York: Viking.

NCTE. 1974. "Students' Rights to Their Own Language." *College Composition and Communication,* 25, 1–32.

Nunberg, Geoffrey. 1983. "The Decline of Grammar." *The Atlantic Monthly,* December 1983, pp. 31–46.

Quirk, Randolph, and Sidney Greenbaum. 1973. *A Concise Grammar of Contemporary English.* New York: Harcourt Brace Jovanovich, Chapter 7.

Schneider, J., and S. Hacker. 1973. "Sex Role Imagery and Use of the Generic 'Man' in Introductory Texts: A Case in the Sociology of Sociology." *The American Sociologist,* 8:12–18.

Scope English, Grammar and Composition, Level Five. 1984. New York: Scholastic Book Services.

Stanley, Julia P. 1978. "Sexist Grammar." *College English,* 39(7):802–811.

Shopen, Timothy, and Joseph M. Williams, eds. 1981. *Style and Variables in English.* Cambridge, MA: Winthrop Publishers, Inc.

Sledd, James. 1962. *Dictionaries and That Dictionary.* Chicago: Scott, Foresman.

Stubbs, M. 1986. *Educational Linguistics.* Oxford: Blackwell.

Trudgill, Peter. 1975. *Accent, Dialect and the School.* London: Edward Arnold.

Winterowd, W. R., and P. Y. Murray. 1985. *English: Writing and Skills.* San Diego, CA: Coronado.

GLOSSARY

Competence: see Chapter 1.

Dialect: see Chapter 13.

Nonstandard: a variety of a language that differs from the standard form.

Register: varieties of a language associated with its use; e.g., different levels of formality, different modes of communication such as reading and writing, various spoken and written genres, the specialized varieties associated with particular occupations and topics. See **dialect.**

Substandard: a term suggesting that one variety of a language is inferior to a standard variety.

INDEX